The
San Francisco
Chronicle
Cookbook Volume II

375 All-New Recipes from
America's Most Innovative
Food Section

The
San Francisco
Chronicle
Cookbook Volume II

edited by Michael Bauer and Fran Irwin

CHRONICLE BOOKS
SAN FRANCISCO

Library of Congress Cataloging-in-Publication Data available.
ISBN 0-8118-3021-7

Printed in the United States of America
Book and cover design by Pamela Geismar
Composition by Candace Creasy, Blue Friday Type & Graphics

Distributed in Canada by Raincoast Books
9050 Shaughnessy Street
Vancouver, BC V6P 6E5

10 9 8 7 6 5 4 3 2

Chronicle Books LLC
85 Second Street
San Francisco, California 94105

www.chroniclebooks.com

Contents

ACKNOWLEDGMENTS vi

INTRODUCTION vii

CHAPTER 1: APPETIZERS 1

CHAPTER 2: SOUPS 31

CHAPTER 3: SALADS 65

CHAPTER 4: PASTA AND GRAINS 93

CHAPTER 5: MEATLESS MAIN COURSES 147

CHAPTER 6: VEGETABLES 185

CHAPTER 7: MEATS 215

CHAPTER 8: POULTRY 253

CHAPTER 9: FISH AND SHELLFISH 301

CHAPTER 10: MORNING REPASTS 333

CHAPTER 11: RELISHES, SAUCES AND CHUTNEYS 371

CHAPTER 12: DESSERTS 399

GLOSSARY OF INGREDIENTS 443

MAIL-ORDER AND ONLINE SOURCES 449

CONTRIBUTORS' NOTES 451

PERMISSIONS 453

INDEX 454

TABLE OF EQUIVALENTS 471

Acknowledgments

Our thanks first have to go out to the Food Department staff, which has made *The San Francisco Chronicle*'s Food Section one of the best in the country: Lynne Bennett, Gerald Boyd, Robin Davis, Tara Duggan, Janet Fletcher, Tilde Herrera, Miriam Morgan, Lesli Neilson, Karola Saekel and Kim Severson. A whole parade of culinary interns from the California Culinary Academy has tested recipes and inspired us to do better by their questions and enthusiasm. They've taken many of the chefs' recipes and turned them from restaurant fare into home fare.

We'd like to thank our editors at *The Chronicle,* Executive Editor Matt Wilson and Managing Editor Jerry Roberts, who have been supportive of our efforts and even stopped by once in a while to taste our food. And we can't forget Rosalie Wright, the former assistant managing editor for Features, who went on to become editor in chief at *Sunset* magazine. She enthusiastically encouraged us to do the first book and remains a steadfast friend and supporter.

We've had lots of encouragement and help from our columnists and contributors: Flo Braker, Ethel Brennan, Georgeanne Brennan, Sharon Cadwallader, Marion Cunningham, Laxmi Hiremath, Jacqueline McMahan, Mai Pham, Shirley Sarvis, Marlena Spieler and Graceanne Walden.

We also would like to thank Sonja Hyams, who made sure we got permission to use all the recipes; Mike Keiser, who helped us get our thoughts on disk; and Bill LeBlond, our editor at Chronicle Books.

And most of all, we thank our readers who have shown their support and trust by using the recipes from the Food Section and giving us feedback.

Introduction

THE SAN FRANCISCO BAY AREA IS THE EPICENTER OF FOOD TRENDS.
Clark Wolf, a well-known New York–based food and restaurant consultant,
claims that San Francisco has become his crystal ball for clients who want a
peek into the future. "San Francisco starts trends," he says, "and New York
grows them."

Probably no other city in the United States flips so freely between
cultures. A Bay Area home cook may serve an Indian curry one night,
Vietnamese noodle soup on another and a perfect roast chicken the next.
It feels completely natural, reflecting what we see on the streets and in the
workplace. This cross-cultural stew makes Bay Area cooks and diners very
food savvy. In offices, at social gatherings and in casual conversations on the
street, the talk almost always turns to food.

The Napa and Sonoma valleys, less than an hour from San Francisco,
give residents quick access to the top wines in the United States, and the best
fruit and vegetables are grown at our doorstep. With artisan producers, great
chefs and inventive cookbook authors, the area is truly a culinary mecca.

Food is more than fuel, it's a lifestyle. This passion makes it pure
pleasure—and sometimes pure hell—to publish the Food Section. Bay Area
residents want recipes that are fresh and inventive, but they're as pressed for
time as people in Chicago or New York. Faxes, cell phones and the Internet
seem to have lengthened our workday, cutting out a chunk of our family time
and cooking time.

Getting the best results for the least amount of effort always has been
an overriding premise in *The Chronicle*'s Food Section. In fact, in 1994 we
launched the "Working Cook" page, which reflects the way people cook
today. Our staff writers develop great recipes that go from stove to table in
about 30 minutes or less. We also offer weekend cooking projects where
leftovers can be frozen and reserved for frantic weeknight meals.

This universal time crunch is also what led us to start our "Tasters'
Choice" column more than a decade ago. Our professional tasting panel
compares and picks the best brands of pasta, ketchup, jarred spaghetti sauce
and other convenience products.

In the last few years, we created even more columns to help readers
cut through the kitchen guesswork. In "The Best Way" series, we baked

potatoes more than a dozen ways to come up with the correct temperature and technique to produce the ultimately fluffy spud (page 172). Scattered throughout this book, you'll find these Best Way tips for everything from dressing a salad (page 67) to sautéing salmon (page 305). You'll also discover myriad tips, techniques and tricks for making cooking easier and a lot more fun.

We've used the same format in this book as we did in the original best-selling *San Francisco Chronicle Cookbook*. We think you'll find the recipes just as distinctive and easy to prepare.

A few things have changed in the Bay Area since the first book was published in 1997. For one, the Internet has dramatically changed the restaurant and cooking scenes. In the first book, we had to think twice about using recipes with hard-to-find ingredients. But today, ordering products online has made life a lot easier. You'll find a list of some of the best resources at the back of the book (page 449). We ordered from many of these companies and found the quality as good as or better than you'll find at many ethnic markets. Still, we have tried to keep the exotica to a minimum.

We've also noticed that breakfast and brunch are becoming a favorite way to entertain. So we've created a new chapter, "Morning Repasts," that covers everything from scrambling an egg (page 367) to making Hot Grilled Blue Cheese Toasts (page 346) and Fig and Chocolate Coffee Cake (page 348).

And, we've seen a resurgence in cocktail parties and multicourse dinner parties, so you'll find a separate "Appetizers" chapter filled with easy-to-make recipes for both stand-up and sit-down occasions.

In the Bay Area, chefs set the trends for home cooks. You'll find more chef recipes this time around, but rest assured, they've been perfected for the home kitchen. *The Chronicle*'s test kitchen is outfitted like a standard house or apartment kitchen. If we can produce great results on a basic electric range, we feel confident that you can, too.

The San Francisco Chronicle Cookbook II may look similar to the first volume, but this is not a revise; you'll find all new recipes and even more useful tips and suggestions.

Between the introduction and the index, we've collected more than 375 recipes from some of the best food minds in the country—from Marion Cunningham, author of the *Fannie Farmer Cookbook*, to Mark Franz, celebrated chef of Farallon. We hope *The San Francisco Chronicle Cookbook II* gives you at least 375 good reasons to head to the kitchen.

Chapter 1

Appetizers

Hors d'oeuvres are back. The cocktail party seems to be making a resurgence. Classic cocktails—Manhattans, Lemon Drops and Cosmos—show up on just about every restaurant menu, and the space devoted to bars in restaurants is growing.

Whether at home or dining out, people love finger food and small portions. Since publishing The San Francisco Chronicle Cookbook *in 1997, we've had many requests from readers for appetizers and other stand-up fare. In the Bay Area, at least, people are entertaining more at home.*

In this chapter we address appetizers in two ways: with a collection of stellar sit-down courses to begin a festive meal, and with stand-up nibbles you might serve at a cocktail party.

Our approach to cocktail fare is relatively uncomplicated. You'll find recipes using olives, which go particularly well with wine and cocktails, and other easy make-ahead nibbles such as a lovely White Bean and Pesto Dip (page 4), Spiced Cheese (page 19) and Chipotle Chicken Wings (page 29).

Some items can pull double duty, either as a sit-down course or as a pass-around treat: Vanilla Shrimp with Avocado-Tarragon Dip (page 22), Morel Quesadillas with Mild Red Chile Sauce (page 16) and Cured Salmon with Green Peppercorns (page 27).

Most appetizers in this chapter are easy to assemble and may be made ahead, so the host can enjoy the party and mingle with the guests.

Colleen McGlynn's Marinated Dry-Cured Olives

Former restaurant chef Colleen McGlynn and her husband, Ridgely Evers, produce olive oil from their 4,500 trees in Healdsburg. McGlynn likes to marinate dry-cured olives, blanching them first to remove some of their salt. These are excellent on their own, or as a "secret weapon" to put zing into a bland dish.

4 cups dry-cured black olives

3 garlic cloves, peeled and crushed

2 rosemary sprigs

2 thyme sprigs

Zest of 1 lemon

Zest of 1 orange

3 fresh or 2 dried bay leaves

4 whole dried red chiles

¾ cup extra virgin olive oil

Fresh lemon juice or red wine vinegar, to taste (optional)

Bring a medium pot of water to a boil over high heat. Add the olives and simmer for 15 seconds, then drain well.

Combine the garlic, rosemary, thyme, lemon and orange zests, bay leaves, chiles and olive oil in a saucepan over low heat. When the mixture is warm, remove from heat. Add the olives and toss to combine.

If the olives need more acidity, add lemon juice or a splash of red wine vinegar.

Let marinate for a few hours at room temperature before serving.

If not serving immediately, cover the olives and store in the refrigerator, but bring to room temperature before serving. They will keep in the refrigerator for up to 1 month.

YIELDS 1 QUART

To determine the best way
to make the classic martini,
The Chronicle's Food
Department evaluated
brands of gin, ingredient
proportions and mixing
methods. In all, we put
10 gins to the test—5 in
the medium-price range
and 5 more-expensive ones.

Using the higher-priced
Bombay Sapphire makes
a smoother drink, but the
moderately priced Gilbey's
still produces a fine classic
cocktail.

We found the best martini
is made with 12 parts gin to
1 part vermouth (¼ cup
to ¾ teaspoon).

Although there's
controversy about whether
to shake or stir, it comes
down to this: If you want
a colder, less alcoholic-
tasting drink, shake it.

Black Olive Tapenade

Here's a basic spread for topping grilled toasts. In the south of France, tapenade almost always is made with capers, but the other additions are open to debate. Tapenade is a welcome partner for any aperitif, from Champagne to lemonade, according to Georgeanne Brennan.

½ pound Mediterranean-style black olives

5 olive oil–packed anchovy fillets or well-rinsed salt-packed anchovies

1 tablespoon drained capers

½ teaspoon minced fresh thyme

1 teaspoon fresh lemon juice

1 to 2 tablespoons olive oil

Using the back of a wooden spoon, press each olive hard enough to crack it open, then remove the pit.

Put the pitted olives, anchovies, capers, thyme and lemon juice in a blender and process until a paste forms. Add the olive oil, a little at a time, until the paste is smooth but not oily.

Or, if you prefer, make the spread in the traditional way using a mortar and pestle, grinding the ingredients together one by one.

If not serving immediately, put the tapenade in a covered jar and store in the refrigerator, where it will keep for up to 3 months.

YIELDS ABOUT ½ CUP

Iron Horse Party Mix

This creative and totally addictive blend of olives, almonds and raisins is served with aperitifs before the annual harvest lunch at Iron Horse Vineyards in the Russian River region of Sonoma County. It's the invention of the winery chef, Mark Malicki.

1 pound black niçoise olives, drained

1 pound green Picholine olives, drained

1 pound golden raisins, plumped in hot water for 20 minutes, drained

1 pound toasted shelled almonds (preferably Mission)

¼ cup olive oil

3 tablespoons toasted fennel seeds

Zest and juice of 2 oranges

∞ Combine the black and green olives, the raisins and almonds in a bowl. Add the olive oil, fennel seeds and orange zest and juice.

Let stand for at least 1 hour before serving.

YIELDS ABOUT 4 POUNDS MIX

White Bean and Pesto Dip

Marlena Spieler's recipe is ideal to smear on bread or crackers, or to use as a dip for a crudité platter. It may be made in a matter of minutes using canned white beans and jarred pesto. The mixture is enlivened with fresh basil and a touch of garlic.

1 to 1½ cups cooked and drained cannellini beans (canned OK)

3 tablespoons basil pesto

1 garlic clove, finely chopped

1 tablespoon chopped fresh basil

∞ Mash the beans with the pesto and garlic in a bowl, or purée in a food processor, then mix in the basil. If the mixture is too thick for dipping, thin with a little water.

SERVES 4

East-West Pesto Dip

Fusion cooking has become trendy in Bay Area restaurants, and it's brought home in this easy takeoff on Italian pesto. Created by Marlena Spieler, the versatile sauce combines mint, cilantro, chile pepper, peanuts and other flavorings. Use it as a dip for oven-roasted vegetable chips, dim sum or chunks of grilled fish speared on toothpicks, or as a sauce on steamed rice noodles.

Leaves from ½ bunch mint, finely chopped (about 6 tablespoons)

Leaves from ½ bunch cilantro, finely chopped (about 6 tablespoons)

1 garlic clove, finely chopped

½ hot green chile, or more, to taste

½ teaspoon finely chopped fresh ginger

2 tablespoons vegetable oil

Juice of ½ lemon

¼ teaspoon sugar

2 to 3 tablespoons water, or as needed

3 tablespoons finely chopped toasted salted peanuts

ۖ Combine the mint, cilantro, garlic, chile, ginger, oil, lemon juice and sugar in a food processor or blender. Process until finely puréed. Continue processing, adding water until the mixture achieves the smooth consistency of a dip.

Transfer to a serving bowl and stir in the peanuts.

SERVES 4

Tomato and Hot Pepper Relish

Joanne Weir, an expert in the cuisines of the Mediterranean, suggests serving this relish as a meze, *or first course, with drinks before dinner. It combines finely chopped tomatoes with olive oil, Italian parsley and onions. For depth, Weir has added two kinds of peppers: hot red pepper flakes and mild green Anaheim chiles.*

2 tablespoons extra virgin olive oil

3 tablespoons chopped Italian parsley

½ cup minced yellow onion

1¼ pounds tomatoes, finely chopped and drained

4 green Anaheim chiles, cored, seeded and minced

½ to 1 teaspoon crushed hot red pepper flakes

5 tablespoons tomato paste

Coarse salt and freshly ground pepper, to taste

◉◉ Combine the olive oil, parsley, onion, tomatoes, chiles, pepper flakes and tomato paste in a bowl. Mix until blended. Season with salt and pepper. Serve with bread or pita triangles.

SERVES 8

Russian Dilled Spinach Dip

This low-fat dip is designed for serving with an assortment of vegetables: red and yellow pepper strips, carrots, cucumbers and celery, to name a few. It's good with low-fat potato chips, too. Creator Marlena Spieler also likes to spoon it over boiled potatoes.

1 cup finely chopped cooked and drained spinach (frozen OK)

3 ounces nonfat sour cream or low-fat yogurt

3 ounces low-fat cottage cheese, mashed lightly with a fork

2 heaping tablespoons reduced-calorie mayonnaise

1 garlic clove, finely chopped

3 or 4 green onions (white and green parts), finely chopped

1 to 2 teaspoons fresh lemon juice, or to taste

Quick Endive Appetizer

Separate the endive into leaves and refrigerate until ready to serve. Arrange the leaves on a platter. To the base of each one add a dollop of sour cream seasoned with chopped Italian parsley and lemon juice. Sprinkle on some salmon roe and serve.

Salt and freshly ground pepper, to taste

3 tablespoons finely chopped Italian parsley

3 tablespoons finely chopped fresh dill, or 1 teaspoon dried dill weed

1 tablespoon chopped fresh tarragon (optional)

⚭ Put the spinach in a bowl. Add the sour cream, cottage cheese and mayonnaise; stir to blend.

Stir in the garlic, green onions, lemon juice, salt, pepper, parsley, dill and tarragon, if desired.

SERVES 4

Chinese Spicy Red Pepper Dipping Sauce

This intense dipping sauce dresses up store-bought Chinese vegetable dumplings. For a chic presentation, Marlena Spieler suggests placing each dumpling in a Chinese soup spoon, then arranging the spoons in spoke-fashion around a bowl of this bright red dipping sauce. Or another idea: Serve the sauce with roasted or steamed sweet potatoes for a novel room-temperature appetizer.

2 or 3 roasted red peppers from a jar

2 garlic cloves, chopped

1 to 2 teaspoons soy sauce

1 to 2 teaspoons Asian sesame oil

1 to 2 teaspoons rice vinegar

1 teaspoon chopped peeled fresh ginger

½ teaspoon sugar, or to taste

3 tablespoons chopped cilantro leaves

⚭ Combine the red peppers, garlic, soy, sesame oil, vinegar, ginger and sugar in a blender or food processor. Process until puréed.

Sprinkle with the cilantro and serve.

SERVES 4

Creamy Brandade of Salt Cod and Potatoes with Garlic Croutons

This traditional French Provençal appetizer, created by Richard Reddington when he was chef at the charming Chapeau restaurant in San Francisco, is creamy and rich. The process of soaking salt cod, then cooking it with milk, garlic and potatoes, takes a little time, but the end result is magnificent. It's just right to serve as an hors d'oeuvre with crispy oven-baked toast rounds.

    1 pound boned salt cod
    2 heads of garlic
    1¼ cups olive oil
    ½ bunch thyme
    1 pound russet potatoes, peeled and cut into eighths
    About 8 cups milk
    Salt and freshly ground pepper, to taste
    2 tablespoons extra virgin olive oil, plus oil for baguette slices
    1 baguette

◉◉ Soak the salt cod in water to cover for 24 hours, changing the water several times.

Break the heads of garlic into individual cloves. Gently smash the cloves, then peel them. Save 1 garlic clove for the croutons. Place the remaining garlic cloves in a saucepan, add the olive oil and simmer gently over low to medium-low heat for 20 minutes, or until the garlic turns golden brown. Remove from heat and add the thyme.

Place the potatoes in a saucepan and add water to cover. Bring to a boil over high heat, then reduce heat to low and simmer until tender; drain. Rice the potatoes and keep them warm.

Drain the salt cod and place in a saucepan. Pour in enough milk to just cover. Bring to a boil over high heat, reduce heat to low and simmer gently for 8 to 10 minutes. Drain and remove the salt cod. Add 1 cup milk to the pan and bring to a boil.

Combine the potatoes, the cod and ¾ cup of the boiling milk, the garlic and its cooking oil (discard the thyme) in a food processor. Process until smooth (don't overprocess or it will become gummy). If the brandade is too thick, add as much of the remaining ¼ cup hot milk as needed. Season with salt, if necessary, and pepper. Stir in the extra virgin olive oil.

Preheat the oven to 400 degrees. Cut the baguette on the bias into croutons. Toss or brush with a little extra virgin olive oil, season with salt and pepper and toast until golden. Rub with the reserved garlic clove.

Divide the brandade among heated plates and surround with croutons.

SERVES 8 TO 10

Libyan Spicy Pumpkin Dip

Serve this zesty Sephardic appetizer with chunks of bread or raw vegetables, such as cucumber slices. Marlena Spieler and her daughter first tasted a similar dip in a Libyan-Jewish restaurant in Jaffa, Israel. Any leftovers will keep for up to 1 week in a covered container in the refrigerator.

> 3 to 4 tablespoons extra virgin olive oil
>
> 1 onion, finely chopped
>
> 5 to 8 garlic cloves, coarsely chopped
>
> 1½ pounds pumpkin, butternut or other winter squash (or sweet potatoes), peeled, seeded and diced
>
> 1 to 2 teaspoons cumin
>
> 1 teaspoon paprika
>
> ¼ to ½ teaspoon dried ginger
>
> ¼ to ½ teaspoon curry powder
>
> ½ cup diced tomatoes (if using fresh, you might need 1 or 2 tablespoons tomato paste to boost the flavor)
>
> ½ red jalapeño or serrano chile, seeded and chopped
>
> Salt, to taste
>
> Pinch of sugar
>
> Juice of ½ lemon, or to taste
>
> 2 tablespoons chopped cilantro

◉◉ Heat the olive oil in a sauté pan over medium-low heat. Add the onion and half of the garlic and sauté for about 10 minutes, until the onion is softened. Add the squash, reduce heat, cover and cook for 10 minutes, or until the squash is about half tender.

Kiwi Antipasto

Georgeanne Brennan wraps slices of peeled kiwi with prosciutto, then tops them with crumbles of fresh goat cheese or blue cheese.

Stir in the cumin, paprika, ginger and curry, then cook until the spices are fragrant. Add the tomatoes, chile, salt and sugar; cook over medium-high heat for about 20 minutes, or until the liquid has evaporated and the squash is very, very tender. Add a few tablespoons of water if needed, so the mixture doesn't dry out and burn.

When the squash is very tender, mash it into a coarse purée using a potato masher. You want a thick, pastelike consistency.

Add the reserved garlic and taste for seasoning, then stir in the lemon juice. Sprinkle with the cilantro and serve at room temperature.

SERVES 4 TO 6

Basic Bruschetta

One of the trendiest appetizers to tease the palate in the last couple of years has been bruschetta, which is slices of toast that are brushed with olive oil, rubbed with garlic, then topped in myriad ways. Here's a recipe for the basic bruschetta with garlic and olive oil (great served with soups and salads). Just about anything can be spooned on top: tomatoes, artichokes or a purée of seasoned white beans.

Day-old dense country-style French or Italian bread

1 garlic clove, halved

Extra virgin olive oil

Salt (optional)

⊚⊚ Cut the bread into ½-inch-thick slices about 3 inches square. The shape of the loaf will determine the shape of your slices. They may be more rectangular than square, which is fine, but don't make them too big to handle easily. Preheat the broiler or a toaster oven, or prepare a charcoal fire (gray-ash stage).

Toast or grill the bread on both sides until golden. While warm, rub one side of each slice with the cut sides of the garlic halves. Drizzle with olive oil, using about 1 teaspoon per slice. Sprinkle with salt, if desired.

SERVES 6 TO 8

Piatti's Bruschetta with Spinach and Lemon

Here is Piatti restaurant's version of bruschetta, which is topped with an enticing mixture of spinach and lemon. Be sure to slice the lemon paper-thin with a sharp knife or mandoline, or it will be too strong.

Juicy Jicama Appetizer

Peel a jicama, then cut it into paper-thin slices. Drizzle with lime juice and add a sprinkling of ground dried red chile and crumbled queso fresco.

1 tablespoon pine nuts

1½ tablespoons extra virgin olive oil

2 large garlic cloves, thinly sliced

½ pound spinach, washed and stemmed

Salt, to taste

½ tablespoon fresh lemon juice

6 Basic Bruschetta (see opposite)

6 paper-thin slices from a small lemon, seeded and halved

1½ tablespoons freshly grated pecorino cheese

Preheat the oven to 300 degrees.

Place the pine nuts in a pie tin and toast in the oven for 8 to 10 minutes, or until golden. Cool.

Heat the olive oil in a large skillet over medium-high heat. When the oil is hot, add the garlic and sauté until it just begins to color. Add the spinach and toss until it just wilts. Season with salt and add the lemon juice; toss briefly. Divide the spinach mixture among the toasts, making sure the garlic is evenly divided. Top with lemon slices. Sprinkle with the pine nuts and pecorino. Serve immediately.

YIELDS 6 BRUSCHETTA

Bruschetta with Prosciutto and Teleme

Janet Fletcher, Chronicle *staff writer and cookbook author, likes to combine salty prosciutto and smooth Teleme cheese. Here, she pairs them as a topping for toasts, then puts them under the broiler until the meat crisps and the cheese melts.*

6 slices (½ inch thick and 3 inches square) of day-old dense French or Italian bread

1½ tablespoons extra virgin olive oil

3 large thin slices prosciutto di Parma, about 3 ounces total, halved

2 ounces cold Teleme cheese, diced

Freshly ground pepper, to taste

Fresh basil leaves for garnish

Preheat the broiler or a toaster oven.

Brush the bread lightly on both sides with the olive oil. Toast on one side, then turn the bread over. On the untoasted side of each slice, put a half-slice of prosciutto, draping so it fits without much overhang. Top each toast with small clumps of cheese, dividing the cheese evenly among the toasts.

Broil until the prosciutto crisps and the cheese melts. Garnish with a grinding of pepper and a few torn basil leaves.

YIELDS 6 BRUSCHETTA

Tecomate and Poblano Chile Crostini

Crostini are similar to bruschetta, but the toasts are generally smaller. Here, chef Dona Savitsky, of Dona Tomas in Oakland, gives porcini mushrooms a Mexican twist with poblano chiles and epazote, a wild weedlike herb sometimes found in Hispanic food stores, specialty stores or garden centers. If you can't find it, just leave it out. If porcini mushrooms are unavailable, use the reconstituted dried variety or any other fresh mushroom.

Easy Fig Crostini

Spread toasted slices of baguette with a thin layer of olive oil. Top with a thin strip of prosciutto and coarsely chopped fresh figs.

1 tablespoon canola oil

1 tablespoon butter

1½ pounds tecomates (porcini mushrooms), thinly sliced

½ cup Mexican crema or crème fraîche

1½ teaspoons chopped epazote

Salt and freshly ground pepper, to taste

36 slices of baguette, toasted

2 poblano chiles, roasted, peeled and cut into ¼-inch strips

Heat the oil and butter in a skillet over medium heat. Add the mushrooms and sauté until tender. Stir in the crema and epazote; season with salt and pepper. Cook for 1 to 2 minutes to combine the flavors. Cool slightly.

Spoon the topping onto the toasts; finish with the chile strips.

YIELDS 36 CROSTINI

Shrimp Crostini with Thai Basil and Kaffir Lime Sauce

The Thai basil and kaffir lime leaves called for in this recipe, from Alexander Ong of Xanadu restaurant in Berkeley, are available in specialty produce markets and Asian grocery stores.

2 tablespoons vegetable oil

3 tablespoons minced fresh ginger

4 garlic cloves, minced

36 medium-size shrimp, shelled and deveined

Juice of 1 lime

½ cup coconut milk

Salt and freshly ground pepper, to taste

2 tablespoons slivered Thai basil leaves

2 tablespoons minced kaffir lime leaves

36 slices of baguette, toasted

Heat the oil in a sauté pan over medium heat. When the oil is hot, add the ginger and garlic; sauté for about 30 seconds, or until aromatic. Add the shrimp and sauté for about 4 minutes, or until they are almost cooked.

Add the lime juice to the pan and cook until it evaporates. Add the coconut milk and cook for 1 to 2 minutes, or until the mixture is slightly reduced. Season with salt and pepper. Add the basil and lime leaves, and mix well.

Place 1 shrimp on each toast, then drizzle lightly with the sauce.

YIELDS 36 CROSTINI

Tips for Making Crostini

Italian and French baguettes (not sourdough) are the best choices for crostini, although other breads such as rye and pumpernickel may be substituted. Use day-old bread if possible because fresh bread may not withstand the weight or moisture of some toppings. Slice crostini no thicker than ¼ inch.

The slices should be small enough to be eaten in 1 or 2 bites. They are traditionally cut straight down but bias cuts are very attractive.

Brush the slices with a judicious amount of olive oil. If desired, sprinkle with a dash of salt and freshly ground pepper and rub with a garlic clove.

Smoked Trout, Asian Pear and Horseradish Cream Crostini

A creamy spread spiked with horseradish and pecans gives a pleasant kick to this crostini from Jennifer Cox of Montage restaurant in San Francisco's Sony Metreon. Crisp slices of Asian pear and flakes of smoked trout are used as the topping, creating an intriguing contrast of textures and flavors. These make a great nibble with mixed drinks or white wine.

1 cup heavy cream

¼ teaspoon sugar

1 tablespoon prepared horseradish

1 tablespoon chopped toasted pecans

1 teaspoon minced lemon zest

¼ teaspoon minced garlic

½ teaspoon apple cider vinegar

Salt and freshly ground pepper, to taste

1 Asian pear, peeled, cored and thinly sliced

Juice of 1 lemon

5 ounces smoked trout

36 slices of baguette, toasted

1 tablespoon minced fresh tarragon leaves

Whip the cream with the sugar in a bowl to firm peaks. Fold in the horseradish, pecans, lemon zest, garlic and vinegar. Season with salt and pepper.

Peel, core and thinly slice the pear, dropping the slices directly into a bowl with the lemon juice to keep them from browning.

Flake the trout into a small bowl.

Spread the horseradish cream in a thin layer on each toast. Top with a slice of Asian pear and a small amount of the flaked trout. Top with tarragon and sprinkle with freshly ground pepper, if desired.

YIELDS 36 CROSTINI

To toast the bread, place slices on a baking sheet in a 400-degree oven for about 10 minutes, or until lightly golden. Cook slightly less if you plan to reheat with toppings. Remove from oven and let cool.

If making crostini ahead of time, cool to room temperature and seal in an airtight plastic container or storage bag. Store at room temperature.

Choose toppings with care. They should be neat and compact so they don't fall off as the crostini are being passed or eaten. Garnish with fresh herbs for color.

Most people will eat 2 or 3 of each hors d'oeuvre. One baguette will yield approximately 36 to 40 toasts.

Morel Quesadillas with Mild Red Chile Sauce

For a great quick meal or an unusual cocktail party nosh, Marlena Spieler likes to top fresh corn or flour tortillas with well-seasoned morel mushrooms, a smear of chile paste and shredded Monterey Jack cheese. Then she pops them under the broiler until they're melty-hot. Cut into pie-shaped wedges to serve to guests.

½ ounce dried morel mushrooms, or about 3 ounces fresh

1 tablespoon olive oil

3 garlic cloves, chopped

Salt, to taste

1 teaspoon ground New Mexico or California chile

1 teaspoon ancho chile powder

¼ teaspoon ground cumin

1 ripe tomato, peeled, seeded and diced

Juice of ¼ lemon, or to taste

Cayenne pepper, to taste

¼ teaspoon dried oregano, or to taste

8 corn or flour tortillas

12 ounces shredded Monterey Jack cheese

1 tablespoon chopped cilantro leaves for garnish

👓 If using dried mushrooms, soak them in hot water for 30 minutes, then drain.

If using fresh mushrooms, soak them in cold water for 30 minutes, then drain well.

Cut the soaked morels into quarters or halves, depending on their size. You want little nuggets of mushroom rather than big chunks.

Heat the olive oil in a skillet over medium heat. Add the morels and half of the garlic and sauté for about 5 minutes, or until the morels are softened and cooked through. Set aside.

Using a mortar and pestle, pound the remaining garlic and a little salt to a purée, then work in the ground chile and chile powder, the cumin, diced tomato and lemon juice. Season the chile paste with salt, cayenne and oregano.

Margaritas

We tried many versions of margaritas using various tequilas, comparing fresh lime juice versus Rose's bottled juice, and using various orange-flavored liqueurs. Although it's traditional, we found the Triple Sec margarita too sweet. On the other end of the spectrum, the Grand Marnier margarita was too tart. Our favorite was the margarita made with Cointreau, which provided the brightest flavor.

Personal preference has a lot to do with whether you like to drink a margarita straight up, on the rocks or made into a slush. In any case, the Food Department agreed that the following recipe was tops:

Margarita

2 ounces 100 percent blue
    agave tequila (such as
    Herradura Silver)
1½ ounces Rose's
    sweetened lime juice
¾ ounce Cointreau
Splash of sweet-and-sour
    mix
Fresh lime juice
Kosher salt

◉◉ Fill a glass or cocktail
shaker with ice. Add the
tequila, Rose's lime juice,
Cointreau and sweet-and-
sour mix. Stir or shake
vigorously. Dip the rim of
a margarita glass into lime
juice and then into salt. Fill
the glass with crushed ice.
Strain the margarita into
the ice-filled glass and serve.

To make a frozen
margarita: Combine the
tequila, Rose's lime juice,
Cointreau and sweet-and-
sour mix in a blender
filled with ice. Blend until
thoroughly mixed. Dip
the rim of a margarita
glass into lime juice and
then into salt. Pour in the
margarita and serve.

SERVES 1

Place the tortillas on baking sheet(s) and smear with a little of the chile
paste. Sprinkle with the morels, scattering them about (they will not cover in a
layer; merely stud the tortillas here and there). Top with the shredded cheese.

Broil until the cheese melts and sizzles. Cut into wedges and serve
immediately, garnished with the chopped cilantro.

SERVES 10 TO 12

Tzatziki

*This traditional Greek yogurt and cucumber dip from Joanne Weir is loaded
with garlic and fresh herbs. Serve with wedges of pita bread, crackers or
chunks of hearty peasant-style bread.*

2 cups plain yogurt
½ cucumber, peeled and seeded
4 garlic cloves, minced
1 tablespoon chopped fresh mint
1 tablespoon chopped fresh dill
1 tablespoon extra virgin olive oil
1 tablespoon fresh lemon juice, or to taste
Coarse salt, to taste

◉◉ Place the yogurt in a sieve lined with a double layer of cheesecloth and let
drain for 8 hours or overnight.

Coarsely grate the cucumber to make 1 cup. Place the grated cucumber
on paper towels and let drain for 30 minutes.

Combine the yogurt, cucumber, garlic, mint, dill and olive oil in a bowl.
Mix well. Add the lemon juice, then season with salt.

SERVES 8

Formaggio alla Griglia con Limone (Grilled Cheese on a Lemon Leaf)

This marvelous appetizer by Marlena Spieler is nothing more than a hunk of cheese placed on a fresh lemon leaf, then pan-grilled, broiled or cooked over an open fire. The melty cheese is scraped off the leaf with the teeth. The leaves protect the cheese against the heat and impart a delicate lemony perfume to the cheese.

> 8 unsprayed lemon leaves, or 16 unsprayed leaves if grilling
>
> 8 ounces cheese (fresh or aged mozzarella, provolone, pecorino, Monterey Jack or similar cheese), cut into eight ½-inch-thick slices

๏๏ Top each leaf with a slice of cheese, then place leaves in a nonstick skillet or on a broiler pan.

Cook over (or under) medium-high heat until the cheese begins to melt and the leaves are lightly browned. If using a skillet, you may need to cover it in order for the cheese to melt a bit; but a lot depends on the type of cheese you are using.

To cook the cheese on a barbecue grill, prepare coals and let them burn down to the gray-ash stage. Use 2 lemon leaves per slice of cheese, one on the top and one on the bottom. This will allow you to turn the little packet so the cheese will melt evenly. Place the cheese packets on the grill, or use a mesh vegetable-grilling rack, and cook, turning the packets once, until the cheese begins to melt and the leaves are lightly browned.

Serve immediately.

SERVES 4

Pairing Wine and Cheese

A cheese course can dress up even the most modest meal. Nick Peyton, owner and cheese master at Gary Danko restaurant in San Francisco, offers these suggestions:

With red Bordeaux: Aged sheep's milk cheese, English farmhouse cheddar and triple crème cheeses such as Explorateur.

With Sauvignon Blanc: Any goat's milk cheese.

With California Pinot Noir: Creamy and mild soft cheeses such as Coulommiers, Reblochon and Morbier.

With Sauternes and other sweet wines: Roquefort and rich cow's milk blue cheeses.

Spiced Cheese

This mashed feta, spiked with garlic and sweet paprika, comes from Cappadocia in central Turkey, where it is served as a spread or a dip. Joanne Weir likes to accompany it with warm pita bread or a sturdy loaf such as sourdough French.

1¼ cups plain yogurt

¼ teaspoon salt

10 ounces feta cheese

2 garlic cloves, minced

½ to ¾ teaspoon cayenne

1 teaspoon sweet paprika

1 tablespoon plus 1 teaspoon extra virgin olive oil

Freshly ground pepper, to taste

Cured black olives for garnish

◉◉ Place the yogurt in a sieve lined with a double layer of cheesecloth and let drain for 4 hours.

Combine the yogurt, salt and feta in a bowl; mash to a smooth paste with a fork. Add the garlic, cayenne, paprika, 1 tablespoon olive oil and pepper; mix well.

Alternatively, this may be prepared in a food processor.

Spread the purée on a serving plate. Drizzle with the remaining olive oil and garnish with olives.

SERVES 8

Storing and Serving Cheese

David Zaft, cheese buyer for the Pasta shop in Oakland, recommends removing cheese from any plastic wrap as soon as you get home. Some experts believe that plastic can impart an unpleasant taste and traps moisture that promotes the growth of mold. He suggests wrapping the cheese in wax paper.

To store: Janet Fletcher recommends storing cheese in the refrigerator's produce bin, which has a higher humidity level.

To serve: Cheese consultant Daphne Zepos says to remove cheese from the refrigerator at least 1 hour before serving; 4 hours is ideal.

Eggplant Caviar with Chipotle Oil

Jacqueline McMahan claims this eggplant spread is addictive—and we have to agree, thanks to the interplay of garlic and smoky chipotle chiles. Serve with toasted pita triangles, thin slices of toasted baguette or warm corn tortillas.

2 large globe eggplants, about 2 pounds total

1 tablespoon fresh lemon juice

⅓ cup olive oil

1 teaspoon red wine vinegar

¾ teaspoon toasted dried oregano

½ to 1 teaspoon salt, or to taste

4 garlic cloves

½ bunch cilantro, finely minced

Chipotle Oil (recipe follows)

Preheat the oven to 350 degrees.

Place the eggplants on a baking sheet and bake for 1 hour, or until the flesh is very tender and the skin is shriveled. Set aside until cool enough to handle.

Scoop out the eggplant flesh; discard any seeds. Place the flesh in the middle of a muslin dish towel. Twist the ends together to squeeze out excess liquid from the eggplant.

Transfer the eggplant flesh to a food processor. Add the lemon juice and, with the processor running, slowly drizzle in the olive oil. Add the vinegar, oregano, salt and garlic; process until the mixture is puréed. Just before serving, stir in the minced cilantro.

The caviar may be made 1 day ahead. Store in a covered container in the refrigerator.

To serve: Spread on toasts or crackers, then sprinkle with a few drops of chipotle oil.

SERVES 4

CHIPOTLE OIL: Combine 1 cup olive oil and 3 slivered dried chipotle chiles in a small saucepan. Use more chiles if you want the oil to be really hot. Heat on low for 5 minutes. Store in a covered glass jar in the refrigerator, where it will keep for up to 1 month. Other uses: Drizzle over steamed vegetables, add sparingly to salsas, use to flavor marinades.

Artichoke Heart Pâté

This tangy pâté, made with marinated artichoke hearts, may be eaten cold with a handful of crisp lettuce leaves. Marlena Spieler also likes to serve it with sliced green apples and crackers. For a warm appetizer, spread the pâté onto thin slices of baguette and broil until sizzling.

1 cup drained marinated artichoke hearts

2 tablespoons pine nuts

3 to 4 tablespoons grated Parmigiano-Reggiano

2 garlic cloves, chopped

1 tablespoon mayonnaise

1 teaspoon Dijon or other mustard

Tiny dash of Tabasco

Freshly ground pepper, to taste

Chop the artichokes and pine nuts to a coarse pâté consistency. (Use a food processor or blender, or chop them by hand.) Add the cheese, garlic, mayonnaise, mustard and Tabasco; mix well. Season with pepper.

SERVES 4

Grilled Plums with Bacon and Goat Cheese

For a sweet and savory appetizer Georgeanne Brennan pits fresh or dried prune plums, tucks a nugget of goat cheese inside, then wraps with bacon. Fasten with a wooden skewer and grill for 2 to 3 minutes, or until the bacon is crispy and the cheese has melted.

Vanilla Shrimp with Avocado-Tarragon Dip

Vanilla is the secret ingredient in this recipe by Michael Bauer. The shrimp are marinated overnight in a mixture of wine, orange juice, lemon zest and a generous sprinkling of red pepper flakes to add a little heat to the blend, but it's the vanilla that imparts an intriguing background flavor. The marinade infuses the shrimp with flavor, so it's a great way to add punch to frozen shrimp. The hot shrimp may be served with the avocado dip (recipe follows) or a mixture of commercial mayonnaise smoothed with lemon juice, minced lemon peel and a generous handful of finely chopped, fresh tarragon leaves.

1½ pounds large shrimp, shelled with tails attached

2 cups white wine (such as Chenin Blanc, Gewürztraminer or Sauvignon Blanc)

½ cup fresh orange juice

Zest of 1 lemon, chopped

Juice of ½ lemon

Generous ½ teaspoon vanilla

1 teaspoon hot red pepper flakes

1½ tablespoons finely chopped fresh tarragon

1 teaspoon kosher salt, plus more, to taste

½ teaspoon freshly ground white pepper

2 garlic cloves, coarsely chopped

2 tablespoons olive oil

Avocado-Tarragon Dip (recipe follows)

◉◉ Rinse the shrimp in cold water and drain. Combine the wine, orange juice, lemon zest, lemon juice, vanilla, pepper flakes, tarragon, 1 teaspoon salt, the pepper, garlic and ½ tablespoon of the olive oil in a large bowl or heavy-duty gallon-size plastic storage bag. Add the shrimp and stir to coat. Marinate for up to 6 hours in the refrigerator.

Drain the shrimp well. Heat ½ tablespoon of the oil in a heavy large skillet over high heat until almost smoking. Working in batches, add the shrimp to the skillet, season with salt and sauté for about 5 minutes, or until the shrimp curl and turn bright pink. Transfer to a serving bowl. Repeat with remaining shrimp, using more oil for each batch.

Serve with avocado dip.

SERVES 10

Avocado-Tarragon Dip

1 ripe avocado, pitted and peeled
Finely chopped zest and juice of ½ lemon
1 tablespoon finely chopped fresh tarragon
½ teaspoon kosher salt
¼ to ½ teaspoon freshly ground white pepper
4 drops of Tabasco

Mash the avocado in a bowl until smooth. Stir in the lemon zest and juice, tarragon, salt, white pepper and Tabasco. Cover and refrigerate.

YIELDS ABOUT 1 CUP

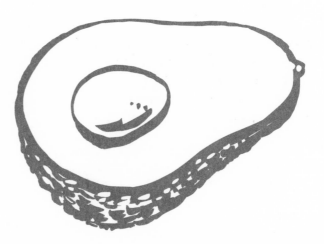

Garlicky Shrimp from a Tapas Bar

These easy-to-make hot shrimp in their shells are reminiscent of ones you'll find in the tiny tapas bars all over Spain. This recipe is from Marlena Spieler.

1 to 1½ pounds large shrimp, in their shells

5 to 8 garlic cloves, chopped

Large pinch of hot red pepper flakes

1 lemon, halved

4 tablespoons olive oil

Salt, to taste

2 tablespoons chopped Italian parsley

◉◉ Combine the shrimp in a bowl with half of the garlic, the pepper flakes, juice of half of the lemon and 2 tablespoons of the olive oil. Season with salt; marinate for at least 30 minutes.

Heat a skillet over high heat until very hot. Add the remaining 2 tablespoons olive oil and the remaining garlic, cook for about 5 seconds, stirring constantly, then reduce the heat to medium and add the shrimp. Sauté, turning occasionally, for 5 minutes, or until the shrimp turn opaque.

Serve hot, sprinkled with the parsley and garnished with the remaining lemon half, cut into wedges for squeezing as desired.

SERVES 4

Quick Vegetable Appetizer

To make cauliflower tapas, Georgeanne Brennan suggests steaming bite-size florets. While still hot, dress them with a vinaigrette made with sherry vinegar, olive oil, salt, freshly ground pepper and hot red pepper flakes. Cool to room temperature and serve.

Stuffed Mussels

Stuffed mussels are popular in Spain and France, where they are served as an appetizer or a first course. In this version, Georgeanne Brennan tops each mussel on its half shell with a mound of herb-seasoned breadcrumbs moistened with tomatoes and olive oil. Then she bakes them until golden brown and serves them hot or at room temperature.

48 mussels, scrubbed and debearded

1¼ to 1½ cups fine breadcrumbs

½ teaspoon salt

½ teaspoon freshly ground pepper

3 tablespoons minced Italian parsley

2 tablespoons minced fresh thyme

4 garlic cloves, minced

1½ tomatoes, peeled, seeded and minced

1½ to 2 tablespoons extra virgin olive oil

Preheat the oven to 500 degrees.

Place the mussels in a baking pan in a single layer. Roast for 8 to 10 minutes, or until the shells open.

Remove from the oven and let cool for about 15 minutes. (Be sure to reserve all juices in the baking pan.)

When the mussels are cool enough to handle, pick up one and pull apart the shells, holding them over the pan to collect the juices. Using a knife, remove the mussel from the shell. Return the mussel to one of the shell halves; discard the other. Repeat with the remaining mussels.

Reduce oven temperature to 450 degrees.

Combine the breadcrumbs, reserved mussel liquid, the salt, pepper, parsley, thyme, garlic and tomatoes in a bowl; mix well. Add enough olive oil to hold the mixture together.

Cover each mussel with about 1 tablespoon of the filling, packing it tightly and mounding the top to the rim of the shell. This will prevent the mussel from drying out in the oven. Place the filled mussels on a baking sheet and bake for 12 to 14 minutes, or until the crumb mixture turns golden brown. If necessary, put them under the broiler for 1 to 2 minutes to finish browning.

Serve hot or at room temperature.

SERVES 8 AS AN APPETIZER; 4 AS A FIRST COURSE

Lucas' Sardinas en Escabeche (Marinated Sardines)

This is a favorite recipe of chef Lucas Gasco of Zarzuela in San Francisco. Joanne Weir suggests serving this as a tapa with fino, manzanilla or amontillado sherry. If you can't get fresh sardines, substitute another white fish such as trout.

> 2 pounds fresh sardines, cleaned and gutted
>
> Salt and freshly ground pepper, to taste
>
> 1 cup all-purpose flour
>
> 4 tablespoons olive oil
>
> 1 yellow onion, thinly sliced
>
> 3 garlic cloves, thinly sliced
>
> 6 peppercorns
>
> 4 whole cloves
>
> 2 bay leaves
>
> 1 small carrot, thinly sliced
>
> 2 thyme sprigs
>
> 4 tablespoons sherry vinegar
>
> ½ teaspoon pimenton (smoked paprika) or sweet paprika
>
> 1½ cups water

From the belly side, split each sardine and remove the backbone. Open flat and rinse well under cold water. Pat dry, then season with salt and pepper.

Put the flour on a plate. Dip both sides of each sardine into the flour, then pat off the excess.

Heat 2 tablespoons of the olive oil in a large skillet over medium-high heat. Add the sardines and fry for 1 minute per side, or until lightly golden, then transfer them to a shallow casserole dish.

Heat the remaining 2 tablespoons olive oil in another large skillet over medium heat. Add the onion and garlic and cook, stirring occasionally, for about 7 minutes, or until the onion is soft and the garlic is lightly golden.

Increase the heat to high, add the peppercorns, cloves, bay leaves, carrot, thyme, vinegar, pimenton and water. Bring to a boil, then boil for 3 minutes. Remove from the heat and pour over the sardines.

The Best Sangria

Here's a great Ruby Red Sangria from Charanga, a pan-Latin restaurant in San Francisco:

> 3 bottles (750ml each) Taylor Hearty Burgundy
>
> 1 orange, cut into ½-inch dice
>
> 1 Granny Smith apple, cut into ½-inch dice
>
> 1 lemon, cut into ½-inch dice
>
> ½ cup sugar

Divide the wine, fruit and sugar between 2 pitchers. Stir to dissolve sugar. Refrigerate and serve.

SERVES 8

Refrigerate the sardines for 12 hours. Bring to room temperature before serving.

SERVES 8

Rose Pistola's Cured Salmon with Green Peppercorns

Like ceviche, this salmon from Rose Pistola restaurant in San Francisco is "cooked" in a citrus marinade. You can use the same technique with halibut.

1 skinless king salmon fillet, in one piece, about 1½ pounds

1¼ cups white wine, plus more if needed

1¼ cups fresh lemon juice, plus more if needed

1 tablespoon kosher salt, plus more if needed

2 small bay leaves

About ½ cup extra virgin olive oil

2 tablespoons plus 2 teaspoons green peppercorns, lightly crushed

Using a very sharp knife, slice the salmon thinly on the diagonal, as for smoked salmon. Arrange the pieces in a single layer in a nonreactive dish.

Combine the wine, lemon juice and salt in a bowl and stir until the salt dissolves. Pour over the salmon, making sure it is completely submerged. Make additional wine–lemon juice mixture if necessary to cover the salmon.

Tear the bay leaves in half and tuck here and here. Cover and refrigerate for about 2 hours, or until the salmon is almost fully "cooked" by the acid.

Drain the slices and divide among serving plates. Top each serving generously with olive oil, then sprinkle with the crushed peppercorns.

SERVES 8

Garlic Chicken Wings with Garam Masala

These chicken wings by Laxmi Hiremath are ideal for a casual cocktail party. They're particularly good with beer, especially Indian beer such as Kingfisher and Taj Mahal, available at some liquor stores, supermarkets and Indian markets.

5 pounds chicken wings, separated at joints, tips discarded

Salt, to taste

2 tablespoons minced garlic

1 tablespoon garam masala

½ cup cider vinegar

½ cup honey

½ cup ketchup

Lemon wedges for garnish

Preheat the oven to 400 degrees.

Season the chicken wings with salt. Line two 10-by-15-by-1-inch baking pans with heavy-duty aluminum foil. Divide the chicken pieces between the two pans.

Bake, stirring gently every 10 minutes, for 35 to 40 minutes, or until golden.

While the chicken wings are baking, combine the garlic, garam masala, vinegar, honey and ketchup in a bowl; stir to blend well.

Pour the sauce over the chicken pieces, dividing it evenly between the two pans. Turn the chicken to coat the pieces evenly.

Return the chicken to the oven and bake for 25 to 30 minutes longer, or until the edges of the wings are lightly browned.

Transfer the wings to a serving platter and garnish with lemon wedges.

Serve hot or at room temperature.

SERVES 4 TO 6

Chipotle Chicken Wings

Few party foods are as irresistible as chicken wings, according to Marlena Spieler. She often combines the winglets and marinade way ahead of time, then pops them into the freezer until the night before the party. Once the wings are defrosted, they're ready to cook.

2 pounds chicken wings (about 10), each cut into 2 pieces

2 tablespoons sugar

Juice of 1 lemon

Coarse sea salt, to taste

1 teaspoon cumin

Several big pinches of cinnamon

Pinch of allspice

3 to 4 tablespoons orange juice

1 or 2 teaspoons grated orange zest

Chipotle sauce or canned chipotle chiles en adobo, to taste

5 tablespoons extra virgin olive oil

Freshly ground pepper, to taste

Fruit salsa or other salsa of choice (homemade or purchased), sprinkled with
   chopped cilantro

◎◎ Combine the chicken wings, sugar, lemon juice, salt, cumin, cinnamon, allspice, orange juice and zest, chipotle sauce, olive oil and pepper in a large bowl. Marinate for 1 to 2 hours in the refrigerator.

If making ahead, transfer to a zip-top plastic freezer bag and freeze for up to 2 months. The night before the party, place the frozen wings in a shallow baking dish and defrost, marinade and all, in the refrigerator.

Preheat the oven to 375 degrees. Bake the wings, turning occasionally, for about 1 hour, or until they are golden and browned in spots, the marinade has turned into a sticky mixture and the oil has separated. If they aren't browned and nicely crispy, either increase the oven temperature or place the wings under the broiler. Pour off and discard the oil before serving.

Serve hot or at room temperature with salsa.

SERVES 2 OR 3

Sautéed Foie Gras with Grapes

Quickly sautéed slices of fresh foie gras make an elegant appetizer for a special occasion. A thin crust forms on the outside, leaving the inside creamy. Classically, large, sweet Muscat grapes are used in this presentation, but other sweet grapes may be substituted. Be careful not to overcook the foie gras or it will melt away, warns Georgeanne Brennan.

- 1 fresh foie gras of duck (about 1 pound)
- 1 teaspoon salt
- 1 teaspoon freshly ground pepper
- 2 to 3 tablespoons fresh grape juice, strained (see Note)
- 2 tablespoons Armagnac or Cognac
- 1 cup Muscat or other sweet grapes, peeled

❧ Separate the small and large lobes of the liver by slicing through with a sharp knife. Cut the lobes lengthwise into ½-inch-thick slices. Remove the exposed nerves with your fingers or the tip of a sharp knife.

Place the slices between layers of wax paper and refrigerate them for 1 hour, or until they are thoroughly chilled and hard. Place a skillet over high heat. Season the foie gras slices with salt and pepper. When the pan is very hot, add the slices and cook them 30 to 40 seconds, then turn and cook another 30 to 40 seconds. Remove them to a platter.

Pour off the fat in the pan; add the grape juice and Armagnac to the pan, scraping up any bits still clinging to the pan. Cook over high heat until the liquid is reduced to about one half. Stir in the grapes and cook, stirring, for about 1 minute.

Arrange the grapes around the platter with the foie gras, and pour the hot pan juices over them.

SERVES 3 OR 4

NOTE: To make fresh grape juice, put peeled and seeded grapes in a blender and process until puréed.

Making Cucumber Vodka

Infusing vodka with flavors of fruit and vegetables is easy and makes the basis for wonderful mixed drinks. You can use cherries, pineapple, vanilla or jalapeños, to name a few.

As an example, here's how to make the cucumber vodka served at Infusion restaurant in San Francisco:

For 1 bottle of vodka (750ml), peel 3 or 4 cucumbers and cut into ⅛-inch-thick rounds (you'll need about 5 cups). Place the cucumber slices in a large, clean glass container and pour in vodka to completely cover them. Cover the container and store at room temperature for 2 weeks. Strain the vodka through a fine-mesh sieve lined with a paper coffee filter or two layers of damp cheesecloth. Pour into a clean bottle (the original vodka bottle is fine), seal tightly and store in the freezer. Serve straight up like a martini, use in a Bloody Mary, or mix with club soda over ice.

Chapter 2

Soups

Soup speaks a universal language of home and hearth—even in our wired, high-tech age.

We've collected a great selection that reflects flavors from around the world: Fresh Cranberry Bean Sambar from India (page 50); Tofu, Cucumber and Chive Soup from Vietnam (page 33); Tomato-Lime Soup with Tapenade from Provence (page 35); Chickpea and Orzo Soup from Egypt (page 44); Guacamole Soup from Mexico (page 36); Arroz Caldo, a rich rice porridge from the Philippines (page 54); and Fish Noodle Soup from Burma (page 60).

In San Francisco, soups tend to be hearty. Moderate daytime temperatures often followed by cool evenings make these a year-round treat. Many recipes in this chapter are a complete meal in a bowl, so they're ideal for the busy cook. Because most freeze well, you can double the recipe and have several different kinds in reserve for a quick weeknight meal.

Cold Cucumber Soup
with Cilantro

Chilled soups are very popular in the Bay Area during the summer, and few are as refreshing as this cucumber soup made with thick and creamy buttermilk. Instead of the traditional dill, Janet Fletcher uses cilantro, and she gives her creation a more complex flavor with the addition of chiles and sun-dried tomatoes.

2 pounds English cucumbers (about 2 cucumbers), peeled and chopped

1 cup coarsely chopped cilantro

½ cup drained oil-packed sun-dried tomatoes

2 large garlic cloves, thinly sliced

1 to 2 jalapeño chiles, seeded and sliced

5 cups buttermilk

Salt, to taste

Using a food processor and working in batches if necessary, purée the cucumbers, cilantro, tomatoes, garlic and 1 chile. Stop the machine and scrape down the sides once or twice. Taste the mixture and add some or all of the second chile, as desired.

With the motor running, add the buttermilk through the feed tube. Blend well.

Transfer the soup to a container; season with salt. Cover and refrigerate until ready to serve.

SERVES 6 TO 8

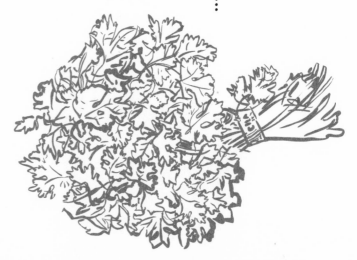

Tofu, Cucumber and Chive Soup

Mai Pham, who is a Chronicle *columnist and owns Lemon Grass restaurant in Sacramento, says this soup is a favorite of her grandmother, who is a vegetarian. To make the vegetable stock, Pham simmers yellow onions, carrots and daikon in water until the liquid is reduced almost by half. Just a teaspoon of sugar and some soy sauce help balance the flavors.*

2 tablespoons vegetable oil

1 shallot, sliced

1 garlic clove, minced

1½ tablespoons soy sauce, or to taste

5 cups vegetable stock, or water

6 ounces firm tofu, cut into 1-inch cubes

1 teaspoon sugar

½ cucumber, halved and sliced

1 cup chive pieces, each about 3 inches long

Salt, to taste

2 green onions (both white and green parts), very thinly sliced

Heat the oil in a medium pot over high heat. Add the shallot and garlic and stir for 10 seconds. Drizzle in the soy sauce, 1 or 2 teaspoons at a time, stirring, letting it sizzle and caramelize.

Add the stock, tofu, sugar and cucumber. Bring to a boil, reduce heat to low and simmer for 5 minutes. Add the chives and cook for 2 minutes.

Taste; season with salt and adjust the other seasonings as needed.

Finish with the green onions.

SERVES 4

Heavenly Corn Soup

Make this ethereal soup anytime you can find the sweetest, most tender corn. Jacqueline McMahan suggests garnishing the creamy soup with the red pepper purée and/or the cilantro cream.

2 tablespoons butter

3 garlic cloves, minced

½ cup chopped sweet white onion, like Vidalia or Maui

8 ears of fresh corn, grated (about 3½ cups)

2½ cups milk

¼ cup whipping cream

1½ teaspoons salt

Minced cilantro and diced tomato for garnish (optional)

Red Pepper Purée Garnish (optional)

1 red bell pepper

1 red jalapeño chile, stemmed and seeded

1 garlic clove

Pinch of salt

1 to 2 teaspoons water

Cilantro Cream Garnish (optional)

½ cup cilantro leaves

1 garlic clove

½ cup sour cream

Pinch of salt

Melt the butter in a heavy 3-quart pot over medium heat. Add the garlic and onion and gently cook for about 5 minutes, or until softened. Do not brown. Stir in the grated corn, any corn juices left in the bowl and the milk. Simmer very gently, stirring frequently, for 15 minutes. Add the cream and salt.

Ladle the soup into bowls. Garnish with cilantro and tomato, if desired. Or drizzle with red pepper purée and/or cilantro cream for a special occasion. (Place the purées in plastic squeeze bottles for easy drizzling.)

To make the red pepper purée: Roast the bell pepper over a gas burner or under the broiler until blackened. Place in a small paper bag, twist shut and let steam for 10 minutes. Remove the pepper and scrape off the blackened skin. Seed and derib the pepper. Purée in a blender with the jalapeño, garlic, salt and water.

To make the cilantro cream: Combine the cilantro, garlic, sour cream and salt in a blender and purée.

SERVES 6

Tomato-Lime Soup with Tapenade

Tomato and lime create an unbeatable combination in this bright Provençal-inspired soup from Marlena Spieler. It's best served with toast spread with tapenade (olive paste).

16 tomatoes, halved

Pinch of sugar

3 tablespoons extra virgin olive oil

1 onion, chopped

6 garlic cloves, chopped

1 cup tomato juice

4 cups chicken or vegetable stock or broth

Juice of ½ lime

4 large slices of country-style bread, stale and/or toasted, halved if desired

6 to 8 tablespoons tapenade (black olive paste) (see page 3)

◎◎ Put the tomatoes in a heavy nonreactive casserole; sprinkle with the sugar and drizzle with the olive oil. Cover the casserole and set over medium-low heat. Pan-roast the tomatoes, turning once or twice, for about 20 minutes, or until they have shrunk and wrinkled somewhat and the juices that have leaked out have intensified. Do not let them burn. About halfway through the roasting, add the onion and half of the garlic, cover and continue roasting.

When the onion is tender but not browned, add the tomato juice and stock. Bring to a boil and cook for 5 to 10 minutes to meld the flavors.

Working in small batches, purée the mixture in a blender or food processor, then return the soup to the pan. Add the lime juice and remaining garlic, then warm through.

Ladle the soup into bowls. Spread each toast generously with the tapenade (you added no salt to the soup, so the salty olives are necessary). Float an olive toast in each bowl.

SERVES 4

Guacamole Soup

In a small cafe in Tonala, Mexico, Jacqueline McMahan discovered this simple yet incredibly delicious soup that begins like guacamole. What makes the soup so good is using perfectly ripe avocados and rich homemade caldo de pollo (chicken stock).

6 cups homemade chicken stock

2 perfectly ripe avocados

1 teaspoon salt

Juice of 1 lime

1 cup shredded cooked chicken breast

About ½ cup chopped cilantro leaves

Lime wedges

Bring the stock to a boil in a pot over high heat while you prepare the avocados.

Halve the avocados and remove the pits. Scoop out half an avocado into each of 4 shallow soup bowls. Mash roughly with a fork as though you were making guacamole. Sprinkle each with a little salt and lime juice; blend well.

Pour 1½ cups of the scalding-hot stock into each bowl. Add ¼ cup shredded chicken and 2 tablespoons cilantro to each.

Pass lime wedges at the table.

SERVES 4

Cabbage Soup with Roquefort

Few combinations are more delightful than cabbage and Roquefort cheese, as evidenced in this rustic soup by Marlena Spieler. From the Auvergne area in France, the soup is amenable to all sorts of additions: cooked white beans, chunks of bacon, bites of potato. The pain levain could be replaced with a baguette or a loaf of country rye if you like.

4 slices of pain levain, each ½ to ¾ inch thick

2 tablespoons butter

1 onion, chopped

1 carrot, peeled and diced

1 celery stalk, diced

½ curly savoy cabbage, or regular cabbage, thinly sliced

1 tablespoon flour

4 cups stock or broth (vegetable, chicken or meat)

3 garlic cloves, sliced

3 tablespoons whipping cream

3 ounces Roquefort, or other strong blue cheese, crumbled

Coarsely ground pepper and salt, to taste, if needed

◎◎ Preheat the oven to 375 degrees. Put the bread on a baking sheet, place in the oven and bake for 20 minutes, or until golden brown. Remove and set aside.

Melt the butter in a large heavy saucepan over medium-low heat. Add the onion, carrot and celery and lightly cook for 8 to 10 minutes, or until the mixture is softened and golden. Add the cabbage, cover and cook for 10 to 15 minutes, or until the cabbage is softened.

Sprinkle the flour over the vegetables, stir well and cook for 2 to 3 minutes longer, then stir in the stock. Bring to a boil, reduce heat to low and simmer, uncovered, for 30 minutes.

Add the garlic and simmer for 10 minutes. Stir in the cream and Roquefort. Season with pepper and, if needed, salt.

Ladle into bowls and serve each with a slice of toasted bread.

SERVES 4

Roasted Eggplant Bisque

This rich, spicy soup comes from chef/owner Chris Rossi of Citron in Oakland.

¼ cup olive oil, plus more for brushing

5 tomatoes

4 large globe eggplants

4 large leeks (white and light green parts only), well rinsed and finely diced

1 tablespoon finely chopped garlic

½ teaspoon cayenne pepper

2 teaspoons paprika

½ cup dry white wine

4 cups chicken stock

2 tablespoons chopped fresh thyme

2 tablespoons chopped fresh oregano

Salt and freshly ground pepper, to taste

Balsamic vinegar, to taste

Extra virgin olive oil for garnish

Fresh basil, cut into chiffonade, for garnish

Preheat the oven to 400 degrees. Brush 2 baking sheets with olive oil.

Halve the tomatoes and place them cut-sides down on one of the baking sheets. Halve the eggplants lengthwise and place them cut-sides down on the other baking sheet. Place the tomatoes on the bottom shelf of the oven and the eggplants on the top shelf. The tomatoes are done when the skins turn darker red and they give off liquid, which will reduce and thicken. Bake the eggplants for about 40 minutes, or until they are very soft.

Let the eggplants cool until you can handle them, then scoop out the pulp, leaving the skin and tops behind.

While the vegetables are baking, start the soup base. Heat the olive oil in a heavy 4-quart pot over medium-high heat. Add the leeks and sauté, stirring occasionally, for about 20 minutes, or until they caramelize slightly. Reduce the heat to medium-low and add the garlic, cayenne and paprika; cook and stir for 5 minutes, taking care that the garlic does not brown.

Add the wine and 3 cups of the chicken stock; bring to a simmer. When the tomatoes are done, add them to the pot along with the eggplant pulp. Add the thyme and oregano and return to a simmer; simmer for 10 minutes.

Working in small batches, purée the soup in a blender until smooth. Strain, if desired.

Return the soup to the pan; season with salt, pepper and balsamic vinegar. Adjust the consistency of the soup with the remaining 1 cup chicken stock as needed.

Serve very hot, garnished with a drizzle of extra virgin olive oil and the basil chiffonade.

SERVES 6 TO 8

Fresh Shelling Bean and Basil Soup

Fresh shelling beans are an autumnal treat in Provence, where market vendors cry out "cocos, get your fresh cocos," referring to the yellowing pods bursting with fresh, round white beans. Georgeanne Brennan loves to pair them with basil in this marvelous soup, which is poured over crisp toasts and finished with a swirl of fresh basil blended with olive oil. While fresh beans are best, dried ones may be used.

Toasts

6 slices of chewy, country-style bread

2 tablespoons olive oil

2 garlic cloves

Soup

1 tablespoon plus ¼ cup extra virgin olive oil

2 garlic cloves, minced

1 yellow onion, minced

5 cups chicken broth

3 to 4 cups shelled white beans or other fresh shelling beans (about 4 pounds before shelling)

1 bay leaf

1 teaspoon freshly ground pepper

Salt, to taste

¼ pound pencil-thin French haricot vert beans, cut into 2-inch lengths (optional)

½ cup basil leaves

To make the toasts: Preheat the oven to 400 degrees.

Place the bread slices on a baking sheet and bake for 15 minutes. Remove from the oven and drizzle with the olive oil. Bake for 5 to 10 minutes longer, or until the toasts are firm and lightly golden. Remove and let cool, then rub both sides of each toast with a garlic clove. Set aside.

To make the soup: Heat the 1 tablespoon olive oil in a heavy soup pot over medium heat. Add the garlic and onion; cook, stirring, for 1 to 2 minutes, or until the onion is translucent.

Add the chicken broth, beans, bay leaf, pepper and salt. Bring to a boil, reduce the heat to low and simmer for 20 minutes, or until the beans are soft. Taste for salt, adding more if needed. Remove the bay leaf.

Remove 1 cup of the beans, purée in a processor or blender, then return them to the pot. Add the haricot vert beans, if desired, and simmer for 3 to 4 minutes, or until they are just tender.

While the beans are cooking, purée the basil and the ¼ cup olive oil in a blender or food processor.

To serve: Place a toast in the bottom of each soup bowl, then ladle in the soup. Add a teaspoon of the basil oil to each, giving half a stir with the spoon to make a swirl.

SERVES 6

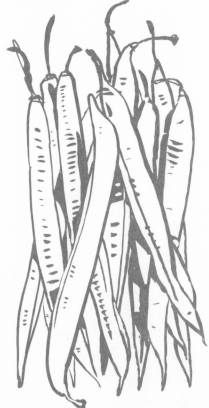

White Bean and Roasted Garlic Soup

Chronicle *staff writer Robin Davis created this heady soup to go with a full-bodied Chardonnay (Franciscan, Steele or Cakebread, for example). It's truly a great combination. Two heads of garlic sounds like a lot, but because they're roasted, the flavor is mellow, not overpowering. For an additional touch, drizzle the finished soup with purchased garlic oil, available at many supermarkets and specialty-foods stores.*

   1 pound great Northern or other small dried white beans

   2 heads of garlic

   3 tablespoons olive oil

   4 ounces pancetta, chopped

   1 large onion, chopped

   8 cups water

   1 bay leaf

   3 tablespoons chopped fresh sage

   Salt and freshly ground white pepper, to taste

   18 fresh sage leaves

Pick over the beans, discarding any broken or withered ones or stones. Put the beans into a large pot, cover with water and let soak overnight. Drain.

Preheat the oven to 400 degrees. Remove the papery outer skin from the garlic heads. Cut off the top ¼ inch. Put the garlic in a small baking dish. Drizzle with 1 tablespoon of the olive oil. Roast for about 30 minutes, or until the garlic is very tender.

When cool enough to handle, squeeze the pulp from the softened cloves into a small dish. Mash into a smooth paste.

Cook the pancetta in a large, heavy saucepan over medium heat until crispy and browned. Using a slotted spoon, transfer the pancetta to paper towels to drain.

Heat the drippings in the saucepan over medium-high heat. Add the onion and sauté for about 5 minutes, or until translucent. Add the garlic paste and stir to combine. Add the water, bay leaf and beans and bring to a boil.

Reduce heat and simmer for about 45 minutes, or until the beans are very tender. Discard the bay leaf. Stir in the chopped sage.

Working in small batches, purée the soup in a blender until smooth. Return the soup to the saucepan. Season with salt and pepper.

Heat the remaining 2 tablespoons oil in a small skillet over medium-high heat. Add the sage leaves and cook for about 30 seconds, or until just crispy. Using tongs, transfer the sage leaves to paper towels to drain.

Ladle the soup into bowls. Top with the fried sage leaves and pancetta.

SERVES 6

Mexican Minestrone with Cilantro Pesto

This may be the best minestrone we've ever eaten. Created by Jacqueline McMahan, it's a hearty meal in a bowl. Chipotle chile gives the broth a pleasant glow, and the topping—a cilantro version of pesto—is nothing less than brilliant. For an even heartier version, sauté slices of spicy sausage (creole or Southwestern-style are good choices) and add to the soup just before serving.

1 tablespoon olive oil

1 cup chopped onions

1 cup chopped red bell pepper

2 leeks (white and light green parts only), well rinsed and chopped (about 1½ cups)

1 tablespoon minced garlic

8 cups vegetable stock, water or chicken broth

2 cups canned crushed tomatoes

1 whole dried chipotle chile

1 teaspoon salt

2 teaspoons pure chile powder

2 teaspoons dried oregano

3 zucchini, trimmed and sliced

6 carrots, peeled and sliced

1½ cups chopped kale leaves

1 cup chopped green cabbage

3 cups cooked pinto beans (homemade or canned, rinsed beans)

1 cup macaroni

Cilantro Pesto (recipe follows)

◉◉   Heat the olive oil in a 5-quart soup pot over medium heat. Add the onions and sauté for 5 to 10 minutes, or until softened. Add the bell pepper and leeks and sauté for 5 minutes, adding the garlic during the last 1 to 2 minutes so it doesn't brown.

Add the stock, tomatoes, chipotle, salt, chile powder and oregano; simmer for 5 to 10 minutes, just to blend the flavors.

Add the zucchini, carrots, kale, cabbage and beans. Simmer for 10 minutes. Add the macaroni and simmer for 8 to 10 minutes, or until it is tender.

Serve in wide soup bowls. Pass the cilantro pesto at the table. But be forewarned! Some pesto addicts like this version so much, they'll not only add it to their soup, they'll also spread it on bread instead of using butter.

SERVES 8

Cilantro Pesto

3 tablespoons olive oil

¼ cup freshly grated Asiago cheese

2 garlic cloves

1 cup cilantro leaves and tender stems

Juice of 1 lime

◉◉   Combine the olive oil, cheese, garlic, cilantro and lime juice in a food processor and purée.

YIELDS ABOUT 1 CUP

Egyptian Chickpea and Orzo Soup

Chickpeas, or garbanzos, and orzo combine in this hearty soup by Marlena Spieler. If you don't have orzo, a pasta that looks like large grains of rice, use spaghetti broken into short lengths before cooking. And if you have any of the ends you've snapped off asparagus, this is a good place to use them. Cut them into thin rounds and add to the soup about 5 minutes before serving. A squeeze of lemon adds a pleasant finishing touch to each bowlful.

6 cups chicken or vegetable broth

2 cups water

6 garlic cloves, thinly sliced

½ onion, chopped

1½ cups cooked drained chickpeas (canned OK)

Salt and freshly ground pepper, to taste

1 teaspoon finely chopped parsley (optional)

6 ounces orzo, or other small soup pasta

2 lemons, cut into wedges

Combine the broth, water, garlic and onion in a saucepan over high heat. Bring to a boil, reduce heat to medium and simmer for about 10 minutes, or until the onion softens.

Add the chickpeas and continue to cook for about 15 minutes, or until the chickpeas are very soft and tender, the soup is well flavored, and the garlic and onions are soft. Season with salt and pepper. Stir in the parsley, if desired.

Meanwhile, bring a large pot of salted water to a boil over high heat. Add the orzo and cook for 6 minutes, or until tender; drain.

Serve the soup in bowls, ladled over the orzo. Top each serving with a wedge or two of lemon to squeeze in, then leave the wedges in the soup to impart their lemony flavor from the rind.

SERVES 4

Chickpea Soup with Kale and Diavolicchio

In some Southern Italian families, homemade chile oil—known as diavolicchio—is always on the table, according to Chronicle *staff writer Janet Fletcher. Make it a couple of days ahead for best flavor, and if you like it, make a lot. Stored in a tightly covered jar in a dark, cool place, the oil will keep for weeks.*

Diavolicchio

½ cup extra virgin olive oil

1 teaspoon hot red pepper flakes

Soup

1 pound dried chickpeas

7 cups water

2 garlic cloves, halved

Salt, to taste

¼ cup olive oil

1 large onion, minced

4 garlic cloves, minced

1 teaspoon minced fresh rosemary

1 teaspoon minced fresh sage

½ cup chopped canned tomatoes

1 pound kale, thick ribs removed

Freshly ground pepper, to taste

◉◉ To make the diavolicchio: Heat the olive oil in a saucepan over medium heat to 165 degrees. Add the pepper flakes. Let cool. Transfer to a clean jar. Cover and let stand for at least 2 days before using.

To make the soup: Pick over the chickpeas, discarding any broken or withered ones or stones. Put the chickpeas in a bowl, cover with water and let soak for 24 hours. Drain and rinse.

Put the chickpeas in a large saucepan; add the water and halved garlic cloves. Bring to a simmer over medium heat, skimming any foam. Cover, adjust the heat to maintain a gentle simmer, and cook the chickpeas for

1 hour or more, depending on their age, or until tender. Season with salt and let them cool in the cooking liquid. Drain when cool, reserving the liquid.

Heat the olive oil in a large pot over medium heat. Add the onion, minced garlic, rosemary and sage. Sauté for about 10 minutes, or until the onion is soft. Add the chickpeas and tomatoes. Sauté for 5 minutes, then set aside.

Chop the kale coarsely and put it in a large skillet with 1 cup of the chickpea liquid. Cover and cook over medium heat for 20 minutes, or until the kale is tender. Drain in a sieve, reserving any liquid.

Transfer the chickpea mixture to a food processor fitted with the steel blade and purée, thinning with some of the reserved chickpea liquid added through the feed tube. Transfer the purée to a large pot and stir in the remaining chickpea liquid, kale liquid and kale. Season with salt and pepper, and heat through.

Serve the soup in warm bowls, drizzling each portion with some of the diavolicchio. Pass additional diavolicchio at the table.

SERVES 6

Cream of Leek Soup with Stilton

Noted teacher Mary Risley, owner of Tante Marie's Cooking School in San Francisco, created this easy, rustic soup that pairs mild leeks and blue cheese. If Stilton is unavailable, use another crumbly blue-veined cheese, such as Roquefort or Maytag Blue.

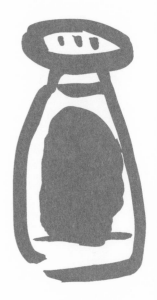

> 1 tablespoon butter
>
> 1 shallot, finely chopped
>
> 2 leeks (white and light green parts only), well rinsed and coarsely chopped
>
> 2 cups low-sodium chicken broth
>
> 2 baking potatoes, peeled and diced
>
> ½ to ¾ cup whipping cream
>
> Salt and freshly ground pepper, to taste
>
> Fresh lemon juice, to taste
>
> 2 ounces Stilton cheese, crumbled

◉◉ Heat the butter in a deep saucepan over medium heat; add the shallot and leeks and sauté, stirring occasionally, for 10 minutes, or until translucent.

Add the broth and potatoes. Simmer briskly for 20 minutes, or until the potatoes are very tender.

Purée using a handheld blender, or pass the soup through a food mill. Add the cream, then season with salt, pepper and lemon juice.

Serve warm and sprinkle each portion with Stilton.

SERVES 4

Wild Mushroom Soup

You can use one or several kinds of wild mushrooms for this easy autumn soup from Denis Soriano formerly of Grand Cafe, a San Francisco brasserie that makes you feel like you're in the heart of Paris.

3 tablespoons butter

3 ounces shallots (about 2 large), chopped

1½ pounds wild mushrooms, cleaned and coarsely chopped

3 cups chicken stock

2 bay leaves

2½ cups whipping cream

Salt and freshly ground pepper, to taste

1 bunch chives, chopped, for garnish

◉◉ Melt the butter in a large, heavy pot over medium heat. Add the shallots and cook for 1 minute, stirring once or twice. Add the mushrooms, increase heat to high and cook, stirring occasionally, for about 5 minutes, or until they release some of their liquid.

Add the stock, bay leaves, cream, salt and pepper. Bring to a boil, reduce heat to low and simmer for 25 minutes.

Remove from heat and let cool for a few minutes. Discard the bay leaves. Working in batches, purée the soup in a blender until very smooth. If you want an even smoother texture, force the soup through a fine sieve.

Reheat gently if necessary.

Serve in bowls or large soup plates; garnish with the chives.

SERVES 4 TO 6

Spicy Sweet Potato Soup

*This rich, smooth soup has a perfect balance of sweet and spicy flavors.
It's ideal for a holiday dinner, says Jacqueline McMahan, and can be made
well ahead and frozen for up to four weeks. To dress it up for any special
gathering, we suggest piping a little sour cream on top of each serving and
garnishing with a tiny sprig of fresh thyme.*

2 tablespoons butter

1 cup chopped onion

2 jalapeño chiles, seeded and chopped

2 teaspoons chopped fresh thyme, or 1 teaspoon dried

3 carrots, peeled and diced

1½ pounds sweet potatoes, peeled and diced

4 cups chicken broth

1 cup milk

¼ to ½ cup whipping cream

1 tablespoon light brown sugar

1 teaspoon salt, or to taste

Healthy pinch of cayenne pepper

4 sprigs fresh thyme for garnish

◌◌ Heat the butter in a soup pot over medium heat until bubbly. Add the
onion and sauté for about 10 minutes, or until caramelized. Add the jalapeños
and thyme; sauté for 1 minute. Stir in the carrots, sweet potatoes and chicken
broth. Simmer for 30 to 40 minutes, or until the vegetables are quite tender.
Use a slotted spoon to transfer the vegetables to a food processor. Purée the
mixture, adding a tiny bit of the liquid to help the process, if necessary, then
return the purée to the pot.

Alternatively, use a handheld blender to purée the soup right in the pot.

Add the milk, cream, brown sugar, salt and cayenne. Heat the soup very
gently for 10 minutes to blend the flavors.

If the soup is too thick, add a little water, broth, milk or cream.

Garnish each serving with a sprig of thyme.

SERVES 8

Pumpkin Soup with Leeks and Chervil

This smooth purée of pumpkin is at once soothing and bland, utterly comforting and delicious contrasted against the dab of crème fraîche and the fragrance of chervil. To add texture, Marlena Spieler sometimes leaves the vegetables in coarse chunks, which creates a strikingly different soup. Both are delightful.

2 to 3 tablespoons butter

1 leek (white and light green parts only), well rinsed and diced

6 garlic cloves, coarsely chopped

12 ounces pumpkin, or other winter squash (such as butternut or kabocha), peeled, seeded and diced

1 potato, 6 to 8 ounces, peeled and diced

6 cups vegetable or chicken stock

2 cups dry white wine, or 1 cup dry vermouth

Grating of nutmeg

Salt and freshly ground pepper, to taste

Garnishes

Crème fraîche, about 1 tablespoon per serving

4 to 6 tablespoons chopped chervil

2 to 3 tablespoons chopped chives

Melt the butter in a heavy soup pot over low heat. Add the leek, garlic, pumpkin and potato. Cover and sweat the vegetables over very low heat for 15 to 20 minutes, or until they are tender but not brown.

Add the stock and wine, bring to a boil over high heat, then reduce heat to low and simmer for about 40 minutes, or until the vegetables are very tender.

Working in batches, purée the soup in a blender or food processor, then season with nutmeg, salt and pepper.

Ladle into bowls and garnish with the crème fraîche, chervil and chives.

SERVES 4 TO 6

Fresh Cranberry Bean Sambar

Sambars—thick lentil and vegetable soups—are mainstays of the Southern Indian vegetarian diet. Laxmi Hiremath finds that meaty cranberry beans adapt well to this classic Indian specialty.

1 tablespoon coriander seeds

1 teaspoon mustard seeds

1 teaspoon fenugreek seeds

2 tablespoons grated coconut (fresh or frozen)

½ teaspoon cayenne pepper

1¾ pounds cranberry beans, shelled (about 3 cups)

1½ teaspoons tamarind concentrate dissolved in ½ cup water

4 cups water

2 tablespoons light brown sugar

1 teaspoon salt, or to taste

Aromatic Oil

2 tablespoons canola oil

½ teaspoon mustard seeds

1 teaspoon cumin seeds

10 fresh kari leaves

⅓ cup sliced shallots

⅓ teaspoon turmeric

◎ Combine the coriander, mustard and fenugreek seeds in a 10-inch nonstick skillet over medium heat. Dry-roast, stirring constantly for 4 to 5 minutes, or until the mixture is aromatic and the mustard seeds pop and splutter. Reduce heat to low. Add the coconut and cayenne; toast, shaking the pan frequently, for about 2 minutes, or until the coconut starts to brown. Remove from heat and cool slightly. Transfer to a coffee mill and grind to a fine powder. (The spice blend may be made ahead and stored in an airtight jar for up to 2 months.)

Combine the cranberry beans, tamarind, water, brown sugar and the spice blend in a Dutch oven over high heat and bring to a boil. Reduce heat to low and simmer for 20 to 25 minutes, or until the beans are tender but not falling apart. Season with salt. Transfer to a tureen.

To make the aromatic oil: Heat the oil in a small skillet over medium-high heat. Add the mustard and cumin seeds. When the seeds begin to pop and splutter, toss in the kari leaves. Stir in the shallots and turmeric. Cook for about 4 minutes, or until the shallots start to brown. Remove from the heat and pour over the sambar. Stir gently and serve.

SERVES 8

Ginger-Tomato Rasam

Rasams are another Southern Indian specialty, but unlike the heartier sambars, these soups are thin, with a pronounced, spicy kick. The most famous rasam is mulligatawny, which was introduced into the Western world by the British. Laxmi Hiremath likes to serve this ginger-tomato rasam in deep bowls or warmed mugs, accompanied by sourdough baguettes.

2 tablespoons unsalted butter

½ teaspoon mustard seeds

½ teaspoon cumin seeds

¼ teaspoon turmeric

10 fresh kari leaves (optional)

1 tablespoon minced fresh ginger

¼ teaspoon freshly ground pepper

1 tablespoon Rasam Powder (recipe follows)

3 tomatoes, cored, peeled, seeded and chopped

1 cup cooked yellow split peas

3 cups water

1 teaspoon salt, or to taste

Chopped cilantro for garnish

Heat the butter in a large, heavy pan over medium heat. Add the mustard and cumin seeds. When the seeds begin to pop and splutter, toss in the turmeric and kari leaves, if desired. Add the ginger and cook, stirring, for 30 seconds. Stir in the pepper and Rasam Powder. Cook and stir for about 1 minute, or until aromatic. Add the tomatoes and cook for about 5 minutes, or until soft.

Add the split peas, water and salt. Bring to a boil, reduce heat to low, cover and simmer for 12 to 15 minutes, or until the flavors blend and the soup has thickened slightly.

Transfer to a tureen and garnish with cilantro.

SERVES 4

Rasam Powder

Toasting whole spices before grinding them gives the finished spice blend an intense aroma and flavor.

2 tablespoons coriander seeds

1 teaspoon cumin seeds

1 teaspoon white peppercorns

1 teaspoon black peppercorns

20 fresh kari leaves

1 dried red chile, broken

◉◉ Combine the coriander and cumin seeds, white and black peppercorns, kari leaves and chile in a 12-inch skillet over medium heat. Dry-roast, stirring constantly, for about 6 minutes, or until the mixture is aromatic and the seeds are lightly browned.

Cool the mixture slightly, then transfer to a spice grinder and grind to a fine powder. Pour into an airtight glass jar.

The Rasam Powder will keep for up to 3 months at cool room temperature, or up to 6 months in the refrigerator.

YIELDS ⅓ CUP

Puy Lentil Soup

This soup by Marlena Spieler is hearty and earthy, with a soft undercurrent of garlic. Bouillon cubes give the stock a layered flavor, and olive oil delicately enriches the mixture.

Croutons

¼ loaf pain levain or baguette, cut into bite-size cubes

Extra virgin olive oil for drizzling

4 to 5 garlic cloves, chopped

Soup

8 ounces lentils de Puy (French green lentils), or regular brown lentils

12 cups water

1 head of garlic, cloves separated, peeled and smashed (10 to 15 cloves)

½ leek (white and light green parts only), well rinsed and chopped

1 celery stalk, diced

1 medium-large potato, peeled and cut into chunks

1 carrot, peeled and diced

4 tablespoons extra virgin olive oil

2 bay leaves

1 or 2 vegetable bouillon cubes

Salt and freshly ground pepper, to taste

∞ To make the croutons: Preheat the oven to 375 degrees. Arrange the bread cubes in a baking dish and drizzle sparingly with olive oil. Bake for 20 minutes, or until the cubes are golden and crispy. Remove from the oven. Toss the toasted bread with the garlic and set aside at room temperature to cool.

To make the soup: Combine the lentils and water in a large soup pot over high heat. Add half of the garlic, the leek, celery, potato, carrot, olive oil and bay leaves. Bring to a boil, then reduce heat to low, cover and simmer until the lentils and vegetables are very tender.

Add the bouillon cubes, extra water if the soup seems too thick, and the remaining garlic. Simmer for about 10 minutes, then season with salt and pepper. Remove the bay leaves. Using a potato masher, mash the soup a bit, breaking up some of the vegetables but leaving others in small pieces—you want a chunky purée.

Ladle the soup into bowls and top with garlic croutons.

SERVES 6

Arroz Caldo (Filipino Rice Porridge)

This porridge, called arroz caldo *or* lugaw *in the Philippines, was created by Noel Advincula, a culinary intern with the Food Department. His recipe features whole, soft kernels of rice suspended in a fragrant golden-yellow broth. Like Chinese* congee, *the soup is soothing and warm, but generous amounts of ginger, fish sauce and lemon juice fill it with exotic Southeast Asian flavors. Noel remembers eating it as a* merienda, *or afternoon snack, in the Philippines and says it also is popular for breakfast.*

3 tablespoons vegetable oil

4 garlic cloves, chopped

1 yellow onion, chopped

2-inch knob fresh ginger, peeled and sliced into coins

2 skinless, boneless chicken breast halves, cut into bite-size chunks

3 tablespoons Asian fish sauce plus more, to taste

1 cup long-grain white rice

5 cups chicken broth

1 teaspoon freshly ground pepper

Pinch of saffron (optional)

2 eggs, in their shells

1 bunch scallions, trimmed and chopped

1 lemon, cut into wedges

Heat the oil in a large, heavy pot over medium heat. Add the garlic, onion and ginger and sauté for about 5 minutes, or until the onion is soft. Add the chicken and sauté for about 1 minute.

Add the fish sauce, rice, broth, pepper and saffron, if desired, and stir well. Bring to a boil over high heat, then add the whole eggs to the pot and boil in their shells for 8 minutes. Stir occasionally to make sure the rice doesn't stick to the bottom of the pot.

Remove the eggs from the pot; set aside. Reduce heat to low and simmer the porridge for about 12 minutes longer, or until the rice is fully cooked. (The porridge should be quite thick, but if you like, thin it with a little water.) Taste and add more fish sauce, if desired.

Peel and halve the eggs.

To serve, discard the slices of ginger, ladle the porridge into soup bowls and top each with chopped scallions, a hard-cooked egg half and a big squeeze of lemon juice.

SERVES 4

Thai Chicken Soup with Coconut Milk and Galangal

The secret of this soup is the galangal or Thai ginger, available fresh or frozen at Asian grocery stores. For the best flavor, give it a few whacks with a knife before adding it to the broth, suggests Mai Pham.

1 tablespoon vegetable oil

1 shallot, thinly sliced

½ teaspoon minced garlic

1 tablespoon minced lemongrass, tender white part only

1 teaspoon hot red pepper flakes, or to taste

1 teaspoon ground chile paste, or to taste

1-inch knob galangal, thinly sliced and bruised with back of a knife

3 cups low-sodium chicken broth

2 tablespoons Asian fish sauce, or to taste

1 teaspoon sugar

2 cups coconut milk

⅓ pound skinless, boneless chicken breasts or thighs, cut into ½-inch cubes

1 cup straw mushrooms, or white mushrooms

½ cup cubed ripe tomato

½ tablespoon fresh lime juice

2 kaffir lime leaves, halved, or 1 teaspoon grated lime zest

6 cilantro sprigs, chopped, for garnish

Heat the oil in a saucepan over medium heat until moderately hot. Add the shallot, garlic, lemongrass, pepper flakes and chile paste; cook for about 30 seconds, or until slightly brown.

Working quickly and without burning the spices, add the galangal, chicken broth, fish sauce, sugar and coconut milk. Bring to a boil; add the chicken, mushrooms and tomato. When it comes to a boil again, turn off the heat and add the lime juice and lime leaves.

Serve immediately, garnished with the cilantro.

SERVES 6

A Quick Chinese Soup

For a quick soup, Marlena Spieler suggests the following: Add a handful of thinly sliced romaine lettuce to about a quart of hot chicken stock and let the lettuce wilt in the heat of the soup. Season with soy sauce, Asian sesame oil and thinly sliced green onions.

Caldo de Tlalpeno

Here's another captivating chicken soup, this one Latin in origin, from Jacqueline McMahan. It features a spicy broth fragrant with epazote and chile powder. The colorful chunks of vegetables, chicken and avocado give it a rib-sticking character. The name means soup in the style of Tlalpan (a region in the state of Michoacan, Mexico).

8 cups homemade chicken stock

1 pound red-skinned or Yukon Gold potatoes, halved

1 green bell pepper, seeded, deribbed and cut into chunks

1 red bell pepper, seeded, deribbed and cut into chunks

2 celery stalks with leaves, thickly sliced

1 epazote sprig

1 large tomato

4 garlic cloves

1 teaspoon salt

1 teaspoon pure mild red chile powder

2 teaspoons chipotle powder

2 teaspoons dried oregano

2 cups shredded, cooked chicken breast

Garnishes

½ cup minced green onions (both white and green parts)

2 cups fresh baby spinach, rinsed in a bowl of warm water

¼ cup cilantro leaves

1 ripe but firm Hass avocado, pitted, peeled and diced

Yellow rice (long-grain white rice to which about 1 teaspoon of turmeric has been added to the cooking water)

Preheat the broiler.

Bring the chicken stock to a simmer in a 4-quart pot over medium-high heat. Add the potatoes, green and red bell peppers, celery and epazote. Simmer for 20 minutes.

Place the tomato and garlic under the broiler and broil just until the tomato chars a little. Transfer the tomato and garlic to a blender, along with the salt, chile powder, chipotle powder and oregano; process to a paste. Stir into the simmering soup. Add the shredded chicken and simmer for 10 minutes, or just until the flavors are blended.

Ladle the soup into wide bowls. Sprinkle each serving with green onions, spinach, cilantro and avocado. The last-minute heat of the soup accentuates the velvety taste of the avocado. Pass the yellow rice at the table so diners can spoon some into their soup.

SERVES 6

Turkey Soup with Wild Rice and Escarole

Here's the perfect solution for what to do with the last of the holiday bird. A whole meal in a bowl, this soup contains chewy wild rice, loads of greens and, of course, moist turkey meat. A dash of hot red pepper flakes gives it a hint of Italy, as does the final dusting of Parmigiano-Reggiano cheese. It was created by Sean Forsha, one of our culinary interns.

1 tablespoon olive oil

1 onion, diced

1½ tablespoons minced garlic

1 teaspoon hot red pepper flakes

6 cups turkey stock (made from the carcass), or unsalted chicken stock

1 cup wild rice, rinsed

8 cups escarole leaves, chopped into 1-inch pieces (about ½ head)

3 cups roughly chopped roasted turkey (white and dark meat)

Salt and freshly ground pepper, to taste

Freshly grated Parmigiano-Reggiano cheese for garnish

◉◉   Heat the olive oil in a large pot over medium heat. Add the onion and cook slowly for about 5 minutes, or until translucent. Add the garlic and pepper flakes and cook until fragrant. Add the stock and bring to a boil. Reduce heat to a simmer, then stir in the wild rice. Simmer, uncovered, for 25 minutes.

Add the escarole and simmer for 20 minutes, or until the rice is tender. Stir in the turkey, season with salt and pepper, and cook until heated through. Ladle into bowls and garnish with grated cheese.

SERVES 6

Spicy Hot-and-Sour Prawn Soup

Tamarind adds richness and color to this spicy soup by Mai Pham. But if you don't have it, simply add more lime juice.

2 tablespoons tamarind pulp

⅓ cup boiling water

1 tablespoon vegetable oil

1 teaspoon finely chopped garlic

½ teaspoon chile paste

½ teaspoon hot red pepper flakes

2 thin slices galangal (fresh or frozen)

1 stalk lemongrass, tender white part only, bruised with the side of a knife and
    cut into 1½-inch pieces

5 cups chicken stock (homemade or low-sodium canned)

2 tablespoons Asian fish sauce

4½ teaspoons sugar

3 kaffir lime leaves, halved

½ cup drained canned straw mushrooms, or 3 ounces white mushrooms, quartered

2 plum tomatoes, seeded and chopped

½ pound shrimp, shelled and deveined

Juice of 1 lime, or to taste

1 scallion, coarsely chopped

8 Thai basil leaves, coarsely chopped

5 cilantro sprigs, chopped

◉◉ Place the tamarind pulp in a small bowl; add the boiling water. Let stand until the pulp has softened, then push the mixture through a sieve. Set aside.

Heat the oil in a saucepan over medium heat. Add the garlic, chile paste and pepper flakes. Stir for about 1 minute, or until fragrant. Add the galangal and lemongrass. Stir for 2 minutes. Add the chicken stock and simmer for 15 minutes.

Bring the soup to a boil over high heat. Add the fish sauce, sugar, lime leaves, mushrooms, tomatoes and tamarind. Add the shrimp and cook for about 2 minutes, or until they just turn pink. The shrimp will continue to cook in the hot broth. Remove the pan from heat, and add the lime juice, scallion, basil and cilantro. Serve immediately.

SERVES 4

Nan Yang's Burmese Fish Noodle Soup (Mohingar)

Unique to Burma, this soup is eaten from morning to night and typically is purchased from a sidewalk vendor. The recipe, adapted for the home kitchen, comes from Philip Chu, owner of Nan Yang restaurant in Oakland.

¼ cup vegetable oil

2 large yellow onions, chopped

6 garlic cloves, minced

1 teaspoon ground turmeric

½ teaspoon paprika

Hot red pepper flakes, to taste

2-ounce knob fresh ginger, peeled

1 stalk lemongrass, tender white part only, split lengthwise

6 cups water

¼ cup Asian fish sauce

1 pound catfish fillets, cut in ½-inch pieces

Salt, to taste

3 bundles (about 10 ounces) Japanese somen, or 10 ounces spaghettini

Garnishes

1 hard-cooked egg, sliced

Coarsely chopped cilantro

Lemon wedges

◎◎ Heat the oil in a soup pot over medium heat. Add the onions and sauté for 5 to 8 minutes, or until softened. Add the garlic, turmeric, paprika and hot pepper flakes; sauté for 1 minute.

Smash the ginger and lemongrass with the side of a cleaver and add to the pot along with the water. Bring to a simmer, then stir in the fish sauce. Cover partially and simmer gently for 15 minutes.

Add the fish and simmer for about 3 minutes, or until it is cooked. Remove the ginger and lemongrass. Season with salt.

While the soup is simmering, bring a large pot of salted water to a boil over high heat. Add the noodles and cook for about 3 minutes, or until just tender. Drain and divide among warm bowls. Top with soup. Garnish with sliced egg and cilantro. Serve with lemon wedges.

SERVES 6

Lamb Shank Soup with Lima Beans

Lamb shanks and lima beans are a dynamic duo in this recipe by Janet Fletcher. Partially cooking the shanks a day ahead allows you to chill the broth and lift off any congealed fat before completing the dish.

1½ cups dried baby lima beans

2 tablespoons olive oil

3 pounds lamb shanks, cut into 1-inch-thick sections

Salt and freshly ground pepper, to taste

1 large onion, chopped

2 garlic cloves, minced

12 cups water

1 bay leaf

½ cup pearl barley

1 pound russet potatoes, peeled and cut into ½-inch dice

1 package (10 ounces) frozen baby lima beans

¼ cup chopped fresh dill

Pick over the dried lima beans, discarding any broken or withered ones or stones. Put the beans in a bowl, add water to cover by 1 inch and let soak overnight. Or quick-soak: Boil the lima beans in a large pot of water for 1 minute, then cover and let stand for 1 hour. Drain beans.

Heat the olive oil in a large skillet over high heat. Add the lamb shanks and season with salt and pepper; reduce the heat to medium and brown the shanks on all sides. Transfer the shanks to a soup pot.

Pour off all but 2 tablespoons of the fat in the skillet. Add the onion and sauté for 8 to 10 minutes, or until soft. Add the garlic and sauté for 1 minute to release its fragrance. Transfer the onion and garlic to the soup pot. Add the water and bay leaf. Bring to a simmer over medium heat, skimming any foam that collects on the surface. Adjust the heat to maintain a gentle simmer and simmer for 1 hour. Cool, then cover and refrigerate overnight.

The next day, lift off and discard any congealed fat on the surface. Return the soup to medium heat and bring just to a simmer. Add the soaked lima beans and the barley, partially cover, adjust the heat to maintain a gentle simmer and simmer for 30 minutes.

Add the potatoes, partially cover the pot and simmer for 15 minutes. Add the frozen lima beans and simmer for about 10 minutes, or until all the beans, barley and potatoes are tender. Remove the bay leaf and stir in the dill. Taste and adjust seasonings as needed.

SERVES 6

Ham Hock and "Peppercorn" Pasta Soup

This rustic recipe was created by Chronicle *staff editor Lesli Neilson. It freezes very well; simply let it cool completely, then transfer to an airtight freezer container to avoid freezer burn.*

2 large smoked ham hocks

4 tablespoons olive oil

2 yellow onions, cut into medium dice

4 garlic cloves, minced

7 celery stalks, cut into ½-inch slices

4 carrots, cut into ½-inch slices

1 cup dry white wine

12 cups vegetable or chicken broth

3½ tablespoons tomato paste

2 bay leaves

3 thyme sprigs

12 peppercorns, crushed

4 parsley stems, finely chopped

12 cups water

2¼ cups acini di pepe pasta

Salt and freshly ground pepper, to taste

◉◉ Remove excess fat from the ham hocks.

Heat the olive oil in a large pot over medium heat. Add the onions and garlic and cook for 3 to 5 minutes, or until translucent. Add the celery and cook for 3 minutes; add the carrots and cook for 3 minutes. Add the ham hocks and stir, allowing all the ingredients to blend. Add the wine, stirring to scrape up the browned bits on the bottom of the pan, and cook for about 5 minutes.

Add the broth, tomato paste, bay leaves, thyme, peppercorns and parsley. Simmer for 45 minutes, or until the ham is tender enough to fall off the bone.

Remove the ham hocks and, when cool enough to handle, remove the meat from the bones and cut into bite-size pieces. Discard bones and return the meat to the soup pot. Discard the bay leaves and thyme sprigs. Add the water and bring to a boil over high heat.

Add the pasta and cook for 13 to 15 minutes, or until al dente. Season with salt and pepper. (You probably won't need much salt.)

SERVES 12

Chapter 3

Salads

The California diet has become a running joke from coast to coast. We're the land of arugula and goat cheese. Instead of fighting that image, we've decided to embrace it. After all, arugula was first imported and sold commercially in the United States by Chronicle *columnist Georgeanne Brennan, and the boutique goat cheese was pioneered by the Bay Area's Laura Chenel. Let's face it, the peppery greens and creamy cheese are an unbeatable combination.*

You'll find much more than arugula and goat cheese, however: Chickpea Salad with Provençal Herbs and Olives (page 82), Minty Thai Chicken Salad (page 86) and Spicy Citrus Couscous Tabbouleh (page 83), for example.

Bay Area salads celebrate the cultures of China, Italy, Mexico and Thailand, to name a few. We haven't forgotten California tradition, either. We've included two updated riffs on the famous Cobb salad (pages 78 and 79), which originated at the Brown Derby Restaurant in Los Angeles. While we don't like to admit we've adopted anything from our state-mates down south, these variations will prove they've made at least a few culinary contributions.

Because of our casual West Coast nature, salads are served in many ways. Some are great side dishes paired with grilled meats; others are an interesting way to start a more formal meal. Still others, such as the Curried Turkey Salad with Apple and Walnuts (page 87), stand alone as a light, refreshing lunch or supper.

Salads lend themselves to experimentation and versatility as you'll see here, from the Warm Brussels Sprout Salad with Bacon and Eggs from Gordon's in San Francisco (page 68) to the amazing Frisee and Corn Salad with Fried Tomatoes from L'Amie Donia in Palo Alto (page 75).

Escarole and Endive Salad
with Bosc Pears

Maria Helm, formerly the chef at PlumpJack Cafe in San Francisco, and now the chef at Sinskey winery (owned by her husband, Robert Sinskey), uses the intense qualities of escarole to play off juicy pears and endive. The toasted walnuts add another dimension to this winter salad. For a heartier version, crumble blue cheese over the top.

1 small head escarole

2 heads Belgian endive

2 ripe Bosc pears, quartered, cored and thinly sliced

½ cup toasted walnut pieces

1 tablespoon walnut oil

Salt and freshly ground pepper, to taste

2 teaspoons sugar

2 tablespoons sherry vinegar

Wash the escarole and endive and drain well. Tear the escarole into bite-size pieces and place in a salad bowl. Cut the endive in half and remove the core. Slice crosswise into ½-inch pieces. Add to the salad bowl along with the pears and walnuts.

Drizzle with the walnut oil and toss. Season with salt, pepper and sugar; toss again. Add the vinegar and toss once more. Taste and adjust seasonings as needed.

SERVES 4 TO 6

Dressing a Salad

Little things really do mean a lot. We tested the premise that salad tastes better when each component is dressed individually.

We made a dressing using 2 parts olive oil to 1 part red wine vinegar and dressed two salads made with baby greens, carrots, cucumbers and tomatoes. We then used exactly the same amount of dressing on each, but for the first salad, we dressed all the ingredients together. For the second salad, we dressed each component separately.

We repeated the experiment several times with the same results: Taking the time to individually dress the components before tossing them together produces a brighter appearance and a fresher taste.

There was also a difference in the "wilt" factor. After letting the salads sit for a few hours, the individually dressed salad retained a brighter appearance. The other salad was limp and tired-looking.

Southeast Asian Summer Salad of Cellophane Noodles and Herbs

Although it's served cold, this noodle salad by Marlena Spieler is light years away from its Western counterparts. The silky noodles are flavored with mint, basil, soy, chile paste and coconut milk balanced by lime. Sprouts and cucumbers give it a cooling crunch. Serve as a salad, or as an accompaniment to simply grilled meats and vegetables.

> 12 ounces cellophane noodles, or thin vermicelli
>
> Handful of bean sprouts
>
> ¼ cup coconut milk
>
> 5 green onions (both white and green parts), thinly sliced
>
> 3 tablespoons light soy sauce, or Asian fish sauce
>
> 1 to 2 tablespoons vegetable oil
>
> 1 tablespoon sugar
>
> 1 tablespoon chile paste, or to taste, or other hot pepper seasoning
>
> 1 tablespoon fresh lime juice
>
> ½ bunch cilantro, leaves only, coarsely chopped
>
> ½ bunch mint (spearmint), leaves only, coarsely chopped
>
> ½ bunch Thai basil, sweet or opal basil, leaves only, coarsely chopped or cut into chiffonade

Garnishes

> ½ English cucumber, seeded and diced
>
> About 6 ounces peanuts, coarsely chopped
>
> 2 limes, cut into wedges

Cook the noodles according to the package directions. If there are no directions, bring a large pot of salted water to a boil over high heat, add the noodles and simmer for about 3 minutes. Remove from heat, add the bean sprouts and let stand in the hot water for a few minutes longer, or until the noodles and bean sprouts are the desired consistency. The noodles should be soft and supple, and the bean sprouts crunchy tender, not soft.

(Alternatively, to keep the sprouts' raw crunchiness, you can add them along with the dressing.)

Drain well and rinse in cold water, then drain again.

Mix the noodles and bean sprouts in a bowl with the coconut milk, green onions, soy sauce, oil, sugar, chile paste and lime juice. Taste and adjust seasonings as needed.

Just before serving, toss the noodles with the cilantro, mint and basil, then transfer to a serving bowl and garnish with the cucumber, peanuts and lime wedges.

SERVES 6

Gordon's Warm Brussels Sprout Salad with Bacon and Eggs

We knew this was a winner when we tested the recipe at The Chronicle; *even avowed Brussels sprout haters came back for more. The combination of tiny individual leaves mixed with bits of bacon, hard-cooked egg and caramelized onion is captivating. It's a best-seller at Gordon's House of Fine Eats in San Francisco, where it was created by chef/owner Gordon Drysdale. This salad is a great way to begin a holiday meal or a cool-weather dinner party.*

Dressing

2 large shallots, diced

4 small garlic cloves, minced

1 teaspoon chopped fresh thyme

¼ cup red wine vinegar

2 tablespoons extra virgin olive oil

Two Easy Salads

Here are two ideas for simple salads from Marlena Spieler:

Potato and Chèvre Salad: Lightly blanch several handfuls of sugar snap peas and toss with cooked, cubed waxy potatoes. Dress with crumbled goat cheese, olive oil, chopped garlic and fresh herbs, such as thyme or marjoram. Add fresh lemon juice, salt and freshly ground pepper, to taste.

Minted North African Cucumber Salad: Arrange thinly sliced cucumbers and bell peppers (red, yellow or green— preferably some of each) on a platter. Top with pitted, halved green olives. Dress with olive oil and white wine vinegar, then garnish with cayenne, chopped cilantro and mint.

Salad

80 Brussels sprouts (about 5 pounds)

1 large red onion

2 tablespoons butter

4 eggs

2 cups herb-flavored artisan bread cubes (¼-inch cubes), crusts removed

4 tablespoons olive oil

1 pound bacon, cut in ½-inch dice

Salt and freshly ground pepper, to taste

◎◎ To make the dressing: Combine the shallots, garlic, thyme and vinegar in a bowl. Let stand for at least 30 minutes, then whisk in the olive oil.

To make the salad: Halve each Brussels sprout. Place cut-side up on a work surface and make a V-shaped cut to remove the core and any stem nubbin. The leaves will fall off and separate. Rinse sprouts and set aside.

Cut the onion, stem to root, into ¼-inch-thick slices. Melt the butter in a skillet over medium heat. Add the onion and sauté, stirring frequently, for about 10 minutes, or until golden and sweet. Set aside.

Place the eggs, still in their shells, in a small saucepan; cover with cold water. Bring to a boil over high heat, remove from heat and let stand for 9 to 11 minutes. The yolks should be firm but slightly undercooked. Peel the eggs and cut each into 8 chunks. Set aside.

Preheat the oven to 450 degrees.

Toss the bread cubes with 2 tablespoons of the olive oil and place in a single layer on a baking sheet. Bake, stirring occasionally, for 10 to 15 minutes, or until golden brown.

Cook the bacon in a sauté pan over medium heat for about 7 minutes, or until golden and crisp. Using a slotted spoon, transfer bacon to paper towels to drain.

Heat the remaining 2 tablespoons olive oil in a large sauté pan over medium-high heat until nearly smoking. Add the Brussels sprout leaves and toss for about 5 minutes, or until wilted. Season with salt and pepper. Add the reserved onion and bacon. Cook, tossing, until hot. Add the vinaigrette and toss to distribute evenly. Add the croutons and eggs, and toss gently to mix.

Serve immediately.

SERVES 8

Mexican Coleslaw

This recipe by Jacqueline McMahan was inspired by a salad created by chef Dean Fearing of the Mansion on Turtle Creek in Dallas, Texas. It is a perfect accompaniment to barbecues.

Dressing

⅔ cup mayonnaise

1 tablespoon maple syrup

½ tablespoon Dijon mustard

1 tablespoon rice vinegar

1 tablespoon fresh lime juice

¼ teaspoon ground cumin

¼ teaspoon salt

1 garlic clove, minced

1 or 2 jalapeño chiles, stemmed, seeded and minced

Slaw

4 cups shredded cabbage

1½ cups shredded carrots

½ cup diced red bell pepper

½ cup minced cilantro

To make the dressing: Mix together the mayonnaise, maple syrup, mustard, rice vinegar, lime juice, cumin, salt, minced garlic and chiles in a bowl. (If you want a mild salad, add just 1 chile.) May be made 1 or 2 days ahead; refrigerate in a covered container.

To make the slaw: Combine the cabbage, carrots, bell pepper and cilantro in a large bowl. Add two thirds of the dressing and toss to combine. (If you like a creamier slaw, add all of the dressing.)

Refrigerate for at least 2 hours before serving.

Keeps well for up to 1 day in the refrigerator.

SERVES 6

Tomato, Lemon, Green Olive and Onion Salad

This salad by Marlena Spieler is embarrassingly simple, but the juxtaposition of flavors is magical. A pinch of sugar, sprinkled on the tomatoes along with salt, is the secret of balancing the flavors.

4 ripe tomatoes, cored and sliced

1 sweet onion, very thinly sliced

Pinch of sugar

Salt, to taste

Pinch of cayenne pepper

1 lemon

12 Mediterranean-type full-flavored green olives

2 tablespoons extra virgin olive oil

Layer the sliced tomatoes on a serving plate with the onion, sprinkling with sugar, salt and cayenne pepper.

Zest the lemon with a grater or a lemon zester and scatter the zest over the tomatoes and onions, then squeeze the juice over the top. Garnish with the olives and drizzle with the olive oil. Refrigerate until ready to serve.

SERVES 4

Plaka Greek Salad

This classic Greek salad, here interpreted by Joanne Weir, is named after a picturesque quarter of Athens. The salad features bite-size cubes of perfectly ripe tomatoes, bell pepper and cucumber, diced onion, kalamata olives and feta cheese. It's a whole meal rolled into one dish. Accompany it with a loaf of country-style bread, a pot of sweet butter and a robust red wine . . . and pretend you're in Athens.

3 large ripe tomatoes (about 2 pounds), coarsely cut into 1- to 1½-inch pieces

1 small red onion, cut into large dice

2 red bell peppers, seeded, deribbed and coarsely cut into 1- to 1½-inch pieces

1 English cucumber, cut into 1-inch pieces

4 tablespoons extra virgin olive oil

2 tablespoons red wine vinegar

Coarse salt and freshly ground pepper, to taste

¾ pound feta cheese

1 cup kalamata olives

1 teaspoon dried Greek oregano

Arrange the tomatoes, onion, bell peppers and cucumber on a serving plate. Drizzle with the olive oil and vinegar. Season with salt and pepper.

Crumble the feta cheese over the top, distributing it evenly. Sprinkle the olives and oregano over the salad and serve immediately.

SERVES 8

BEST WAY:
Red Wine Vinaigrette

Although a vinaigrette is simple to make, finding the proper balance can be tricky: The type of oil and vinegar used, the proportion of each, and the amount and timing of adding the salt all make a difference.

After testing many brands, we chose mild Fini Extra Virgin Olive Oil and Eden Select Red Wine Vinegar.

The best vinaigrette uses 2 parts olive oil to 1 part vinegar. Put the vinegar in a bowl and begin whisking. Slowly add the oil in a steady stream to form an emulsion. When all the oil is incorporated, add 1 teaspoon of kosher salt and continue to whisk for a few seconds. Add freshly ground black pepper, to taste, and whisk again.

Celery Root, Mache and Blood Orange Salad

In this eye-catching salad by Georgeanne Brennan, celery root takes on the vibrant red color of the blood orange in the dressing. The crisp, pungent celery root makes a delicious flavor combination with the nutty-tasting greens and the sweet oranges.

1 celery root

4 blood oranges

3 tablespoons finely grated regular orange zest

1 tablespoon sherry vinegar

2 to 3 tablespoons walnut oil, or extra virgin olive oil

Freshly ground pepper, to taste

4 cups mache, or mixed baby greens

A Green, Green Dressing

Add a handful of fresh tarragon to your favorite vinaigrette, along with a little cooked, well-squeezed spinach. Purée until the mixture turns the color of a field of greens.

◐ Peel the celery root and, using a mandoline or a knife, cut the root into thin julienne strips. Put the strips in a bowl of ice water. Set aside.

Squeeze and strain the juice of 1 orange into a small bowl. Add half of the orange zest, the vinegar, walnut oil and pepper. Mix with a fork. Taste, adding more oil if too tart. Set aside.

Peel the remaining oranges, cutting away all the white pith. Slice the oranges and remove the seeds with the tip of a knife.

Drain and dry the celery root. Arrange the mache on individual salad plates. Arrange a layer of orange slices on or around the mache.

Put the celery root in the bowl with the orange juice dressing and toss to coat. Distribute the celery root evenly atop the mache. Finish each plate with the remaining orange zest.

SERVES 4

Fennel and Dry Goat Cheese Salad with Lemon Vinaigrette

The combination of lemon and fennel is the crux of this simple salad by Georgeanne Brennan. Paper-thin slices of crunchy, licoricelike fennel are tossed with a tangy lemon–olive oil dressing, then topped with shavings of dry goat cheese and lots of coarsely ground black pepper.

2 fennel bulbs

½ to 1 pound dry goat cheese, or dry Monterey Jack cheese, in 1 chunk

¼ cup fresh lemon juice

½ teaspoon salt

½ cup extra virgin olive oil

2 tablespoons chopped Italian parsley

2 teaspoons freshly ground pepper

◉◉ Remove any tough or discolored leaves from the fennel and discard them, as well as the stalk. Slice the fennel bulbs in half lengthwise. Then slice each half crosswise into paper-thin slices. Set aside.

Using a sharp knife, shave paper-thin slices from the cheese.

Mix together the lemon juice, salt and olive oil in a bowl. Stir in the parsley.

Put the fennel in a bowl and toss it with the vinaigrette. Mound the fennel on a serving platter or on individual salad plates. Sprinkle with pepper and top with thin shavings of cheese.

Serve at room temperature.

SERVES 4

Asparagus and Goat Cheese

One of Marlena Spieler's favorite combinations is just-cooked asparagus drizzled with vinaigrette. Serve alongside a disk of warm goat cheese, lightly browned in the oven.

After experimenting with various ways of storing lettuce for up to a week at a time, we found these methods work the best.
For iceberg lettuce: Store the head of lettuce in a self-sealing, nonperforated plastic bag in the crisper drawer. Do not core or wash it if you plan to keep it for more than two days. Wash the lettuce right before using.
For mixed baby greens: Wash greens, pat with paper towels or dry in a salad spinner and place in a self-sealing, nonperforated plastic bag in the refrigerator. To prevent bruising, handle the greens as little as possible.

Frisee and Corn Salad with Fried Tomatoes

The flavor contrast of corn and frisee, and the temperature contrast of cool greens against hot fried tomatoes dusted in cornmeal, make this salad truly spectacular. It's the brainchild of Donia Bijan, chef at the charming L'Amie Donia in Palo Alto. If you can't find frisee—a type of chicory with fine, lacy, blanched leaves—substitute six handfuls of mixed baby greens.

2 small heads frisee

2 ears of yellow corn

6 tablespoons extra virgin olive oil

2½ tablespoons balsamic vinegar

3 shallots, minced

Salt and freshly ground pepper, to taste

1 cup yellow cornmeal

Pinch of sugar

Olive oil for frying

6 large slices beefsteak tomato, each about ⅓ inch thick

1 dozen fresh basil leaves

◉◉ Core the frisee and separate the heads into individual leaves. Discard any tough, dark green leaves. Put the pale leaves in a large mixing bowl and set aside.

Bring a large pot of water to a boil over high heat. Cut the corn kernels from the cobs. Blanch corn in the boiling water for 2 minutes. Drain and transfer to ice water to stop the cooking. When cool, drain again and set aside.

Whisk together the extra virgin olive oil, balsamic vinegar and shallots in a bowl. Season with salt and pepper. Set aside.

Put the cornmeal in a small bowl and season with salt, pepper and sugar. Stir to blend.

Heat a large nonstick skillet over high heat. Add a generous film of olive oil. When the oil is hot, dip the tomato slices 1 at a time in the cornmeal, coating both sides. Fry 3 slices at a time so you don't crowd the pan, browning slices on both sides. Transfer them as they are done to a platter. Wipe the pan clean before frying the second batch.

While the tomatoes are frying, tear the basil leaves into small pieces and add to the frisee, along with two thirds of the corn kernels. Add the vinaigrette and toss to coat. Transfer to a large serving platter. Top with the fried tomatoes and sprinkle with the remaining corn kernels.

SERVES 6

Green Papaya Salad

This recipe is from Gary Woo, consultant for Moki's Sushi and Pacific Grill in San Francisco. Green papaya is available in Asian markets. To make the salad, however, you need a mandoline to produce thin, uniform shreds of papaya, carrot and cucumber. For a more substantial salad or a lunch main course, add cooked shellfish or shredded cooked chicken, if you like.

1 green papaya, about 1½ pounds, peeled and seeded

1 carrot

1 cucumber

1 cup finely chopped cilantro leaves

1 small red bell pepper, seeded, deribbed and julienned (optional)

4 teaspoons minced garlic

2 teaspoons salt

3½ tablespoons sugar

3 cups distilled vinegar

Freshly ground pepper, to taste (optional)

Shred the papaya, carrot and cucumber on a mandoline. Put in a salad bowl and toss with the cilantro and bell pepper, if desired. Stir in the garlic, salt, sugar, vinegar and pepper, if desired. Set aside for a couple of hours to let the flavors combine.

SERVES 6 TO 8

Summer Fruit Salad with Feta and Cilantro

This is Georgeanne Brennan's version of a salad she enjoyed at a beachside stand in Puerto Vallarta. For best results, use fruit that is sweet and ripe but not overly soft.

2 cups thinly sliced nectarines or peaches

¾ cup cantaloupe cubes

¾ cup honeydew cubes

¼ cup fresh lime juice (about 6 limes)

2 tablespoons chopped cilantro

½ teaspoon freshly ground ancho or other dried chile, or to taste

¼ cup crumbled feta cheese, or queso fresco

Cilantro sprigs for garnish

Combine the nectarines, cantaloupe and honeydew cubes, lime juice and chopped cilantro in a serving bowl. Gently stir to mix. Add the chile and mix gently. Add the cheese and mix gently again. Garnish with the cilantro sprigs.

SERVES 4 TO 6

A Fine Fruit Salad

Mix together a cup each of blackberries and cubed ripe cantaloupe. Add fresh lemon juice, to taste, and let stand for about 5 minutes.

Cobb Salad Brown Derby

This is based on the original Cobb salad recipe that appeared in Jean Anderson's American Century Cookbook *in 1997, although it was probably first published in* The Brown Derby Cookbook *in 1949. Robin Davis simplified it a bit for the home cook.*

Brown Derby French Dressing

1 tablespoon water

6 tablespoons red wine vinegar

½ teaspoon sugar

1 teaspoon fresh lemon juice

1½ teaspoons Worcestershire sauce

½ teaspoon dry mustard

1 small garlic clove, minced

½ cup olive oil

½ cup vegetable oil

Salt and freshly ground pepper, to taste

Salad

2 cups chopped iceberg lettuce (about ¼ head)

2 cups chopped curly endive (about ½ small bunch)

4 cups finely chopped romaine lettuce

2 plum tomatoes, seeded and chopped

2 cooked chicken breast halves (preferably roasted), skinned, boned and cubed

6 bacon slices, crisply cooked and crumbled

1 avocado, halved, pitted, peeled and cubed

3 hard-cooked eggs, peeled and chopped

½ cup crumbled Roquefort cheese

2 tablespoons chopped fresh chives

∞ To make the dressing: Combine the water, vinegar, sugar, lemon juice, Worcestershire sauce, mustard and garlic in a bowl. Gradually whisk in the olive and vegetable oils. Season with salt and pepper.

To make the salad: Combine the iceberg lettuce, curly endive and romaine in a bowl. Add half of the dressing and toss to coat. Arrange on a platter.

The Best Avocado

Jacqueline McMahan says one of the best pairings is balsamic vinegar and avocado. Simply place a tiny pool of aged balsamic vinegar in the cavity of a ripe avocado half. It makes a heavenly lunch.

Arrange the tomatoes, chicken, bacon, avocado, eggs and cheese in strips over the salad. Sprinkle with the chives. Drizzle with the remaining dressing.

SERVES 4 TO 6 AS A MAIN COURSE

French-Style Cobb Salad

Robin Davis also created this updated version of a Cobb salad with a nod to France. It combines cubes of beets, creamy goat cheese, tiny golden tomatoes and duck confit. To remove the excess fat from the confit, briefly plunge the duck pieces into boiling water, then pat dry. Duck confit is available in some specialty markets. If desired, smoked chicken or chicken confit may be substituted.

3 medium-size beets, trimmed

¼ cup chopped fresh tarragon

¼ cup fresh lemon juice

¾ cup olive oil

Salt and freshly ground pepper, to taste

8 cups arugula, or 2 cups arugula mixed with 6 cups baby greens

1½ cups shredded duck or chicken confit, or smoked chicken

1 cup crumbled soft fresh goat cheese

2 hard-cooked eggs, peeled and chopped

1 cup golden currant tomatoes, or small golden cherry tomatoes, halved

Place the beets in a heavy saucepan and cover with 2 to 3 inches of water. Bring to a boil over high heat, reduce heat to low and simmer for about 45 minutes, or until tender when pierced with a knife. Drain. When cool enough to handle, peel and cut into ½-inch dice.

Mix the tarragon and lemon juice in a small bowl. Gradually whisk in the olive oil until well blended. Season with salt and pepper.

Place the arugula in a bowl. Add half of the dressing and toss to coat. Transfer to a platter. Arrange the beets down the center of the salad. On one side, arrange the duck confit and goat cheese; on the other side, arrange the eggs and tomatoes. Drizzle with the remaining dressing.

SERVES 4 AS A MAIN COURSE

Black Bean and Corn Salad

The dazzling contrast of bright yellow corn against earthy black beans makes this salad look as exciting as it tastes. Created by Angel Perez, deli manager of Oakville Grocery in the Napa Valley, it's great with sandwiches or as a side dish at a cookout.

2½ cups dried black beans

1 carrot, halved

1 celery stalk, halved

1 onion, halved

2 thyme sprigs, plus 1½ teaspoons minced fresh thyme

2 oregano sprigs, plus 1½ teaspoons minced fresh oregano

Salt, to taste

2 to 3 canned chipotle chiles en adobo

3 garlic cloves, minced

½ cup olive oil

1 red bell pepper, seeded, deribbed and diced

1 yellow bell pepper, seeded, deribbed and diced

½ onion, minced

Kernels from 3 small ears of corn

½ cup fresh lemon juice

½ bunch cilantro, chopped

½ bunch green onions (both white and green parts), chopped

Freshly ground pepper, to taste

Pick over the beans, discarding any broken or withered ones or stones. Put beans in a bowl, add water to cover by 1 inch and let soak overnight. Drain.

Put the beans in a large saucepan with the carrot, celery, onion, and thyme and oregano sprigs. Add water to cover by 1 inch and bring to a simmer over medium heat. Cover and adjust heat to maintain a gentle simmer. Cook for 45 minutes or more, depending on age of beans, or until tender. Season with salt 20 minutes before the beans are done. Let the beans cool in the broth, then discard the carrot, celery, onion and herbs.

Purée the chipotle chiles and garlic in a blender.

Heat the olive oil in a large skillet over medium heat. Add the red and yellow bell peppers, onion, and minced thyme and oregano; sauté for about 3 minutes, or until the vegetables are slightly softened.

Add the corn and sauté for 3 or 4 minutes, or until it no longer tastes raw but is still slightly crunchy.

Stir in the chipotle-garlic paste and cook for about 3 minutes longer to blend the flavors. Transfer to a bowl.

Drain the beans and add to the bowl.

Just before serving, add the lemon juice, cilantro and green onions and stir to mix. Season with salt and pepper.

SERVES 10 TO 12

Chickpea Salad with Provençal Herbs and Olives

This chickpea salad from Joanne Weir gets a boost from a generous dose of fresh herbs, niçoise olives and red onion. Serve at room temperature to begin a casual meal, or as an accompaniment for roast chicken or grilled pork.

1 cup dried chickpeas

5 tablespoons red wine vinegar

4 garlic cloves, minced

4 tablespoons extra virgin olive oil

Salt and freshly ground pepper, to taste

1 tablespoon chopped fresh mint

1 tablespoon chopped fresh basil

1 teaspoon chopped fresh thyme

1 teaspoon chopped fresh rosemary

1 teaspoon chopped fresh oregano

2 tablespoons chopped fresh Italian parsley

⅓ cup black niçoise olives, pitted

1 small red onion, diced

◎◎ Pick over the chickpeas, discarding any broken or withered ones or stones. Put the chickpeas in a bowl, cover with water and let soak overnight.

The next day, drain the chickpeas and place in a saucepan. Add water to cover by 2 inches. Simmer, uncovered, for 45 to 60 minutes, or until the skins begin to crack and the beans are tender. Drain and place in a bowl.

Whisk together the vinegar, garlic and olive oil in a bowl. Season with salt and pepper, then add to the hot chickpeas. Stir until chickpeas are coated with dressing. Let cool to room temperature.

Add the mint, basil, thyme, rosemary, oregano, parsley, olives and onion to the chickpeas; toss well. Taste and season with salt and pepper, if needed.

SERVES 8

Making Tuscan Pinzimonio

One of Marlena Spieler's favorite salads is the classic Tuscan *pinzimonio*. It's simple and delicious, especially when eaten outdoors under the shade of a grand old tree.

Wash and prepare an array of fresh vegetables: carrots, celery, bell peppers, fennel, endive, turnips, cabbage, jicama and radishes, for example. Some vegetables may need to be blanched and then chilled, such as sugar snap peas, asparagus or green and yellow wax beans. Set out a basket of warm grilled bread, a cruet of fragrant olive oil, lemon wedges and kosher salt.

To eat *pinzimonio*, each diner is given a saucer-size plate. The idea is to tip one's plate a little, pour on a few spoonfuls of oil and then sprinkle with salt and a squeeze of lemon juice (some Tuscans omit the lemon). Stir the oil mixture with a piece of vegetable or a chunk of bread. Your dressed vegetable (or bread) is ready to eat, and you're ready to start again.

Spicy Citrus Couscous Tabbouleh

This classic Middle Eastern dish, created by Marlena Spieler, is given a whole new attitude with the addition of citrus and chile.

1 cup couscous

3 cups boiling water

4 garlic cloves, chopped

1 to 2 teaspoons ground red chile

½ to 1 teaspoon ground cumin

2 green onions (both white and green parts), thinly sliced

½ jalapeño chile, seeded and chopped

3 to 4 tablespoons chopped cilantro

Juice of 1 orange, or to taste

Juice of 1 lemon, or to taste

2 tablespoons extra virgin olive oil

Salt and freshly ground pepper, to taste

◉◉ Place the couscous in a bowl and pour the boiling water over it. Cover and let stand for 5 to 10 minutes. Test to see if it is tender. If not, let it stand longer. Drain well.

Mix the couscous in a bowl with the garlic, ground chile, cumin, onions, jalapeño, cilantro, orange and lemon juices, olive oil, salt and pepper. Taste and adjust seasonings as needed.

Cover and refrigerate if made ahead. Bring to room temperature before serving.

SERVES 4

Lush Yogurt Rice

An addictive mixture of cooked white rice, crunchy cucumber, fiery chile and cool yogurt, this Indian "salad" by Laxmi Hiremath is a perfect remedy for hot weather. It makes a unique side dish for a picnic or a barbecue. In addition to grapes, it's good with almost any summer fruit: peaches, nectarines, pineapple, melon, mango or papaya, but it may be best with early summer Babcock peaches.

1 teaspoon grated fresh ginger

1 fresh hot green chile, stemmed, seeded and minced

½ teaspoon ground cumin

2 cups cooked basmati or California long-grain white rice, cooled to room temperature

1 cup chopped English hothouse cucumber

¼ teaspoon salt, or to taste

1 teaspoon sugar

1 cup plain yogurt (nonfat or low fat), stirred

2 tablespoons sour cream (optional)

2 tablespoons coarsely chopped peanuts

½ tablespoon chopped cilantro for garnish

2 small clusters green grapes for garnish

Combine the ginger, chile and cumin in a large bowl. Add the rice and cucumber and toss gently to mix. Sprinkle in the salt and sugar and mix well. Fold in the yogurt, sour cream, if desired, and the peanuts.

If not serving immediately, cover and refrigerate.

May be made 1 day in advance. You may want to add more yogurt before serving.

Garnish with the cilantro and grape clusters just before serving.

SERVES 2 OR 3

Potato Salad with Asparagus and Pesto Vinaigrette

Robin Davis is from the Midwest, but her version of potato salad is given a sophisticated turn with the addition of asparagus and pesto. It's unusual enough for a summer dinner party, but it also makes a delicious accompaniment to a family picnic. Try to serve this as soon as it has been made because the pesto will discolor when exposed to air. Or, you can assemble all the parts and refrigerate separately (press plastic wrap directly onto the surface of the pesto), then toss together when you're ready to serve.

½ pound asparagus, trimmed and cut into 2-inch lengths

2 pounds red-skinned potatoes (about 6 large), cut into ½-inch-thick slices

2 garlic cloves, peeled

¾ cup packed basil leaves

¼ cup packed Italian parsley leaves

¼ cup toasted walnuts

2 tablespoons fresh lemon juice

½ cup extra virgin olive oil

¼ cup freshly grated Parmigiano-Reggiano cheese

Salt and freshly ground pepper, to taste

◐ Bring a large pot of salted water to a boil. Add the asparagus and cook for about 3 minutes, or until bright green and just tender. Using a slotted spoon, transfer the asparagus to a bowl of cold water. Drain.

Add the potatoes to the boiling water. Return to a boil. Cook for about 10 minutes, or until just tender. Drain the potatoes. Run under cold water until cool. Drain well.

Meanwhile, finely chop the garlic in a food processor. Add the basil, parsley, walnuts and lemon juice and process until finely chopped. With the processor running, gradually add the olive oil and process until the mixture is emulsified. Stir in the cheese. Season with salt and pepper.

Toss the asparagus with 2 tablespoons pesto. Arrange in the center of a platter. Toss the potatoes with the remaining pesto. Arrange around the asparagus.

SERVES 6

Basil Vinegar

Put 1 cup loosely packed green or purple basil leaves in a widemouthed jar with a lid. Fully cover with 3½ cups distilled white wine vinegar. Cover and place the jar in a sunny location. Let stand for about 10 days, or until the vinegar is infused with the flavor of basil. Strain and discard the leaves. Bottle in sterilized jars, seal and store in a cool, dark place. This same technique also may be used with other herbs, says Georgeanne Brennan.

Minty Thai Chicken Salad

The unmistakable flavor of kaffir lime leaves, available in some Asian markets, gives Mai Pham's chicken salad a distinctive edge. Make sure to shred the leaves very thinly so the intense aroma and flavor are evenly distributed in the salad. To turn this into a delicious vegetarian dish, substitute tofu for the chicken.

1 tablespoon vegetable oil

2 garlic cloves, minced

1 shallot, sliced

2 teaspoons hot red pepper flakes, or to taste

⅔ pound skinless, boneless chicken breasts or thighs, minced

2 tablespoons Asian fish sauce, or to taste

2 teaspoons light brown sugar

1 tablespoon water, if needed

¼ cup fresh lime juice

3 teaspoons toasted rice powder (optional)

2 tablespoons thinly sliced yellow onion

1 tablespoon minced lemongrass

2 kaffir lime leaves, finely slivered

2 cups very finely shredded green cabbage

2 plum tomatoes, seeded and cut into thin wedges

⅓ cup mint leaves

Boston or red lettuce leaves

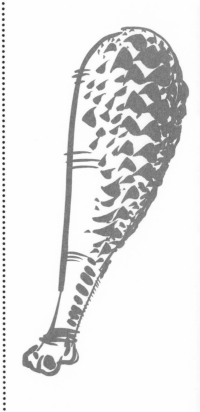

Heat the oil in a small sauté pan over medium heat. Add the garlic, shallot and pepper flakes and stir for about 20 seconds, or until fragrant. Add the chicken, fish sauce and sugar. If the pan becomes too dry, add the water. Cook for about 2 minutes longer, or until the chicken is done. Transfer to a mixing bowl.

Add the lime juice, toasted rice powder, if desired, the onion, lemongrass, lime leaves, cabbage, tomatoes and mint leaves. Toss gently.

Serve on plates lined with lettuce leaves.

SERVES 4

Curried Turkey Salad
with Apple and Walnuts

California Culinary Academy graduate Sean Forsha used leftover turkey to make this wonderful filling for pita bread. To add texture and color, garnish each sandwich with alfalfa or radish sprouts and tomato slices.

⅓ cup mayonnaise

2½ teaspoons curry powder, toasted (see Note)

¼ teaspoon fresh lemon juice

Pinch of cayenne pepper

2 cups cubed roasted turkey

1 cup peeled, cored and diced red apple

1 celery stalk, diced

½ cup peeled, seeded and diced cucumber

¼ cup chopped toasted walnuts

Salt and freshly ground pepper, to taste

6 pita breads

Alfalfa or radish sprouts for garnish

Tomato slices for garnish

◎◎ Combine the mayonnaise, curry powder, lemon juice and cayenne pepper in a bowl; stir to blend.

Combine the turkey, apple, celery, cucumber and walnuts in a bowl. Fold in the dressing. Season with salt and pepper.

Cut the pita breads in half. Spoon the salad into the halves and garnish with sprouts and tomato slices.

SERVES 6

NOTE: Toast the curry powder in a small nonstick skillet over low heat, stirring often, for 1 minute, or until just fragrant. This will help remove the raw flavor.

Vietnamese "Shaking" Beef Salad

In Vietnam, bo luc lac *often is accompanied by a simple dipping sauce made with salt, freshly cracked black pepper and a squeeze of lime. But Mai Pham likes to toss the greens and onion with a dressing so the flavors will permeate the mix. This dish makes a great appetizer and, with a bowl of steamed rice, a satisfying entree as well.*

Dressing

1 teaspoon minced garlic

1 teaspoon minced fresh chile (any variety)

2 tablespoons fresh lime juice

2 tablespoons Asian fish sauce

2 tablespoons sugar

Salad

1½ cups watercress, torn into bite-size sprigs

2 cups butter lettuce, or other lettuce, torn into bite-size pieces

¼ cup thinly sliced red onion

Salt and freshly ground pepper, to taste

Beef

2 to 3 tablespoons vegetable oil

2 garlic cloves, sliced

1 pound beef sirloin or flank steak, cut into ⅛-inch-thick slices

2 tablespoons oyster sauce

¼ cup bite-size fresh pineapple pieces, each about ⅛ inch thick

20 Thai basil leaves, halved

To make the dressing: Combine the garlic, chile, lime juice, fish sauce and sugar in a bowl. Mix well. Set aside.

To make the salad: Gently combine the watercress, lettuce and onion in a bowl. Season with salt and pepper, then place on a platter.

To make the beef: Heat the oil in a skillet over high heat. Add the garlic and stir quickly for about 10 seconds, or until fragrant. Add the beef and oyster sauce and cook for 2 minutes. Add the pineapple and cook, stirring, for about 1 minute, or until the beef is done and the pineapple is just hot. Transfer to a mixing bowl.

Marion Cunningham's Tips for Making the Perfect Salad

Discard any blemished, yellowed, limp or wilted greens.

Rinse all fresh, raw ingredients under cold running water.

Dry all rinsed greens with paper towels or cloth towels, or use a salad spinner. Salad dressings won't adhere to wet leaves.

Vary your salads by including different greens, either by themselves or in combination. Try small spinach leaves, watercress, red oak leaf and small amounts of fresh herbs like basil or fennel.

Don't put the dressing on a tossed green salad until you are ready to serve it.

If you are making a salad using cooked ingredients, add the dressing earlier so it penetrates the ingredients and fully flavors the salad.

Add half of the dressing and the basil leaves to the beef and toss gently to combine. Arrange the beef in the center of the salad and drizzle the remaining dressing over the top.

SERVES 4

Penne with Three Herbs, Capers and Tuna

We've had so many bad versions of cold pasta salads that we'd come to the conclusion pasta should only be served hot. This salad from Georgeanne Brennan made us reconsider. Capers and herbs give the blend a piquant flavor, and the addition of tuna raises it to main-dish status. To make a vegetarian version, substitute grilled red bell peppers and Mediterranean-style black olives for the tuna.

6 ounces oil-packed tuna, preferably olive-oil packed

½ pound penne

2 tablespoons fresh lemon juice

2 tablespoons extra virgin olive oil

½ teaspoon freshly ground pepper

½ teaspoon salt

2 teaspoons vinegar-packed capers

¼ cup chopped parsley

¼ cup chopped basil

¼ cup chopped cilantro

◖◗ Drain the tuna of as much of its oil as possible. Put the tuna in a bowl and, using a fork, break it into flakes. Set aside.

Bring a large pot of salted water to a boil over high heat. Add the pasta and cook for about 12 minutes, or until al dente. Drain well.

Put the penne in a salad bowl and add the lemon juice, olive oil, pepper and salt. Mix well, then add the capers, parsley, basil, cilantro and tuna and mix again. Serve at room temperature.

SERVES 4

Wilted Cabbage Salad with Bacon and Cashel Blue Cheese

This cabbage salad, by Kerry Heffernan of Autumn Moon in Oakland, is about as rustic and delicious as you'll find. You may use any blue cheese, such as Stilton or Roquefort, in place of the Irish farmhouse cheese.

Dressing

7 ounces bacon, cut into 2-inch pieces

2 tablespoons extra virgin olive oil

1 garlic clove, chopped

1 small white onion, sliced

3 tablespoons apple cider vinegar

Salt and freshly ground pepper, to taste

Salad

2 tablespoons extra virgin olive oil

1 head savoy cabbage, thick ribs removed, leaves sliced

1 carrot, julienned

Leaves from 3 Italian parsley sprigs

½ head radicchio, thinly sliced

½ cup crumbled Cashel blue cheese, or more, to taste

To make the dressing: Sauté the bacon in the olive oil over medium heat until the bacon begins to crisp up. Remove the bacon with a slotted spoon to paper towels to drain.

Add the garlic and onion to the pan and sauté for 1 minute. Remove from heat and carefully add the vinegar. Scrape the bottom of the pan to loosen any juices, then season with salt and pepper.

To make the salad: Heat the olive oil in a large skillet over medium heat. Add the cabbage and carrot all at once. Cook, stirring, for about 2 minutes, or until the cabbage wilts. Transfer to a large bowl. Add the parsley, radicchio, reserved bacon and the cheese to the warm cabbage mixture; toss with the dressing.

Divide the salad among warmed plates.

SERVES 6

Grilled Tuna Salad with Bok Choy and Papaya

Mounds of thinly sliced bok choy tossed with napa cabbage and a soy sauce–based dressing make a delicious background for sweet papaya and grilled tuna in this recipe by Georgeanne Brennan. You may substitute grilled shrimp or chicken for the tuna, if you like.

2 baby bok choy

3 cups very thinly sliced napa cabbage

¼ cup light soy sauce

3 tablespoons fresh lemon juice

1½ teaspoons sugar

2 tablespoons sesame seeds

¾-pound tuna steak

½ teaspoon salt

½ teaspoon freshly ground pepper

2 papayas, peeled, seeded and thinly sliced

◎◎ Prepare a hot wood or charcoal fire in a grill or preheat a gas grill to high heat.

Cut the stems of the bok choy into ¼-inch-thick slices, julienne the leaves and put them in a bowl with the cabbage.

Combine the soy sauce, lemon juice and sugar in a small bowl. Pour over the bok choy and cabbage and mix gently.

Heat a skillet over medium heat and add the sesame seeds, shaking the pan until the seeds are lightly browned. Be careful not to burn them. Add half of the sesame seeds to the salad and stir to mix. Reserve the remaining seeds.

Season both sides of the tuna with the salt and pepper. Clean the grill with a damp cloth and rub it with oil. Cook the tuna 2 to 3 minutes per side. It should remain rare in the middle. Remove the tuna and let it stand a few minutes before slicing it into ¼-inch-thick strips.

Divide the salad evenly among serving plates and top each with equal portions of tuna and papaya. Sprinkle with the reserved sesame seeds.

SERVES 4

Hot-and-Spicy Calamari Salad

Thai salads are Mai Pham's favorite foods. In summer, she cools her palate with a big serving of this hot-and-spicy salad and a side of steamed rice. Instead of calamari, you could substitute chicken or shrimp or even a combination of seafood or meats. If you can't find tamarind pulp, add more lime juice.

Dressing

1½ tablespoons Asian fish sauce

1 teaspoon palm sugar or brown sugar

1 tablespoon tamarind pulp, soaked in 3 tablespoons hot water, then pushed through
    a fine-mesh sieve

½ teaspoon ground chile

3 Thai bird chiles, or 1 serrano, chopped

2 tablespoons fresh lime juice, or to taste

Salad

⅔ pound calamari, cleaned

¼ small red onion, thinly sliced (about ¼ cup)

1 lemongrass stalk, tender white part only, sliced into paper-thin rings

1 large plum tomato, cut into thin wedges

3 or 4 romaine lettuce leaves, shredded

½ cup mint leaves

To make the dressing: Combine the fish sauce, sugar, tamarind, ground chile, chopped chile and lime juice in a mixing bowl; set aside so the flavors can develop.

To make the salad: Cut the calamari bodies into ½-inch rings. Leave the tentacles whole.

Bring a pot of water to a boil over high heat. Add the calamari and blanch for about 10 seconds, or until just done but still tender. Drain, then rinse under cold running water to stop the cooking. Set aside.

Just before serving, combine the calamari, onion, lemongrass, tomato, lettuce, mint and the dressing in a large bowl; toss gently.

SERVES 4

Chapter 4

Pasta and Grains

Ready to be tempted?

Creamy Lemon Spaghetti with Olives and Basil (page 94); Orecchiette with Broccoli Rabe and Turnips (page 103); Lamb Ravioli with Yogurt, Garlic and Mint (page 120).

Today it seems that everyone loves pasta. In the Bay Area, cooks have widened their repertoire considerably in the last few years. Udon and cellophane noodles from Asia have become just about as common as Italian spaghetti or fettuccine. Like their Italian counterparts, many are simple to prepare but spiced in less-familiar ways, such as Cold Udon Noodles with Morels and Fresh Peas (page 97) and Chinese Noodles with Five-Spice Shiitake Mushrooms (page 98).

While most recipes in this chapter are simple and straightforward, a few will take a considerable amount of time, such as the Duck Bolognese (page 123) from Donna Scala of Bistro Don Giovanni in Napa. It takes a while to cook, but after one bite of this rich, earthy sauce, you'll be glad you took the time to make it.

Two other Italian staples, risotto and polenta, are fast becoming everyday staples, as well. Like pasta, both beg to be dressed up. We have recipes that combine risotto with asparagus (page 138), with green garlic and spinach (page 139), with piquant green olives (page 140) and with pumpkin (page 141). And if you crave polenta, you'll find ways to give it a twist: served soft and creamy with walnuts (page 144) or studded with sweet bursts of corn and fiery jalapeño (page 145).

In addition, you'll find recipes using many other grains, including barley and cracked wheat, in the Meatless Main Courses chapter.

Creamy Lemon Spaghetti with Olives and Basil

This is wonderfully smooth and creamy even though it contains just a tiny bit of cream. It can be as puckery-tart as you like, depending on how much lemon juice you use. Marlena Spieler combines the pasta with slivers of black olive and sweet basil to add a Mediterranean twist. However, the basic recipe is versatile, and you may substitute other herbs or vegetables such as peas or green beans for an easy weeknight meal.

12 ounces spaghettini

4 tablespoons sour cream, crème fraîche or whipping cream

Salt and freshly ground pepper, to taste

Zest of 1 lemon, cut from the lemon into long strips with a zester

3 tablespoons olive oil

Juice of 2 lemons

4 ounces freshly grated Parmigiano-Reggiano cheese, or other grating cheese, plus
     more for serving

2 garlic cloves, chopped

20 to 25 kalamata olives, or other brined black olives, pitted and slivered

¼ cup basil leaves, torn into large pieces

Lemon wedges

◎◎ Bring a large pot of salted water to a boil over high heat. Add the pasta and cook for about 10 minutes, or until al dente, then drain and return to the pot. Toss with the sour cream, then with salt, pepper and lemon zest.

Working quickly, toss with the olive oil, lemon juice, cheese, garlic and olives. Transfer to a serving dish and scatter the basil over the top.

Serve immediately, with lemon wedges and extra cheese for those who desire it. The lemon strips are not meant to be eaten.

SERVES 4

Making a Chiffonade

Here's a simple way to cut large-leafed herbs such as basil or mint. Stack the leaves on top of each other, about 10 at a time. Roll lengthwise into a tube, with the middle vein in the center. Using a very sharp knife, start at the pointed end of the rolled leaves and slice as thinly as possible. You'll end up with long ribbons of herbs, perfect for enlivening pasta, salads or vegetables.

Delfina's Spaghetti

The secret to this simple and delicious recipe, by Craig Stoll of Delfina restaurant in San Francisco, is partially cooking the pasta in water, then finishing the cooking in the pasta sauce. The recipe yields enough sauce for 8 servings (it's easier to make in a larger quantity). You will need only half of the sauce for the amount of pasta called for here. Ladle the remaining sauce into an airtight container and freeze for up to 2 months.

½ cup extra virgin olive oil

4 garlic cloves

Kosher salt, to taste

2 cans (28 ounces each) peeled whole tomatoes (such as Di Napoli)

3 cups water

Freshly ground pepper, to taste

Hot red pepper flakes, to taste

½ bunch fresh basil (leaves only), torn into small pieces

1 pound spaghetti

Freshly grated Parmigiano-Reggiano cheese

Peeling Tomatoes

Remove the core and cut an "X" into the bottom of each tomato. Drop into rapidly boiling water for 10 seconds, or until you begin to see the skin peel away from the sides. Drain and plunge tomatoes into ice water. The skin will then slip off easily.

⚭ Heat the olive oil in a large heavy saucepan over medium-low heat. Smash the garlic with the side of a chef's knife; sprinkle with salt. Add to the oil. Cover and cook slowly for about 10 minutes, or until tender but not browned.

Meanwhile, remove the seeds from the tomatoes, breaking up tomatoes slightly with your hands. Add the tomatoes, their juices and the water to the saucepan. Increase heat to medium-high. Season lightly with salt, pepper and pepper flakes. Bring to a boil. Skim the foam that rises to the top, being careful not to skim the oil. Reduce heat to medium-low and simmer, stirring occasionally, for about 2 hours, or until the sauce is reduced by about two thirds and the oil is emulsified into the sauce. Remove from heat.

Pass two thirds of the sauce through a food mill fitted with the medium blade. Stir this purée into the remaining sauce, then stir in the basil.

Bring a large pot of salted water to a boil. Add the pasta and cook for 6 minutes. Drain, reserving 1½ cups of the cooking water.

Set 2 large, heavy skillets over medium-high heat. Place a generous ½ cup of the sauce and ¼ cup of the reserved cooking water in each. Divide the pasta between the skillets. Cook, stirring frequently, until the pasta is cooked through and the sauce clings to the pasta, adding more cooking water if necessary. Adjust seasonings. Divide pasta among serving plates. Sprinkle with cheese.

SERVES 4, WITH LEFTOVER SAUCE

Spaghetti with Marinated Fennel, Tomato and Olives

A cool, fresh "salad" of marinated fennel and tomato makes an inviting sauce for pasta in warm weather, says Janet Fletcher. The vegetables aren't cooked, but they are warmed gently when added to the hot pasta.

1 fennel bulb (about 1 pound after removing stalks), quartered and cored

1 pound tomatoes, peeled, seeded and chopped

6 tablespoons extra virgin olive oil

4 garlic cloves, minced

Salt, to taste

Hot red pepper flakes, to taste

White wine vinegar, to taste

1 pound spaghetti

20 black olives, pitted and coarsely chopped

2 tablespoons chopped Italian parsley

◉◉ Slice the trimmed fennel bulb as thinly as possible. A mandoline or Japanese vegetable slicer is helpful for this, but you can use a sharp knife. Transfer the fennel to a large bowl; add the tomatoes, olive oil and garlic. Season with salt, pepper flakes and a splash of vinegar. Stir, then set aside for 2 to 3 hours.

Bring a large pot of salted water to a boil over high heat. Add the pasta and cook until al dente. Drain and return it to the pot. Add the olives, parsley and the fennel-tomato mixture; toss well and serve.

SERVES 4 TO 6

Cold Udon Noodles with Morels and Fresh Peas

This dish is perfect for a picnic, says Brenda Buenviaje, the former chef of Oritalia, a stylish East-West restaurant in San Francisco. Pack it into a sturdy plastic container and refrigerate until you're ready to leave.

3 tablespoons butter

1 teaspoon minced garlic

½ small onion, thinly julienned

¼ cup Shaoxing rice wine

2 cups sliced morel mushrooms

1 cup fresh peas (about 1 pound unshelled)

½ cup vegetable stock or water

1 tablespoon fresh lemon juice

5 tablespoons low-sodium light soy sauce, or to taste

2 tablespoons vegetable oil

1 pound udon noodles, cooked al dente, rapidly cooled in ice water and drained

4 cups young spinach leaves

3 tablespoons thinly sliced scallions

Melt the butter in a sauté pan over medium-high heat; add the garlic and onion and sauté for about 10 minutes, or until the garlic is toasted and the onion is lightly caramelized. Add the rice wine and cook, stirring to dislodge all the browned bits on the bottom of the pan.

Add the morels and peas; simmer for 5 minutes. Add the stock and simmer for 5 minutes longer, or until the peas are tender. Add the lemon juice and soy sauce. Set aside.

Heat another sauté pan over high heat until very hot, then add the vegetable oil. Add the cooked and drained noodles and stir-fry for 1 minute.

Add the morel mixture and the spinach. Stir-fry over high heat until the noodles absorb the cooking liquid. Toss in the scallions.

Transfer to a plastic container and let cool. Cover tightly and refrigerate until ready to serve or pack for a picnic.

SERVES 4 TO 6

Chinese Noodles with Five-Spice Shiitake Mushrooms

Staff writer Tara Duggan created this quick and unusual recipe for The Chronicle's *Working Cook column. The simple-to-prepare dish can be on the table in 30 minutes. It incorporates five-spice powder, a Chinese spice mixture made of ground star anise, cinnamon, Sichuan peppercorns, fennel seeds and cloves. Heady and rich, the seasoning brings an intense earthiness to the blend.*

2½ cups water

½ ounce dried shiitake mushrooms

1 pound fresh Chinese chow mein noodles

2 shallots

2 garlic cloves

⅓ pound fresh shiitake mushrooms

1 tablespoon butter

2 tablespoons vegetable oil

1 teaspoon Chinese five-spice powder

2 tablespoons soy sauce

1 tablespoon Shaoxing rice wine or dry sherry

2 green onions (both white and green parts), thinly sliced

1 tablespoon sesame seeds (optional)

Using Asian Glass Noodles

Kirk Webber, the innovative chef at Cafe Kati in San Francisco, always has Asian glass noodles in his pantry for an easy meal at home.

With just a dip in hot water, the noodles can become the base for a hot or cold supper. For a hot, quick meal, stir in a little chicken stock, soy sauce, green onion and a handful of stir-fried bok choy or other vegetables.

To make a cold salad, chill the noodles and toss with soy sauce, sesame oil, chopped vegetables and slivered chicken.

◉◉ Bring a large pot of salted water to a boil over high heat. Meanwhile, bring the 2½ cups water to a boil in a small saucepan over high heat. Add the dried shiitakes, cover, reduce heat to low and simmer for 3 minutes. Strain the liquid into a bowl, then squeeze the mushrooms over the bowl. Set aside both mushrooms and liquid.

Cook the noodles in the large pot of boiling water until tender according to package directions. Drain and rinse under cold running water. Drain well.

Mince the shallots and garlic. Remove the caps from the fresh and dried shiitakes and slice into thin strips.

Heat the butter and 1 tablespoon of the oil in a wok or large saucepan over medium heat. Add the five-spice powder and shallots and sauté, stirring frequently, for about 2 minutes, or until tender.

Add the garlic and sauté for 2 minutes. Increase the heat to medium-high and add the fresh and dried shiitakes with ½ cup of the reserved mushroom-soaking water. Sauté, stirring frequently, for about 3 minutes, or until the mushrooms are tender.

Add the soy sauce and rice wine. Increase the heat to high and sauté, stirring, for 1 minute. Add the remaining mushroom-soaking water (except the last few tablespoons, which might contain dirt particles). Remove the mushroom mixture from the pan and set aside.

Heat the remaining 1 tablespoon oil in the pan over high heat. Add the noodles; sauté, stirring, for 1 minute. Add the mushroom mixture and green onions. Stir quickly to heat through, then sprinkle with the sesame seeds, if desired.

SERVES 4

Cellophane Noodles with Black Mushrooms

These hot noodles are an interesting departure from the standard pasta most Americans are used to. Mai Pham seasons the noodles with soy sauce, tiger lily buds and black mushrooms. For best flavor and texture, cook the noodles until they have completely expanded and absorbed all the sauce.

2 tablespoons vegetable oil

2 shallots, sliced

8 black mushrooms, soaked in hot water for 30 minutes, drained, stemmed and halved or quartered

20 dried tiger lily buds, soaked in hot water for 30 minutes, drained (optional)

1 teaspoon hot red pepper flakes

2 tablespoons soy sauce, or to taste

3 ounces cellophane noodles, cut into 10-inch lengths, soaked in hot water for 30 minutes, drained

1¼ cups low-sodium chicken broth

½ cup julienned carrots, blanched

⅔ cup canned bamboo shoot strips, parboiled and drained

2 heads baby bok choy, cut diagonally into 2-inch strips

Salt and freshly ground pepper, to taste

10 Thai or sweet basil leaves

Heat the oil in a skillet over high heat. Add the shallots and toss for about 10 seconds, or until fragrant. Add the black mushrooms, tiger lily buds, if desired, and pepper flakes; stir for 30 seconds. Sprinkle the soy sauce, several teaspoons at a time, directly on the skillet bottom so it can caramelize.

Quickly add the noodles and, using chopsticks or tongs, stir to coat.

Add the chicken broth. Reduce heat to low and cook for 10 minutes. Add the carrots, bamboo shoots and bok choy; cook for 5 to 7 minutes, or until the vegetables are done and the noodles have absorbed all the liquid.

Adjust seasonings with salt and pepper. Add the basil leaves just before serving.

SERVES 4

Pappardelle with Arugula, Cherry Tomatoes and Breadcrumbs

Janet Fletcher created this fresh pasta dish using warm tomatoes and wilted arugula. The sauce is a simple blend of oil, garlic and hot red pepper flakes. Toasted breadcrumbs, sprinkled on just before serving, add a pleasing crunch.

1 pound fresh egg pasta in sheets

½ cup olive oil

½ cup fine fresh breadcrumbs (see Note, page 108)

4 garlic cloves, minced

Pinch of hot red pepper flakes

1 pound cherry tomatoes, halved

Salt, to taste

½ pound arugula, thick stems removed

Using a fluted pastry wheel, cut the pasta into ½-inch-wide strips. Set aside on a baking sheet.

Heat 1 tablespoon of the olive oil in a skillet over medium-low heat. Add the breadcrumbs and stir to coat evenly with oil. Cook, stirring often, for about 10 minutes, or until the crumbs are an even golden brown. Set aside.

Bring a large pot of salted water to a boil over high heat.

Heat 6 tablespoons of the olive oil in a large skillet over medium heat. Add the garlic and pepper flakes and sauté for about 5 minutes, or until the garlic colors slightly. Add the cherry tomatoes and season generously with salt. Cook briefly until they just begin to lose their shape.

Add the arugula and toss with tongs. It will barely fit in the skillet at first but will quickly begin to wilt. Cook, tossing with tongs, until the leaves are wilted but not completely collapsed, then reduce the heat to low to keep the sauce warm. Taste and adjust seasonings.

Add the pasta to the boiling water and cook until al dente. Drain and return to the pot. Add the remaining 1 tablespoon olive oil and toss to coat. Add the sauce and toss again. Transfer to warm plates. Top each portion with breadcrumbs.

SERVES 4 TO 6

Orecchiette with Fava Beans and Frisee

Fava beans, which have a short season in the spring, are the caviar of the vegetable world. They have to be taken from their pods, then the thick skin on each lima-shaped bean must be removed. It's a time-consuming task, so it's best to showcase them in a simple fashion, as in this pasta from Janet Fletcher. The beans are combined with frisee and prosciutto, plus a little olive oil to carry the flavor. Choose pods with beans that are fully developed but not too large. To speed preparation, recruit a helper for shelling and peeling the beans.

3 pounds fava beans

6 tablespoons olive oil

2 large shallots, minced

2 ounces prosciutto, minced

Salt, to taste

Pinch of hot red pepper flakes

⅓ pound young frisee, coarsely chopped

2 tablespoons chopped Italian parsley

1 pound orecchiette (ear-shaped pasta)

∞ Remove the fava beans from their fuzzy pods. Bring a medium-size pot of water to a boil over high heat. Add the favas and blanch for 1 to 2 minutes, or until they lose their raw taste (remove one with a slotted spoon and pinch it open to test). Drain the beans and transfer to a bowl of ice water. When cool, drain again. Peel the beans by pinching open the end opposite the one that connected the bean to the pod. The peeled bean will slip out easily. Set aside.

Heat 4 tablespoons of the olive oil in a large skillet over medium heat. Add the shallots and sauté for about 2 minutes, or until softened. Add the prosciutto and fava beans; season generously with salt and add a pinch of pepper flakes. Toss to coat with seasonings. Add the frisee and toss, then cover the skillet and cook for 3 to 5 minutes, or until the frisee is just tender. Stir in the parsley. Taste and adjust the seasonings. Keep the sauce warm.

Bring a large pot of salted water to a boil over high heat. Add the pasta and cook for about 11 minutes, or until al dente. Drain and return it to the

BEST WAY:
Precooking Pasta

We wanted to see if the harried cook could precook pasta on the weekend and reheat it during the week when hunger is at a maximum and time is at a minimum.

While boiling pasta just before serving is the optimum, we found a way to make precooked pasta taste good.

Undercook the pasta slightly so it is firmer than al dente.

Drain the water immediately and quickly rinse the pasta with cold water to stop the cooking process.

Toss the pasta with a little olive oil, and store in an airtight, roomy plastic bag or other container. The pasta will keep up to six days in the refrigerator.

When ready to serve, warm the sauce and add the pasta. You can also dip pasta in boiling water, although it takes more time than rewarming with the sauce.

pot. Add the remaining 2 tablespoons olive oil and toss, then add the sauce and toss again. Serve immediately on warm plates.

SERVES 4 TO 6

Orecchiette with Broccoli Rabe and Turnips

Broccoli rabe, a slightly bitter Italian vegetable, has become the rage these days, and this once hard-to-find vegetable now is available in many supermarkets. It pairs superbly with ear-shaped pasta and turnips in this recipe by Janet Fletcher.

¾ pound turnips

1½ to 1¾ pounds broccoli rabe

6 tablespoons extra virgin olive oil

Salt, to taste

1 pound orecchiette (ear-shaped pasta)

4 garlic cloves, minced

¼ teaspoon hot red pepper flakes

☙ Peel the turnips and cut them into ¾-inch pieces; set aside. Trim the broccoli rabe, removing any stems, thick or thin, that feel tough. Cut a slit in any remaining stems that are larger than a pencil; set aside.

Bring a large pot of salted water to a boil over high heat.

Meanwhile, heat 1 tablespoon of the olive oil in a skillet over medium-high heat. Add the turnips, season with salt, and sauté for 4 to 5 minutes, or until they are nicely browned in spots. If they are still underdone, cover, reduce the heat to low and steam them until they are just tender. Do not overcook. Leave the turnips in the skillet and remove from the heat.

When the water boils, add the broccoli rabe and cook for about 3 minutes, or until the stems are just tender. Use tongs to transfer the broccoli to a sieve to drain. Add another cup of water to the pot and return it to a boil. Add the pasta and cook for about 11 minutes, or until al dente.

While the pasta is cooking, add the garlic and pepper flakes to the turnips and sauté them briefly over medium heat to release the garlic fragrance.

Chop the broccoli rabe coarsely and add it to the skillet along with the remaining 5 tablespoons olive oil. Season with salt and stir to coat with seasonings. Cook over medium heat until the mixture is hot throughout.

Drain the pasta and return it to the pot. Add the broccoli mixture and toss well. Serve in warm bowls.

SERVES 4

Sicilian Tomato Pesto with Linguine

Italians like their pasta simply sauced, and this straightforward pesto from Joanne Weir illustrates why you don't need a lot of extra ingredients to make a delicious pasta.

¼ cup pine nuts

4 cups basil leaves

3 garlic cloves, minced

⅓ cup extra virgin olive oil

1 cup freshly grated Parmigiano-Reggiano cheese

⅛ teaspoon crushed hot red pepper flakes

2 large vine-ripened tomatoes, peeled, seeded, chopped and drained

Coarse salt and freshly ground pepper, to taste

1¼ pounds linguine

Heat a skillet over medium-high heat. Add the pine nuts and cook, stirring constantly, for 3 to 4 minutes, or until they turn golden. Remove them from the pan immediately.

Place the basil leaves, garlic, pine nuts and olive oil in a blender or food processor and blend at high speed until smooth. Stop and scrape down the sides. Add half of the cheese and the red pepper flakes and pulse a few times to make a thick paste. Transfer to a bowl and fold in the tomatoes. Season with salt and pepper.

Bring a large pot of salted water to a boil over high heat. Add the pasta and cook for 7 to 9 minutes, or until al dente. Drain, toss with the pesto and serve immediately, sprinkled with the remaining cheese.

SERVES 8

Penne with Butternut Squash, Turkey, Currants and Spinach

Here's a great way to use up leftover turkey or chicken. In this recipe by Food Department intern Sean Forsha, the squash is roasted before being blended with the other ingredients. The combination of spinach and currants gives the dish a special appeal. And instead of cheese, sprinkle on toasted pecans before serving.

Butternut Squash

1½ pounds butternut squash, peeled and cut into medium dice

1 tablespoon olive oil

1 tablespoon minced garlic

Salt and freshly ground pepper, to taste

Pasta

1 pound penne or rigatoni

1 tablespoon olive oil

1 shallot, thinly sliced

½ cup dry white wine

1½ cups turkey stock (made from the carcass), or low-sodium chicken broth

1 teaspoon finely chopped Italian parsley

1 teaspoon finely chopped fresh sage

⅓ cup currants, plumped in warm water, drained

1 tablespoon butter

6 cups stemmed and cleaned spinach leaves

2 cups shredded roasted turkey, or chicken, white meat preferred

Salt and freshly ground pepper, to taste

¼ cup toasted and roughly chopped pecans

To make the squash: Preheat the oven to 400 degrees.

Combine the butternut squash, olive oil, garlic, salt and pepper in a large bowl; toss to combine. Transfer to a baking pan and bake for 30 minutes, or until the squash is tender but not mushy.

To make the pasta: While the squash is roasting, bring a large pot of salted water to a boil over high heat. Add the pasta and cook for about 7 minutes, or until al dente. Drain, return it to the pot, cover and set aside.

Heat the olive oil in a large pan over medium heat. Add the shallot and cook for about 3 minutes, or until softened. Add the wine and cook until reduced by half. Add the stock, parsley, sage and drained currants and cook for 2 minutes. Swirl in the butter, then add the spinach, turkey and squash. Season with salt and pepper.

Toss the sauce with the pasta and top with the toasted pecans.

SERVES 4

Whole-Wheat Spaghetti with Chard

Robust whole-wheat pasta is a perfect match for chard with red pepper flakes and anchovies in this recipe by Janet Fletcher.

2 bunches (12 ounces each) green Swiss chard

⅓ cup plus 2 tablespoons olive oil

4 garlic cloves, minced

3 to 4 anchovy fillets, minced

¼ teaspoon hot red pepper flakes

Salt, to taste

1 pound whole-wheat spaghetti

Separate the chard leaves from the ribs and wash them separately in a sink filled with cold water. Lift out of the water and drain well. Put the leaves in a large pot with just the water clinging to them. Cover and cook over medium heat, stirring occasionally, for about 5 minutes, or until the leaves are wilted and tender. Drain and cool, then squeeze gently to remove excess moisture but do not squeeze dry. Chop the leaves medium-fine.

Cut the chard ribs into ½-inch dice; set aside.

Heat ⅓ cup of the olive oil in a large skillet over medium heat. Add the garlic and sauté for 1 minute to release its fragrance. Add the anchovies and pepper flakes and sauté, stirring, until well blended. Add the chopped chard, season well with salt and stir to coat with seasonings. Keep warm.

Bring a large pot of salted water to a boil over high heat. Add the chard ribs and pasta. Cook until the pasta is al dente. Remove about ½ cup of the

Mincing Garlic

To keep the garlic from clinging to the knife blade while chopping, sprinkle a little salt over the roughly chopped cloves and continue to mince. The salt granules will also capture the juice from the garlic, intensifying its flavor.

cooking water, then drain the pasta and chard ribs and return them to the pot. Add the remaining 2 tablespoons oil and toss to coat. Add the chard mixture and toss again, adding a little cooking water if needed to moisten the pasta. Serve immediately on warm plates.

SERVES 4 TO 6

Perciatelli with Anchovies and Breadcrumbs

Many people shy away from anchovies, but this simple pasta dish by Janet Fletcher celebrates this much-maligned ingredient. The flavor of the fish is mellowed by the pasta and breadcrumbs. This makes an easy starter, main course or side dish for grilled fish or fowl. Perciatelli, also called bucatini, look like hollow strands of thick spaghetti.

¼ cup plus 2 teaspoons extra virgin olive oil

⅓ cup fine breadcrumbs (see Note)

Salt, to taste

1 pound perciatelli, or spaghetti

3 garlic cloves, minced

4 anchovy fillets, minced

2 tablespoons minced Italian parsley

Freshly ground pepper, to taste

Heat 2 teaspoons of the olive oil in a skillet over medium heat. Add the breadcrumbs, season with salt and sauté, stirring constantly, until golden brown. Transfer to a bowl and let cool.

Bring a large pot of salted water to a boil over high heat. Add the pasta and cook until al dente.

While the pasta cooks, heat the remaining ¼ cup olive oil in a large skillet over medium-low heat. Add the garlic and sauté for 1 minute to release its fragrance. Add the anchovies and sauté, mashing them with a wooden spoon, until they dissolve in the oil. Add the parsley, season with salt and pepper and remove from heat.

When the pasta is ready, transfer it directly from the pot to the skillet with long tongs. The pasta should be dripping wet. Toss to coat with seasonings. Add ¼ cup of the breadcrumbs and toss again. Serve in warm bowls, topping each portion with a few of the remaining breadcrumbs.

SERVES 4

NOTE: To make fine breadcrumbs, preheat the oven to 325 degrees. Make coarse crumbs from day-old crustless bread in a food processor. Spread crumbs on a baking sheet and bake for about 15 minutes, or until dry. Let cool, then process again until fine.

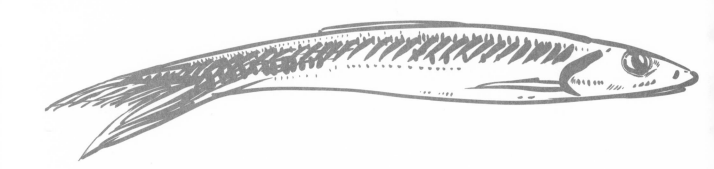

Jalapeño Macaroni

Jacqueline McMahan gives a Latin twist to the all-American macaroni and cheese. Here she seasons it with both Tabasco and canned jalapeños, then smooths it out with butter, milk, eggs and both sharp cheddar and queso fresco, a soft Mexican cheese.

8 ounces elbow macaroni

1 tablespoon butter

2 garlic cloves, minced

1 teaspoon salt

1 teaspoon Tabasco

2 cups grated sharp cheddar cheese

1 tablespoon olive oil

½ cup finely chopped onion

1 cup chopped tomatoes (canned OK)

2 canned jalapeño chiles, minced

1½ cups milk

2 eggs

¼ cup crumbled queso fresco

Preheat the oven to 350 degrees. Butter a deep, 1½-quart baking dish.

Bring 2 quarts salted water to a boil in a large pot over high heat. Add the pasta and cook for 8 to 10 minutes. Drain. Transfer to a bowl and add the butter, garlic, salt and Tabasco; toss to combine. Stir in the grated cheddar cheese.

Heat the olive oil in a sauté pan over medium heat. Add the onion and sauté for about 10 minutes, or until softened. Add the tomatoes and jalapeños. Simmer for 5 minutes, then add to the pasta and stir to combine. Spoon into the prepared baking dish.

Combine the milk and eggs in a blender, process until smooth, then pour over the pasta. Bake for 25 minutes.

Remove from the oven and let stand for 10 minutes to absorb excess liquid. Sprinkle with the queso fresco.

SERVES 6 TO 8

Judy Rodgers' Ricotta Gnocchi

At Zuni Café in San Francisco, chef Judy Rodgers sauces these feather-light gnocchi with melted butter and sage leaves, or with braised fava beans, peas or wilted spinach. They're as light and delicious as any we've found.

1 pound fresh ricotta, drained (see Note)

7 tablespoons freshly grated Parmigiano-Reggiano cheese

1 tablespoon butter, melted

About 1 tablespoon all-purpose flour, plus flour for coating gnocchi

Salt, to taste

2 eggs

◎◎ Using a spatula, press the ricotta through a sieve to make it smooth. Stir in the Parmigiano-Reggiano, butter and 1 tablespoon flour. Season with salt. Stir in the eggs. You can make the gnocchi right away, but refrigerating the dough for at least 1 hour will make it easier to handle.

Bring 2 large pots of salted water to a gentle simmer.

Using 2 soupspoons, shape about 1 tablespoon of the dough into an oval dumpling. Drop into a bowl of flour, turn to coat, then lift out and gently shake off excess flour. Transfer to a baking sheet.

Test the consistency of the dough by adding the first dumpling to the simmering water, adjusting the heat so the water stays below a boil. Cook for 6 minutes, then remove the dumpling with a slotted spoon. If the dumpling holds together in the water, the dough is firm enough; if not, add a little more flour.

When all the gnocchi are formed, divide them between the 2 pots of simmering water, adjusting the heat so the water stays just below a boil. Cook for 6 minutes, then transfer with a slotted spoon to warm bowls, draining well.

Add sauce (see headnote) and serve immediately.

YIELDS ABOUT 36 GNOCCHI; SERVES 6 AS A FIRST COURSE

NOTE: To drain ricotta, line a sieve or colander with dampened and wrung-out cheesecloth. Place the colander in a bowl, then scoop the ricotta into the colander. Bring the ends of the cheesecloth up over the ricotta. Place a plate on top and weight with a heavy can. Refrigerate for 8 to 24 hours.

Light-as-a-Cloud Gnocchi with Gorgonzola Cream

There are all kinds of gnocchi made with cream puff (or pâté à choux) dough. But this version is an all-time favorite of Joanne Weir. It's a great make-ahead dish—just simmer the gnocchi and then refrigerate until you're ready to use them. Then, all you have to do is make the simple cream sauce, toss with the gnocchi and bake.

1⅔ cups milk

¾ cup unsalted butter

¾ teaspoon coarse or kosher salt, plus more, to taste

1⅓ cups all-purpose flour

6 eggs

2 cups whipping cream

6 ounces Gorgonzola, crumbled

Freshly ground pepper, to taste

¼ cup grated Parmigiano-Reggiano cheese

☙ Combine the milk, butter and ¾ teaspoon salt in a saucepan over medium-high heat and bring to a boil. Immediately remove the pan from the heat and add the flour all at once. Mix vigorously with a wooden spoon until it forms a ball.

Place the dough in a mixing bowl. Add the eggs, 1 at a time, beating well with a wooden spoon after each addition. The mixture should be very thick and smooth.

Bring a large pot of salted water to a boil over high heat. Reduce the heat to a simmer. Fit a large pastry bag with a ¾- to 1-inch plain round tip. Fill the pastry bag with the dough.

Holding the pastry bag in one hand, start squeezing out the dough over the simmering water. Using a knife, cut off 1-inch pieces of dough into the simmering water. Do not crowd the pot. Slowly simmer the gnocchi for 10 minutes, or until they begin to puff and are slightly firm. Remove the gnocchi from the water with a slotted spoon, draining well; let cool.

Preheat the oven to 425 degrees.

Combine the cream and Gorgonzola in a large saucepan over medium-high heat; bring to a boil. Reduce heat to low and simmer for 5 to 10 minutes, or until the cream has reduced by one fourth. Season with salt and pepper. Pour the sauce over the gnocchi and mix carefully. Transfer to a 13-by-9-inch baking dish (you'll have a full single layer). Sprinkle with the Parmigiano-Reggiano.

Bake for 10 to 14 minutes, or until the gnocchi puff and turn golden brown. If the gnocchi have not turned golden, run them under the broiler.

SERVES 10

Crab Pasta

Georgeanne Brennan prepares this simple yet elegant crab dish for special dinners. If you're having a crab feast, you can make this pasta with the leftovers.

2 tablespoons butter

4 tablespoons olive oil

½ teaspoon salt

½ teaspoon freshly ground pepper

½ teaspoon hot red pepper flakes

1 garlic clove, minced

¼ cup dry white wine

1 pound fresh garlic fettuccine

½ to ¾ cup cooked crabmeat

1 tablespoon minced Italian parsley

Melt the butter in a saucepan over medium heat. Add the olive oil, salt, pepper, pepper flakes and garlic. Cook, stirring, for 4 to 5 minutes, or until the garlic is translucent. Add the wine and cook for 3 to 4 minutes longer. Keep warm.

Bring a large pot of salted water to a boil over high heat. Add the pasta and cook for about 5 minutes, or until tender. Drain and transfer to a serving bowl.

Spoon 2 tablespoons of the hot butter sauce over the pasta and toss to coat. Add the crabmeat and toss again, then pour on the remaining hot butter sauce. Top with the parsley.

SERVES 4 OR 5

Rice Stick Noodles with Grilled Pork and Lime Vinaigrette

This exotic and delicious dish by Tara Duggan can be on the table in 20 minutes. If you don't want to heat up a grill, use a grill pan or quickly stir-fry the pork in a hot wok or a large nonstick skillet.

⅓ cup lime juice (about 3 limes)

¼ cup plus 1 tablespoon rice vinegar

2 tablespoons Asian fish sauce

4 teaspoons sugar

1 teaspoon salt

¼ cup peanut or vegetable oil

1 teaspoon Asian sesame oil

1 pork tenderloin, about 1 pound, cut into thin rounds

Salt and freshly ground pepper, to taste

12 ounces rice stick noodles

1 cucumber, cut into half-moons

6 green onions (both white and green parts), trimmed and cut thinly on the bias

½ cup roasted and lightly salted peanuts, roughly chopped

Prepare a fire in a grill, letting the coals burn down to the gray-ash stage. Bring a large pot of water to a boil over high heat.

Mix together the lime juice, ¼ cup of the vinegar and the fish sauce in a bowl. Add the sugar and salt; stir until dissolved. Whisk in the peanut and sesame oils. Set aside.

Season the pork pieces generously with salt and pepper. Grill the pork for 1 to 2 minutes per side, or until just cooked through. Set aside.

Add the noodles to the boiling water and cook according to package directions. Drain and rinse briefly to cool, then drain well, shaking the colander vigorously.

Toss the sliced cucumber with the remaining 1 tablespoon rice vinegar. Combine the cucumber, pork, noodles and most of the green onions and some of the chopped peanuts in a large bowl; toss to combine. Add the vinaigrette and toss again. Sprinkle with the remaining green onions and peanuts.

SERVES 4

Easy Pad Thai

When Mai Pham is in a hurry, more often than not she'll turn to this recipe. Not only is it simple, but it also uses easy-to-find ingredients. The secret ingredient: ketchup. You have to try it to believe how delicious it is. For extra flavor, try sprinkling fresh herbs on top. You may substitute any meats or vegetables for the shrimp topping.

2½ tablespoons vegetable oil

¼ cup sliced yellow onion

2 teaspoons minced garlic

¼ cup ketchup

1½ tablespoons Asian fish sauce

1 tablespoon sugar

½ teaspoon hot red pepper flakes, or to taste

½ pound dried rice stick noodles (⅛ inch thick), boiled for about 90 seconds, rinsed and drained

¼ to ½ cup chicken broth

1 egg

⅓ pound cooked small shrimp

⅓ cup chopped roasted peanuts

3 cups bean sprouts

2 green onions (both white and green parts), cut into 3-inch lengths

4 lime wedges

∞ Heat the oil in a wok or large pan over medium heat. Add the onion and garlic and stir for about 20 seconds, or until fragrant. Add the ketchup, fish sauce, sugar and pepper flakes; cook over low heat for about 2 minutes, or until slightly reduced.

Stir in the noodles and cook for 1 minute. Sprinkle with chicken broth, 2 tablespoons at a time and only as needed. Cook for 2 to 3 minutes, or until the noodles are done but still a little firm.

When the pan becomes dry, push the noodles to the edges and crack the egg into the center. (If necessary, add a little oil.) Scramble the egg and cook until set. Fold into the noodles.

Add the cooked shrimp. Using chopsticks, toss to blend ingredients into the noodles. Sprinkle half of the peanuts, 2 cups of the bean sprouts and the green onions on the noodles and toss gently.

Serve immediately, finished with the remaining bean sprouts, peanuts and the lime wedges.

SERVES 4

Emerald Fire Noodles

Cecilia Chiang of San Francisco's Betelnut loves her noodles simple and delicious, inspiring this creation by former chef Barney Brown. The herbs and spices give the soft, silken noodles a delightful lift. Spinach noodles are available in Asian and other specialty markets.

2 tablespoons vegetable oil

1 teaspoon grated fresh ginger

2 garlic cloves, finely chopped

1 teaspoon red curry paste, or to taste

1 tablespoon Asian fish sauce

2 teaspoons oyster sauce

¼ cup unsweetened coconut milk

1 pound thin spinach noodles, freshly cooked and drained

1 cup coarsely chopped mixed fresh herbs, such as Thai basil, mint, cilantro and/or
    Chinese garlic chives

½ cup bean sprouts

½ tablespoon chopped serrano or jalapeño chile, or to taste

Heat the oil in a wok or large sauté pan over medium heat. Add the ginger, garlic and red curry paste and stir for about 3 minutes, or until aromatic.

Add the fish sauce, oyster sauce and coconut milk; simmer for 3 minutes.

Increase heat to high and add the noodles, herbs, bean sprouts and chile. Toss until the noodles are heated through and well coated with the sauce.

SERVES 4

O Chame's Soba with Salmon and Bean Sprouts

This Japanese noodle soup from David Vardy of O Chame in Berkeley is easy to make once you assemble the ingredients. Both the kelp, which gives the broth a silky texture, and the shaved bonito flakes are available in Japanese markets. The method for boiling the noodles calls for adding cold water during the cooking, which is thought to help them cook more evenly without becoming soggy.

1 piece thick kombu (dried kelp), about 2 by 4 inches

8 cups water

2 ounces dried shaved bonito, or a mixture of bonito and mackerel (see Note)

½ cup mirin (sweet sake)

¼ cup Japanese soy sauce

1 tablespoon kosher or sea salt, or more, to taste

Japanese seven-spice mixture (shichimi) (optional)

1⅓ cups bean sprouts

4 salmon fillets, ¾ pound total

400 grams (14 ounces) dried soba (Japanese buckwheat noodles)

¼ cup chopped green onion (both white and green parts)

Combine the kombu and water in a saucepan over medium heat. Slowly bring to a simmer. Just before it simmers, remove the kombu. Don't allow it to boil. Discard the kombu. Add the shaved bonito, bring the water to a boil and skim the foam that collects on the surface. Remove from heat and let stand 1 minute, then strain through a cheesecloth-lined sieve. Press on the bonito flakes with a wooden spoon to release the moisture, then discard them.

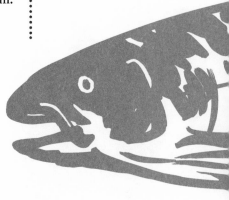

Return the broth to a clean saucepan and add the mirin, soy sauce and 1 tablespoon salt. Bring to a gentle simmer over medium heat; adjust heat to simmer very gently for about 2 minutes. Taste and add more salt if needed. The broth needs to be salty or it will taste bland when combined with the noodles. Keep warm.

Bring a medium pot of water to a boil over high heat. Add a few dashes of seven-spice mixture, if desired, then add the bean sprouts and blanch for 30 seconds. Drain.

Preheat the broiler. Bring a large pot of water to a boil over high heat. Season the salmon with salt, then broil until done to your liking.

While the salmon cooks, add the soba to the boiling water. When the water returns to a boil, add 1 cup of cold water. Cook until the noodles are just tender, adding 1 cup of cold water whenever the water returns to a boil. Drain the noodles and divide them among deep bowls.

Top the noodles with broth, then with salmon, bean sprouts and the green onions.

SERVES 4

NOTE: Shaved bonito can be fine or coarse. Use coarse bonito in this recipe so you can strain it out easily.

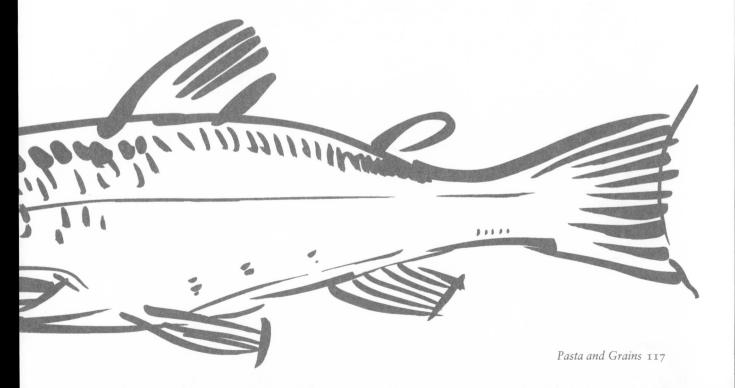

Kasma Loha-unchit's Garlic Noodles (Bamee Haeng)

Kasma Loha-unchit, an Oakland cooking teacher and cookbook author, often takes these cool noodles to potlucks. They may be topped with pork, roast duck, chicken or sautéed shrimp.

½ cup peanut oil

1 large head of garlic, cloves separated, peeled and chopped

1 pound fresh thin Chinese-style egg noodles

4 cups bean sprouts

8 green onions (white and most of the green part), thinly sliced

¼ cup chopped and firmly packed preserved Tianjin vegetable (see Note)

2 to 3 tablespoons Asian fish sauce, or to taste

2 to 3 teaspoons sugar (optional)

Hot red pepper flakes, to taste

12 to 15 leaves of romaine or leaf lettuce, torn into bite-size pieces

Leaves from 1 small bunch cilantro, plus a few sprigs for garnish

½ cup coarsely chopped dry-roasted unsalted peanuts

1 pound Chinese-style barbecued pork, roast duck, chicken, sautéed shrimp, cooked crabmeat, tofu or other topping

Condiments

Hot red pepper flakes

Pickled hot peppers

Crushed chile sauce

Chopped peanuts

Pickled garlic

Asian fish sauce

Sugar

๑๑ Heat the oil in a wok or skillet over medium-low heat. Add the garlic and cook, stirring frequently, for about 10 minutes, or until golden brown. Set aside.

Bring a large pot of water to a boil over high heat. Add the noodles and cook for 3 to 5 minutes, or until done to your liking. Drain well. Transfer them to a large bowl and add the garlic and oil, the bean sprouts, green onions, preserved vegetable, fish sauce, sugar, if desired, and pepper flakes. Toss well to wilt the bean sprouts and green onions. Taste and adjust seasonings. Add the lettuce and cilantro leaves, reserving sprigs for garnish. Toss well.

Transfer to a serving platter. Sprinkle with the chopped peanuts and top with the barbecued pork or other topping. Garnish with the reserved cilantro sprigs.

Serve warm or at room temperature with small dishes of condiments for each diner to add to taste.

SERVES 6

NOTE: Look for preserved Tianjin vegetable (salted cabbage) in a small crock in Asian markets.

Bruce Cost's Beijing Noodles with Meat Sauce

These Chinese noodles by Asian cooking expert Bruce Cost feature a sauce of ground pork shoulder. Other elements that give the sauce character include rice vinegar, chile and sesame oils, bean sauce and generous doses of fresh ginger and garlic.

¼ cup Chinese rice vinegar

1 tablespoon Asian chile oil

2 tablespoons peanut oil

1 tablespoon minced fresh ginger

1 tablespoon minced garlic

1 pound ground pork shoulder

¼ cup Chinese whole bean sauce

2 teaspoons sugar

1 tablespoon Chinese or Japanese sesame oil

½ cup thinly sliced green onions (white and most of the green part)

1 pound fresh Chinese-style egg noodles

Whisk together the rice vinegar and chile oil in a small bowl. Set aside. Bring a large pot of water to a boil over high heat.

Heat the peanut oil in a large skillet over medium-high heat. Add the ginger and sauté for about 15 seconds, then add the garlic and sauté briefly to release its fragrance.

Add the pork and cook, stirring, until the meat has changed color, but do not let it brown. Add the bean sauce and sugar. Cook, stirring, until the meat is evenly seasoned. Stir in the sesame oil and green onions. Turn off the heat.

Add the noodles to the boiling water and cook for 3 to 5 minutes, or until tender. Drain and toss with the meat sauce. Serve on warm plates. Pass the spicy rice vinegar at the table to be added to taste.

SERVES 4

Lamb Ravioli with Yogurt, Garlic and Mint

Joanne Weir gives a Mediterranean slant to ravioli stuffed with seasoned lamb and bathed in a cooling yogurt sauce. Serve this dish as a starter or a main course.

4 cups plain yogurt

1¾ cups all-purpose flour

½ cup whole-wheat flour

½ teaspoon salt, plus more, to taste

1 egg

1 egg yolk

½ cup water

1 cup chicken broth

4 garlic cloves, minced

2 tablespoons extra virgin olive oil

Freshly ground pepper, to taste

½ pound ground lean lamb

½ small onion, grated

3 tablespoons minced Italian parsley

Rice flour as needed

¼ cup coarsely chopped mint for garnish

Home cooks can use white
truffle oil to add a whiff
of luxury to simple dishes.
But don't overdo it—a few
drops per portion usually
is enough.

With hot foods, add the
oil at the end of cooking to
conserve its power.

Try white truffle oil
drizzled over:
◎◎ Fettuccine with
mushrooms, or any other
pasta where you want an
earthy nuance of flavor
◎◎ Sliced prosciutto or
salami
◎◎ Teleme or fontina
cheese
◎◎ Celery root purée
◎◎ Mashed potatoes
◎◎ Winter squash soup
◎◎ Baked halibut or
sea bass
◎◎ Scrambled eggs or
omelets

To store the oil: Truffle
oil gradually loses its
intensity and, like any
oil, eventually goes rancid.
Either refrigerate it after
opening to prolong its life,
or keep it in a cool, dark
place. In any case, use it
within 3 to 6 months after
opening for maximum
flavor.

◎◎ Place the yogurt in a cheesecloth-lined strainer and let drain for 1 hour.

While the yogurt is draining, combine the all-purpose and whole-wheat flours and ½ teaspoon salt on a work surface. Make a well in the center. Mix together the whole egg, egg yolk and water in a bowl; pour into the well. Using a fork, gradually bring the flour into the well to mix together. Using a pastry scraper and your hands, gather the mixture into a ball and knead for 2 to 3 minutes. It will be a rough dough. Wrap in plastic wrap and let rest at room temperature for 30 minutes.

Pour the chicken broth into a saucepan and reduce over high heat to ½ cup. Combine half of the broth, the drained yogurt, garlic and olive oil in a bowl. Mix with a wooden spoon until light and creamy. Season with salt and pepper. Set the sauce aside at room temperature.

Combine the lamb, onion and parsley in a bowl; season with salt and pepper. Knead together for 2 minutes; set the filling aside.

Divide the dough into 4 equal pieces. Cover with an inverted bowl so the dough doesn't dry out.

Lightly dust a work surface and rolling pin with rice flour. Place 1 piece of dough on the surface and roll out until you can almost see the outline of your hand through it.

Alternatively, use a pasta machine, rolling the dough to about 1/16 inch thick.

Cut the dough into 2½-inch squares. Place a scant ½ teaspoon of the filling in the center of each square. Lightly mist the squares using a spray bottle filled with water. Fold each square in half to form a triangle. Press together to seal edges. Place the ravioli on a floured baking sheet in a single layer. Repeat with the remaining dough.

Bring a large pot of salted water to a boil over high heat. Drop the ravioli into the water and simmer, stirring occasionally, for 3 to 5 minutes, or until the pasta is cooked. Carefully remove ravioli with a large slotted spoon and toss with the remaining reduced chicken broth.

To serve, toss the ravioli with the yogurt sauce. Transfer to a platter and garnish with the mint.

SERVES 8

Pasta with Saffron-Scented Cream, Peas and Prosciutto

This easy pasta is noteworthy for its rustic triad of flavors: Saffron gives the creamy sauce a bright yellow herbal hue, peas add a sweet freshness and prosciutto contributes a salty, meaty accent. Marlena Spieler likes to use fettuccine or other flat, tender pasta with this sauce. Other options include farfalle—bow tie–shaped pasta—or tiny rice-shaped orzo.

   4 to 6 pinches of saffron threads

   3 shallots, chopped

   4 garlic cloves, chopped

   3 tablespoons butter

   1½ cups whipping cream

   8 ounces tiny peas (frozen, or fresh and blanched)

   1 pound fresh fettuccine

   6 tablespoons grated Asiago, pecorino or Parmigiano-Reggiano cheese,
      plus more for garnish

   3 ounces prosciutto, cut into julienne strips

◉◉ Lightly toast the saffron in a dry heavy pan over medium-low heat until it is just fragrant. Remove from the heat and let it cool for 1 to 2 minutes. Remove the saffron to a plate.

Add the shallots, garlic and butter to the pan. Cook over medium heat for about 5 minutes, or until they are softened, then pour in the cream and cook for about 5 minutes. Add the toasted saffron and peas to the cream sauce. Set the sauce aside in a warm spot.

Bring a large pot of salted water to a boil over high heat. Add the pasta and cook for 5 to 7 minutes, or until al dente, then drain.

Toss the pasta with the sauce, cheese and half of the prosciutto.

Serve on heated plates, topped with the remaining prosciutto and grated cheese as desired.

SERVES 4 TO 6

Duck Bolognese

OK, let's admit it up front: Donna Scala's Duck Bolognese takes a long time to make and is relatively expensive. Scala prepares it at her Bistro Don Giovanni in Napa, where she has lots of help. Frankly, we were skeptical that it would be worth the effort when we tested it in The Chronicle's *kitchen. At first bite, we thought, "Humm, this pasta is pretty good." With the second bite, we crowed, "It's delicious!" By the third bite, we couldn't stop eating it.*

1 small yellow onion

2 small leeks (white and light green parts only), trimmed and well rinsed

3 celery stalks

2 tablespoons olive oil

1½ tablespoons chopped garlic

2 bay leaves

1½ pounds ground duck meat (see Note)

1 pound ground pork

¼ cup brandy

8 cups veal or beef broth, or unsalted chicken broth

1½ tablespoons chopped fresh sage

1½ tablespoons chopped fresh thyme

1¼ tablespoons ground juniper berries

1 tablespoon cracked pepper

2½ cups chopped drained tomatoes

1 cup Picholine olives, or other green olives, pitted and chopped

½ cup dry red wine

2 pounds rigatoni

¼ cup whipping cream

Salt, to taste

1½ cups grated provolone cheese

◉◉ Roughly chop the onion, leeks and celery. Working in batches, place the vegetables in a food processor and process into small dice.

Heat the olive oil in a large stockpot over medium heat. Add the diced vegetables, the garlic and bay leaves; sauté for 5 minutes. Add the ground duck and pork; sauté for about 10 minutes, or until no longer pink. Do not sear the meat. Skim off all fat in the pan.

Add the brandy, stirring to dislodge all the browned bits on the bottom of the pan. Add the broth, sage, thyme, juniper berries, pepper, tomatoes, olives and wine. (If you have the duck bones, add them to the pot—they will enrich the sauce and give it extra flavor and body.) Simmer over low heat for 2 hours, stirring occasionally and skimming off the fat.

If the sauce is not thick enough, strain into a large sauté pan and reduce rapidly over high heat. Return the reduced sauce to the stockpot, making certain you get all of the syrupy glaze out of the sauté pan.

Preheat the oven to 350 degrees.

Bring a large pot of salted water to a boil over high heat. Add the pasta and cook according to package directions. Drain. Transfer the pasta to a large ovenproof casserole.

If you have added duck bones to the sauce, remove them. Add the cream to the sauce and stir to mix well; taste and adjust seasonings with salt, if needed. Pour the sauce over the pasta, add half of the grated cheese and mix well. Sprinkle the remaining cheese over the top.

Bake until everything is hot throughout and the cheese has melted.

SERVES 8

NOTE: If you don't wish to use duck, substitute an equal amount of ground beef, pork or veal.

Italian-Style Tomato Sauce

Use this all-purpose sauce by Janet Fletcher on short or long dried pasta shapes, in lasagna or with store-bought ravioli. You can also embellish the sauce with chopped olives, capers, sautéed mushrooms, chickpeas, canned tuna or homemade meatballs.

3 tablespoons olive oil

½ red onion, minced

1 celery stalk, minced

1 small carrot, minced

2 garlic cloves, minced

1 tablespoon minced Italian parsley

1¾ pounds ripe plum tomatoes, chopped

⅛ teaspoon hot red pepper flakes

Salt, to taste

Heat the olive oil in a skillet over medium heat. Add the onion, celery, carrot, garlic and parsley; sauté for about 15 minutes, or until the vegetables are soft.

Add the tomatoes, pepper flakes and salt. Cook at a brisk simmer for 15 minutes, stirring often and adding water as needed to thin. The tomatoes will collapse and form a thick sauce. Pass the sauce through a food mill into a bowl, then return to a clean skillet. Taste and adjust seasonings.

YIELDS 2 CUPS

Tomato and Pancetta Sauce

Here's another versatile sauce by Janet Fletcher, featuring tomato and pancetta,
an Italian-style bacon. Serve over bucatini (hollow spaghetti-like strands) to
make the classic Bucatini all'Amatriciana. If you can't find bucatini (also
known as perciatelli), substitute spaghetti or linguine. The sauce also is ideal
as a base for braising chicken wings or thighs.

2 tablespoons olive oil

3 ounces pancetta, minced

½ onion, minced

1½ pounds ripe plum tomatoes, peeled, seeded and chopped

Salt and freshly ground pepper, to taste

Heat the olive oil in a large skillet over medium heat. Add the pancetta
and sauté for about 3 minutes, or until it softens and renders some of its fat.

Add the onion, reduce heat to medium-low and sauté for about 5 minutes,
or until the onion softens. Add the tomatoes and season with salt and pepper.
Increase the heat to medium and cook briskly, stirring often, for 15 to
20 minutes, or until the tomatoes collapse and form a sauce. Add water
as needed to thin the sauce. Taste and adjust seasonings.

YIELDS 1½ CUPS

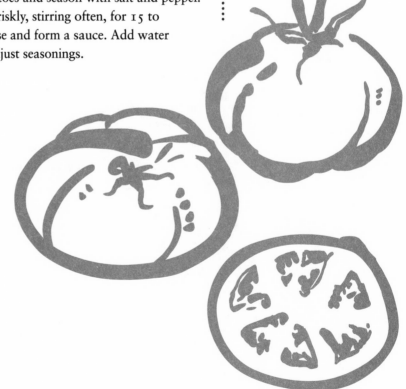

All-American Spaghetti Sauce

This is the type of sauce Americans expect to find in "authentic" Italian restaurants. It's easy and utterly delicious. Janet Fletcher's recipe calls for Italian-style sausage flavored with fennel, but if you can't find that, use another variety of sausage and add ½ teaspoon fennel seeds, lightly crushed with a mortar and pestle or in a spice grinder, to the tomato purée.

2 pounds ripe plum tomatoes

2 tablespoons olive oil

½ onion, chopped

2 garlic cloves, minced

¾ pound Italian-style fennel sausage, removed from casings

Pinch of hot red pepper flakes

2 tablespoons minced Italian parsley

1 bay leaf

Salt, to taste

Quarter the tomatoes and put in a saucepan. Cover and cook over medium heat, stirring occasionally, for 15 to 20 minutes, or until the tomatoes soften and render their juices. Pass through a food mill into a bowl.

Heat the olive oil in a large skillet over medium-low heat. Add the onion and garlic and sauté for about 5 minutes, or until the onion is soft.

Add the sausage, breaking it up with a fork, and cook gently until it changes color; do not allow it to brown.

Add the tomato purée, pepper flakes, parsley and bay leaf. Bring to a gentle simmer, partially cover and simmer for 45 minutes. Season with salt. Remove bay leaf.

YIELDS 3 CUPS

Tomato and Almond Pesto

Pesto, a classic uncooked Italian sauce consisting of basil, olive oil, garlic, Parmigiano-Reggiano cheese and pine nuts, has become the model for many creative variations. Here, Janet Fletcher uses the traditional basil but adds tomatoes and almonds to create this excellent pasta sauce. Toss room-temperature sauce with 1 pound cooked pasta, short or long. If necessary, moisten the dish with a little of the pasta-cooking water.

⅔ cup almonds

1 pound ripe plum tomatoes, peeled and seeded

1 cup lightly packed basil leaves

2 garlic cloves, thinly sliced

⅓ cup extra virgin olive oil

Salt, to taste

Hot red pepper flakes, to taste

◉◉ Preheat the oven to 325 degrees.

Bring a small pot of water to a boil over high heat. Add the almonds and boil for 1 minute, then drain. Immediately transfer the nuts to a clean dishtowel and rub to remove the skins. By hand, remove any skins that don't slip off easily.

Spread the nuts on a baking sheet, place in the oven and toast for 15 to 20 minutes, or until lightly colored and fragrant. Let cool.

Combine the tomatoes, almonds, basil and garlic in a food processor. Pulse until well chopped. With the motor running, add the olive oil through the feed tube. Stop the machine and scrape down the sides of the bowl once or twice. Purée until the sauce is nearly smooth but still has some texture.

Transfer to a bowl and stir in a generous amount of salt and a pinch of pepper flakes.

YIELDS 2 CUPS

How to Prepare
Rice for Cooking

To ensure fluffy, tender and evenly cooked grains, follow these precooking steps:

Cleaning: Like other grains and legumes, rice may include unhulled grains, stones, stems and tiny travelers. To remove them, spread rice on a white dinner plate or cookie sheet. Work a small portion of the rice at a time across to the opposite side of the plate, picking out any foreign matter.

Washing: Place the rice in a large bowl and pour in cold water to cover. Swish the grains with your fingertips to release starches and to encourage any husks to float to the surface. Pour off the milky water. Wash two or three times until the water runs clear.

Soaking: Soak the rice briefly (15 minutes to 1 hour) before cooking to encourage the grains to relax and absorb moisture. This allows the rice to expand into long, thin grains that will not break during cooking. After soaking, drain the rice and save the soaking water to use as cooking water (this preserves all of the nutrients).

Stir-Fried Black, White and Red Rice

In this recipe by Janet Fletcher, the three rices must be cooked separately because the darker colors "bleed." They may be cooked several hours ahead, however, then combined just before serving. To make a Chinese-style stir-fry, use peanut oil instead of butter and add a beaten egg, peas and chopped ham.

½ cup Bhutanese red rice

½ cup kalijira ("baby basmati") rice

½ cup Chinese black rice

2½ tablespoons unsalted butter, or olive oil

½ large onion, minced

Salt, to taste

⅓ cup toasted pine nuts

2 tablespoons minced Italian parsley

Wash all the rices separately. To wash, put the rice in a bowl and cover with cold water. Swish with your fingers, then pour off the cloudy water. Repeat until the water is no longer cloudy. Drain well in a sieve.

To cook the red rice: Bring ¾ cup lightly salted water to a boil in a small saucepan over high heat. Add the red rice, stir, cover and reduce heat to low. Cook for 20 minutes, then remove from heat and let stand for 10 minutes. Uncover and fluff the rice with a fork.

To cook the kalijira rice: Bring ½ cup plus 2 tablespoons lightly salted water to a boil in a small saucepan over high heat. Add the kalijira rice, stir, cover and reduce heat to low. Cook for 12 minutes, then remove from heat and let stand for 5 minutes. Uncover and fluff the rice with a fork.

To cook the black rice: Bring ¾ cup lightly salted water to a boil in a small saucepan over high heat. Add the black rice, stir, cover and reduce heat to low. Cook for 35 minutes, then remove from heat and let stand for 10 minutes. Uncover and fluff the rice with a fork.

Heat the butter in a large skillet over medium heat. Add the onion and sauté for about 8 minutes, or until soft and sweet. Add the red rice and kalijira rice. Stir until the grains are separate, well blended and hot. Add the black rice, season with salt and continue stirring until the three grains are well blended and hot. Stir in the pine nuts and parsley.

SERVES 6

Oven-Baked Quinoa Pilaf

Almost any grain can be used for a pilaf, but Robin Davis is partial to quinoa, used extensively in South American cuisine. The grain, somewhat like couscous, is considered a complete protein because it contains all eight essential amino acids. The oven technique reduces the risk of burning the quinoa, which can happen easily on the stovetop.

2 tablespoons butter

1 shallot, finely chopped

2 cups canned low-salt chicken broth

1 teaspoon dried thyme

1 cup quinoa, rinsed

¼ cup currants

½ cup toasted slivered almonds

Preheat the oven to 350 degrees.

Melt the butter in a heavy ovenproof saucepan over medium-high heat. Add the shallot and sauté for 5 minutes. Add the broth, thyme, quinoa and currants. Bring to a boil. Cover the pan tightly and transfer it to the oven.

Cook for about 25 minutes, or until the liquid is absorbed and the quinoa is tender. Remove from the oven and let stand, covered, for 5 minutes. Fluff the pilaf with a fork. Transfer to a serving bowl. Sprinkle with the almonds.

SERVES 6

How to Cook Rice

Here is how Indian cooking expert Laxmi Hiremath cooks rice:

General directions for all white rice (except Cal Riso): Rinse rice well before cooking to remove surface starch. Drain well. Bring water (amounts follow) to a boil. Add salt, if desired. Add rice, stir once and return to a boil. Cover and reduce heat to low. Cook for designated time (see below). Remove from heat and let rest, covered, for 5 to 10 minutes.

Cal Riso: 1 cup rice to 3 cups liquid. Cooking time: About 25 minutes. Do not rinse rice first. Cal Riso may be used in any risotto recipe.

Chinese black rice: 1 cup rice to 1¾ cups water. Cooking time: About 35 minutes.

Bhutanese red rice: 1 cup rice to 1½ cups water. Cooking time: About 20 minutes.

Kalijira ("baby basmati") rice: 1 cup rice to 1¼ cups water. Cooking time: About 12 minutes.

Texas jasmine rice: 1 cup rice to 1½ cups water. Cooking time: 18 minutes.

Arroz Rojo

Arroz rojo, or red rice, is a dish made special by an early-California rancho seasoning paste. Jacqueline McMahan suggests serving it as a side dish with grilled fish or barbecued meats. However, it's so good that diners often eat it up and ignore everything else.

1 tablespoon olive oil

1 cup long-grain white rice

½ cup chopped onion

1⅔ cups water

¼ cup seasoning paste (recipe follows)

Heat the olive oil in a heavy saucepan over medium-high heat. Add the rice and sauté until the grains are coated with oil and have turned opaque, adding the onion toward the end. Add the water and seasoning paste. Bring to a simmer, cover tightly, reduce heat to low and cook for about 18 minutes. Check after 15 minutes (you can peek without ruining the rice). If the rice is tender, turn off heat, replace lid and allow rice to steam in its own heat for 5 to 10 minutes before serving.

SERVES 6

NOTE: To create another soothing comfort-type dish, stir 2 or 3 sliced cooked sausages and 3 cups hot, spicy black beans into the rice at serving time. This becomes a quick Mexican-style jambalaya.

Seasoning Paste

2 tablespoons minced garlic

1 tablespoon pure chile powder

3 tablespoons puréed canned chipotle chiles en adobo

2 teaspoons dried oregano

½ teaspoon freshly ground pepper

½ teaspoon crushed cumin seeds

1 teaspoon kosher salt

½ cup water

@@ Put the garlic, chile powder, chipotles, oregano, pepper, cumin, salt and water in a food processor. Grind into a thick paste. You will not use all of the paste in the above recipe. Refrigerate the remainder in a covered container. It keeps well for 2 to 3 weeks. Use as a marinade for chicken, fish, pork or beef (adding lime juice and olive oil for a more liquid marinade).

YIELDS ABOUT ¾ CUP

Lemon-Asparagus Rice Pilaf

The combination of flavors in this rice dish by former Food Department editorial assistant Tilde Herrera is amazing. The lemon adds a brightness right on top, backed by the richness of the rice and the freshness of the asparagus. It's great as a vegetarian main course, or as a side dish with grilled chicken or poached salmon.

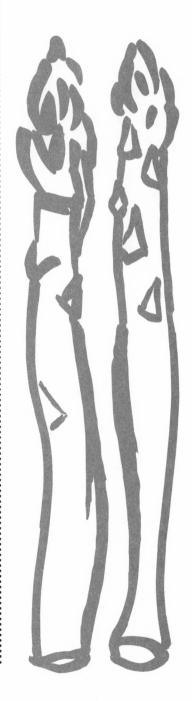

2½ cups vegetable or chicken broth

2 tablespoons olive oil

2 large shallots, minced

1½ cups basmati rice

¼ cup fresh lemon juice

½ teaspoon salt

Freshly ground pepper, to taste

1 pound thin asparagus

Finely minced zest of 1 lemon (2 to 3 teaspoons)

@@ Heat the broth in a large, wide pot over high heat.

Heat the olive oil in a Dutch oven over medium heat. Add the shallots and sauté for about 2 minutes, or until tender. Add the rice and stir until all the grains are coated with oil. Add the heated broth, the lemon juice, salt and a few grindings of pepper. Stir and bring to a boil. Reduce heat to low, cover and simmer for 10 minutes.

While the rice is cooking, snap the tough ends off the asparagus and discard. Cut the asparagus spears into 1-inch lengths, but leave the tips whole.

After the rice has cooked for 10 minutes, stir in the lemon zest and asparagus. Return to a simmer, cover and cook for about 10 minutes longer, or until the rice is tender.

Let stand, covered, for a few minutes before serving.

SERVES 4

Malabar Coconut Rice

The Malabar Coast is a historic spice trade center in what is now the state of Kerala in Southern India. This area's lush tropical landscape is dotted with swaying coconut palms, and Keralite cooks use the milk and meat of coconuts in all sorts of dishes, including rice dishes like this one by Laxmi Hiremath.

1½ cups basmati rice

1½ tablespoons mild vegetable oil

¼ cup whole cashews

½ teaspoon mustard seeds

1 to 2 fresh hot green chiles, stemmed and slit lengthwise

10 fresh kari leaves

2 cups unsweetened coconut milk

¾ cup water

¾ teaspoon salt, or to taste

2 tablespoons grated fresh or flaked unsweetened coconut

Wash the rice in several changes of cold water. Soak in water to cover for 15 minutes to 1 hour. Drain and set aside.

Heat the oil in a heavy saucepan over medium heat. Add the cashews and fry for 4 to 5 minutes, or until lightly browned. Remove with a slotted spoon and set aside. Add the mustard seeds to the pan; when the seeds begin to sizzle and splutter, add the chiles and kari leaves. Cook, stirring, for 1 minute, then add the rice. Stir and fry for about 5 minutes, or until the rice grains are glistening and coated with oil.

Mix together the coconut milk and water in a bowl; add to the rice, sprinkle in the salt and bring to a boil. Reduce heat to low; cover and simmer for about 15 minutes, or until the rice is tender and the liquid is absorbed. Remove rice from heat and let stand, covered, for 5 minutes.

Fluff the rice with a fork. Remove the chiles, if desired. They are not meant to be eaten. Transfer the rice to a heated serving dish and top with the fried cashews and coconut.

Serve hot, warm or at room temperature.

SERVES 6

Mango Rice with Macadamia Nuts

This elegant tropical pilaf by Laxmi Hiremath is seasoned with aromatic sweet spices. Serve it with grilled meats or roasts.

1 cup basmati rice

1 large ripe mango

1¾ cups water

2 tablespoons desi ghee

¼ cup macadamia nuts

Seeds from 4 green cardamom pods, ground

¼ teaspoon cinnamon

⅛ teaspoon nutmeg

½ teaspoon salt

¼ cup stemmed, pitted and quartered Bing cherries

◎ Wash the rice in several changes of cold water. Soak in water to cover for 15 minutes to 1 hour. Drain and set aside.

Peel the mango and separate the flesh from the pit in large chunks. Cut flesh into cubes. Set aside some of the prettier ones and place the remainder in a blender. Add ¾ cup of the water and process until the mango is puréed. Set aside.

Preparing Perfect Basmati Rice

Basmati is sold under many brand names, including Tilda, Pari and Dehra Dun. Look for bags that indicate the rice has been aged, which gives the grains a better flavor and texture. If the information is not on the label, ask the grocer.

Here's how to cook it:
Water: The amount of water used will vary depending upon the variety and age of the rice and the depth and weight of the pan. As a general guideline, decide if you like your rice soft or firm, then gradually adjust the amount of water you use: 1¾ cups water to 1 cup basmati rice produces just-tender rice. If you like a very firm texture, use 1½ cups water.
Pan: A heavy pan with a tight-fitting lid will distribute the heat evenly. If your rice is cooking unevenly (perhaps the top

layer is not cooked), then the lid is not fitting tightly enough. Use a kitchen towel as an inside cover; it stops the steam from condensing inside the lid and dripping back into the rice.

Cooking: Follow package directions for cooking times. Do not stir or disturb the rice as it cooks. Removing the lid will let steam escape, and the rice will cook unevenly. Let the cooked rice rest, covered, for a few minutes before serving.

Tips for fluffy rice: Stir-frying the rice in a little oil or desi ghee before adding water will make the grains fluffy and separate.

A few drops of oil, butter or desi ghee and a teaspoon of fresh lime juice added at the start of cooking also help the rice grains to remain separate and light during cooking.

Heat the desi ghee in a saucepan over medium heat. Add the nuts and fry for 4 to 5 minutes, or until golden brown. Remove with a slotted spoon and set aside.

Add the rice to the pan. Stir and fry for about 4 minutes, or until the grains are coated with desi ghee and start to glisten. Add the cardamom, cinnamon and nutmeg and cook, stirring, for 1 minute. Stir in the mango purée, the remaining 1 cup water and the salt. Bring to a boil, reduce heat to low, cover and simmer for 15 minutes.

Remove rice from heat and let stand, covered, for 5 minutes.

Uncover, lightly fluff rice with a fork and transfer to a heated serving platter. Fold in the reserved mango pieces and cherries. Sprinkle the reserved nuts over the top.

SERVES 4

Rice with French Green Lentils

This comforting combination of rice and legumes is a spin-off of a classic Indian dish, adapted to California tastes by Laxmi Hiremath. The turmeric in the dish turns it a pale ocher color. Serve it as part of an Indian meal, or as a Western-style accompaniment to roasted meats, poultry or game.

1 cup basmati rice

¼ cup French green lentils

1 teaspoon coriander seeds

½ teaspoon cumin seeds

1 tablespoon grated fresh or flaked unsweetened coconut

1½ tablespoons mild vegetable oil

½ teaspoon mustard seeds

2 large garlic cloves, thinly sliced

1-inch piece fresh ginger, peeled and minced

10 kari leaves (optional)

⅛ teaspoon turmeric

2¼ cups water

½ teaspoon salt, or to taste

Sliced cherry tomatoes for garnish

⊚⊚ Combine the rice and lentils in a bowl. Wash in several changes of cold water. Add water to cover by at least 2 inches. Let soak for 1 to 2 hours. Drain and set aside.

Toast the coriander and cumin seeds in a small skillet over medium heat for about 5 minutes, or until aromatic. Add the coconut and toast for 2 minutes. Let cool, then grind to a fine powder in a spice grinder or coffee mill reserved for spices. Set aside.

Heat the oil in a heavy saucepan over medium-high heat. Add the mustard seeds, and when they sizzle and splutter, stir in the garlic, ginger, kari leaves, if desired, and turmeric. Cook, stirring, for about 1 minute, or until the mixture is aromatic and the garlic is lightly browned. Add the rice and lentil mixture. Fry, stirring, for 4 to 5 minutes, or until the rice grains are glistening and coated with oil.

Add the water, salt and spice blend. Bring to a boil, reduce heat to low, cover and cook for 20 minutes, or until the lentils are tender and all the water is absorbed. Remove from heat and let stand, covered, for 5 minutes. Fluff lightly with a fork and transfer to a warmed serving platter. Garnish with the tomatoes.

SERVES 4

Clay-Pot Rice with Chicken and Black Mushrooms

This delicious clay pot dish is from Mai Pham. The chicken is added before the rice is completely cooked so it can fully absorb all the juices and flavor.

½ pound skinless, boneless chicken thighs, cut into bite-size pieces

1 teaspoon Chinese five-spice powder

1 tablespoon soy sauce

1 teaspoon Asian fish sauce

2 teaspoons cornstarch

1½ cups long-grain white rice, rinsed and drained

3 cups low-sodium chicken broth

½ teaspoon turmeric

2 tablespoons vegetable oil

Adding Pizzazz to White Rice

Here are some great ideas from Laxmi Hiremath for perking up white rice: **Aromatic rice:** Heat 1 tablespoon oil, butter or desi ghee in a heavy saucepan. Stir in a 1-inch piece of cinnamon stick, 4 whole cardamom pods, 1 or 2 bay leaves, and 3 or 4 whole cloves; add 1 cup uncooked rice and stir-fry for 4 to 5 minutes over medium heat. Add 1¾ cups water; bring to a boil, reduce heat, cover and cook until rice is tender and liquid has been absorbed (cooking time depends on type and age of rice). Remove spices before serving.

2 garlic cloves, minced

2 tablespoons minced fresh ginger

6 dried black mushrooms, soaked in hot water for 30 minutes, drained and halved

1 cup canned bamboo shoot slices, rinsed and drained

Salt and freshly ground pepper, to taste

1 green onion (white and most of the green part), thinly slivered

Cilantro leaves

◉ Combine the chicken, five-spice powder, soy sauce, fish sauce and cornstarch in a mixing bowl and set aside to marinate.

Put the rice in a nonstick skillet over low heat and cook, stirring, for 3 to 4 minutes, or just until it turns opaque.

Transfer the rice to a Chinese sandy clay pot or medium-size saucepan. Add 2 cups of the chicken broth and the turmeric; stir to blend well. Bring to a boil, reduce heat to very low and cover with the pot's lid.

While the rice is cooking, heat the oil in a wok or skillet over high heat. When hot, quickly stir in the garlic, ginger and black mushrooms. Stir for 30 seconds, or until fragrant, then add the chicken. Reduce heat to medium and cook for 2 minutes. Add the bamboo shoots and ½ cup of the chicken broth. Remove from heat and gently fold the chicken and vegetables into the rice. Cover and continue to cook until the rice is done. Total cooking time for the rice should be 19 to 20 minutes. If the rice appears dry, add a little broth.

Season with salt and pepper. Finish with the green onion and cilantro and serve.

SERVES 4

Yellow rice: Add a pinch of turmeric to the boiling water before adding the rice. The cooked rice takes on a beautiful yellow hue without altering the taste.
Saffron rice: Toast a few saffron threads in a small skillet over low heat. Crush saffron with the back of a spoon, and soak in 2 tablespoons hot milk or water for 15 minutes. Stir into the rice while it's cooking.
Multicolored rice: Some pilafs in Indian restaurants contain rice of different colors. This is a simple trick. Sprinkle hot cooked rice randomly with tiny drops of food coloring and mix gently. You can also toss together plain white and yellow rice.

Asparagus Risotto

This delightful version of risotto is from Weezie Mott, an Alameda cooking teacher.

2 pounds slender fresh asparagus

4 tablespoons butter

1 onion, preferably sweet, such as Vidalia or Maui, chopped

6 cups chicken broth

2 cups Cal Riso rice, or Italian Arborio, carnaroli or vialone nano

¼ cup whipping cream

⅓ cup freshly grated Parmigiano-Reggiano cheese

A few drops of truffle oil (optional)

Salt and freshly ground pepper, to taste

◉◉ Holding an asparagus spear in both hands, bend it until it breaks naturally at the point where it becomes tough. Discard the tough end. Repeat with remaining spears. Line up the trimmed spears and cut off the top 2½ inches. Set those tips aside. Coarsely chop the remainder of the spears.

Bring a pot of salted water to a boil over high heat. Add the tips and boil for 3 minutes. Drain and transfer to a bowl of ice water to cool quickly. When cold, drain again. Melt the butter in a saucepan over medium heat. Add the onion and chopped asparagus pieces and sauté for about 10 minutes, or until the onion is golden and the asparagus is soft.

Meanwhile, bring the broth to a simmer in a saucepan over medium-high heat; adjust heat to keep it barely simmering.

Add the rice to the onion mixture and stir to coat with butter. When the rice is hot, add 1 cup of the hot broth and cook until absorbed, stirring constantly. Add more broth, ½ cup at a time, stirring constantly and adding broth only when the previous addition has been absorbed. Cook for about 25 minutes, or until the rice is tender and creamy but al dente.

Remove rice from heat and stir in the cream, cheese, asparagus tips and truffle oil, if desired. Season with salt and pepper. Serve immediately.

SERVES 6

Green Garlic and Spinach Risotto

Green garlic is a harbinger of spring in Northern California. When it starts to come into the farmers' markets, Janet Fletcher likes to make this risotto.

2 tablespoons olive oil

2 to 2½ cups thinly sliced green garlic (white and pale green part only, tough outer layer removed)

4 ounces baby spinach leaves, washed and thick stems removed

2 tablespoons unsalted butter

1½ cups Arborio rice

½ cup dry white wine

About 4 cups chicken broth, hot but not simmering

¼ cup freshly grated Parmigiano-Reggiano cheese

Salt and freshly ground pepper, to taste

◉◉ Heat the olive oil in a 4-quart saucepan over medium heat. Add the garlic, stir to coat with oil, cover and reduce heat to low. Cook, stirring occasionally to prevent the garlic from sticking, for about 15 minutes, or until the garlic is softened.

Meanwhile, put the spinach and 1 tablespoon of the butter in a food processor. Process until finely chopped.

Add the rice to the saucepan and cook, stirring constantly, for about 2 minutes, or until hot throughout. Add the wine and simmer, stirring, until it evaporates. Begin adding the hot broth, ½ cup at a time, stirring constantly and adding more broth only when the previous addition has been absorbed. Cook for 20 to 22 minutes, or until the rice is al dente and has absorbed all or most of the broth.

When the rice is, in your judgment, a minute away from doneness, stir in the spinach-butter mixture. Cook, stirring, for about 1 minute, then remove from heat and stir in the remaining 1 tablespoon butter and the cheese. Taste and adjust seasonings with salt and pepper. Serve in warm bowls.

SERVES 4

How to Store Green Garlic

Because it's so moist, green garlic, which is tender, fresh and mild, is much more perishable than dried bulb garlic. Treat it like a flower: Leave the roots on, stand the shoots up in a glass of water in the refrigerator and cover with a plastic bag.

Alternatively, place the garlic and a damp paper towel in a plastic bag and store in the vegetable bin. Either way, the garlic should last at least a week.

The white and pale-green shaft is entirely edible, although some cooks like to remove an outer layer or two if it feels tough.

Anne Gingrass's Green Olive Risotto

If you love olives, this simple risotto from Anne Gingrass, the former chef/owner of Hawthorne Lane in San Francisco, is pure heaven. The olives are balanced by a touch of Parmigiano-Reggiano cheese and Italian parsley. A squeeze of lemon gives the dish a last-minute vibrancy.

4 tablespoons extra virgin olive oil

¼ cup finely diced yellow onion

1 cup Arborio rice

¼ cup white wine

3 to 3½ cups chicken broth, brought to a simmer

¼ cup finely chopped pitted green olives, such as Picholine

2 tablespoons chopped Italian parsley

1 tablespoon grated Parmigiano-Reggiano cheese

Fresh lemon juice, to taste

Salt and freshly ground pepper, to taste

◉◉ Heat 1 tablespoon of the olive oil in a saucepan over medium heat. Add the onion and sauté for about 5 minutes, or until softened. Add the rice and cook, stirring, until it is hot throughout. Add the wine and cook, stirring, until it evaporates.

Begin adding the hot broth, ½ cup at a time, stirring constantly and adding more broth only when the previous addition has been absorbed. After 10 minutes, stir in the olives. Continue cooking for a total of 20 to 25 minutes, or until the rice is creamy and al dente, neither soupy nor stiff.

When the rice is done, remove the pan from the heat and stir in the parsley, cheese and the remaining 3 tablespoons olive oil. Season with lemon juice, salt and pepper.

SERVES 4

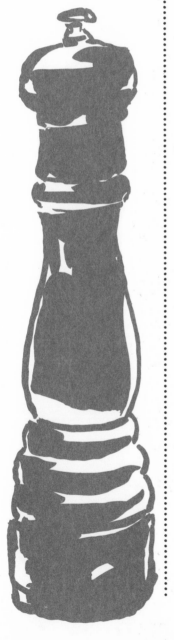

Carol Field's Creamy Pumpkin-Flavored Risotto

Carol Field, an expert on Italian cuisine, created this risotto, which doesn't require constant stirring and undivided attention. It's a simple preparation an Italian nonna *might fix for her grandchildren.*

14 ounces pumpkin, or butternut squash, seeded

2 tablespoons extra virgin olive oil

5 tablespoons unsalted butter at room temperature

1 white or yellow onion, finely chopped

¾ cup minus 1 tablespoon (5 ounces) carnaroli, vialone nano or Arborio rice

2 cups chicken broth

Salt and freshly ground pepper, to taste

2 tablespoons finely chopped Italian parsley

½ cup freshly grated Parmigiano-Reggiano or grana cheese

◉ Bring a pot of water to a boil over high heat. Cut the unpeeled pumpkin into thick slices and add to the boiling water. Cook until a knife pierces the flesh easily. Drain, peel and cut into small dice. There should be about 3 cups.

Meanwhile, warm the olive oil and 1 tablespoon of the butter in a heavy pot over medium heat. Add the onion and sauté for 7 to 10 minutes, or until it is limp and translucent. Add the rice, the diced squash and the broth to the pot. Bring to a boil over high heat, cover, reduce heat to low and cook for 15 to 18 minutes, or until the rice has absorbed the broth.

Season with salt and pepper. Stir in the parsley, the remaining 4 tablespoons butter and the cheese. Serve immediately.

SERVES 4 TO 6

Mussel Risotto

This risotto by Georgeanne Brennan is a great way to use leftover mussels and their broth.

1½ cups broth left over from cooking mussels

3 cups water

3 tablespoons butter

2 tablespoons extra virgin olive oil

½ onion, minced

1 garlic clove, minced

2 cups Arborio rice

Salt (optional)

1 teaspoon chopped fresh thyme

¼ cup freshly grated Parmigiano-Reggiano cheese

24 shelled cooked mussels

◉◉ Combine the broth and water in a saucepan over medium-high heat; bring to a simmer. Adjust heat to maintain a low simmer.

Heat 2 tablespoons of the butter and all of the olive oil in another saucepan over medium heat. When the butter foams, add the onion and garlic; sauté for 2 to 3 minutes, or until translucent. Add the rice and cook, stirring, for 1 to 2 minutes, or until the grains are coated with the butter-oil mixture. Add ½ cup of the hot broth. Cook over medium heat, stirring constantly while the rice absorbs the broth. When the liquid is nearly absorbed, add about ¼ cup more broth. Continue to cook and stir, adding the remaining broth in 2 or 3 additions, as needed.

After about 25 minutes, when the rice is almost done and nearly all of the liquid has been absorbed, taste. The grains should offer scant resistance when crunched between your teeth. Add salt, if needed, and stir in the thyme, cheese, the remaining 1 tablespoon butter and the mussels. Cook for 2 to 3 minutes longer, or just until the cheese has blended in and the risotto is deliciously creamy.

Spoon onto warmed plates and serve immediately.

SERVES 4

Winter Wild Mushroom Risotto

Eric Tucker of Millennium in San Francisco enriches this vegan risotto by adding cashew "cream," a blend of ground cashews and water. Tucker likes to use a mix of wild mushrooms, including black chanterelles if he can find them. Sometimes he adds an ounce of dried porcini to the vegetable stock for added flavor and depth. At the restaurant, Tucker serves this risotto over braised kale or mustard greens, with French green lentils alongside. To make the dish even more special, drizzle a few drops of white truffle oil over the risotto just before serving.

About 8 cups vegetable or mushroom stock, or canned broth

3 tablespoons dry sherry, or dry red wine

2 tablespoons olive oil

6 shallots, finely chopped

12 ounces mixed fresh wild mushrooms (such as chanterelle, crimini and shiitake), tough stems removed, chopped

2 teaspoons chopped fresh thyme

2 cups Arborio rice

¾ cup water

½ cup raw cashews

⅛ teaspoon nutmeg

Salt and freshly ground pepper, to taste

2 tablespoons chopped fresh chives

1 tablespoon grated lemon zest

◉◉ Bring the stock to a simmer in a heavy saucepan over medium-high heat. Remove from heat. Cover to keep warm.

Heat the sherry and olive oil in a large, heavy saucepan over medium-high heat. Add the shallots and sauté for about 5 minutes, or until tender and beginning to brown. Reduce heat to medium, add the mushrooms and thyme and sauté for 5 minutes. Add the rice and stir well.

Add enough stock just to cover. Cook, stirring, until most of the stock is absorbed.

Add enough stock to cover again. Continue cooking and stirring, adding stock as necessary, for about 20 minutes, or until the rice is tender but still firm to the bite. Remove from heat.

Combine the water and cashews in a food processor and purée until smooth. Add to the rice mixture along with the nutmeg. Cook, stirring, over low heat for 5 minutes. Season with salt and pepper.

Sprinkle with the chives and lemon zest.

SERVES 6

Michelle Anna Jordan's Soft Polenta with Walnuts

Michelle Anna Jordan, a cookbook author and Chronicle *North Bay restaurant reviewer, created this soft, creamy polenta dish. The walnuts are a simple addition but add loads of flavor.*

6 cups water

2 teaspoons kosher salt, plus more, to taste

1 cup coarse-grind polenta, such as Golden Pheasant or Guisto's

2 tablespoons butter

4 ounces dry Monterey Jack or Parmigiano-Reggiano cheese, grated

Freshly ground pepper, to taste

3 to 4 ounces Gorgonzola

Best-quality extra virgin olive oil, to taste

2 ounces walnut halves or pieces, lightly toasted

Bring 3 cups of the water to a rolling boil in a heavy pot over high heat; have the remaining 3 cups water simmering in another saucepan. Add the 2 teaspoons salt to the boiling water and stir rapidly with a whisk in the same circular direction to create a vortex. Pour the polenta into the vortex in a thin, steady stream, whisking continuously to prevent lumps. Continue to whisk after all the polenta has been added; reduce heat to low so the mixture simmers slowly.

When the polenta begins to thicken, trade the whisk for a long-handled wooden spoon. Add 1 cup of the simmering water and continue to stir until the grains of polenta are tender and the mixture pulls away from the sides of the pot. Add more simmering water as needed for the proper consistency.

The polenta should be soft and creamy but not soupy. (Most types of polenta will take 20 to 30 minutes, but a few types may take as long as 60 minutes.)

Add the butter and the Jack cheese; stir thoroughly. If the polenta seems a little stiff, add ½ cup of the simmering water and simmer 5 minutes longer.

Remove the polenta from the heat. Add several grindings of pepper. Taste and season with salt, if needed.

Ladle into warm soup bowls, top each portion with some of the Gorgonzola, drizzle with olive oil, scatter walnuts on top and serve immediately.

SERVES 3 OR 4

Quick Oven Polenta

This no-fuss method of making soft polenta was first shown to us by Gary Danko, chef/owner of Gary Danko restaurant in San Francisco. It's even easier than the stovetop method.

Heat 2 to 4 tablespoons olive oil in a large ovenproof pan over medium-high heat. Add 1 cup polenta, stirring to coat with the oil, and cook until heated through. Gradually stir in 6 cups boiling water and return to a boil. Add about 2 teaspoons salt. Cover the pan and place in a 350-degree oven for 35 to 40 minutes. The polenta should mound slightly when done. Remove from oven and whisk until well blended. The polenta may be cooked a couple of hours ahead and held in a water bath.

To make a water bath: Select a pan that will easily hold the pan of polenta. Fill the larger pan about one third of the way up with water. Bring almost to a boil and reduce heat. Place the pan containing the polenta into the pan of hot water.

SERVES 4 TO 6

Corn and Jalapeño Polenta

Jacqueline McMahan likes to serve this spicy polenta with grilled or roasted meats.

1 tablespoon butter
½ cup minced white onion
2 jalapeño chiles, seeded and finely minced
1½ cups chicken broth
⅓ cup dry white wine
½ cup polenta, or coarsely ground cornmeal
2½ cups grated fresh corn (about 5 ears)
½ teaspoon salt
1 tablespoon snipped chives
Olive oil for frying

Grease an 8-by-13-inch baking pan.

Heat the butter in a wide, deep skillet over medium-low heat. Add the onion and chiles and sauté for about 7 minutes, or until softened. Do not let them brown. Add the chicken broth and wine. Simmer for 3 to 4 minutes. Slowly stir in the polenta and cook, stirring, for 10 minutes.

Add the corn and simmer over low heat for 15 minutes, or until a spoon drawn through the polenta to the bottom of the pan leaves a track. Stir in the salt and chives.

Pour the polenta into the prepared pan. Let cool, then cover well with plastic wrap and refrigerate until chilled.

Just before serving, cut into 8 squares and carefully remove with a wide spatula (because of the corn, this polenta is fragile).

Heat a little olive oil in a nonstick skillet over medium-high heat. Add a few polenta squares (do not crowd the pan) and fry, turning once, until golden brown on both sides. Continue frying the remaining squares, adding more olive oil as needed.

SERVES 8

Saffron and Raisin Couscous with Fresh Mint

This simple combination created by Georgeanne Brennan is highlighted with the flavor of mint. It makes a wonderful bed for grilled chicken or vegetables.

2 cups water

½ teaspoon saffron threads

1 teaspoon extra virgin olive oil

½ teaspoon salt, plus more, to taste

1½ cups couscous

¼ cup raisins

3 tablespoons chopped fresh mint

Bring the water to a boil in a saucepan over high heat. Add the saffron. Remove from heat and let stand 30 minutes.

Return the pan to the heat and bring to a boil again. Add the olive oil, salt, couscous and raisins. Remove from heat, cover and let stand for 5 minutes.

Using a fork and your fingertips, fluff the couscous to separate the grains. Taste and add more salt, if needed. Stir in the mint. Cover and refrigerate for several hours, allowing the flavors to blend.

Serve chilled or at room temperature.

SERVES 8

Chapter 5

Meatless Main Courses

In the Bay Area, meatless meals are politically correct, and surveys show that the majority of residents try to go meatless at least one day a week. Chefs and home cooks have become clever in devising recipes that feature hearty fare with the same satisfying quality found in meat.

Meatless main courses are so prevalent that it's hard to separate them into a single chapter—you'll discover many more examples in Pasta and Grains and in the Vegetables chapters. Most dishes in this chapter constitute a meal in themselves: rib-sticking stews, hearty casseroles and savory gratins.

Here, you'll find Lentil and Squash Lasagna with Caramelized Onions (page 182), Black Bean and Sweet Potato Stew (page 148), Portobello-Polenta Pie (page 168), Wild Mushroom Bread Pudding (page 167) and Millet and Kale Gratin (page 161). Many of these combinations are versatile, too, and they make ideal side dishes to meats, poultry and fish.

You'll even savor a couple of marvelous pizzas (pages 176 and 179), as well as Morels in Brandy Cream on Toast (page 165) and a refined Potato and Goat Cheese Galette (page 172).

As in other chapters, many dishes carry an international pedigree: Fresh Corn Tamales (page 151), Yellow Curry with Mixed Vegetables, Tofu and Thai Basil (page 174), Malaysian Coconut Curry of Autumn Vegetables (page 175) and Vegetarian Corn Biryani (page 156).

In addition, many of these dishes make great leftovers and are even better the second time around.

Black Bean and Sweet Potato Stew

This hearty vegetarian stew was created by Robin Davis to go with a rich Syrah wine. The spicing is mild, so the flavor of the wine remains robust. However, if you'd rather serve it with beer, feel free to add more cayenne or a seeded and diced jalapeño chile. The stew is best made a day ahead.

1 pound black beans

1 poblano chile

2 tablespoons olive oil

1 large onion, diced

2 garlic cloves, minced

1½ teaspoons cumin seeds

½ teaspoon ground coriander

¼ teaspoon cayenne pepper

2 cans (14½ ounces each) diced peeled tomatoes with their juices

4 cups water

1 teaspoon dried oregano

1 bay leaf

1 sweet potato, peeled and cut into ½-inch cubes

Sea salt or kosher salt and freshly ground pepper, to taste

Steamed white rice for serving

Chopped cilantro for garnish

1 lime, cut into wedges, for garnish

👓 Pick over the beans, discarding any broken or withered ones or stones. Rinse beans, place in a large pot and add enough water to cover by 3 inches. Let soak overnight. Drain.

Roast the poblano chile over a gas burner or under the broiler until blackened on all sides. Place in a paper bag, seal and set aside for 10 minutes to steam. Remove the blackened skin, then stem and seed the chile. Cut into ½-inch dice.

Heat the olive oil in a large, heavy saucepan over medium-high heat. Add the onion and sauté for about 5 minutes, or until translucent. Add the garlic and cook, stirring, for 2 minutes. Add the cumin seeds, coriander, cayenne and diced chile and cook, stirring, for about 30 seconds, or until fragrant. Add the and let stand, covered, for 1 hour.

Rinse beans with cold water and cook according to package directions, adding salt at the end of cooking. If you intend to use the beans in salads, salting 30 minutes into the cooking produces a better appearance with far fewer split skins.

How to Cook Beans

Simmer the beans gently in their cooking liquid. Do not boil. When the liquid in the pot gets low, add hot (not cold) water.

To add a flavor punch to a pot of beans, fry a chopped onion in olive oil until it deeply caramelizes with some brown spots. Add to the beans during the last 30 to 40 minutes of cooking time. This trick gives the beans a complex, rich flavor—especially useful when you're not adding meat to the beans.

Don't add too many different ingredients when cooking a pot of beans. They get confused.

Don't add salt until the end of cooking (or during the last 30 minutes of cooking if the beans are to be used in salads).

beans, tomatoes and their juices, the water, oregano and bay leaf. Bring to a boil, reduce heat to low and simmer for 45 minutes.

Add the sweet potato and simmer for about 30 minutes, or until the beans and potato are tender. Season with salt and pepper.

Divide the rice among serving bowls. Ladle the stew over the rice and garnish with the cilantro and lime wedges.

SERVES 4 TO 6

Cianfotta Lucana (Eggplant, Tomato, Pepper and Potato Stew)

Pino Spinoso, the chef at Tiramisu restaurant in San Francisco, fondly remembers this family recipe for cianfotta. *For a simple supper, the stew was followed by cheese. However, it's a versatile dish. It makes a great accompaniment to meat or fish, or a sauce for pasta. Some cooks add capers or fresh ginger.*

2 red bell peppers

2 yellow bell peppers

3 tomatoes

½ cup extra virgin olive oil

1 red onion, chopped

1 pound russet potatoes, peeled and cut into walnut-size cubes

Salt and freshly ground pepper, to taste

3 cups warm water

3 Japanese eggplants, cut into ¾-inch cubes

👓 Roast the bell peppers over a gas burner, under the broiler or on a grill until the skins blister and char. Place in a plastic bag, seal and set aside for 15 minutes to steam. Then peel, stem, seed and derib. Cut the peppers into strips. Set aside.

Bring a pot of water to a boil over high heat. Blanch the tomatoes by plunging them into the boiling water for 15 seconds, then into ice water. Drain, then peel, seed and dice. Set aside.

Heat 1 tablespoon of the olive oil in a large pot over medium heat. Add the onion and sauté for about 5 minutes, or until translucent. Add the potatoes and season with salt and pepper. Add the warm water and simmer slowly for 20 minutes, stirring occasionally. Add the tomatoes and simmer for 5 minutes longer.

Heat 2 tablespoons of the olive oil in a large skillet over medium-high heat. Add the pepper strips and sauté until softened, then add them to the potato mixture.

Add the remaining oil to the skillet and, when hot, add the eggplant cubes and fry until golden brown. Add the eggplant to the potato mixture and cook for a few minutes longer, or until the potatoes and eggplant are soft, the liquid has been absorbed and the flavors are well blended.

SERVES 6

Roasted Winter Roots with Whole Garlic Heads

All the ingredients in this easy dish by Georgeanne Brennan may be cooked in the oven at the same time. The root vegetables become soft and succulent while roasting, and those with a high sugar content—carrots, parsnips and onions—caramelize and turn sweet. The heads of garlic, roasted alongside the vegetables, become a self-contained spread that is delicious on country-style bread. Be sure to allow one garlic head for each person.

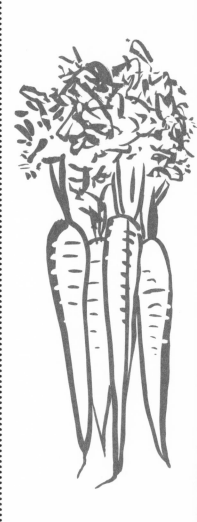

4 carrots, about ½ pound total

2 parsnips, about ½ pound total

2 turnips, about 1 pound total

1 rutabaga, about 1 pound

2 yellow onions, about ¾ pound total

3 russet potatoes, about 1¾ pounds total

4 heads of garlic, about ½ pound total

⅓ cup olive oil

1½ teaspoons salt

1 tablespoon freshly ground pepper

4 fresh thyme sprigs, or 1 teaspoon dried

4 fresh rosemary sprigs, or 1 teaspoon dried

4 fresh sage sprigs, or 1 teaspoon dried

👁👁 Preheat the oven to 350 degrees.

Peel the carrots, parsnips, turnips and rutabaga. Cut the carrots into 2-inch lengths. Halve the parsnips crosswise, separating the tapering root end from the thick upper portion. Cut the upper portion lengthwise into 2 pieces. Quarter the turnips and rutabaga. Peel the onions but do not cut off the root ends. Quarter the onions lengthwise.

Scrub the potatoes and cut them lengthwise into quarters, then in half. Cut off the upper quarter of the garlic heads, leaving the heads intact, skin and all.

Combine half of the olive oil, the salt, pepper, thyme, rosemary and sage in a large bowl. Add all of the vegetables, including the garlic. Stir them until they are well coated with the seasoned oil.

Arrange the vegetables in a single layer on 2 baking sheets. Roast for 30 minutes. Stir the vegetables and baste with some of the remaining olive oil. Continue roasting, stirring once or twice and basting with olive oil, for 30 to 45 minutes longer, or until all the vegetables are tender and are easily pierced with a fork. Remove from the oven and transfer to a platter.

Serve hot or at room temperature.

SERVES 4

Fresh Corn Tamales

These vegetarian tamales are a favorite of Jacqueline McMahan, who grew up on the last-remaining rancho in California.

12 ears of yellow corn

1 cup butter at room temperature

1¼ cups yellow cornmeal

⅓ cup sugar

1½ teaspoons salt

3 tablespoons whipping cream

4 ounces cheddar cheese, cut into 15 sticks

1 can (7 ounces) mild green chiles, or 6 charred and peeled fresh Anaheim chiles, cut into strips

👓 Carefully remove the corn husks by trimming off the ends of each ear of corn so you can easily unfurl the husks without tearing them. Put the widest and largest husks in a large bowl and discard the remaining ones. Pour boiling water over the husks and let soak for 1 hour, or until they become pliable.

Cut the corn off the cobs by standing each ear in a large bowl and cutting off the kernels with a sharp knife. Coarsely purée the kernels in a food processor.

Put the butter in a bowl and beat with an electric mixer until smooth, then slowly beat in the cornmeal, sugar, salt, cream and puréed corn. Blend until well mixed. Drain the corn husks on paper towels.

Set up an assembly line: the husks, corn dough, cheese sticks, green chile strips and cotton string for tying the tamales.

Place a wide corn husk on a work surface (overlap 2 if 1 isn't wide enough). Place about ½ cup dough in the center of the husk. Add 1 cheese stick and 2 strips of green chile. Fold over the top and bottom of the husk, then overlap the sides to form a square package. The corn dough is leakier than regular masa dough, so carefully fold the tamale into a package. Tie with string. Repeat with the remaining ingredients to make 15 tamales.

Place the tamales in a tamale steamer (or a vegetable steamer or stacked Chinese steamer). Steam for 50 minutes.

YIELDS 15 MEDIUM-SIZE TAMALES

NOTE: You may make these a day in advance. Steam them, let cool, then cover and refrigerate. To reheat, steam for 10 minutes. Or, wrap the cooled steamed tamales and freeze for up to 2 months.

Making Masa Dough

If you go to a Mexican market to buy fresh masa for making tamales, be sure you get a freshly ground product (not more than one day old), says Jacqueline McMahan. Also be sure you're not getting "masa preparada," a mixture of lard, masa, salt and seasonings.

If freshly ground masa is not available, you can make your own from dried masa harina, which can be found at most supermarkets (look for Quaker and Maseca brands):

Add 1⅓ cups warm (100-degree) water to 2 cups masa harina tortilla flour; mix first with a spoon, then with your hands to form a very soft dough. Knead in the bowl for about 3 minutes. Cover with plastic wrap and let stand for at least 30 minutes. Yields 1 pound prepared masa.

Kasha and Vegetable Casserole

The nuttiness of kasha brings out the best in vegetables. This recipe by Robin Davis was designed as a meatless main course, but it also could be served as a side dish to something hearty like steak.

2 cups water

1 teaspoon salt, plus more, to taste

1 cup kasha

1 cup small broccoli florets

1 cup small cauliflower florets

1 cup carrot pieces, each ½ inch long

2 tablespoons olive oil

1 onion, chopped

2 garlic cloves, minced

Freshly ground pepper, to taste

Vegetable-oil cooking spray

1 cup whole-milk ricotta cheese

1 egg

1 tablespoon chopped fresh thyme

½ cup freshly grated Parmigiano-Reggiano cheese

⊚⊚ Combine the water and 1 teaspoon salt in a small, heavy saucepan and bring to a boil over high heat. Add the kasha. Reduce heat to low, cover and simmer for about 30 minutes, or until the grains are very tender.

Combine the broccoli, cauliflower and carrot in a vegetable steamer. Cover and steam above boiling water for about 5 minutes, or until crisp-tender. Heat the olive oil in a large, heavy skillet over medium-high heat. Add the onion and sauté for 5 minutes. Add the garlic and cook, stirring, for 2 minutes. Stir in the vegetables and kasha. Season generously with salt and pepper.

Preheat the oven to 350 degrees. Spray a 1½-quart baking dish with vegetable-oil cooking spray.

Whisk together the ricotta, egg and thyme in a small bowl to blend. Stir into the kasha mixture. Spoon the mixture into the prepared pan. Sprinkle with the cheese.

Bake for about 30 minutes, or until the top is golden brown.

SERVES 4 AS A MAIN COURSE; 6 AS A SIDE DISH

The Red Enchiladas

This family recipe of Jacqueline McMahan's dates from about 1850 and has remained unchanged. Every woman who married into the family was taught how to make "The Red Enchiladas." Red enchiladas, along with sarsa (recipe, page 382), are indigenous to the California ranchos, and no barbecue was ever complete without them. One of the nicest things about these enchiladas is that they may be made, one step at a time, over a period of days. The sauce may be made 2 days in advance. The filled enchiladas (unbaked) keep for up to 3 days in the refrigerator.

3 tablespoons mild olive oil, or lard

5 onions, chopped

Salt and freshly ground pepper, to taste

1 tablespoon dried oregano

4 cups Red Chile Sauce (recipe follows), warmed

10 flour tortillas, the thinnest you can find (homemade, if possible)

1½ pounds sharp cheddar cheese, grated

1 cup pitted black olives

Preheat the oven to 350 degrees. Grease a 4-quart rectangular baking dish.

Heat the olive oil in a large skillet over low heat. Add the onions and sauté slowly, stirring frequently, for about 10 minutes, or until softened and translucent. Season with salt and pepper and stir in the oregano.

Spoon ½ cup of the chile sauce onto a wide dinner plate. Dip both sides of a tortilla in the sauce. Place ½ cup of the cheese, a couple of olives and ⅓ cup of the sautéed onions down the middle of the tortilla. Fold the sides of the tortilla over the filling. Place the enchilada folded-edges down in the baking dish. Repeat with the remaining tortillas.

Pour the remaining ½ cup sauce over the enchiladas. Sprinkle with the remaining cheese and olives. Bake for 20 minutes.

YIELDS 10 ENCHILADAS

Red Chile Sauce

This sauce by Jacqueline McMahan was a staple of the rancho. It was used for enchiladas and chile colorado and was spooned over eggs.

10 dried California chiles (mild), or New Mexico chiles (hotter), or a combination

4 guajillo chiles

2 ancho chiles

2 garlic cloves

3 tablespoons olive oil

3 tablespoons all-purpose flour

1 teaspoon dried oregano

1 tablespoon cider vinegar

1 teaspoon salt

Rinse the chiles; remove the stems and shake out some of the seeds. Place the chiles and garlic in a large bowl and cover with boiling water. Cover and let soak for 30 minutes to 1 hour.

Purée the chiles and garlic in a blender in batches, using about ½ cup fresh water for each batch. Add more water if the purée is too thick. Strain the mixture, pressing with a wooden spoon.

Heat the olive oil in a skillet over medium-high heat; stir in the flour and cook for about 10 minutes, or until golden. Do not let it burn. Add the oregano, chile purée, vinegar and salt. Reduce heat to low and simmer for 20 minutes. Add a little water if the mixture gets too thick.

YIELDS 4 TO 5 CUPS SAUCE

Making Chile Purée

Rinse 8 dried California (mild) or New Mexican (hot) chiles, then break in half. Place in a large bowl and add boiling water to cover. Cover and let steep for 1 hour, pushing the chiles down into the water from time to time. When the chiles have softened, remove them from the soaking water, reserving the water. Remove the stems and some of the seeds. Place the chiles and remaining seeds (the exact number is up to you— the more seeds you use, the hotter the purée) in a blender, add 1 cup water (use the soaking water if it isn't bitter) and process until completely smooth. Yields about 2½ cups chile purée, depending on size of chiles. Note: The purée freezes well.

Vegetarian Corn Biryani

This fragrant casserole by Laxmi Hiremath features layers of rice and a fresh corn mixture seasoned with spices, cashews and currants.

1 cup basmati rice

1¼ cups water

½ cup low-fat or whole milk

¾ teaspoon salt

3 ears of corn, husks and silks removed

1 tablespoon mild vegetable oil

2 bay leaves

½ cup chopped onion

1 teaspoon minced garlic

⅛ teaspoon turmeric

2 tablespoons chopped cashews

1 tablespoon currants or raisins

½ teaspoon ground cumin

½ teaspoon ground coriander

½ cup chopped tomato

∞ Place the rice in a large bowl and pour in cold water to cover. Swish the grains with your fingertips. Drain, then wash 2 or 3 more times until the water runs clear. Soak the rice in a bowl of water for 15 minutes to 1 hour. Drain.

Combine the water and milk in a heavy saucepan and bring to a boil over high heat. Add the rice and ½ teaspoon of the salt. Reduce heat to low, cover and cook for about 10 minutes, or until the rice is just tender.

Meanwhile, grate the corn on the coarse side of a box grater, or use a small sharp knife to cut off just the tips of the kernels, then scrape the milky centers out of the kernels that remain on the cobs into a bowl.

Heat the oil in a heavy sauté pan over medium-high heat. Add the bay leaves, onion and garlic. Cook, stirring, for 3 to 4 minutes, or until the onion starts to brown. Add the turmeric, cashews, currants, cumin and coriander. Cook, stirring, for 2 to 3 minutes. Add the tomato, corn and the remaining ¼ teaspoon salt; mix well. Reduce heat to medium, cover and cook for 6 to 8 minutes, or until the mixture is soft.

Position a rack in the center of the oven; preheat to 350 degrees.

To assemble: Make alternate layers of the rice and the corn mixture in a 2-quart heat-proof glass baking dish, finishing with a layer of rice.

Cover tightly with foil and bake for 15 minutes. Remove from the oven and let stand, covered, for 5 minutes before serving.

SERVES 4

NOTE: The dish may be made 1 day ahead. Let cool in the baking dish, cover and refrigerate. Reheat in the oven or microwave.

Super-Rica Rajas

Some cooks just char the chiles, cut them into strips (or rajas) *and mix them with cheese and cream. But Santa Barbara's Super-Rica Taqueria, the now-famous taco stand that Julia Child visits from time to time, adds a twist. What makes these rajas so special are the onions, which give off their sweetness as they're cooked with the chiles. Rajas are good with a variety of foods: alongside grilled meats, enclosed in a soft taco, or layered with rice and corn in Arroz con Rajas y Crema (see recipe, page 159).*

3 teaspoons canola oil, or olive oil

2 cups thinly sliced mild onions, with slices halved so onion strands aren't too long

6 poblano chiles

3 garlic cloves, minced

1 bay leaf

1½ teaspoons fresh thyme leaves

⅔ cup vegetable broth

½ pound mozzarella cheese, or Mexican asadero cheese, grated or cut into small pieces

¼ cup whipping cream (optional but fantastic; or use thick Mexican crema if you can find it)

Salt, to taste

⊚⊚ Heat the oil in a heavy nonstick skillet over medium-low heat; add the onions and sauté slowly for at least 15 minutes, or until very soft and translucent. Let them brown a little to add flavor.

Meanwhile, prepare the chiles. Quickly char the chiles on a rack over a gas burner, under the broiler or on a grill until they blister and blacken without burning. Place in a plastic bag, seal and set aside for 15 minutes to steam, then peel, stem and seed. It's easier to use your fingers to tear off the chile from its stem, then pull out the heavy seed pod. Hold the chile under cold running water to rinse off any remaining seeds. Pat dry.

Cut the chiles into long strips. Add to the onions and sauté for about 5 minutes. Add the garlic, bay leaf, thyme and broth. Simmer for about 15 minutes longer, or until there is very little liquid left in the pan.

BEST WAY:
Cooking Long-Grain Rice

It sounds simple, but it isn't—what's the best way to cook white, enriched long-grain rice so it maintains distinct grains and is not sticky?

We tested 15 batches of rice to find out. We used different proportions of rice to water and various cooking methods: baked in the oven, simmered on the stove and steamed in a rice cooker.

In the process, we found the proportions often listed on the package—1 cup rice to 2 cups water—consistently produced sticky rice. To ensure that grains stay separate, we found the best ratio was 1 cup rice to 1¼ cups water. The traditional stovetop method produces good results, but this way is even better:

Stir in the cheese and cream, if desired. Simmer until the cheese is melted and blended with the rest of the ingredients. Taste and season with salt, if needed.

SERVES 4 GENEROUSLY

Arroz con Rajas y Crema

Rice with chile strips and cream is a favorite dish in Mexico for large groups and buffets, says Jacqueline McMahan. It may be made ahead and refrigerated for several hours or overnight before baking.

1 cup sour cream

1 garlic clove, minced

2 green onions (white and most of the green part), minced

2 tablespoons minced cilantro

2 cups cooked long-grain rice (1 cup raw rice cooked in 2 cups water, vegetable broth or chicken broth)

Super-Rica Rajas (see recipe, page 158)

1 cup fresh corn kernels, or frozen niblet kernels

Cilantro leaves for garnish

Preheat the oven to 350 degrees. Oil a 2-quart, deep baking dish or spray with olive oil mist.

Blend together the sour cream, garlic, green onions and minced cilantro in a bowl. Set aside.

Place half of the rice in the bottom of the prepared dish. Top with half of the rajas. Layer on all of the corn kernels. Spread half of the sour cream mixture on top of the corn. Layer the remaining rice over the sour cream, then top with the remaining rajas. Spread the remaining sour cream mixture over the top. Cover and bake for 30 minutes (45 minutes to 1 hour if made ahead and refrigerated).

Garnish with cilantro leaves and serve.

SERVES 6

Preheat the oven to 350 degrees. Place 1 cup white long-grain rice and ½ teaspoon kosher salt in a small, ovenproof baking dish. Add 1¼ cups boiling water, stirring once to dissolve the salt. Cover the dish first with heavy-duty plastic wrap and then with aluminum foil, making sure the plastic is completely covered by the foil. Bake for 30 to 35 minutes, or until all the water is absorbed.

Remove the rice from the oven and let it rest for 5 minutes. Stir gently, then cover the dish loosely with the plastic wrap and let the rice rest 5 minutes longer before serving. Yields approximately 3½ cups. (Note: To double the amount, use 2 cups rice, 2½ cups water and 1 teaspoon kosher salt.)

Short Rice with Long Beans

This Parsi recipe is from Niloufer Ichaporia King, a San Francisco rice authority. Parsis are an ethnic minority from the Indian state of Gujarat. Serve this dish as a vegetarian meal with yogurt and cucumbers. It's also good with grilled meat, fish or prawns.

> 2 cups kalijira ("baby basmati") rice
>
> 1 cup husked red lentils (masoor dal), or husked mung beans (mung dal)
>
> ½ pound yard-long beans
>
> 4 tablespoons plus 2 teaspoons clarified butter, or vegetable oil
>
> 2-inch piece cinnamon stick
>
> 6 to 8 peppercorns
>
> 5 whole cloves
>
> 3 whole cardamom pods
>
> 1 teaspoon cumin seeds
>
> 1 small onion, finely chopped
>
> 2 green serrano chiles, slit
>
> ½ teaspoon ground turmeric
>
> 3¾ cups water
>
> 1½ to 2 teaspoons salt

Wash the rice in a bowl of cold water and drain well. Swish the dal in a large bowl of water, remove bits of husk and chaff that float to the surface, then drain.

Bring a pot of salted water to a boil over high heat. Cut the long beans into pea-size pieces; you should have about 2 cups. Add the beans to the boiling water and cook for about 3 minutes, or until crisp-tender; drain and transfer to ice water. When cool, drain again.

Heat 4 tablespoons clarified butter in a saucepan over medium-high heat. When hot, add the cinnamon, peppercorns, cloves, cardamom and cumin. Cook until the seeds begin to pop.

Add the onion, chiles and turmeric. Cook until the onion is soft and browning around the edges. Add the drained rice and dal. Add the water and 1½ teaspoons salt. Bring to a boil, cover tightly and reduce heat to low. Cook for 15 minutes, then remove from heat and let stand for 10 minutes.

Heat the remaining 2 teaspoons clarified butter in a skillet over medium-high heat. When hot, add the long beans, season with remaining ½ teaspoon salt and toss for about 1 minute, or until hot. Add them to the rice and dal and fluff with chopsticks.

Remove the whole spices, if desired, or warn diners to look out for them. They are not meant to be eaten.

SERVES 6

Millet and Kale Gratin

Just about any hearty green will work in this recipe by Robin Davis. It's a delightful meatless main course, or a side dish for roast chicken or fish.

4 cups water

1 teaspoon salt, plus more, to taste

1 cup millet

2 tablespoons olive oil

2 shallots, finely chopped

2 garlic cloves, minced

2 pounds kale (about 2 bunches), stemmed and coarsely chopped

Freshly ground pepper, to taste

Vegetable-oil cooking spray

1½ cups grated fontina cheese

2 tablespoons butter

1½ cups fresh breadcrumbs

¼ cup freshly grated Romano cheese

◎◎ Combine the water and 1 teaspoon salt in a small, heavy saucepan over high heat. Bring to a boil. Add the millet and boil, stirring frequently to prevent sticking, for about 30 minutes, or until tender. Transfer to a large bowl.

Preheat the oven to 400 degrees. Spray a 1½-quart baking dish with vegetable-oil cooking spray.

Heat the olive oil in a large, heavy skillet over medium-high heat. Add the shallots and sauté for about 5 minutes, or until translucent. Add the garlic and sauté for 2 minutes. Working in batches, add the kale and sauté for about 5 minutes per batch, or until just wilted. When each batch is cooked, transfer to the bowl with the millet. Stir the kale into the millet. Season generously with salt and pepper.

Layer half of the millet mixture into the prepared pan. Sprinkle with the fontina. Layer in the remaining millet mixture.

Melt the butter in a medium, heavy skillet over medium heat. Add the breadcrumbs and stir until just beginning to brown. Spoon the breadcrumbs over the millet. Sprinkle with the Romano cheese.

Bake for about 30 minutes, or until the topping is brown and the mixture is bubbling.

SERVES 4 AS A MAIN COURSE; 6 AS A SIDE DISH

Chile Relleno Casserole

You can make this dish using fresh green chiles, but if you're pressed for time, canned roasted and peeled chiles work almost as well, says Jacqueline McMahan. For a non-vegetarian version, try adding sautéed crumbled chorizo or other spicy sausage to the egg mixture.

8 whole Anaheim chiles, charred, peeled and seeded; or 2 cans (7 ounces each) whole green chiles, drained, rinsed and patted dry

½ pound Monterey Jack cheese, or asadero cheese, cut into 8 sticks

3 eggs

1 jalapeño chile, seeded and minced

¼ cup all-purpose flour

½ teaspoon salt

¾ cup milk

1 cup grated cheddar cheese

◉◉ Preheat the oven to 350 degrees. Oil a 9-by-13-inch baking dish.

Stuff each Anaheim chile with a cheese stick and place it in the baking dish.

Beat together the eggs, jalapeño, flour, salt and milk in a bowl; pour over the chiles. Sprinkle the cheese over the top.

Bake for about 35 minutes, or until golden brown. Let cool for 10 minutes before serving.

SERVES 4 TO 6

To Char or Not to Char

When you chop or mince fresh Anaheim chiles to add to a dish, they don't necessarily have to be charred and peeled. You won't have the smoky caramelized flavor, but you will still have the heat and the crunch. Sometimes crunch is good.

Roasted Portobellos with Pink Peppercorns

This dish by Marlena Spieler is super easy to prepare and strikingly delicious. You may use any mature mushroom in place of portobellos. Similarly, if you don't have chervil, use fresh tarragon. And if you don't have fresh tarragon, use chopped parsley and chives; this recipe is very adaptable.

4 portobello mushrooms, or other mature flat mushrooms

5 garlic cloves, chopped

6 tablespoons extra virgin olive oil

2 tablespoons balsamic vinegar

Salt, to taste

3 tablespoons pine nuts

1 to 2 teaspoons pink peppercorns

1 tablespoon chopped fresh chervil and/or tarragon

⊚⊚ Preheat the broiler or preheat the oven to 400 degrees.

Place the mushrooms on a plate and sprinkle with the garlic, olive oil, balsamic vinegar and salt; marinate for 30 minutes.

Lightly toast the pine nuts in a dry heavy skillet over medium-high heat, tossing and turning the nuts every few moments, until they are golden and lightly browned in spots. Remove from the skillet and set aside.

Transfer the mushrooms gill-side up to a shallow baking pan and broil or bake until browned. Turn the mushrooms and broil or bake until the tops are lightly browned and the mushrooms are just tender. This should take 10 to 15 minutes total. If broiling the mushrooms, watch carefully so they don't burn.

Sprinkle with the pine nuts, pink peppercorns and chervil and/or tarragon.

SERVES 4

Potato and Portobello Mushroom Casserole

Here's a simple recipe from one of San Francisco's best French chefs, Hubert Keller of Fleur de Lys. If you want to splurge, add some shaved fresh black truffles to the mushrooms and sauté them together, Keller says.

3 pounds russet potatoes

½ cup minced onion

3 tablespoons finely diced carrot

3 tablespoons finely diced celery

1 leek (white part only), well rinsed and julienned

4 garlic cloves, minced

3 tablespoons olive oil

2 portobello mushrooms, stems and gills removed, sliced

Salt and freshly ground pepper, to taste

½ cup white wine

1½ cups vegetable broth

Preheat the oven to 400 degrees.

Peel and wash the potatoes. Slice them into rounds about ⅛ inch thick. Toss the potatoes in a large mixing bowl with the onion, carrot, celery, leek and garlic.

Heat the olive oil in a sauté pan over high heat. When the oil is very hot, add the mushrooms and toss constantly for 2 to 3 minutes, or until they are moist and tender. The heat should remain high but the mushrooms should not brown. Remove the mushrooms from the pan, season with salt and pepper and set aside.

Arrange half of the potato mixture in a shallow earthenware or glass casserole dish about 6-by-9-by-2 inches. Season with salt and pepper. Layer half of the mushrooms over the potato mixture. Cover with the rest of the potato mixture, season with salt and pepper, then top with the remaining mushrooms. Pour in the wine and broth. The liquid should come about halfway up the sides of the potatoes and mushrooms.

Seal the casserole very tightly with 2 or 3 layers of aluminum foil, making sure no steam can escape during baking.

Bake for about 1¼ hours, or until the potatoes are tender and can be cut easily with a fork.

Serve directly from the casserole.

SERVES 4

Morels in Brandy Cream on Toast

Shirley Sarvis, a wine- and food-matching expert from San Francisco, originally designed this recipe to complement a Sanford Barrel Select Chardonnay. The amount of butter and the cooking time may vary depending on the moisture content of the mushrooms.

5 tablespoons unsalted butter

½ pound small fresh morel mushrooms (or slightly larger ones, halved or quartered lengthwise), brushed clean and tough parts removed

1½ tablespoons minced shallots

5 tablespoons brandy

1 cup whipping cream

Salt, to taste

8 toast points (recipe follows)

About ⅛ teaspoon cayenne pepper

2 teaspoons minced curly parsley

Melt the butter in a medium-large, heavy skillet over medium heat. Add the morels and sauté, stirring, for about 7 minutes, or until they begin to soften. Stir in the shallots and heat through. Add the brandy and cook until reduced to a syrup over the morels.

Add the cream and simmer until the liquid has reduced to the consistency of heavy cream. Season with salt.

Arrange 2 toast points, slightly overlapping, on each plate. Spoon the morels and sauce over the toasts. Sprinkle with the cayenne, then the parsley.

SERVES 4

TO MAKE TOAST POINTS: Preheat the oven to 300 degrees. Trim crusts from thickly sliced firm-textured non-sourdough white bread, such as French sandwich or farm-style white. Cut into 3-inch triangles. Place on a baking sheet. Bake, turning occasionally, for 15 to 20 minutes, or until crisp and lightly browned.

NOTE: You can use year-round market mushrooms if you wish. Follow the recipe above except use 3 tablespoons butter; ½ pound white mushrooms, thinly sliced; 1 tablespoon minced shallots; 3 tablespoons brandy; ½ cup whipping cream; 6 toast points; about ¹⁄₁₆ teaspoon cayenne; and 1 teaspoon minced curly parsley. Serves 3.

Wild Mushroom Bread Pudding

Philippe Striffeler, chef at the Nikko Hotel's restaurant, Anzu, in San Francisco, serves this bread pudding with steak, pork, veal and chicken. We find that it stands proudly on its own.

4 tablespoons butter

¼ cup minced shallots

6 ounces assorted mushrooms, cleaned and cut into medium dice

½ cup Madeira

1 cup milk

1 cup whipping cream

6 egg yolks, beaten

¼ bunch Italian parsley, finely chopped

1½ teaspoons chopped fresh thyme

Salt and freshly ground pepper, to taste

1½ teaspoons porcini powder (optional)

6 ounces brioche loaf, cut into ½-inch-thick slices and crusts removed

◉◉ Melt the butter in a large sauté pan over low heat. Add the shallots, cover and gently simmer for 1 minute. Add the mushrooms, increase heat to medium-high and cook, stirring occasionally, until softened and dry. Add the Madeira and cook until it evaporates. Add the milk and cream and heat to near boiling.

Put the egg yolks in a large bowl and whisk the mushroom mixture into the yolks. Add the parsley, thyme, salt, pepper and porcini powder, if desired.

Preheat the oven to 300 degrees. Coat a large, shallow casserole with butter.

Layer one third of the bread slices into the casserole. Pour in half of the mushroom custard. Layer half of the remaining bread over the custard; pour in the remaining custard. Top with the remaining bread. Let stand for 10 to 15 minutes. Moisten with additional cream if the top of the pudding seems dry.

Place the casserole in a large baking pan. Pour in enough hot water to come one third of the way up the sides of the casserole. Bake for about 1 hour, or until firm.

Let cool for 10 to 15 minutes, then cut into squares and serve.

SERVES 6

Portobello-Polenta Pie

This deliciously homey dish with goat cheese comes from chef Kerry Heffernan of Autumn Moon Cafe in Oakland. The pie isn't much for looks, but the taste and texture are marvelous. Heffernan likes to serve this savory main course with a green salad.

Marinara Sauce

2 tablespoons extra virgin olive oil

1 tablespoon roughly chopped garlic

1 can (16 ounces) crushed tomatoes with their juices

1 tablespoon chopped fresh basil

Salt and freshly ground pepper, to taste

1 tablespoon dry red wine

Pinch of sugar

Polenta

2 tablespoons unsalted butter

2 teaspoons minced garlic

3½ cups water

1 teaspoon salt

1 cup polenta

Filling

2 tablespoons olive oil

2 cups sliced stemmed portobello mushrooms

½ cup chopped pitted kalamata olives

2 tablespoons chopped fresh basil

½ teaspoon chopped fresh thyme

½ cup crumbled soft fresh goat cheese

1 cup grated mozzarella cheese

1 cup freshly grated Parmigiano-Reggiano cheese

◎◎ To make the sauce: Heat the olive oil in a heavy saucepan over medium heat. Add the garlic and stir for about 3 minutes, or until golden. Using a slotted spoon or skimmer, remove and discard the garlic. Add the tomatoes and their juices and the basil to the saucepan. Season lightly with salt and pepper. Bring to a simmer, reduce heat to low and simmer for 10 minutes, stirring occasionally. Add the wine and simmer for 5 minutes.

Purée the sauce in a food processor or blender. Adjust seasoning with salt, pepper and sugar.

To make the polenta: Butter a 9-inch glass baking pan. Melt the butter in a heavy saucepan over medium heat. Add the garlic and sauté for about 3 minutes, or until golden. Add the water and salt and bring to a boil. Slowly add the polenta in a continuous stream, whisking constantly. Reduce heat to low and cook, stirring, for about 20 minutes, or until the polenta is very thick. Pour into the prepared baking pan, making the sides slightly higher than the center.

Position the broiler rack at least 8 inches from the heat source; preheat the broiler. Or preheat the oven to 400 degrees.

To make the filling: Heat the oil in a large, heavy skillet over medium heat. Add the mushrooms and sauté for about 5 minutes, or until tender. Spoon over the polenta. Sprinkle with the olives, basil, thyme, goat cheese, marinara sauce, mozzarella and Parmigiano-Reggiano.

Broil until the cheese is fully melted and golden brown, watching carefully to avoid burning. Or bake for about 20 minutes, or until the cheese melts.

Let stand for 5 minutes, then cut into squares and serve.

SERVES 4 TO 6

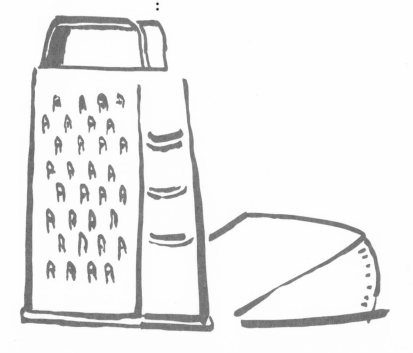

Polenta Baked with Vegetables

Marion Cunningham, author of the Fannie Farmer Cookbook, *calls polenta the Italian version of our cornmeal mush. Whatever name you use, it has become a staple in many households. Cunningham's version of polenta baked with vegetables is a very satisfying dish, and it's easy to make. All it takes is stirring together cornmeal, salt, olive oil and water in a baking dish, adding a few vegetables, then, after about an hour of baking, sitting down to supper. If you have any leftover polenta, you can enjoy it by cutting it into squares and frying it in olive oil until golden on both sides.*

1 large red tomato

1 green bell pepper

1 bunch fresh spinach, or ½ box frozen chopped spinach (thawed)

1 yellow onion

1 cup polenta

3¼ cups lukewarm water

1¼ teaspoons salt

¼ cup olive oil

½ cup grated Parmigiano-Reggiano cheese

◍ Position the rack in the center of the oven and preheat to 350 degrees. Core the tomato, then cut into bite-size pieces.

Stem the bell pepper and halve lengthwise; store half of the pepper for future use. Seed, derib and chop the remaining half.

If using fresh spinach, remove any large, tough stems and wash the leaves. Pile about half of the spinach on a cutting board and chop into pieces the size of large postage stamps. Press the leaves firmly into a measuring cup and measure out 1½ cups of chopped spinach. Wrap and store any extra spinach for future use.

Matching Wine and Food

To make your recipes as full-flavored and wine-friendly as possible, be sure each dish has a bitter, sour, sweet, salty and umami (a meaty, savory flavor) component (see page 298).

To do this, try the following:

Taste the dish just before serving, then add a squeeze of lemon and a dash of salt to bring out full flavors.

At the table, if the accompanying wine tastes too aggressive, add some lemon juice or rice vinegar and salt or soy sauce to the food.

If a dish tastes too acidic and the accompanying wine tastes flat, add a pinch of sugar to the food.

If using frozen spinach, be sure it is defrosted and squeeze out any excess water with your hands.

Peel the onion and halve it lengthwise from the stem down. Store half of the onion for future use. Chop the remaining half.

Put the polenta, water, salt and olive oil into an 8-inch square baking dish and stir with a fork until blended. Add the tomato, pepper, spinach and onion and stir to distribute the vegetables evenly.

Bake for 30 minutes, then check to see if the liquid is boiling around the edges of the pan. If so, leave the temperature as is. If not, increase the oven temperature to 400 degrees. Bake for 15 minutes longer, or until all the water has been absorbed—that's your signal the polenta is done.

Remove the pan from the oven, sprinkle the cheese evenly over the top and let stand for 5 minutes. Cut the polenta into squares, lift portions with a spatula and serve warm.

SERVES 4 AS A MAIN COURSE; 6 AS A SIDE DISH

Potato and Goat Cheese Galette

Donia Bijan, chef/owner of L'Amie Donia in Palo Alto, created this crisp potato galette using a skillet filled with alternating layers of thinly sliced potatoes, butter and goat cheese.

2½ pounds Yukon Gold potatoes
½ cup unsalted butter
⅓ pound goat cheese
Salt and freshly ground pepper, to taste
1 tablespoon coarsely chopped fresh thyme

◉◉ Preheat the oven to 400 degrees.

Using a mandoline or other vegetable slicer or a sharp knife, slice the potatoes about ⅛ inch thick.

Using 1½ tablespoons of the butter, grease the bottom and sides of a 10-inch ovenproof skillet. Using half of the sliced potatoes and working from the outside in, cover the bottom of the skillet with concentric rings of potatoes, overlapping the slices slightly and allowing each successively smaller ring to slightly overlap the previous one. Dot the potatoes with 2 tablespoons of the butter. Sprinkle the goat cheese evenly over the potatoes, then flatten the clumps of cheese with your fingers to make an even layer. Season with salt and pepper and scatter half of the thyme over the goat cheese. Cover with the remaining potato slices, again arranging them in neat concentric rings of overlapping slices.

Melt the remaining butter in a small skillet over medium heat, then drizzle it evenly over the top. Season with salt and pepper and sprinkle with the remaining thyme.

Bake the galette for about 1¼ hours, or until golden brown on top and sizzling hot. Insert a sharp knife through the galette to make sure all the potatoes are tender and cooked through.

Cool in the pan for 5 minutes, then invert onto a serving platter and cut into wedges.

SERVES 6

BEST WAY:
Baking Potatoes

In a three-step process, we cooked potatoes 14 ways, testing oven temperature, cooking time and cooking style. We wrapped, oiled, buttered, salted—and left some completely plain. We even tried the microwave.

Using medium-size russets, we achieved the best results with a plain potato, pierced with a fork to let steam escape. Baked at 350 degrees for 1½ hours, the potato emerged with a great flavor and a light, fluffy texture. In addition, the skin was crisp but chewable.

The microwaved potato was the worst, coming out limp and gluey.

If you're in a time crunch, try microwaving the potato for 5 minutes, then place it in a 350-degree oven for 10 minutes. The oven helps crisp the skin and dry out the flesh.

Tarte Tatin of Celery Root, Leek and Potato

Store-bought puff pastry works well to crown this rustic vegetable tart from Marlena Spieler. It also makes a wonderful accompaniment to tarragon-roasted chicken.

6 ounces celery root, peeled

1 large russet potato, peeled

2 tablespoons butter

1 leek (white part only), well rinsed and chopped, or 4 shallots, chopped

Salt and freshly ground pepper, to taste

2 garlic cloves, chopped

1 teaspoon chopped fresh tarragon leaves

A few drops of lemon juice

10 to 12 ounces puff pastry dough

Tarragon sprigs for garnish (optional)

∞ Preheat the oven to 375 degrees.

Thinly slice the celery root and potatoes. Heat the butter in a skillet over medium-high heat until it foams. Then add the celery root and potatoes and cook for about 5 minutes, or until they are golden but not cooked through. Add the leek and cook a few minutes longer. Season with salt and pepper. Fold in the garlic and chopped tarragon, then the lemon juice. Arrange the celery root and potatoes evenly in a 12-inch pie pan.

Roll out the pastry on a floured board into a circle slightly larger than the diameter of the pie pan. Gently fit the pastry over the top of the vegetables, letting the excess hang over the sides of the pan. Trim the pastry even with the edge of the pan, then roll the edges facing inward. The pastry will have a sort of border that covers the vegetables but doesn't go up the sides of the pan.

Bake for about 30 minutes, or until the pastry is golden brown. The vegetables will be tender and creamily cooked through.

Invert the tart onto a serving plate. Pluck off any pieces of potato or celery root that cling to the bottom of the pan and arrange them on the tart.

To serve, cut into wedges and garnish with tarragon sprigs, if desired.

SERVES 4

Yellow Curry with Mixed Vegetables, Tofu and Thai Basil

Traditionally, Thai curry is prepared by stirring the paste into the coconut milk and allowing the mixture to sizzle until fragrant. However, you can't find commercial pastes in the United States that are as aromatic as the ones in Thailand. Mai Pham compensates for this difference by browning shallots and curry paste in a little oil, giving the dish an even more delightful fragrance. Please note that a little fish sauce is used in the sauce, so technically, this is not a vegetarian dish.

1 tablespoon vegetable oil

1 tablespoon minced shallots

2 tablespoons Thai yellow curry paste, or to taste

2 cups unsweetened coconut milk

2 tablespoons Asian fish sauce

1½ tablespoons light brown sugar

2 carrots, peeled and cut into ¼-inch rounds

2 cups broccoli florets

2 chayote squash, peeled and cut into 1-inch cubes

6 ounces firm tofu, cut into cubes

2 kaffir lime leaves, cut into thin slivers

⅓ cup loosely packed Thai basil leaves

☙ Heat the oil in a nonstick wok over medium heat. Add the shallots and curry paste and stir for about 1 minute, or until fragrant.

Skim off the top creamy part of the coconut milk (about ½ cup) and add to the wok. Let the mixture bubble and sizzle for 2 minutes, or until fragrant. Add the remaining coconut milk, the fish sauce, brown sugar and carrots. Reduce the heat to low and simmer for 5 minutes.

Add the broccoli, chayote and tofu; cook until the vegetables are slightly softened. Remove from heat. Add the lime leaves and basil.

SERVES 4

Malaysian Coconut Curry of Autumn Vegetables

This creamy curry, crafted by Marlena Spieler, is extremely versatile; you may add, substitute or delete vegetables at will. If you want to add meat or seafood, consider strips of chicken breast or prawns in the shell. Tofu also adds more substance to this already-rich dish. Serve with rice and naan or warmed flour tortillas.

5 shiitake mushrooms, fresh or dried

3 tablespoons dry-roasted peanuts

1 stalk lemongrass (tender white part only), finely chopped, or 2 to 3 teaspoons chopped lemon zest

4 shallots, or 1 onion, chopped

6 garlic cloves, chopped

2 to 3 red jalapeño chiles, seeded and chopped

6 tablespoons chopped cilantro

½ teaspoon turmeric

¼ teaspoon curry powder

2 to 3 tablespoons vegetable oil

1 Japanese eggplant, cut into chunks

¼ pound winter squash, peeled, seeded and cut into chunks

2 potatoes, peeled and cut into bite-size chunks

Salt and freshly ground pepper, to taste

1½ to 2½ cups vegetable stock

½ pound green beans, trimmed and cut into 1-inch lengths

1 pound tomatoes, peeled, seeded and diced

1 cup unsweetened coconut milk

Juice of 1 lemon

Several handfuls of fresh basil, torn or coarsely chopped

◉◉ If using dried shiitakes, rehydrate them in 1 cup hot water. Let soak while you make the curry paste and cook the other vegetables.

To make the curry paste, combine the peanuts, lemongrass, shallots, garlic, chiles, cilantro, turmeric, curry and 1 to 2 tablespoons of the oil in a blender or food processor; process into a paste.

Heat the remaining 1 to 2 tablespoons oil in a heavy skillet over low heat. Add the curry paste and cook, letting the mixture fry, for 7 to 8 minutes, or until it is fragrant and the solids have separated from the oil.

Add the eggplant, squash and potatoes; cook for a few minutes, then season with salt and pepper. Add 1½ cups of the stock. Raise heat to high and cook for about 10 minutes. Add the green beans and tomatoes and cook, stirring, for a few minutes longer.

Cut the mushrooms into bite-size pieces and add them to the skillet. If using fresh shiitakes, add the remaining 1 cup stock. If using dried mushrooms, add the strained mushroom-soaking liquid.

Simmer the vegetables a few minutes longer, or until the beans are cooked through.

Reduce the heat to low, stir in the coconut milk and simmer for a few minutes, or until the sauce is somewhat thickened. Stir in the lemon juice and basil.

SERVES 4

Three-Cheese Pizza with Arugula

A classic sauce made with fresh tomatoes underlies the melting Romano, Parmigiano-Reggiano and mozzarella cheeses on this simple pizza by Georgeanne Brennan. Young arugula leaves scattered across the top at serving time add a peppery tang.

Pizza Crust Dough (recipe follows)

Sauce

2 tablespoons olive oil

1 garlic clove, minced

5 pounds very ripe tomatoes, peeled, seeded and chopped

½ teaspoon salt

½ teaspoon freshly ground pepper

½ to 1 tablespoon sugar (optional)

1 tablespoon minced fresh thyme

2 tablespoons cornmeal

Topping

4 tablespoons olive oil

4 ounces grated Romano cheese

4 ounces grated Parmigiano-Reggiano cheese

8 ounces mozzarella cheese, cut into thin slices

1 tablespoon freshly ground pepper

16 young arugula leaves

Prepare the pizza crust dough.

To make the sauce: Heat the olive oil in a saucepan large enough to hold all the tomatoes. Add the garlic and sauté over medium heat for 2 to 3 minutes, being careful not to brown it. Reduce heat to low, add the tomatoes and simmer for 30 minutes.

Taste the sauce and add the salt, pepper and sugar, if desired. Continue cooking for 30 minutes to 1 hour, depending upon the type of tomato, or until the sauce thickens. Skim any clear liquid off the sauce. Stir in the thyme and cook for 10 minutes longer. (Yields about 3 cups.)

Preheat the oven to 500 degrees.

Dust two 12-inch or four 6-inch pizza pans with the cornmeal. Fit the pizza dough into the pans.

To make the topping: Brush half of the olive oil over the crusts. Spread each crust with 4 to 5 tablespoons of the tomato sauce. Divide the cheeses evenly among the crusts. Season with the pepper.

Bake the pizzas on the upper rack of the oven for 10 to 12 minutes, or until the crusts are lightly browned and the cheeses are bubbling.

Remove from oven and drizzle with the remaining olive oil. Strew the arugula leaves over the top.

YIELDS TWO 12-INCH PIZZAS OR FOUR 6-INCH PIZZAS

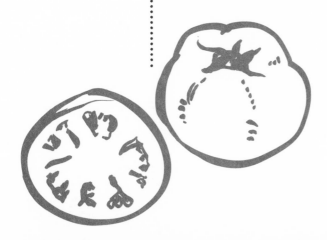

Pizza Crust Dough

2 envelopes active dry yeast

1 cup warm water (105 degrees)

1 teaspoon sugar

1 teaspoon salt

2 tablespoons olive oil

3 cups all-purpose flour, plus more if needed

◉◉ Dissolve the yeast in the water in a small bowl. Add the sugar and let stand for about 5 minutes, or until foamy.

Processor method: In a food processor fitted with a dough blade, combine the yeast mixture, salt, 1 tablespoon of the olive oil and 3 cups flour. Process until the ingredients come together into a ball. If the dough is too wet, add more flour, a little at a time, until the dough has a smooth, firm texture. Continue to process for 3 to 4 minutes after the ball is formed, or until the dough is smooth and silky but firm. Turn out the dough onto a well-floured work surface and knead for 6 to 7 minutes, or until elastic.

Hand method: Follow the same steps as the processor method, but use only 2 cups flour to start and work the ingredients together in a bowl with a fork or your fingertips. Gradually add more flour until the dough forms a stiff ball. Knead the dough on a well-floured work surface for 6 to 7 minutes, or until it is smooth and elastic.

Oil a large bowl with the remaining 1 tablespoon olive oil. Place the dough in the bowl and turn to coat the surface with oil. Cover the bowl with a clean cloth and let stand in a warm place for 1 to 1½ hours, or until the dough has doubled in size.

Punch down dough in bowl, cover and let it rest for 30 minutes before shaping the crusts.

YIELDS ENOUGH DOUGH FOR TWO 12-INCH OR FOUR 6-INCH PIZZAS

Green Garlic Pizza

You will need a baking stone to re-create the crisp crust on this pizza by
Janet Fletcher, adapted from San Francisco's Universal Cafe.

Dough

1½ teaspoons active dry yeast

¾ cup warm water (105 degrees)

1 tablespoon olive oil

1 teaspoon salt

About 1¾ cups unbleached all-purpose flour

Topping

⅓ pound Yukon Gold potatoes, peeled and cut into ⅛-inch-thick slices

2 tablespoons olive oil, plus more for brushing dough

Salt and freshly ground pepper, to taste

½ pound green garlic, leafy greens removed, white and pale green parts
        sliced lengthwise, then into ½-inch widths

Coarse cornmeal (polenta) for dusting baking sheet

½ pound whole-milk mozzarella, coarsely grated

3 ounces goat cheese, crumbled

2 teaspoons minced fresh thyme

Pinch of hot red pepper flakes (optional)

∞ To make the dough: Sprinkle the yeast over the warm water in a large
bowl. Let stand for 2 minutes. Stir with a fork to dissolve the yeast. Let stand
for 10 minutes. Whisk in the olive oil and salt. Add 1½ cups of the flour,
stirring with a wooden spoon.

Turn the dough out onto a lightly floured work surface. Knead for 6 to
8 minutes, or until smooth and elastic, adding as much of the remaining
¼ cup flour as needed to keep the dough from sticking. Shape into a ball,
transfer to an oiled bowl, turn to coat with oil and cover tightly with plastic
wrap. Place in a warm spot and let rise for 2 hours.

Punch down dough, then reshape into a ball. Cover with plastic wrap and
let rise for 4 hours.

To make the topping: Preheat the oven to 400 degrees.

Toss the potatoes with ½ tablespoon of the olive oil, then season with
salt and pepper. Arrange on a baking sheet in a single layer. Bake for about

10 minutes, or until the potatoes are done but not brown. Watch carefully, as they burn easily. Use a spatula to transfer them to a plate.

Increase the oven temperature to 550 degrees and preheat a baking stone for at least 20 minutes.

Heat 1½ tablespoons of the olive oil in a skillet over medium-low heat, add the green garlic, season with salt and pepper and sauté for 5 to 8 minutes, or until softened. Let cool.

Dust a rimless baking sheet with cornmeal. Punch down dough and place on a lightly floured surface. Roll the dough into a 13- to 14-inch round. Transfer to the baking sheet.

Working quickly so the dough doesn't stick, top first with the mozzarella, then with the sliced potatoes, green garlic, crumbled goat cheese, thyme and pepper flakes, if desired. Brush the rim with olive oil. Carefully slide the pizza onto the hot baking stone.

Bake for about 8 minutes, or until the crust is browned and the topping is bubbling. Use the baking sheet to transfer the pizza to a cutting board.

YIELDS ONE 13- TO 14-INCH PIZZA

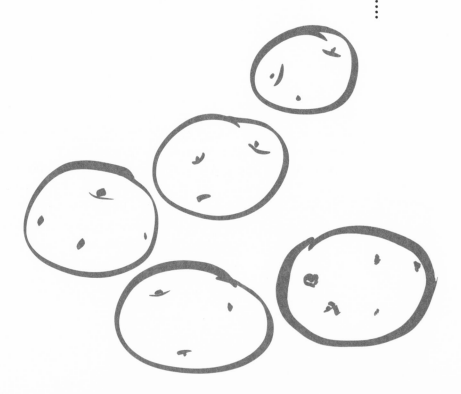

Potato Gnocchi with Asparagus and Tomatoes

This easy tomato sauce by Marlena Spieler makes asparagus the star. The dish is elegant enough for company, yet fast enough for a quick weeknight meal. Packaged gnocchi work fine in this dish.

1 to 1½ pounds asparagus

6 tablespoons olive oil

1 onion, chopped

8 garlic cloves, chopped

2¼ pounds vine-ripened tomatoes, or 2 cans (14 ounces each) tomatoes, diced, with their juices

Salt and freshly ground pepper, to taste

Pinch of sugar to balance the acidity of the tomatoes, if needed

1½ to 2 packages potato gnocchi, 12 ounces total

Several handfuls of fresh basil leaves, torn

8 tablespoons coarsely shredded Parmigiano-Reggiano, pecorino or other grating cheese

இ Snap off the tough ends of the asparagus. Peel the remaining stalks. Cut the tips and peeled stalks into bite-size lengths; set aside.

Heat the olive oil in a skillet over medium-low heat, add the onion and lightly sauté for 5 to 7 minutes, or until softened. Add the garlic and tomatoes and their juices and cook for about 10 minutes, or until the tomatoes have concentrated into a richly flavored sauce.

Add the asparagus and season the sauce with salt, pepper and sugar, if needed. Cook until the asparagus is crisp-tender, then set aside.

Bring a large pot of salted water to a boil over high heat, add the gnocchi and cook according to package directions, or until just tender. Drain. Toss the gnocchi with the sauce and sprinkle with the basil and cheese.

SERVES 6

Lentil and Squash Lasagna with Caramelized Onions

The combination of lentils and squash at first may seem strange, but believe us, the finished product is superb. The dish is great served fresh from the oven, or it may be frozen and reheated for a quick weeknight meal, says Chronicle *writer Tara Duggan.*

Vegetables

7 pounds butternut squash

4 tablespoons olive oil

Salt and freshly ground pepper, to taste

4 onions, thinly sliced

8 garlic cloves, minced

1 tablespoon fresh thyme leaves, finely minced

Lentils

2¼ cups French green lentils (see Note)

2 celery stalks, halved

1 carrot, peeled and halved

1 onion, halved

1 bay leaf

1 teaspoon salt

18 sheets lasagna (about 1 pound)

Béchamel Sauce (recipe follows)

1½ cups grated Parmigiano-Reggiano cheese

◔◔ To make the vegetables: Preheat the oven to 375 degrees. Line large baking sheets with foil or parchment paper.

Halve the butternut squash. Discard seeds. Brush the exposed halves with 2 tablespoons of the olive oil and season with salt and pepper.

Place the squash halves cut-sides up on the baking sheets. Bake for about 30 minutes, or until the thickest part of the squash is tender when pierced with the tip of a sharp knife. Do not let them get completely soft. Remove from oven and let cool.

How to Cook Legumes

Here are the basic instructions from Laxmi Hiremath for cooking legumes used in sambars and rasams, the homey lentil soups of Southern India.

Pink lentils: For ½ cup, use 1¼ cups water. Simmer for 20 minutes. Yields approximately 1 cup.

Split peas and yellow lentils (toor dal): For 1 cup, use 2 cups water. Simmer for 30 minutes. Yields approximately 2½ cups.

Yellow mung beans (mung dal): For ¼ cup, use 1 cup water. Simmer for 20 minutes. Yields approximately 1 cup.

When cool, scoop out the flesh into a bowl. Break into small pieces and season with salt and pepper.

Heat the remaining 2 tablespoons olive oil in a large nonstick sauté pan over medium-high heat. Add the onions and cook, stirring often, for about 10 minutes. Add the garlic and thyme and continue to cook for 15 to 20 minutes, or until the onions are golden brown and very sweet.

To make the lentils: While the squash is roasting, place the lentils in a small saucepan with the celery, carrot, onion, bay leaf and salt. Add enough water to cover the vegetables completely. Bring to a boil over high heat, reduce heat to low and simmer for 15 to 20 minutes, or until the lentils are completely tender. Remove the vegetables and bay leaf, strain out any liquid and adjust the seasonings as needed.

Bring a large pot of salted water to a boil over high heat and cook the lasagna noodles for about 8 minutes, or until al dente. Drain, then spread out to dry on a baking sheet so the noodles won't stick to each other.

Reduce the oven temperature to 350 degrees.

Mix together the squash, lentils, caramelized onions and half of the béchamel sauce in a bowl. Divide this mixture into 3 equal parts. Spread one third of the vegetable mixture in an oversized lasagna pan (or use an 8-by-8-inch pan plus a 9-by-13-inch pan). Sprinkle with ⅓ cup of the cheese. Cover with a layer of lasagna noodles. Trim noodles as needed.

Repeat layers two more times. Spread the remaining béchamel over the last pasta layer. Sprinkle with the remaining cheese. Bake for 20 to 25 minutes, or until heated through and golden brown on top.

Let rest for 10 minutes, then cut and serve.

SERVES 12

NOTE: French green lentils are available in upscale supermarkets and specialty stores. Do not substitute any other lentils, which become mushy when cooked.

Béchamel Sauce

This recipe makes just enough sauce for the Lentil and Squash Lasagna.

1 bay leaf
½ onion
1 whole clove
6 cups milk
6 tablespoons butter
7 tablespoons all-purpose flour
Pinch of nutmeg
Salt and freshly ground white pepper, to taste

☙ Place the bay leaf on the outside of the onion half, then pierce it with the clove to attach. Add this piquet and the milk to a small saucepan. Simmer over medium-low heat for 20 minutes.

Meanwhile, make the roux. Melt the butter in a heavy-bottom sauté pan over low heat. Slowly incorporate the flour, stirring constantly. Continue cooking, stirring constantly, for 4 to 5 minutes. Remove from heat. Strain the milk and discard the onion piquet.

Whisk the milk into the roux a little at a time. Bring to a simmer, reduce heat to very low and cook, stirring often, for 15 minutes. Stir in the nutmeg and season with salt and white pepper.

Chapter 6

Vegetables

California cooks have access to some of the best specialty produce in the world, but on a day-to-day basis, we still eat a lot of broccoli, cauliflower and zucchini, just like the rest of the country.

However, creative cooks have discovered ways to coax the best out of everything. For example, who would have thought zucchini could be sexy? It takes on a sophisticated aura when cooked Mediterranean-style with olives and lemon (page 209). You'll feel like you've tasted it for the first time when it's served raw in a refreshing pairing with apples and mint (page 210), and it lends a juicy wholesomeness to a rich casserole with a corn and basil sauce under a bubbling blanket of cheese (page 211).

We'll also show you how to add extra zest to sweet potatoes, which have been forever slandered by their association with marshmallows at Thanksgiving. They take on a unique dimension when matched with smoky chipotles in a gratin (page 205), or paired with roasted red pepper, lime and chiles (page 204) in a flavored butter that helps to balance the inherent sweetness of this tuber.

We also offer a timesaving technique that allows the busy cook to partly cook marinated vegetables ahead of time (page 212). Just before serving, you can toss them on an outdoor grill or stovetop grill pan. Savvy hosts will serve them at dinner parties and cocktail gatherings, either warm or at room temperature. This ease of preparation and versatility make them ideal for a picnic, too.

Vegetable gratins are another way to give common ingredients a starring role. We include some with potatoes and mushrooms (page 201) and butternut squash (page 207).

You'll discover uncommon ways to cook just about every common vegetable. And not one of them is boring.

Asparagus, Artichokes and Peas

Two of our favorite ingredients, asparagus and artichokes, are combined with sweet English peas in this simple vegetable dish by Marlena Spieler. It's equally good served warm or at room temperature.

1 to 1½ pounds thin asparagus, tough ends snapped off

2 tablespoons olive oil, or as needed

8 to 10 small artichoke hearts, fresh and blanched, or frozen

1 cup peas (frozen OK)

1 garlic clove, chopped

Salt and freshly ground pepper, to taste

Pinch of sugar

1 teaspoon chopped fresh marjoram, or 1 tablespoon chopped basil

◉◉ Bring a pot of salted water to a boil over high heat. Add the asparagus and cook for about 2 minutes, or until it is crisp-tender and bright green. Drain.

Heat the olive oil in a sauté pan over medium-high heat. Add the artichoke hearts, peas and garlic. Cook for about 5 minutes, then add the asparagus and warm through. Season with salt, pepper, sugar and marjoram.

SERVES 4

Asparagus with Pesto

Toss asparagus with pesto, to taste, a little olive oil and minced garlic. Grill over hot coals until the asparagus is lightly charred. Serve as is, or toss with more pesto.

Green Bean Gremolata

Still-crunchy green beans, cooled to room temperature, are bursting with flavor, thanks to an easy topping of lemon zest, parsley and Parmigiano-Reggiano cheese. This creation is by Kirk Webber of Cafe Kati in San Francisco.

½ pound green beans

2 tablespoons extra virgin olive oil

1 tablespoon minced garlic

Zest of 2 lemons

½ bunch Italian parsley, leaves only, chopped

2 tablespoons freshly grated Parmigiano-Reggiano cheese

½ teaspoon salt

¼ teaspoon freshly ground pepper

Bring a pot of salted water to a boil over high heat. Add the green beans and cook for 1 minute; drain and plunge into ice water. Drain well. Transfer to a heated serving bowl.

Heat the olive oil in a sauté pan over medium-high heat. Add the garlic and sauté, stirring constantly, for 3 to 5 minutes, or until very fragrant and cooked through. Do not let it brown. Pour over the beans and toss to combine. Add the lemon zest, parsley, cheese, salt and pepper and toss again.

Serve warm or at room temperature.

SERVES 2

Swiss Chard with Peppers and Walnuts

The triad of flavors in this recipe by Sharon Cadwallader is superb, plus the dish is easy and may be made ahead.

> 3 large bunches Swiss chard, about 1½ pounds total
>
> 4 tablespoons olive oil
>
> 2 red bell peppers, stemmed, seeded, deribbed and coarsely chopped
>
> 1 cup finely chopped green onion (white part only)
>
> 1 cup chicken or vegetable broth
>
> 1 to 2 tablespoons balsamic vinegar
>
> 1 cup coarsely chopped walnuts
>
> Salt and freshly ground pepper, to taste

Wash the chard well and dry. Trim off any tough ends, then chop coarsely.

Heat 2 tablespoons of the olive oil in a large nonstick skillet over medium-high heat. Add the peppers and green onion and sauté for 2 minutes.

Add the remaining oil and the chard; sauté for 6 to 8 minutes. Add the broth and simmer until the chard is tender and the broth has cooked away (pour off any excess liquid). Sprinkle with vinegar and toss with the nuts. Season lightly with salt and pepper.

Serve at room temperature.

SERVES 6

Mediterranean-Style Marinated Red Beets

The intriguing combination of coriander, cumin and tarragon brings out the best in beets in this lemon and olive oil–based dressing created by Hoss Zare of Zare restaurant in San Francisco.

2 garlic cloves

1 shallot

⅓ cup fresh lemon juice

¾ teaspoon cumin seed, toasted and ground

¼ teaspoon toasted and ground coriander

½ teaspoon turmeric

¼ cup chopped fresh tarragon

½ teaspoon salt

½ teaspoon freshly ground pepper

2 tablespoons honey

1 cup extra virgin olive oil

6 red beets, about 8 ounces each

Finely chop the garlic and shallot in a blender. Add the lemon juice, cumin, coriander, turmeric, tarragon, salt, pepper and honey. Process until well blended. With the motor running, start adding the olive oil very slowly. (To keep the mixture from breaking, add the oil slowly at first and wait until it is fully incorporated before adding more. This process is similar to making mayonnaise.) Once all the oil is incorporated, set the dressing aside.

Bring a pot of salted water to a boil over high heat. Peel the beets and cut into ¼- to ½-inch slices, then into cubes. Add to the boiling water and cook for 10 minutes, or until the beets are just tender. Drain and plunge into ice water to stop the cooking. Drain well.

Transfer the beets to a bowl, add the dressing and toss gently.

The beets may be served immediately, but for the best flavor, cover and marinate for up to 24 hours before serving. Refrigerate the beets if you plan to marinate them longer than 1 hour.

SERVES 6

Brussels Sprouts with Toasted Hazelnut Butter

Marlena Spieler serves these every Thanksgiving. After years of struggling to keep the sprouts hot until serving time, she discovered that she likes them even better at room temperature.

2 pounds Brussels sprouts, trimmed

Pinch of salt, plus more, to taste

Pinch of sugar

⅔ cup hazelnuts

½ cup unsalted butter

Freshly ground pepper, to taste

∞ Cut an "X" in the bottom of each sprout. Bring a pot of water to a boil over high heat. Add a pinch each of salt and sugar, then add the sprouts and cook for 5 to 6 minutes, or until just tender and bright green. Drain and set aside. They will continue to cook a bit from their internal heat, so do not overcook.

Toast the hazelnuts in a heavy dry skillet over medium heat, tossing every so often so they don't burn (or toast them in a 400-degree oven for about 10 minutes). You want them to have some brown spots fairly evenly placed. The skins will begin to shrink and pull away. Remove from the heat and pour into a clean towel. Placing your hands outside the towel, vigorously rub the nuts together to remove the skins. Coarsely chop the hazelnuts.

Place a heavy skillet over medium-high heat. When hot, add the butter. Reduce heat to medium or medium-low so the butter will gently brown and take on a nutlike aroma and flavor. Be careful it does not burn.

Toss the sprouts with the browned butter and the hazelnuts, shaking to coat well. Season with salt and pepper.

SERVES 4 TO 6

Braised Cucumbers in Dill

Here's a quick recipe for using cucumbers from Georgeanne Brennan. Peel and halve cucumbers lengthwise, scrape out the seeds with a spoon and cut cucumbers into thin half-moon slices. Sauté in a little butter over medium-high heat for 1 minute. Add a little chicken broth and cook for 2 to 3 minutes longer or until the stock forms a glaze on the cucumbers. Sprinkle with chopped dill and serve warm.

Belgian Endive with Prosciutto

Sweet-salty prosciutto and a creamy sauce make a fetching counterpoint to the slightly bitter taste of Belgian endive in this recipe by Georgeanne Brennan. The dish is baked in a casserole until the endive nearly melts under the seductive brown, bubbly crust.

8 heads Belgian endive

3½ tablespoons butter

3 tablespoons all-purpose flour

½ teaspoon salt, or to taste

¼ teaspoon freshly grated nutmeg

⅛ teaspoon cayenne pepper

1 cup milk

¼ cup freshly grated Parmigiano-Reggiano cheese

4 ounces thinly sliced prosciutto

2 tablespoons grated Swiss cheese

½ tablespoon freshly ground pepper, or to taste

◉◉ Preheat the oven to 375 degrees.

Using a small, sharp knife, cut out the inverted V-shaped cores of the Belgian endive by cutting around at the base. Set the cored endive aside.

To make the sauce, melt 2 tablespoons of the butter in a saucepan over medium heat. When the butter begins to foam, remove the pan from the heat and whisk in the flour, salt, nutmeg and cayenne pepper until a paste forms. Return the pan to medium heat and gradually whisk in the milk in a steady stream. Reduce the heat to low and stir until there are no lumps. Simmer, stirring occasionally, for about 15 minutes, or until the sauce is thick enough to coat the back of a spoon and has lost the taste of flour.

Stir in the Parmigiano-Reggiano cheese and continue to cook for 2 to 3 minutes, or until the cheese has just melted into the sauce. Taste and adjust seasonings with salt, if needed.

Using ½ tablespoon of the butter, grease the bottom and sides of a shallow ovenproof casserole just large enough to hold the endive snugly. Arrange the endive in the casserole and top with the slivers of prosciutto. Pour the sauce over the top. Cut the remaining 1 tablespoon butter into small bits and dot the surface, then strew the Swiss cheese over the top.

Bake for 25 to 30 minutes, or until the endive is completely tender and the surface has formed a bubbly, slightly golden crust.

Season with pepper and serve hot.

SERVES 4 TO 6

Cauliflower in the Style of Puebla

This spicy rendition of cauliflower is a favorite of Jacqueline McMahan.

1 head cauliflower, trimmed

2 tablespoons olive oil

1 cup chopped onion

3 tomatoes, peeled, seeded and chopped

2 garlic cloves, minced

1 jalapeño chile, seeded and minced

2 whole cloves

1 cinnamon stick

2 bay leaves

Topping

2 tablespoons chopped Italian parsley

1 garlic clove, minced

¾ cup coarse breadcrumbs (see Note)

¼ cup grated Asiago cheese

Preheat the oven to 350 degrees.

Place the cauliflower in a steamer insert above a pot of simmering water. Cover and steam for 8 minutes, or until just barely tender. Separate into small florets.

Heat the olive oil in a skillet over medium-low heat. Add the onion and sauté, stirring frequently, for about 10 minutes, or until golden. Stir in the tomatoes, cook for 1 minute, then add the garlic, chile, cloves, cinnamon and bay leaves. Simmer for 10 minutes. Discard the cloves, cinnamon stick and bay leaves.

Place half of the sauce in a 9-by-13-inch baking dish. Arrange the cauliflower on top. Pour the remaining sauce over the cauliflower.

To make the topping: Mix together the parsley, garlic and breadcrumbs in a bowl; sprinkle over the cauliflower and sauce. Scatter the cheese over the top.

Bake for 10 to 15 minutes, or until the cauliflower is hot and the topping is golden.

SERVES 4 TO 6

NOTE: Make coarse, fluffy breadcrumbs from French or Italian bread that is 2 to 3 days old but not completely dried out. Place small pieces of bread, crusts removed, in a food processor. Process just until you have coarse yet fluffy crumbs.

Toasting Breadcrumbs

A slice of bread will yield about ⅓ cup crumbs. Tear the bread into pieces and put in a blender or food processor. Pulse several times to make the crumbs. To toast, spread the crumbs on a baking sheet and put in a 250-degree oven for about 10 minutes, or until golden.

Fennel Choucroute

After baking for 2 hours, julienned fennel soaks up the rich flavors of saffron, honey, orange and Pernod in this unusual dish from Donia Bijan of L'Amie Donia in Palo Alto. It's an ideal accompaniment to sausages, ham, pork chops or duck breast.

6 smoky bacon slices

1 large white onion, halved and thinly sliced

Olive oil

6 fennel bulbs, trimmed and cut into fine julienne

Zest of 2 oranges

6 thyme sprigs

¼ teaspoon saffron threads

¾ cup honey

2 cups fresh orange juice

¼ cup Pernod

Salt and freshly ground pepper, to taste

◉◉ Preheat the oven to 350 degrees.

Cut 2 of the bacon slices into ¼-inch strips. Cook gently in a Dutch oven over medium-low heat until the fat renders out. Add the onion and a drizzle of olive oil and sauté for about 10 minutes, or until soft and translucent.

Add the fennel, orange zest, thyme, saffron and honey. Stir with a wooden spoon until the fennel begins to soften. Stir in the orange juice and Pernod and season with salt and pepper. Using the back of the spoon, pat the fennel down to make the surface even. Arrange the remaining 4 bacon slices over the top, and cover with foil or a lid.

Bake for 2 hours. The fennel will be tender, very aromatic and should melt in your mouth. Remove the bacon strips before serving.

This dish may be made ahead. Store in a covered container in the refrigerator and reheat before serving.

SERVES 6 TO 8

Charred Corn with Chile Butter

This is the perfect vegetable for the outdoor grilling season. Everyone garnishes their corn by pulling back the husks, drizzling on some crema, and sprinkling on crumbled queso cotija, a Mexican cheese (see Note). This simple recipe was created by Jacqueline McMahan.

½ cup butter

3 garlic cloves

2 teaspoons ground New Mexican chile, such as Dixon

2 to 3 soft chipotle chiles (dried or en adobo)

8 ears of white or yellow corn, with husks intact

1 cup Mexican crema

1 cup finely crumbled queso cotija (see Note)

Prepare a medium-hot wood or mesquite fire in an outdoor grill.

Meanwhile, combine the butter, garlic, ground chile and chipotles in a food processor and blend just to combine. Set aside.

Carefully peel back the corn husks so you don't tear them. Remove all of the silks but keep the husks intact. Rub about ¾ tablespoon of the chile butter over the kernels of each ear, then pull up the husks, smoothing them over the ears.

Grill the ears, turning frequently, for about 15 minutes. The husks will char and smoke a bit, lending even more flavor to the corn.

Pass the crema and cheese at the table.

SERVES 8

NOTE: Queso cotija, sold in Mexican markets, comes in small, firm rounds. It is not a melting cheese but is crumbly. Sprinkle over corn, tacos, enchiladas, salads and such. It is fairly salty, so use sparingly. In a pinch, feta may be substituted.

BEST WAY:
Cooking Corn

Boiling is probably the most popular way to cook corn, but some cooks swear that steaming or microwaving yields the best results.

To determine which method is best, we cooked fresh corn 10 ways. We tested not only the cooking methods, but also when to add salt (or sugar) and whether leaving the corn in the husk during cooking had any benefit. It didn't.

No one in the Food Department liked the microwaved version, and some liked the boiled version, but the clear winner was the steamed corn. Not only did steaming produce a bright color,

Corn Pudding

Here's a quick and easy vegetable casserole by Jacqueline McMahan. It was one of her father's favorite dishes, and she remembers making it on his 80th birthday.

12 ears of fresh corn

2 tablespoons butter

½ teaspoon salt

1 teaspoon sugar

½ cup whipping cream

2 green Anaheim chiles, charred, peeled and seeded

∞ Preheat the oven to 350 degrees.

Remove the kernels of corn by using a corn grater or by rubbing the ears against the large holes of a box grater. Do this over a big bowl to catch all the juices.

Melt the butter in a shallow 2-quart casserole dish. Add the grated corn, corn juices, salt, sugar and cream. Blend together. Cut the chiles into strips and poke them into the corn. Cover with foil or a tight-fitting lid.

Bake for 25 minutes, checking at least once to make sure the corn stays creamy. Add a little more cream if the dish starts to dry out.

SERVES 6 TO 8

it also enhanced the sweet corn flavor. Since the corn was cooked in only an inch of boiling water, it took less time than the more traditional way of boiling corn in water to cover.

Here's how to steam corn:

Remove the husks and silks from the ears of corn. Fill a large pot with 1 inch of cold water. Place the pot over high heat and bring the water to a rapid boil. Place the corn in the pot, stacking the ears on top of each other, if necessary. Cover the pot with a tight-fitting lid and steam over high heat for 7 minutes. Remove the corn from the pot and serve. Add butter and salt, if you like.

A Guide to Asian Vegetables

Asian eggplant: This sleek, slender variety comes in shades ranging from amethyst to deep purple to nearly black. More delicate-tasting than the common globe eggplant, it requires less cooking time.

The Asian variety doesn't need to be peeled. It's great in stir-fries, stews and curries. One of the best ways to cook Asian eggplant is to steam or grill, either whole or sliced, then drizzle with Vietnamese dipping sauce and scallion oil.

Bitter melon: Called *fu gwa* in Chinese and *kho qua* in Vietnamese, bitter melon resembles a small cucumber covered with smooth bumps and ranges from pale to deep green. It's extremely bitter but quite delicious. In Asia, it's believed to purify the food and is often served to expectant moms. Markets usually sell bitter melons 8 to 10 inches long, but they're sometimes available much smaller. Smaller ones are better for stuffing.

To stuff, cut a long slit, spoon out the seeds and fill with a meat mixture. To stir-fry, halve the melons, remove the seeds and cut into thin slices.

If you want to reduce the bitterness, choose melons that are pale green rather than dark green and scrape off the white membrane inside. Salting them before cooking also helps.

Bottle gourd: Also called *po qwa* in Chinese and *trai bau* in Vietnamese, this vegetable tastes like summer squashes. The elongated pear-shaped fruit is usually sold when it's about 12 inches long. It has thick, light-green skin with soft white flesh.

To use, peel and cut into pieces. This vegetable is amenable to all types of cooking—steaming, braising, stir-frying and stewing. Undercook it a tad to retain its delicate flavor.

Chayote: In Asia, this pear-shaped vegetable often is covered with tiny thorns, which makes peeling a little tricky. But the variety sold in this country has smooth, pale-green skin. Chayote tastes like squash but is more delicate and firm. It's excellent steamed or used in stir-fries, soups, stews and casseroles. The flavor is better if the vegetable is cooled a bit before serving.

Chinese mustard: Called *gai choy* in Chinese, this mustard cabbage is highly nutritious. Though the whole cabbage can be eaten, some Chinese restaurants serve only the crunchy stems. To distinguish *gai choy* from other leafy varieties such as bok choy and *choy sum*, look for the thick, almost knobby stem and the semi-closed head. Other varieties have straight stems. Chinese mustard is great in stir-fries and soups.

Chrysanthemum: Called *tong ho* in Chinese and *tan o* in Vietnamese, edible chrysanthemum leaves resemble the common flower-garden type but are a different variety. They quickly wilt when cooked, much like spinach, but the delightful floral-mustard flavor sets them apart. They're best in soups or simply steamed. If you're lucky enough to find very fresh young leaves, try tossing a few into a salad.

Long beans: Also called *dau dua* or "chopstick beans" in Vietnamese and *dow gok* in Chinese, these beans—which grow as long as 3 feet—are available in three varieties: pale green, dark green and sometimes dark purple. Dark green are the best, and only buy them if they're young and slender, no thicker than chopsticks.

Cut into 3- to 4-inch pieces (not shorter, because they are long beans) and blanch them before tossing into stir-fries. They can withstand longer cooking than most green beans without getting mushy, and longer cooking imparts a deeper flavor. Long beans are also great in salads and stews.

Luffa squash: A cross between a squash and okra, luffa has a delightful earthiness. Also called *sze qwa* in Chinese and *muop* in Vietnamese, luffa is an elongated, often slightly curved vegetable with thick, dark-green skin and narrow ridges running its entire length. To uncover the delicious flesh, first peel the tough ridges, then the whole squash. The tender flesh takes well to sauces, so it's wonderful in stir-fries and soups. Roll-cuts are best because of the vegetable's soft, spongy texture.

Taro: This prized starchy root shows up at the produce section in two varieties: small (the size and shape of an egg) and a large variety measuring up to 7 inches in diameter. Both are protected by brown, shaggy skin. The small taro has soft, almost mushy light-purple flesh, while the large has dense, whitish flesh with purple or reddish veins. Similar to potato, taro has a distinctively delicate nuttiness.

Small taro may be steamed or boiled whole, then added to soups, stuffings and stews. Peel and slice the large variety before cooking. When making curries, add taro toward the end so it doesn't overcook and thicken the entire dish.

Water spinach: Called *ong choy* in Chinese, *rau muon* in Vietnamese and *pak boong* in Thai, this vegetable is beloved in much of China and Southeast Asia. The stems and leaves are simply steamed and dipped in sauces or added to stir-fries and soups. The Vietnamese shred the hollow, crunchy (and oftentimes tough) stems into thin slivers. Once soaked in water, the feathery slivers curl and crisp and are wonderful additions to salads.

Grilled Asian Eggplant with Chile-Lime Sauce and Scallion Oil

Peeling grilled or broiled eggplants can be a little messy, but it's worth the effort, promises Mai Pham. This method adds a deliciously smoky quality to the flesh, which is accented with a sweet-sour chile sauce and scallion-scented oil.

Chile Sauce

1 garlic clove, minced

2 or 3 Thai bird chiles, or 1 serrano, finely chopped

2 tablespoons sugar

3 tablespoons Asian fish sauce

2 tablespoons fresh lime juice

2 tablespoons water

Scallion Oil

3 tablespoons vegetable oil

3 scallions, cut into thin rings

1½ pounds Asian eggplants

Prepare a medium-hot fire in an outdoor grill, or preheat the broiler.

To make the chile sauce: Combine the garlic, chiles, sugar, fish sauce, lime juice and water in a small bowl; stir well to blend. Set aside.

To make the scallion oil: Heat the oil in a small saucepan over medium heat. Add the scallions and stir for about 20 seconds, or until they turn bright green and fragrant. Immediately transfer to a bowl. Set aside to cool.

Grill or broil the eggplants, turning from time to time, for 15 to 20 minutes, or until they are just tender.

When cool enough to handle, use a fork to peel off the charred skins. Arrange the eggplants on a platter and drizzle the chile sauce and scallion oil over them.

SERVES 4

Asian Greens with Garlic

Blanching is the key to this delicious recipe by Mai Pham. This allows the greens to be cooked quickly, before they turn soggy and lose their flavor. When stir-frying the greens, make sure the pan is hot and use lots of garlic. The recipe works with any leafy green, including gai lan *(Chinese broccoli),* gai choy *(Chinese mustard) and* ong choy *(water spinach).*

⅔ pound Chinese mustard or other Asian greens

2 tablespoons vegetable oil

2 garlic cloves, sliced

1 tablespoon oyster sauce

2 to 3 tablespoons chicken broth or water

Pinch of salt

⊚⊚ Separate the stems from the mustard greens and cut the greens on the diagonal into ⅔-inch-thick slices. Bring a large pot of water to a boil over high heat. Blanch the greens in the water for about 20 seconds, or until the leaves just wilt and turn bright green. Drain and set aside.

Heat the oil in a large skillet over high heat. Working quickly, add the garlic and stir for about 20 seconds, or until fragrant. Add the mustard greens, oyster sauce and broth. Cook, stirring, for 1 to 2 minutes, or until the vegetables are done but still green and crunchy. Transfer to a serving plate. Season with salt.

SERVES 4

Sauté of Summer Greens

The earthiness of greens is tempered by toasted pine nuts, capers and currants in this recipe from Heidi Krahling of Insalata's restaurant in San Anselmo. Anchovies and garlic add a depth of flavor but do not overpower the dish. This may be served as a side dish, or spooned on toasted or grilled bread for a wonderful appetizer.

4 pounds baby kale, escarole or Swiss chard

4 tablespoons extra virgin olive oil

2 garlic cloves, peeled and lightly crushed

6 anchovy fillets, finely chopped

1 tablespoon capers (preferably salted), rinsed and drained

½ cup currants, soaked in warm water and drained

½ cup toasted pine nuts

Zest of 3 lemons, finely chopped

Salt and freshly ground pepper, to taste

◉◉ Wash the greens and remove stems, stalks and tough leaves. Bring a large saucepan of water to a boil over high heat. Add the greens and simmer until tender. Drain and refresh in cold water. Drain again. Squeeze out the water and chop coarsely if serving greens as a side dish, or chop finely if serving greens on toast as an appetizer.

Heat the olive oil in a large skillet over medium-high heat. Add the garlic and sauté until lightly browned. Discard the garlic.

Add the greens and stir for 1 minute to evaporate excess moisture. Add the anchovies and capers and cook, stirring, for 30 seconds.

Transfer mixture to a bowl and let cool. Stir in the currants, pine nuts, lemon zest, salt and pepper.

Serve warm or at room temperature.

SERVES 4

Spicy Asian Pan-Fried Okra

Even those who dislike okra might change their minds once they try this dish from Arnold Wong of Eos Restaurant & Wine Bar in San Francisco. The vegetable takes on a silken texture when cooked in this spicy Asian-inspired sauce.

Sauce

¾ cup soy sauce

½ cup oyster sauce

2 tablespoons Asian fish sauce

¼ cup white rice vinegar, or distilled vinegar

¼ cup dry sherry

¼ cup light brown sugar

¼ cup honey

½ bunch basil, leaves only, finely minced

¼ bunch mint, leaves only, finely minced

⅓ bunch cilantro, finely minced

3 serrano chiles, seeded and finely minced

1 tablespoon finely minced garlic

1 tablespoon finely minced fresh ginger

1½ tablespoons Asian chile sauce

Zest of 1 lime, finely minced

Juice of 3 limes

½ tablespoon freshly ground pepper

2 teaspoons hot red pepper flakes

3 pounds young okra

⅔ cup canola or other light-tasting oil, plus more if needed

3 plum tomatoes, thinly sliced, for garnish

1 bunch scallions, thinly sliced on the diagonal, for garnish

◙◙ To make the sauce: Combine all the sauce ingredients in a bowl and whisk to combine. There should be about 3 cups. (You will need only half of the sauce for this recipe. Store the remainder in a covered container in the refrigerator for up to 1 week. May be used in other vegetable stir-frys.)

Wash the okra and trim a little off the stem tips. Split each pod lengthwise.

Heat the oil in a wok or a large skillet over high heat until it just begins to smoke.

Add the okra and stir-fry for 5 to 7 minutes, tossing until the cut sides begin to color slightly. Add more oil if necessary while frying. Remove the okra to a sieve; drain off oil in the pan.

Return the okra to the pan. Add 1½ cups of the sauce and cook, stirring and tossing, for about 5 minutes, or until the okra is coated with sauce and the sauce has begun to thicken and caramelize slightly.

Transfer to a serving bowl and garnish with the tomatoes and scallions. Serve hot, warm or at room temperature.

SERVES 6

Potato and Wild Mushroom Gratin

This potato gratin makes the perfect accompaniment to a roast chicken or even turkey, says Marlena Spieler.

3 pounds potatoes, peeled and thinly sliced

¼ ounce dried cepes or porcini, broken into tiny pieces

10 shallots, chopped

3 garlic cloves, chopped

3 to 4 tablespoons butter, cut into small bits

Salt and freshly ground pepper, to taste

1 cup whipping cream

Put the potatoes in a large container and add cold water to cover. Let stand for at least 30 minutes. Drain well and pat dry. (You may omit this step, but soaking the potatoes makes the gratin lighter and finer.)

Preheat the oven to 350 degrees.

Butter a gratin dish large enough to hold all of the potatoes, then layer in the potatoes, dried mushrooms, shallots, garlic and butter, seasoning each layer with salt and pepper. Top the gratin with the last bits of butter.

Pour the cream over all, then bake the gratin for about 1 hour, or until the potatoes are golden brown on top and tender when pierced with a sharp knife.

SERVES 4

Zarzuela's Patatas al Ajillo (Potatoes with Garlic)

Hot cubes of fried potatoes are doused in a wonderful garlic sauce in this recipe from Zarzuela restaurant in San Francisco. Serve it as a tapa with a fino sherry, or as a side dish with roasted or grilled meats.

Peanut oil for deep-frying

3 large baking potatoes, peeled and cut into 1-inch cubes

Coarse salt, to taste

1½ tablespoons olive oil

3 garlic cloves, minced

Pinch of crushed hot red pepper flakes

½ teaspoon chopped Italian parsley

3 tablespoons sherry vinegar

๑๑ Pour ½ inch of the peanut oil into a deep, heavy saucepan over high heat; heat to 350 to 375 degrees. Add the potatoes and cook for 3 to 4 minutes, or until tender. Remove the potatoes with a slotted spoon to paper towels to drain briefly. Transfer to a serving plate and season with salt.

Heat the olive oil in a large skillet over medium-low heat. Add the garlic and stir for about 30 seconds, or until soft. Add the pepper flakes and stir together. Remove from heat and stir in the parsley and sherry vinegar. Pour over the potatoes and serve immediately.

SERVES 8 AS A TAPA

BEST WAY:
Mashed Potatoes

It took two days and 25 pounds of potatoes to come up with the formula for the perfect mashed potatoes. We tried mashing by hand, in a mixer, food mill and food processor. We tried different amounts of butter and cream. We salted at the start, middle and end, and we tried different cooking methods. Ultimately, the hand-mashed version won. Here's the recipe:

The Best Mashed Potatoes

1 pound russet potatoes (about 2 potatoes)
1 teaspoon salt, plus more, to taste
¼ cup whipping cream
2 tablespoons butter

๑๑ Peel the potatoes and cut into eighths. Put in a large pot and cover with cold water. Add 1 teaspoon salt and bring to a simmer over medium-high heat. Simmer for about 7 minutes, or until the potatoes are cooked through. Drain the potatoes in a large colander and shake to remove excess moisture.

Meanwhile, warm the cream in a saucepan over low heat. Or pour the cream into a microwave-safe container and microwave for 30 seconds.

Transfer the potatoes to a large bowl and mash with a handheld potato masher until they reach the texture you like. Stir in the butter and cream and adjust the seasoning with salt.

SERVES 4

NOTE: To reheat mashed potatoes, place in a microwave-safe bowl, cover with plastic wrap and microwave on high for 2 minutes, or until heated through.

Herb-Rubbed Oven Fries

These roasted potatoes from Georgeanne Brennan are crisp and delicious. They may be finished with a drizzle of fragrant olive oil.

1 cup Italian parsley leaves

¼ cup fresh sage leaves

¼ cup fresh marjoram or oregano leaves

¼ cup fresh thyme leaves

4 russet potatoes, cut lengthwise into ½-inch-wide pieces

2 tablespoons olive oil

1 teaspoon salt

1 teaspoon freshly ground pepper

⊚⊚ Preheat the oven to 350 degrees.

Combine the parsley, sage, marjoram and thyme in a blender or food processor and mince them.

Place the potatoes on a baking sheet and rub them with the olive oil, salt and pepper. Add the herbs, turning the potatoes to coat them with the mixture. Not all of the herbs will stick, but the remaining ones will stay on the baking sheet to flavor the potatoes as they cook.

Bake, turning the potatoes occasionally, for about 45 minutes, or until they are crisp on the outside and tender when pierced with the tip of a sharp knife.

SERVES 4

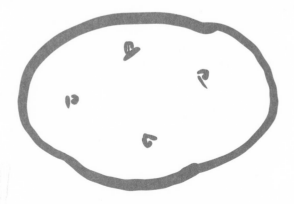

Roasted Sweet Potatoes with Red Pepper-Chile-Lime Butter

The addition of spicy chile and acidic lime gives sweet potatoes a whole new appeal. Created by Marlena Spieler, these are a great alternative to the traditional Thanksgiving side dish topped with marshmallows. They're also particularly good with roast chicken or duck.

4 sweet potatoes, preferably red-orange fleshed and narrow in width

1 roasted red bell pepper, peeled, seeded, deribbed and diced (roast your own or use a jarred one)

4 garlic cloves, chopped

1 to 2 tablespoons extra virgin olive oil

1 teaspoon mild chile powder, such as ancho, New Mexico, California or pasilla

¼ teaspoon ground cumin, or to taste

½ cup unsalted butter at room temperature

Salt, to taste

Fresh lime juice, to taste

◉◉ Preheat the oven to 400 degrees.

Put the sweet potatoes on a baking sheet and roast for about 40 minutes, or until they are just tender.

Meanwhile, mix the roasted pepper with the garlic, olive oil, chile powder and cumin in a bowl, then work the mixture into the softened butter. Season with salt and lime juice. Transfer the butter to a small bowl or crock. (If made ahead, transfer to a piece of plastic wrap, roll it into a log and refrigerate until chilled; cut into slices to serve.)

When the sweet potatoes are done, peel and cut into thick slices. Pile the potatoes into a warmed serving bowl. Pass the seasoned butter at the table.

SERVES 4 TO 6

Sweet Potato Gratin with Chipotles

Here, sweet potatoes are paired with chipotle, which adds a smoky, spicy edge to the dish. Even though this recipe calls for a whopping amount of cream, it is worth every gram of fat. Jacqueline McMahan guarantees it.

1½ tablespoons butter at room temperature

2 to 3 tablespoons puréed canned chipotle chiles en adobo

4 cups whipping cream

8 large sweet potatoes, peeled and thinly sliced (about 8 cups)

Salt and freshly ground pepper, to taste

Preheat the oven to 350 degrees.

Rub the butter over the inside of a shallow 4-quart casserole. (It must be shallow so the cream can reduce and turn golden and crusty.) Stir the puréed chipotles into the cream.

Bring a large pot of water to a boil over high heat. Add the sweet potato slices and cook for 15 minutes. Drain well.

Arrange a single layer of sweet potatoes in the casserole; pour 1 cup of the chile-cream over them. Season with salt and pepper. Repeat layering, ending with chile-cream.

Bake for 45 minutes to 1 hour, or until the potatoes are lightly browned and bubbling.

Serve warm.

SERVES 8

Steamed New Potatoes with Lemon-Caper Sauce

Here's another idea for potatoes from Georgeanne Brennan: Steam new potatoes in their jackets for 10 to 15 minutes, or until just done. Melt a nubbin or so of butter in a saucepan; add the juice of half a lemon and a tablespoon of capers. Pour over the potatoes.

Roasted New Potatoes with Sage

Rub largish new potatoes with olive oil, suggests Georgeanne Brennan, then sprinkle generously with salt and pepper. Pack snugly in a baking dish and stick sprigs and leaves of sage between them. Roast in a 350-degree oven for 45 minutes to 1 hour, or until the outsides are crisp and the insides are creamy.

Braised Garden Spinach

Here's a simple and absolutely superb way to cook spinach, compliments of Georgeanne Brennan.

1½ teaspoons salt

6 bunches fresh spinach, washed and stemmed

¼ cup olive oil

3 garlic cloves

½ teaspoon freshly ground pepper

Juice of 1 lemon

◈◈ Bring a large pot of water to a boil over high heat and add 1 teaspoon of the salt. Add the spinach, pushing the leaves under the water with a wooden spoon. It may seem like the spinach won't fit, but the leaves cook down quickly. Cook for about 2 minutes, or until the leaves are wilted but still bright green. Drain, then rinse the leaves under cold water. Squeeze them dry with your hands.

Heat the olive oil with the garlic in a large skillet over medium heat. When it is hot, add the spinach, the remaining ½ teaspoon salt and the pepper. Reduce the heat to low and cover for about 1 minute. Remove the cover and stir, then add the lemon juice. Discard the garlic cloves.

SERVES 6

Grilled Winter Squash with Cumin

Slice winter squash or pumpkin into ½- to ¾-inch pieces. Dress with a little olive oil, lots of chopped garlic, cumin, salt and freshly ground pepper or hot red pepper flakes, to taste. Oregano and thyme are optional. Grill over medium coals, turning until tender. It's delicious with anything Mexican or Indian.

Fallen Butternut Squash Gratin

You'd be hard-pressed to find a squash preparation better than this moist soufflélike concoction created by David Kinch at the marvelous Sent Sovi restaurant in Saratoga. It has just the right hit of sweetness enhanced by aromatic spices and toasty pecans. The gratin will rise a little in the oven but will fall when removed.

6 medium-size butternut squash

½ cup honey

3 tablespoons all-purpose flour

1 teaspoon salt

¼ teaspoon grated nutmeg

¼ teaspoon cinnamon

3 eggs, separated

¼ cup chopped pecans

Preheat the oven to 350 degrees. Butter a 9-inch-diameter gratin dish or baking pan. Line a large baking pan with parchment paper.

Halve the squash and scoop out the seeds. Place the halves cut-sides down on the parchment-lined pan and bake for about 30 minutes, or until soft. Let the squash cool. Spoon out the flesh and purée it in a food processor. (You should have about 3 cups squash purée.)

Combine the squash purée, honey, flour, salt, nutmeg, cinnamon and egg yolks in a mixing bowl; blend well.

Beat the egg whites to stiff peaks in a bowl. Carefully fold into the squash mixture until no streaks of white remain. Pour the gratin mixture into the prepared pan. Sprinkle the nuts over the top.

Bake for about 45 minutes, or until golden.

SERVES 6

Sweet Cinnamon Tomatoes

When it's impossible to find a good tomato, Jacqueline McMahan has the solution with this recipe: Dip slices of firm tomato in cinnamon-sugar and sauté them in butter. They go very well with spicy foods, and make a wonderful accompaniment to scrambled eggs or omelets.

2 tomatoes, barely ripe and firm

¼ cup fresh lemon juice

½ cup sugar

½ teaspoon cinnamon

Pinch of salt

2 to 4 tablespoons butter

Cut off the ends of the tomatoes and discard. Cut the tomatoes into ⅓-inch slices. Place in a flat glass dish and pour the lemon juice over them. Marinate for 5 minutes, then turn the slices. Combine the sugar, cinnamon and salt on a plate and stir to blend.

Drop 2 or 3 tomato slices at a time into the sugar mixture, turning the slices over to coat both sides.

Heat 2 tablespoons of the butter in a skillet over medium heat. When the butter is bubbly hot, add a few tomato slices and sauté, turning once, until golden brown on both sides. Transfer to paper towels to drain. Repeat with the remaining tomatoes, adding more butter to the skillet as needed.

SERVES 4

Asparagus with Tarragon Mayonnaise

For a quick vegetable side dish or party appetizer, Georgeanne Brennan recommends steaming asparagus spears until tender, then running them under cold water and setting aside. Stir together minced tarragon leaves, mayonnaise, a little lemon juice and freshly ground pepper. Serve the asparagus with a spoonful or two of the tarragon mayonnaise alongside.

Roasted Asparagus

Here's a clever idea from Georgeanne Brennan: Pour balsamic vinegar to a depth of ½ inch in a shallow baking dish; add a little olive oil, salt, freshly ground pepper, chopped fresh tarragon and asparagus spears. Let marinate for an hour or so, then transfer to a baking sheet and roast in a 400-degree oven for about 20 minutes, or until tender.

Greek Taverna-Style Zucchini with Lemon

Zucchini can be a relatively dull vegetable, but in this simple preparation, Marlena Spieler brings it to life with the addition of garlic, olives and lemon juice.

4 zucchini, halved lengthwise, then cut into large chunks

3 garlic cloves, chopped

Large pinch of salt

Large pinch of dried oregano, or other herb such as thyme or herbes de Provence

Juice of ½ lemon

4 tablespoons olive oil

Freshly ground pepper, to taste

15 olives (green, black or a combination) for garnish

◎ Bring a pot of salted water to a boil over high heat. Add the zucchini and cook for 10 to 15 minutes, or until it is quite soft. Drain.

Crush the garlic, preferably in a mortar and pestle, with the salt, then rub it onto the cut surfaces of the zucchini. Sprinkle with oregano, lemon juice and olive oil. Season with pepper.

Garnish with the olives and serve at room temperature.

SERVES 4

Zucchini with Apple and Mint

Here's a unique preparation for zucchini from Mark Lusardi, who owns Emma Restaurant in San Francisco. Apples, mint and freshly squeezed lime juice give raw zucchini a masterful flavor punch. It's great with grilled chicken or fish.

4 green and/or yellow zucchini

2 Gravenstein or other crisp apples

Juice of 2 limes, or to taste

Salt and freshly ground pepper, to taste

8 fresh mint leaves

◉◉ Scrub the zucchini, then trim off the stem and blossom ends. Cut into very long, thin, matchstick strips, stopping when the core and seeds are reached. Put zucchini in a bowl. Peel and core the apples, then cut into julienne strips. Add to the zucchini, then pour in the lime juice; toss to coat. Season with salt and pepper.

Stack the mint leaves and slice into very fine strips (chiffonade). Add to the zucchini mixture and toss to combine.

SERVES 4 TO 6

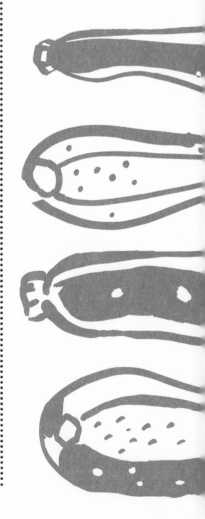

Mexican Zucchini and Corn Gratin

In this recipe by Jacqueline McMahan, zucchini is sautéed, placed in a casserole and topped with a creamy corn and basil sauce. Then it's sprinkled with cheese and broiled until bronzed and bubbly.

1 tablespoon butter

½ cup diced onion

4 zucchini, about 1½ pounds total, cut into small dice

Salt and freshly ground pepper, to taste

Corn-Basil Sauce

1 tablespoon butter

1½ cups grated fresh corn

1 tablespoon yellow cornmeal

½ cup milk

½ teaspoon salt

2 red jalapeño chiles, seeded and minced

2 tablespoons slivered basil leaves

1½ cups grated fontina or Monterey Jack cheese

❧ Preheat the broiler to medium. Butter an 8-inch square baking pan.

Melt the butter in a sauté pan over medium heat. Add the onion and zucchini and sauté for about 10 minutes, or until the zucchini is golden but still al dente. Season with salt and pepper. Place in the prepared baking pan.

To make the sauce: Melt the butter in a saucepan over medium heat. Add the grated corn, cornmeal, milk, salt and chiles. Simmer until thickened. Remove from heat and add the basil.

Pour the corn sauce over the zucchini. Sprinkle with the grated cheese and broil until the cheese is bubbly and golden brown.

SERVES 6

Marinated Vegetables in a Grill Pan

Microwaving prepared vegetables in a marinade infuses them with flavor and allows you to finish them in a grill pan in a matter of minutes. The vegetables may be marinated and microwaved 1 day ahead, stored in the refrigerator, then grilled as needed. Just about any combination of vegetables will work, including asparagus, red onions and carrots. Cooking times may vary. This recipe is from Michael Bauer.

> Asian or Italian marinade (recipes follow)
>
> 1 red bell pepper, stemmed, seeded, deribbed and cut lengthwise into 8 strips
>
> 1 green bell pepper, stemmed, seeded, deribbed and cut lengthwise into 8 strips
>
> 2 zucchini, cut lengthwise into 4 slices
>
> 2 yellow squash, cut lengthwise into 4 slices
>
> 1 eggplant, cut into ¼-inch rounds
>
> 2 portobello mushrooms, cleaned and cut into ¼-inch strips
>
> Vegetable or olive oil

∞ Prepare the marinade. Place the bell peppers in a flat, microwave-safe dish and pour in half of the marinade, making sure to coat the pieces well.

Place the zucchini, squash, eggplant and mushrooms in another microwave-safe dish and pour in the remaining marinade.

Tightly cover both dishes with plastic wrap.

Microwave the peppers for 6 minutes; microwave the other vegetables for 4 minutes. They should still be a little crisp.

Brush a grill pan with oil and place over high heat until the pan is hot. Or prepare an outdoor grill, letting the coals burn down to the gray-ash stage.

Working in batches, place a single layer of vegetables (reserving the marinade) in the grill pan (or on a vegetable-grilling rack on the barbecue, if grilling). Cook for 2 to 3 minutes, or until you see charred grill marks on the bottom side of the vegetables. Turn and grill other side for 2 to 3 minutes.

Serve the marinade on the side as a dipping sauce.

SERVES 4 TO 6

Vegetables on the Grill

Most vegetables cook easily on the barbecue; a light brushing of oil or a little time in a simple marinade is all they need. A feast of grilled vegetables is irresistible, and leftovers are terrific additions to pastas, salads, sandwiches and soups. Vegetables can be cooked on hot or cooler coals; just keep checking for doneness.

Some vegetables— peppers, eggplant, zucchini and other summer squashes, potatoes, fennel—can be cooked either whole or sliced.

Many salad vegetables are delicious when grilled, especially endive and radicchio. Asparagus is an amazement.

Solid, starchy or stringy vegetables need to be partly cooked (parboiled) before grilling. Plunge them whole into boiling water for 8 to 10 minutes, then drain (slice afterward if you wish) and marinate before grilling to desired doneness:

Artichokes: After parboiling, marinate in olive oil, lemon and herbs.

Beets: After parboiling, marinate or baste with olive oil and lemon.

Broccoli: Parboil briefly, then marinate in a little teriyaki sauce and a dash of balsamic vinegar.

Carrots: After parboiling, baste with a little butter seasoned with preserved ginger and garlic.

Corn: If it's older, parboil briefly; if young and tender, just cook husked ears on the grill, brushed with a little olive oil or butter and dusted with cumin and chili powder.

Garlic: After parboiling briefly, marinate whole heads in a little olive oil, salt and thyme; or, for real decadence, use duck fat and chicken stock.

Leeks: Parboil whole, then marinate in a little olive oil and lemon juice.

Potatoes: After parboiling, marinate in olive oil, lemon juice and herbs.

If you're not parboiling them, whole potatoes, whole sweet potatoes, large pieces of winter squash and whole eggplant are best cooked over indirect heat in a covered grill.

Small vegetables—cherry tomatoes, whole peeled shallots—need to be skewered so that they don't fall through the grill. Green beans should be cooked in a grilling basket for the same reason. Or, use a fine-mesh screen made just for this purpose.

Asian Marinade

 1 teaspoon minced fresh ginger
 2 garlic cloves, minced
 ½ cup soy sauce
 1 teaspoon rice wine vinegar
 ⅛ teaspoon Asian sesame oil
 ½ teaspoon fresh lemon juice
 2 tablespoons chopped cilantro

Combine the ginger, garlic, soy sauce, vinegar, sesame oil and lemon juice in a bowl. Mix well.

Sprinkle the cilantro over the grilled vegetables.

YIELDS A GENEROUS ½ CUP

Italian Marinade

 1 garlic clove, minced
 ¼ cup balsamic vinegar
 ¼ cup olive oil
 ½ teaspoon fresh lemon juice
 ½ teaspoon salt
 ¼ teaspoon freshly ground pepper
 2 tablespoons chopped basil

Combine the garlic, vinegar, olive oil, lemon juice, salt and pepper in a bowl. Mix well.

Sprinkle the basil over the grilled vegetables.

YIELDS A GENEROUS ½ CUP

Roasted Onions, Potatoes, Carrots and Fennel

Georgeanne Brennan's roasted vegetables are imbued with the flavor of freshly ground spices as they cook to tenderness. Feel free to vary the seasonings, depending on your mood.

1 tablespoon whole cloves

1 tablespoon fennel seeds

1 teaspoon salt

1 teaspoon peppercorns

1 tablespoon dried winter savory

2 white or yellow onions

2 carrots

2 potatoes

1 fennel bulb

Olive oil for baking sheet

2 to 3 tablespoons water

Preheat the oven to 350 degrees.

Combine the cloves, fennel seeds, salt, peppercorns and winter savory and grind to a near powder in a coffee mill reserved for spice grinding.

Cut the onions lengthwise into quarters. Cut the carrots into 2-inch lengths, then cut the lengths in half. Cut the potatoes lengthwise into quarters, sixths or eighths, depending on their size. Cut the fennel lengthwise into quarters or sixths, depending on its size. Place the vegetables in a bowl and rub them with the herb and spice mixture. Let stand for 30 minutes.

Lightly grease a baking sheet with olive oil. Place the vegetables in a single layer on the baking sheet and bake for 45 minutes. Sprinkle with the water and bake for 30 minutes longer, or until the vegetables are tender.

SERVES 4 TO 6

Chapter 7

Meats

The popularity of lamb in the Bay Area can't be overstated; it's almost as popular as beef and pork, but it still has a special cachet that often makes it dinner-party fare. It could be a Roasted Leg of Lamb with Potatoes and Onions (page 243) for a crowd, Tunisian-Style Grilled Lamb Chops (page 244) for an outdoor affair, or an Indian Tagine of Meatballs and Peas (page 250) for a warming cool-night repast.

Beef still is king, however, especially for a hurry-up meal, as in our Pan-Grilled Steaks with Toasted Walnuts and Roquefort-Shallot Butter (page 216), or a simple stir-fry of Beef with Green Beans, Lime Leaves and Chiles (page 224). Both of these dishes are also suitable for guests, and so is the long-cooked Pot Roast with Caramelized Onion Sauce and Roasted Winter Vegetables (page 220).

In this chapter, you'll also be inspired by some intriguing flavor combinations using pork. Nancy Oakes, the chef/owner of Boulevard, has created a vanilla brine that brings out a sweet, rich undercurrent in the meat (page 235). For a more robust flavor, we've included a recipe for Cider-Cured Pork Chops served at 42 Degrees restaurant (page 234) and easy Lavender, Thyme and Rosemary Pork Chops (page 236).

Pan-Grilled Steaks with Toasted Walnuts and Roquefort-Shallot Butter

This is a simple bistro-style dish that Marlena Spieler came across in Paris. The combination of shallots, nuts and blue cheese is irresistible.

3 ounces shelled walnut pieces

6 ounces Roquefort cheese, crumbled

6 tablespoons unsalted butter

2 to 3 shallots, chopped

2 garlic cloves, chopped

2 tablespoons Cognac or brandy

Salt and freshly ground pepper, to taste

1 tablespoon chopped chives

4 small, very tender steaks (rib-eye or filet mignon), 5 to 6 ounces each

Handful of frisee or arugula leaves, lightly dressed with a few drops of
    olive oil and balsamic vinegar

◉◉ Toast the walnuts in a dry skillet over medium-high heat, tossing and turning every so often so they do not burn. When they are toasted and lightly browned, transfer them to a plate and set aside.

Combine the Roquefort with 4 tablespoons of the butter, the shallots, garlic, Cognac, salt, pepper and chives. Refrigerate. If making ahead of time, spoon it onto a piece of wax paper, then roll it up into a log and refrigerate. When ready to serve, unroll and slice the butter into coins.

Pat the steaks dry with a paper towel, then season with salt and pepper.

Melt the remaining 2 tablespoons butter in a heavy skillet over medium-high heat. When it is foaming and hot, add the steaks, 1 or 2 at a time. Cook for about 2 minutes per side, depending on thickness, or until browned on both sides but rare on the inside.

Serve the steaks piping hot, each with a generous nugget of Roquefort butter on top, a scattering of toasted walnuts and a handful of the dressed salad leaves.

SERVES 4

Grilling Times for Beef

Hamburgers: Cook over medium-hot coals, allowing about 10 minutes per side for well done. (If your family insists on rare, which is no longer considered safe, you can lessen the time.) Initial searing is a good way to get a nice smoky, crusty exterior.

Steaks: Sear for 1 minute per side over medium-hot to hot coals, then cook for 4 minutes per side for rare, 6 to 7 minutes for medium and 8 minutes for well-done.

Beef Kebabs: Grill over medium-hot coals for 3 to 4 minutes per side for rare, up to 6 to 7 minutes for well-done.

Skirt steaks (or the original fajita): Cook this cut whole over medium-hot coals for 4 to 5 minutes per side, or until it is browned on the outside but rare on the inside.

Whole fillet. Cook a 2- to 3-pound fillet, covered, over medium-hot coals for about 20 minutes. Turn periodically. Before slicing and serving, let rest on a platter for about 10 minutes.

Cognac-Pepper Steaks

Created by Shirley Sarvis, this is the perfect dish for a romantic dinner for two. To crack the peppercorns, chop with a sharp French chef's knife, or use a mortar and pestle and a pounding motion, or put the peppercorns in a plastic bag and pound with a mallet or hammer.

2 filets mignons, 6 ounces each and 1¼ to 1½ inches thick, brought to near
  room temperature
Salt, to taste
1 teaspoon halved or cracked black peppercorns
About 1 tablespoon clarified butter, or ½ tablespoon olive oil plus ½ tablespoon
  unsalted butter
¼ cup Cognac
6 tablespoons whipping cream
Watercress for garnish

◉◉ Wipe the steaks dry. Season with salt, then press the pepper into the flat surfaces.

Heat the butter in a heavy skillet over medium-high heat. When hot, add the steaks. Cook, turning the steaks occasionally, for 3 to 4 minutes total for rare, or until well browned on both sides (or done to your liking). Increase heat if necessary to achieve a rich brown exterior and the doneness you wish. Transfer the steaks to warm plates.

Remove any fat and burned (not browned) particles from the pan. Let the pan cool a little, then add the Cognac and cream; cook, stirring, until the sauce has reduced to the consistency of heavy cream. Season with salt; pour over steaks. Garnish generously with watercress.

SERVES 2

Roasted Beef Tenderloin with Red Pepper–Goat Cheese Sauce

This roasted beef tenderloin, created by Robin Davis, is perfect to show off a big Cabernet Sauvignon. The goat cheese mellows the flavors and adds a sophisticated edge to the dish.

1 red bell pepper

2 shallots, roughly chopped

1 tablespoon balsamic vinegar

2 tablespoons olive oil

1 beef tenderloin, about 3 pounds

Kosher or sea salt and freshly ground pepper, to taste

¼ cup dry red wine

¼ cup soft fresh goat cheese

2 tablespoons chopped chives

Preheat the oven to 500 degrees.

Roast the bell pepper over a gas burner or under the broiler until blackened on all sides. Seal in a paper bag and let steam for 10 minutes. Peel, stem, seed, derib and quarter the pepper. Transfer the pepper to a food processor. Add the shallots and balsamic vinegar and process until puréed. Set aside.

Heat the olive oil in a large, heavy roasting pan over high heat. Season the beef with salt and pepper. Add the beef to the pan and brown on all sides, for about 8 minutes. Transfer the pan to the oven and roast for 25 to 30 minutes, or until an instant-read thermometer inserted into the thickest part of the meat registers 130 degrees for medium-rare. Transfer the meat to a platter and tent with aluminum foil to keep warm.

Place the roasting pan over medium-high heat. Add the wine and bring to a boil, stirring to scrape up any browned bits. Add the red pepper purée and return to a boil. Strain the mixture into a small saucepan. Bring to a simmer over medium heat, then remove from heat. Add the goat cheese and stir until melted and smooth. Season with salt and pepper and stir in the chives.

Slice the meat and arrange on the platter. Drizzle with sauce.

SERVES 8

Roast Beef and Yorkshire Pudding

Here's a classic recipe from Mary Risley, founder of Tante Marie's Cooking School in San Francisco. It's served with a creamy horseradish sauce.

Sauce

¼ cup prepared horseradish

1 tablespoon white wine vinegar

1 teaspoon sugar

¼ teaspoon dry English mustard

½ teaspoon salt

½ teaspoon freshly ground white pepper

½ cup whipping cream

1 standing 3-rib roast, about 8 pounds

Yorkshire Pudding

2 eggs

½ teaspoon salt

1 cup all-purpose flour

1 cup milk

2 tablespoons roast beef drippings

◉◉ To make the sauce: Spoon the horseradish into a square of double-layer cheesecloth and squeeze dry. Place in a small bowl and add the vinegar, sugar, dry mustard, salt and pepper. Mix thoroughly. Beat the cream to soft peaks in a chilled bowl; fold into the horseradish. Transfer to a sauceboat, cover and refrigerate until ready to serve.

Preheat the oven to 450 degrees.

Place the roast fat-side up in a shallow roasting pan. Roast for 20 minutes, then reduce the oven temperature to 325 degrees and continue roasting, without basting, for about 1½ hours, or until the beef is done to your liking. For rare, an instant-read thermometer inserted into the thickest part of the roast, away from the bone, should register 125 to 130 degrees.

Transfer the roast to a heated platter and let it rest for at least 15 minutes before carving.

To make the Yorkshire pudding: Combine the eggs, salt, flour and milk in a blender and process on high speed for 2 to 3 seconds. (Or, use a handheld rotary beater or wire whisk.) Refrigerate for at least 1 hour.

As soon as the beef comes out of the oven, increase the oven temperature to 400 degrees.

Pour 2 tablespoons of the beef drippings into a 10-by-15-by-2½-inch roasting pan. Place over medium heat until the fat sputters.

Briefly beat the batter again and pour into the roasting pan. Place in the middle of the oven and bake for 15 minutes. Reduce the oven temperature to 375 degrees and bake for 15 minutes longer, or until the pudding has risen over the rim of the pan and is crisp and brown.

Using a sharp knife, divide the pudding into portions and serve immediately with the beef. Pass the sauce at the table.

SERVES 8

Pot Roast with Caramelized Onion Sauce and Roasted Winter Vegetables

This homey pot roast is as warming as a cozy fire. Robin Davis likes to serve it with a big, hearty Syrah.

5 tablespoons olive oil

1 tri-tip or bottom round of beef, about 3 pounds

Kosher salt and freshly ground pepper, to taste

4 onions, sliced

1 teaspoon sugar

2 celery stalks, sliced

2 carrots, sliced

8 garlic cloves, sliced

2 cups dry red wine (preferably Syrah)

BEST WAY:
Caramelizing
Onions

The proper cooking technique and patience are the secrets to making perfectly caramelized onions.

To find the best method, *The Chronicle*'s Food Department tested which type of fat is best, the amount of heat needed to get good color and how long the onions should cook. We used one medium-size yellow onion, thinly sliced (approximately 2 cups), as our standard measurement.

For best results, cook the uncovered onions slowly in butter over medium-low heat for 1 hour. Here are other factors to consider:

4 cups beef stock

2 cans (each 14¼ ounces) diced peeled tomatoes with their juices

2 bay leaves

1 teaspoon dried marjoram

1 teaspoon dried oregano

1 teaspoon fennel seeds

2 carrots, cut into 3-by-½-inch sticks

2 parsnips, cut into 3-by-½-inch sticks

18 small red-skinned potatoes

◦◦ Preheat the oven to 375 degrees.

Heat 2 tablespoons of the olive oil in a Dutch oven over medium-high heat. Season the meat with salt and pepper. Add the meat to the Dutch oven and brown on all sides, 10 to 12 minutes. Transfer the meat to a platter.

Reduce heat to medium and heat 2 tablespoons of the oil in the Dutch oven. Add the onions and cook slowly, stirring frequently, for about 30 minutes, or until golden brown. Sprinkle with the sugar and cook for about 10 minutes, or until deep golden brown.

Add the celery, sliced carrots and garlic and stir briefly. Add the wine, increase heat to high, and bring to a boil, stirring to scrape up any browned bits. Put the beef atop the vegetables. Add the beef stock, tomatoes and their juices, bay leaves, marjoram, oregano and fennel seeds. Bring to a boil. Cover and transfer to the oven. Cook for 2 to 2½ hours, or until the meat is very tender.

Combine the carrot sticks, parsnips and potatoes on a large baking sheet. Drizzle with the remaining 1 tablespoon olive oil. Season with salt and pepper. Roast at 375 degrees for about 30 minutes, or until tender and golden brown.

Transfer the meat to a platter. Tent with aluminum foil to keep warm. Strain the cooking liquid into a saucepan. Skim any fat that rises to the surface. Boil over high heat for about 30 minutes, or until reduced by half and slightly thickened. Season with salt and pepper.

Slice the meat across the grain and transfer to a platter. Arrange the roasted vegetables around the meat. Spoon the sauce over the meat.

SERVES 6

The size and style of the pan is vital. A standard sauté pan with a heavy, flat bottom and without a nonstick coating works the best. The larger the surface area, the more consistently the onions will cook, and they'll finish with a better texture.

As the onions cook, they will dry out around the edges. Deglazing the pan often using a liquid—stock, wine or water—will help moisten the onions and improve their finished texture. Stir every 2 to 3 minutes, as needed. Stirring too often decreases the coloring, while not stirring often enough can result in scorching.

Daube of Beef Auberge d'Aillaine

Joanne Weir's beef daube, marinated and cooked in red wine, is great served with egg noodles and freshly grated Parmigiano-Reggiano.

Marinade

1 (750ml) bottle dry red wine, such as a Côte du Rhône

2 yellow onions, quartered

3 carrots, peeled and cut into 2-inch pieces

4 garlic cloves, crushed

5 peppercorns, lightly crushed

3 whole cloves

1 strip orange peel, 3 inches long

4 pounds lean beef chuck, cut into 2-inch pieces

Daube

3 tablespoons olive oil

3 ounces smoked bacon, diced

1¼ cups peeled, seeded and chopped tomatoes

3 garlic cloves, minced

6 Italian parsley sprigs

Large pinch of dried thyme

2 bay leaves

1 strip orange peel, 3 inches long

Salt and freshly ground pepper, to taste

Beef stock, as needed

¼ cup pitted niçoise olives

◉◉ To make the marinade: Combine the wine, onions, carrots, crushed garlic, peppercorns, cloves and orange peel in a large bowl. Add the meat, mix well, then cover and refrigerate for 24 hours, stirring occasionally.

To make the daube: Remove the meat, onions and carrots from the marinade. Strain the remaining marinade and discard anything left in the strainer. Reserve the marinade.

Pat the meat, onions and carrots dry. Warm the olive oil in a large, heavy pot over medium-high heat. Add the meat in a single layer and sauté for 12 to 15 minutes, or until browned on all sides. Remove the meat and set aside.

Add the onions and carrots to the pot and sauté for about 6 minutes, or until browned. Reserve the onions and carrots separately from the meat.

Preheat the oven to 300 degrees.

Bring a saucepan of water to a boil over high heat. Add the bacon and blanch for 20 seconds. Drain. Combine the bacon, onions, carrots, tomatoes and minced garlic in a bowl. Spoon half of this mixture into the pot. Layer in the meat, then add the parsley, thyme, bay leaves and orange peel. Season with salt and pepper. Add the remaining tomato mixture, then pour the reserved marinade over all.

If needed, add enough stock to bring the level of liquid almost up to the top of the solids. Bring to a boil over high heat on the stovetop. Cover and bake for 3 to 3½ hours, or until the meat is very tender and can be easily pierced with a skewer.

Skim off as much fat as possible. Discard the bay leaves and orange peel. Add the olives.

Ladle some of the juices into a saucepan and reduce over medium-high heat by about two thirds. Pour juices back into the stew, taste and season with salt and pepper as needed.

SERVES 10

Beef and Shiitake Skewers

For an easy and delicious combination, marinate cubes of steak in a mixture of olive oil seasoned with salt, freshly ground pepper and fresh herbs for at least 1 hour. Thread on skewers with shiitake mushrooms. Brush steak and mushroom skewers often with the oil during grilling.

Beef with Green Beans, Lime Leaves and Chiles (Nua Pad Ki Mow)

Mai Pham created this delicious stir-fry. Be sure to drain the beans well before adding them to the pan as any excess water will dilute the sauce and make it bland.

½ pound green beans, tipped, tailed and cut diagonally into 3- to 4-inch lengths

1 pound beef sirloin, cut into thin strips about 3 inches long and ¼ inch thick

2 teaspoons Asian fish sauce

1 teaspoon soy sauce

2 teaspoons oyster sauce

¼ teaspoon freshly ground white pepper

2 tablespoons vegetable oil

3 garlic cloves, sliced

¼ cup low-sodium chicken broth, or water

2 or 3 Thai bird chiles, or 1 jalapeño or serrano chile, seeded and chopped

3 kaffir limes leaves, thinly slivered

½ red bell pepper, stemmed, seeded, deribbed and thinly sliced

4 cilantro sprigs for garnish

◉◉ Bring a pot of salted water to a boil over high heat. Add the beans and blanch for 1 minute. Drain and plunge into a bowl of cold water to stop the cooking. Drain well. Set aside.

Place the beef in a mixing bowl. Add the fish sauce, soy sauce, oyster sauce and white pepper; toss to coat. Set aside.

Heat the oil in a wok over high heat. When the oil begins to smoke, quickly add the garlic and beef; stir-fry for 2 minutes. If the pan gets too dry, add 1 to 2 tablespoons of chicken broth. Add the chiles, lime leaves, green beans and bell pepper; cook for about 2 minutes, or until the meat is just done and the vegetables are hot and slightly softened. If desired, add the remaining broth to the pan to create extra sauce.

Garnish with the cilantro sprigs.

SERVES 4

Thai Red Curry with Beef and Kabocha Squash

Red curry, with its deep smoky flavors of dried red chiles, complements meats like beef, lamb and duck. If you can't find kabocha, says Mai Pham, substitute another winter squash. Like many curries, this dish tastes even better the day after it has been made.

1½ cups unsweetened canned coconut milk

1 to 1½ tablespoons red curry paste

⅔ pound beef sirloin, cut into ¼-inch-thick slices

⅓ cup chicken broth, or water

1 kabocha squash, about 1½ pounds, or other winter squash, peeled and cut into
    ¾-inch cubes (about 2 cups)

1½ tablespoons Asian fish sauce

1 tablespoon palm sugar, or cane sugar

½ teaspoon sweet paprika

⅔ cup fresh peas, blanched, or frozen peas

2 kaffir lime leaves, thinly slivered

½ cup Thai basil leaves, halved

◉◉ Scoop out ⅔ cup of the thick cream from the can of coconut milk and heat in a pot over medium heat. Stir for 3 to 4 minutes, or until it bubbles and becomes fragrant. Add the curry paste and cook, stirring, for 1 to 2 minutes, or until the mixture becomes very aromatic.

Add the beef slices and stir to coat evenly with the paste. Increase the heat to high and add the remaining coconut milk, the chicken broth, squash, fish sauce, sugar and paprika. Cook for 2 to 3 minutes, then reduce heat to low and simmer, covered, for 15 minutes, or until the beef is done and the squash is tender.

Stir in the peas, kaffir lime leaves and half of the basil. Transfer to a serving bowl and scatter the remaining basil on top.

SERVES 4

Stir-Fried Flank Steak with Bok Choy

This quick Chinese stir-fry makes a great dish for a dinner party, served with a bright, fruity Merlot, says Robin Davis.

3 tablespoons black bean garlic sauce

2 tablespoons hoisin sauce

1 tablespoon soy sauce

1 teaspoon Chinese five-spice powder

1 teaspoon Asian sesame oil

1 teaspoon freshly cracked pepper

½ teaspoon chile paste

1 flank steak, about 1 pound

4 tablespoons vegetable oil

1 pound bok choy, trimmed and cut crosswise into 1-inch pieces

¼ cup water

2 tablespoons rice vinegar

2 teaspoons cornstarch mixed with 1 tablespoon water

Steamed white rice, or cooked Asian noodles

Toasted sesame seeds for garnish

Chopped green onion tops for garnish

◐ Combine the black bean sauce, hoisin, soy sauce, five-spice powder, sesame oil, pepper and chile paste in a small bowl; blend well. Rub the mixture on both sides of the steak. Place in a large baking dish. Cover and refrigerate for 4 hours or overnight.

Remove the meat from the refrigerator and scrape off the marinade; reserve marinade. Wrap the meat in plastic and place in the freezer for 30 minutes. Cut the meat across the grain into thin slices.

Heat 2 tablespoons of the oil in a large, heavy skillet or wok over high heat. Add the beef and stir-fry for 2 minutes. Using a slotted spoon, transfer the beef to a platter. Reduce heat to medium-high and heat the remaining 2 tablespoons oil in the skillet. Add the bok choy and stir-fry for 2 minutes. Mix the reserved marinade with the water and vinegar. Add to the skillet and bring to a boil. Stir for about 3 minutes, or until the bok choy is crisp-tender.

Marinade for Beef and Lamb

This red-wine marinade from Marlena Spieler brings out the best of lean cuts of beef and lamb, enhancing rather than masking the flavor, and keeping the meat deliciously juicy. It's designed for about 2 pounds of meat.

Red Wine Marinade: Combine 4 tablespoons wine, 4 tablespoons olive oil, 2 finely chopped shallots, 2 finely chopped garlic cloves, 1 tablespoon chopped fresh herb of choice (rosemary or thyme is good) and salt and freshly ground pepper, to taste. Marinate for 30 minutes to 2 hours.

Stir the cornstarch-water mixture to recombine and add to the skillet. Bring to a boil. Return the beef to the skillet and stir for about 2 minutes, or until it is heated through and the sauce thickens.

Spoon the rice onto a heated platter. Top with the beef and bok choy. Garnish with sesame seeds and green onions.

SERVES 4

Hamburgers with Portobellos and Pink Peppercorn–Tarragon Butter

Marlena Spieler adds a twist to the everyday hamburger with a splash of white wine for succulence. Other alcohol, such as vermouth or sherry, may be used. However, avoid red wine, which results in a purple hue and an inferior taste. The pink peppercorn–tarragon butter is lovely melted onto the burgers and mushrooms. You can substitute just about any herb for the tarragon.

7 garlic cloves, crushed with 1 or 2 pinches of salt

4 shallots, finely chopped

4 to 6 tablespoons dry white wine, or vermouth

2 pounds ground beef

Salt and freshly ground pepper, to taste

6 tablespoons unsalted butter at room temperature

1 teaspoon pink peppercorns

2 tablespoons chopped fresh tarragon leaves

1 or 2 drops of fresh lemon juice

4 medium-size portobello mushrooms

◉◉ Combine half of the garlic, half of the shallots and the wine in a bowl. Let stand for about 5 minutes. The wine will be absorbed somewhat by the shallots.

Mix the meat with the garlic-shallot mixture, season with salt and form into 4 patties. Season generously with pepper.

Combine the butter with the remaining garlic and shallots, then work in the pink peppercorns, tarragon, salt, pepper and lemon juice. Set aside.

Prepare a fire in a grill. Let the coals burn down to the gray-ash stage.

Smear the gill side of the mushrooms with a little of the seasoned butter and place gill-side down on the grill. Grill for a few minutes to seal in flavors, then turn the mushrooms gill-side up and move them to the cooler edge of fire to roast until the hamburger patties are done; juices will accumulate in the caps, so do not turn them again.

Meanwhile, grill the patties until they are crusty brown on the outside and done to your liking on the inside.

Remove the patties and mushrooms from the grill, and serve everything topped with a dab of the flavored butter.

SERVES 4

Braised Oxtails with White Beans and Salsa Verde

This rich and satisfying dish by Janet Fletcher is the ultimate comfort food. The meat is so tender it falls off the bone, and the pungent sauce magically plays off the sweetness of the meat.

Beans

¾ pound large dried white beans, such as cannellini, Emergo or Gigante

6 cups water

1 onion, peeled and halved

1 bay leaf

Salt and freshly ground pepper, to taste

3 tablespoons extra virgin olive oil

2 garlic cloves, minced

¾ cup chopped canned tomatoes

Oxtails

1 tablespoon olive oil

3 to 3½ pounds oxtails, cut into 1-inch lengths

Salt and freshly ground pepper, to taste

¾ cup water

12 thyme sprigs

Salsa Verde

½ cup minced Italian parsley

½ cup extra virgin olive oil

6 anchovy fillets, minced

3 tablespoons capers, chopped

3 tablespoons fine breadcrumbs

1 large garlic clove, minced

1½ tablespoons red wine vinegar

Salt, to taste

To make the beans: Pick over the beans, discarding any broken or withered ones or stones. Put the beans in a bowl, add water to cover by 1 inch and let soak overnight. Drain and place in a large pot. Add the water, onion and bay leaf. Bring to a boil over high heat, skimming any foam that collects on the surface; partially cover and reduce heat to maintain a slow simmer. Cook for 1 hour or more (cooking time will depend on the age of the beans), or until the beans are tender. Season with salt and pepper and let cool in the cooking liquid. Drain when cool, reserving the liquid. Discard the bay leaf and onion.

Heat the olive oil in a large skillet over medium heat. Add the garlic and sauté for 1 minute to release its fragrance. Add the tomatoes and cook for about 3 minutes to soften slightly. Add the beans and enough of the reserved cooking liquid to make them brothy. Cover and simmer gently for about 15 minutes to blend the flavors. Taste and adjust seasonings. Reheat the beans just before serving.

To make the oxtails: Preheat the oven to 325 degrees.

Heat the olive oil in a large skillet over high heat. Add the oxtails (in batches if necessary), season well with salt and pepper, reduce heat to medium and cook for about 10 minutes, or until the oxtails are well browned on both sides. Transfer the oxtails to a baking dish just large enough to hold them in a single layer.

Pour off any fat in the skillet. Return the skillet to high heat, add the water and deglaze, scraping the bottom of the pan with a wooden spoon to dislodge and dissolve any flavorful bits. Pour over the oxtails, scatter the thyme sprigs in the dish, cover and bake for 2¼ to 2½ hours, or until the oxtails are tender.

To make the salsa verde: Combine the parsley, olive oil, anchovies, capers, breadcrumbs, garlic and vinegar in a bowl. Season with salt.

To serve: Divide the oxtails among warmed serving plates, leaving the fat behind in the baking dish. Top the oxtails with a generous spoonful of salsa verde. Spoon the beans around the meat.

SERVES 6

Veal Braised with Cognac

This is an Italian home-style dish created by Shirley Sarvis. The sauce should be uneven in texture; a brisk whisking smooths it enough. Accompany with roasted potatoes, and for the wine, perhaps a Barbaresco.

1 boneless veal shoulder roast, 2½ to 3 pounds, rolled and tied

Olive oil

Salt and freshly ground pepper, to taste

3 to 4 teaspoons dried sage

⅓ cup Cognac

4 cups milk, warmed

3 to 4 teaspoons chopped fresh rosemary needles, or 1½ teaspoons crumbled dried rosemary

8 garlic cloves, minced

◎◎ Preheat the oven to 350 degrees.

Wipe the meat dry, then rub with a generous amount of olive oil. Season well with salt and pepper and rub with the sage.

Place the roast in an oiled Dutch oven. Cover and bake for about 2 hours, or until browned, turning the roast halfway through the cooking time. (If the juices begin to dry out, add a little water.) Transfer the roast to a plate; set aside.

Put the pan over medium-high heat and add the Cognac. Cook, stirring, until the liquid reduces to ¼ cup. Stir in ½ cup of the milk, the rosemary and garlic. Return the veal to the pan, cover and bake for about 1 hour longer, or until the meat is very tender. If necessary, add more milk to keep ½ inch of liquid in the pan.

Remove the roast to a warm platter and let rest for 10 to 15 minutes. Add the remaining milk to the pan and cook over high heat, whisking, until the sauce turns light brown, is as thick as heavy cream and has reduced to about 2 cups. Season with salt and pepper.

Carve the veal, divide among warmed plates and spoon some of the sauce over each serving.

SERVES 6

Pork Loin Stuffed with Chile-Glazed Prunes

Prunes and pork are a classic French combination, but in this recipe, Georgeanne Brennan has given the combo an innovative Southwestern twist.

1 pork loin or butt roast, 5 to 6 pounds, boned

1½ teaspoons salt

1½ teaspoons freshly ground pepper

3 dried chiles negros, or pasilla chiles, stemmed, seeded and ground to powder

12 pitted prunes

½ cup water

1 tablespoon sugar

1 teaspoon dried oregano

⅔ cup crème fraîche, or ⅔ cup sour cream plus 1 teaspoon distilled white vinegar

∞ Preheat the oven to 350 degrees.

Place the meat flat on a work surface and, using a very sharp knife, butterfly it. Open it out and pat dry.

Rub the inside surface with half of the salt and pepper and ½ teaspoon of the chile powder.

Combine the prunes and water in a saucepan over medium heat; cook for 3 to 4 minutes. Remove the prunes with a slotted spoon and set aside. Measure the liquid in the pan and add enough water to make ½ cup. Return the prune-cooking liquid to the saucepan and add the sugar, all but 1½ tablespoons of the chile powder, the oregano and prunes. Cook over medium-low heat for about 15 minutes, stirring occasionally. The prunes will absorb some of the liquid, so be careful not to burn them.

When the prunes are shiny and glazed, remove them from the pan. Reserve the remaining glaze in the pan. Let the prunes cool for 10 minutes, then quarter them. Cover one side of the butterflied roast with the prunes. Starting from a short end, roll up the meat and tie with kitchen string every 2 inches. The ends of the roast may need to be fastened with skewers or sewn together.

Gently rub the outside of the roast with the remaining salt, pepper and 1 tablespoon of the chile powder.

Grilling Times for Pork

Loin or rib chops: For 1-inch-thick chops, sear both sides, then cook over medium-hot coals for 6 to 8 minutes per side. **Spareribs:** Cook—preferably covered, over indirect heat—over medium-hot coals for 1 to 2 hours for baby back ribs, or until tender. Alternatively, parboil the ribs, then barbecue them over hot coals, covered or uncovered, for about 10 minutes per side. **Kebabs:** Cook, covered or uncovered, over medium coals for 5 to 6 minutes per side. **Sausage:** Grill over medium-hot coals for 6 to 7 minutes per side, and check to make sure they're cooked through (same for beef and poultry sausage).

Add 1 to 2 tablespoons of water to the remaining prune glaze to thin it to a thick syrup. Drizzle this over the roast.

Place the meat on a rack in a shallow roasting pan. Roast, basting occasionally with the pan juices, for 1½ to 2 hours, or until an instant-read thermometer inserted into the thickest part of the meat registers 150 to 155 degrees.

Remove the roast from the oven, cover loosely with aluminum foil and let stand for 15 minutes.

To serve, carve into ½-inch-thick slices. Garnish each slice with a dollop of crème fraîche and a dusting of chile powder.

SERVES 6

Pork Loin Roast with Ginger-Orange Glaze

Rum and ginger add a zesty zing to pork loin in this recipe by Shirley Sarvis. Part of the glaze is used to coat the meat before cooking, and the rest becomes the sauce. Accompany with hot cornbread and steamed spinach.

One 6-rib pork loin roast, about 6 pounds, trimmed of all excess fat, chine bone
    removed (for easy carving), brought to near-room temperature
Ginger-Orange Glaze (recipe follows)
Golden (medium) rum, as needed
Salt and freshly ground pepper, to taste

◉◉ Preheat the oven to 325 degrees.

Wipe the pork dry. Place fat-side up on a rack (or standing on its ribs) in a shallow roasting pan. Bake for 15 minutes. Spoon part of the glaze over the top of the roast (use only enough glaze to cover the top). Continue roasting, spooning on a little more glaze every 15 minutes, for about 1¼ hours, or until an instant-read thermometer inserted into the thickest part of the roast registers 140 degrees. Remove from the oven and let rest in a warm place for 15 minutes.

Measure the remaining glaze into a saucepan. For each ¼ cup glaze, add 2 teaspoons rum. Place over medium heat and cook, stirring, until heated through.

Carve the pork and divide among heated plates. Serve with roasted glaze and all carving juices. Pass the remaining glaze at the table. Offer salt and pepper at the table.

SERVES 6

Ginger-Orange Glaze

To grate ginger, use a handheld grater with ¼-inch (maximum) holes.

¼ cup grated orange zest

2 cups fresh orange juice

¼ cup finely grated fresh ginger

2 tablespoons light brown sugar

⅓ cup golden (medium) rum

◉ Combine the orange zest, orange juice, ginger and brown sugar in a heavy saucepan. Bring to a boil over medium-high heat and boil, stirring occasionally, until reduced to about 1⅓ cups. Stir in the rum and reduce to 1⅓ cups.

YIELDS 1⅓ CUPS

Quick Sauce for Pork

Here's a quick way to dress up pork from Marion Cunningham: Mix together 6 tablespoons jalapeño jelly and ⅓ cup sour cream in a small saucepan over very low heat. Stir to blend and warm slightly. When blended, remove from heat.

42 Degrees' Cider-Cured Pork Chops

Brining is one of the best ways to add flavor to meat. These delicious cider-cured pork chops are served at 42 Degrees in San Francisco.

Brine

4 cups water

2 cups hard cider

½ cup salt

½ cup light brown sugar

10 peppercorns

4 bay leaves

½ bunch fresh thyme

1 onion, chopped

1 carrot, peeled and chopped

1 celery stalk, chopped

1 apple, peeled and chopped

4 center-cut pork loin chops, each 1¼ to 1½ inches thick

Olive oil as needed

◎ To make the brine: Combine all brine ingredients in a saucepan and bring to a boil over high heat. Remove from heat and let cool. When cool, refrigerate until cold.

Add the pork chops to the cold brine. Weight with a plate if necessary to keep the chops completely submerged. Refrigerate for 1 to 2 days.

Remove the chops from the brine and pat them dry. Heat 2 skillets over medium-high heat. Add just enough olive oil to coat the bottom of each skillet. When the skillets are hot, add the chops and reduce heat to medium-low. Cook for 10 minutes, then turn and cook for about 10 minutes longer, or until the chops are no longer pink at the bone.

SERVES 4

Brine-Time Tips

Here are some tips to start you brining:

A heavy-duty plastic tub, earthenware crock, stainless-steel bowl or even a re-sealable plastic bag can work as a brining container as long as the meat is fully submerged. Weight with a plate if necessary to keep the meat fully covered with the brine. Always refrigerate the meat while brining.

To determine how much brine you'll need, place the meat in your container and add water to cover. Remove the meat and measure the water.

Although some cooks prefer lighter or heavier brines, we've found that 1 cup of salt per gallon of water is a happy medium. Use kosher salt, which has no additives.

Experiment with seasonings. Salt is essential, but everything else is optional. Consider garlic, ginger, fresh herbs, juniper berries, clove, cinnamon sticks, vanilla beans, mustard seeds, coriander seeds, star anise, hot red pepper flakes or Sichuan peppercorns. To give pork a sweet edge and encourage browning, add ½ cup sugar to each 2 quarts of water.

You don't need to rinse meat after you remove it from the brine unless the brine is highly salted (more than 1 cup salt per gallon).

Don't salt brined meat before cooking; it is already salted throughout.

Don't reuse brine.

Brining Times for Pork

⊚⊚ Whole pork tenderloin: 12 hours
⊚⊚ Pork chops (1¼ to 1½ inches thick): 1 to 2 days
⊚⊚ Whole pork loin: 2 to 4 days

Nancy Oakes' Vanilla Brine

Vanilla is a natural with pork. This recipe from Nancy Oakes of Boulevard restaurant in San Francisco makes enough brine for a 4- to 6-pound boneless pork loin; or 6 center-cut pork loin chops, each 1¼ to 1½ inches thick; or 4 pork tenderloins, 1 to 1¼ pounds each.

> 9 cups boiling water
> ½ cup sugar
> ½ cup kosher salt
> 2 tablespoons coarsely cracked pepper
> 2½ teaspoons vanilla

⊚⊚ Combine the boiling water, sugar, salt, pepper and vanilla in a bowl, small crock or heavy-duty plastic container; stir to dissolve the salt and sugar. Let cool, then refrigerate until cold.

Add pork of choice (see headnote). Weight with a plate if necessary to keep the meat completely submerged.

Refrigerate 3 days for pork loin, 1 to 2 days for chops and 12 hours for tenderloin. Stir the brine each day and turn the pork occasionally.

Roast or grill pork loin or tenderloins. Grill chops or panfry according to directions in 42 Degrees' Cider-Cured Pork Chops (see page 234).

Lavender, Thyme and Rosemary Pork Chops

The addition of lavender brings a perfumed sweetness to the pork and pan juices in this recipe by Georgeanne Brennan. Serve with fluffy mashed potatoes.

½ teaspoon dried lavender flowers, minced

2 teaspoons fresh thyme leaves, minced

1 teaspoon fresh rosemary leaves, minced

4 pork chops, each ½ inch thick

1 teaspoon salt

½ to ⅔ cup water, dry vermouth or dry white wine

½ teaspoon freshly ground pepper

◎◎ Combine the lavender, thyme and rosemary in a bowl, then rub each chop with an equal amount of the mixture, pressing it into the meat.

Scatter the salt in a heavy skillet and place over high heat. When the salt is nearly smoking (or when a drop of water sizzles and sputters when dropped in the skillet), place the chops in the skillet and sear for 2 to 3 minutes, or until nicely golden. Turn the chops and sear the other side.

Pour the water into the skillet and deglaze the pan, stirring to scrape up any browned bits from the bottom. Add the pepper. Reduce the heat to low, cover with a tight-fitting lid and simmer for about 10 minutes, or until the chops are done to your liking.

Transfer the chops to a warm platter. Increase the heat to medium-high and reduce the cooking juices to 4 tablespoons, stirring constantly.

Pour the juices over the chops and serve.

SERVES 4

Cooking Times for Pork Chops

Fried pork chops retain their tenderness and moisture when they aren't cooked to death. Cook over medium-high heat.

◎◎ ½-inch-thick chops: About 5 minutes per side

◎◎ ¾-inch-thick chops: 8 minutes per side

◎◎ 1-inch-thick chops: 10 minutes per side

Pork, Chorizo and Hominy Stew

Janet Fletcher created this marvelous stew, which seems to telescope the seductive, soulful flavors of Mexico. Serve with warm corn tortillas. Canned chipotle chiles en adobo are available in Mexican markets.

Broth

2 pounds baby back ribs, sliced into individual ribs

12 cups water

1 onion, halved

3 garlic cloves, peeled and lightly crushed

12 peppercorns

2 bay leaves

Salt, to taste

Stew

½ pound Mexican-style chorizo sausage

Olive oil as needed

1 onion, minced

½ green bell pepper, stemmed, seeded, deribbed and diced

2 garlic cloves, minced

1 teaspoon dried Mexican oregano

1 teaspoon ground toasted cumin seeds (see Note)

1 tablespoon all-purpose flour

¼ cup chopped cilantro leaves

1 tablespoon finely minced canned chipotle chiles en adobo, or more, to taste

1 can (14½ ounces) whole hominy, rinsed and drained

Salt, to taste

◉ To make the broth: Put the ribs in a large pot and add the water. Bring to a simmer over medium heat, skimming any foam that collects on the surface. Add the onion, garlic, peppercorns and bay leaves. Adjust heat to maintain a bare simmer and cook for 2 hours. Season with salt.

Let the ribs cool in the broth, then strain, reserving the ribs and broth separately. You should have about 8 cups broth. Discard the onion, garlic, peppercorns and bay leaves.

To make the stew: Slit open the chorizo casing and crumble the sausage into a large pot. Cook over medium heat, breaking up the sausage with a wooden spoon, until it has rendered its fat and is hot throughout. Strain in a sieve. Measure the rendered fat and add enough olive oil to make ¼ cup.

Return the fat to the pot and set over medium heat. When hot, add the onion, bell pepper, garlic, oregano and cumin; sauté for 5 to 10 minutes, or until the onion is soft. Add the flour and cook, stirring, for 1 minute. Add 7 cups of the reserved broth, the cilantro and chipotle. Bring to a simmer. Add the reserved pork ribs and return to a simmer. Partially cover, reduce heat to low and cook for 15 minutes.

Add the hominy and chorizo, partially cover and cook for 15 minutes. The pork should be completely tender and beginning to pull away from the bone. Season with salt. Cool, then refrigerate.

Lift off and discard any congealed fat on the soup's surface. Reheat the soup, adding more broth if necessary. Taste and adjust seasonings.

SERVES 4 TO 6

NOTE: Toast whole cumin seeds in a small skillet over medium heat until lightly colored and fragrant. Grind to a powder in a mortar and pestle or in a spice grinder.

Foothill Cafe Ribs

Jerry Shafer of Foothill Cafe in Napa covers these delicious ribs with a dry rub before grilling. He then serves them with a zesty Caribbean barbecue sauce. For a larger crowd, this recipe may easily be doubled or tripled.

Ribs

4 teaspoons sugar

4 teaspoons paprika

2 teaspoons salt

2 teaspoons ground cumin

2 teaspoons freshly ground pepper

2 teaspoons pure chile powder

1 teaspoon ground ginger

1 slab baby back pork ribs, about 1¾ pounds

½ cup water

Juice of 1 lemon

All About Rubs

Marinades aren't the only way to add flavor to grilled foods. Dry rubs, pastes and glazes all do the same job in different ways.

Dry rubs are great for long-cooked foods that are fatty enough to hold in their own moisture. Ribs are terrific with a dry rub: The spices permeate the meat for the long fire-roasting, and the dry spice rub leaves the meat crisp and crusty. Dry rubs can be applied to meats well before cooking, so the flavors can permeate the meat, or they can be added right before grilling.

A dry rub can be turned into a paste with the addition of a small amount of liquid—oil, yogurt, fruit juice, vinegar or some combination of these. Pastes can be left on overnight so the flavors permeate the meat, or they can be added right before grilling.

Glazes are similar to pastes but they are sweet, often based on chutneys or jams combined with tangy ingredients such as mustard or vinegar. They must be used at the very end of cooking because the sugar in the glaze quickly chars and burns.

Cajun Dry Rub: Combine 2 tablespoons paprika; 1 tablespoon each of cumin, thyme, onion powder, garlic powder, dried oregano; 1 teaspoon each of freshly ground black pepper, cayenne pepper; salt, to taste.

Mediterranean Sage Paste: Blend together 5 chopped garlic cloves, 2 to 3 tablespoons chopped sage leaves, 1 teaspoon fennel seeds, 1 tablespoon chopped Italian parsley, 3 tablespoons extra-virgin olive oil, 1 tablespoon balsamic vinegar or dry white wine, 1 tablespoon ouzo (optional), salt and freshly ground pepper, to taste.

Mexican Chili Paste: Mix together 5 chopped garlic cloves, 4 tablespoons chile powder, 1 teaspoon cumin, ½ teaspoon cinnamon, ½ teaspoon dried oregano, ½ teaspoon salt, 2 to 3 tablespoons beer and/or orange juice.

Mango Chutney–Mustard Glaze. Combine 3 tablespoons mango chutney, 2 tablespoons Dijon mustard, 1 tablespoon orange marmalade or apricot jam, several drops hot sauce and fresh lemon or lime juice.

Barbecue Sauce

4 teaspoons pineapple juice

4 teaspoons dark rum

4 teaspoons Caribbean hot sauce

2 teaspoons light brown sugar

Juice of 1 orange

Pinch of ground allspice

To make the ribs: Combine the sugar, paprika, salt, cumin, pepper, chile powder and ginger in a small bowl. Rub the mixture over both sides of the ribs. Cover and refrigerate for 4 hours.

Prepare a medium-low fire in a barbecue grill.

Place the ribs on the grill, cover and cook for 20 minutes. Turn the ribs over.

Combine the water and lemon juice in a bowl. Brush over the ribs. Cover and cook for 20 minutes. Continue cooking, turning and basting with lemon water, for 30 to 60 minutes, or until the ribs are tender.

To make the barbecue sauce: Combine the pineapple juice, rum, hot sauce, brown sugar, orange juice and allspice in a serving bowl; stir to blend.

Serve the ribs with the sauce on the side.

SERVES 2

Polenta Pie with Pork in Salsa Verde

This party-size version of the classic Mexican pork in green chile sauce is streamlined for the busy cook by Tara Duggan. It takes only a fraction of the time to make. The secret? Using a tender cut of pork and a store-bought salsa verde. It's great to make a large batch on the weekend and freeze the rest for effortless weeknight dinners.

Pork in Salsa Verde

3 pounds boneless pork butt or shoulder, cut into ¾-inch cubes, fat trimmed

Salt and freshly ground pepper, to taste

About 6 tablespoons vegetable oil

1 large red onion, chopped

8 garlic cloves, minced

3 serrano chiles, seeded and minced

1 tablespoon dried Mexican oregano, crumbled

3 cups chicken broth

2 pints fresh salsa verde, or jarred tomatillo or green chile salsa

Polenta

4 cups water

2 cups whipping cream

2 teaspoons salt

2 cups polenta

2 teaspoons dried Mexican oregano, crumbled

1 cup grated queso fresco

⅔ cup sour cream

1 cup grated queso fresco

Asian-Style Pork Burgers

Make ground pork patties seasoned with chopped green onion, garlic and soy sauce with a pinch of sugar and just enough cornstarch to hold the mixture together. Brush with soy sauce; grill over white ash–covered coals for about 10 minutes; turn and grill for 10 minutes longer. Serve with hoisin, cucumber spears and cold rice noodles tossed with soy sauce and sesame oil.

To make the pork in salsa verde: Season the pork with salt and pepper. Place a large, heavy stockpot over medium-high heat. When quite hot, add enough oil to coat the bottom of the pot. When the oil is almost smoking, carefully add the pork in batches. Do not crowd the pan or the meat will stew instead of fry. Brown the pork for 5 minutes; stir and brown for 5 minutes longer, or until the pork is golden brown on both sides. Remove the pork from pot with a slotted spoon to a bowl. Repeat with the remaining pork, adding more oil if necessary, until all the meat has been browned; set aside.

Add the onion to the pot and sauté in any remaining oil for 5 to 10 minutes, or until tender. Scrape the bottom of the pot with a wooden spoon to dislodge the browned bits of pork. Add the garlic, chiles and oregano and sauté for 2 minutes, stirring occasionally.

Return the pork to the pot. Add the chicken broth and salsa verde. Bring to a boil, then reduce heat and simmer, uncovered, for about 1 hour and 15 minutes, or until the meat is very tender. During cooking, keep an eye on the level of liquid. If the meat is not submerged, add water. When the pork is tender, season with salt and pepper.

To make the polenta: Preheat the oven to 375 degrees.

Combine the water, cream and salt in a saucepan, place over high heat and bring almost to a boil. Combine the polenta, oregano and queso fresco in a large mixing bowl; stir until combined. Stir into the hot liquid, making sure to incorporate all of the ingredients and smooth out any lumps. Pour evenly into two 13-by-9-inch baking pans.

Bake for 10 minutes. Stir, then bake for 25 minutes longer.

Reduce the oven temperature to 350 degrees. Ladle the stewed pork over the polenta. Dot with the sour cream, top with the queso fresco and bake for 20 minutes, or until heated through.

SERVES 12

Lamb Klephtiko

Boneless leg of lamb is seasoned with a garlic-herb mixture, then wrapped in parchment paper and roasted at a low temperature. It's an unusual treatment, which infuses the lamb with loads of character. Joanne Weir created this recipe from a dish served at Stoyanof's, a family-owned Mediterranean restaurant in San Francisco that is now closed.

8 garlic cloves, thinly sliced

3 bay leaves, ground to a powder in a mortar and pestle or spice grinder

½ teaspoon cinnamon

1½ teaspoons dried oregano

Coarse salt and freshly ground pepper, to taste

1 leg of lamb, 5 to 6 pounds, boned and excess fat removed

2 tablespoons extra virgin olive oil

∞ Preheat the oven to 200 degrees.

Combine the garlic, bay leaves, cinnamon, oregano, salt and pepper in a small bowl; stir well to blend.

Make 1-inch slits in the lamb with a small, sharp paring knife; insert the garlic slices and herb mixture into the slits. Roll up the lamb and tie with kitchen string (tie it as you would a package). Rub the outside of the roast with the olive oil, then season with salt and pepper. Wrap the lamb in a large piece of parchment paper and seal the edges by folding well so steam will not escape.

Place the parchment package on a rack in a roasting pan. Add water to the pan to come almost up to the level of the rack. Do not let it touch the parchment package. Place in the oven and bake for 4 hours, adding more water to the pan as necessary.

At the end of the roasting time, open the package and transfer the roast to a cutting board. Slice the lamb and place on a heated platter. Drizzle with the juices remaining in the package.

SERVES 8

Grilling Times for Lamb

Chops: For 1½-inch-thick chops, sear and cook over medium-hot coals for 4 to 5 minutes per side for rare, 5 minutes for medium, and up to 8 minutes for well-done.

Butterflied leg of lamb: Indirect cooking is an excellent way to grill this cut, and it provides drippings for a sauce. Cook, covered, over hot coals, for about 20 minutes per side. You want the outside brown and slightly charred, the inside still pink or rosy, according to taste.

Lamb breast or ribs: Best cooked indirectly and covered, over medium or low coals, for 1 to 1½ hours, or until the meat is crisply browned on the outside and much of the fat has melted away. Discard drippings.

Roasted Leg of Lamb with Potatoes and Onions

Many years ago, the people of Provence used the village baker's oven to cook special dishes such as this one, says Georgeanne Brennan. The potatoes, which have been simmered in broth, are finished in the oven while the lamb roasts on top of them. It's a great dish for a party, because the lamb and potatoes are cooking while you spend time with your guests. Plus the meat and potatoes perfume the house with mouth-watering aromas.

1 tablespoon butter

2½ pounds baking potatoes, peeled and very thinly sliced

2½ large yellow onions, very thinly sliced

1½ cups beef broth

1 leg of lamb, bone in, about 5 pounds

1 tablespoon olive oil

1½ teaspoons mixed dried thyme, rosemary, winter savory and marjoram

½ teaspoon salt

¾ teaspoon freshly ground pepper

3 garlic cloves, cut into fine slivers

Butter a baking dish large enough to hold the lamb.

Preheat the oven to 400 degrees.

Combine the potatoes, onions and broth in a saucepan and bring to a boil over high heat. Reduce heat to low and simmer for 10 minutes. Remove the potatoes and onions with a slotted spoon and spread them evenly in the baking dish, then pour the broth over them. Bake for 20 minutes.

While the potatoes are baking, prepare the lamb by making 20 to 25 1-inch-deep slits in the meat with a sharp knife. Rub the lamb with the olive oil, herbs, salt and pepper. Insert the garlic slivers into the slits. Place the lamb atop the bed of potatoes and onions and return to the oven.

Reduce the oven temperature to 375 degrees.

Bake for about 1 hour, or until an instant-read thermometer inserted into the thickest part of the meat, away from the bone, registers 125 to 130 degrees for medium-rare. For medium, roast 15 minutes longer, or to 135 to 145 degrees. Remove from the oven, cover loosely with aluminum foil and let stand for 15 to 20 minutes.

To serve, remove the lamb from the baking dish and carve it into thin slices. Top the potatoes with the lamb slices, pour over any carving juices and bring to the table. Scoop up the potatoes and lamb slices with a serving spoon onto warmed plates.

SERVES 6 TO 8

Tunisian-Style Grilled Lamb Chops

In creating this recipe, Georgeanne Brennan was inspired by the grill stands found all over Tunisia. Here, the chops are marinated overnight. Grinding the spices yourself makes a big difference in maximizing the benefit of the sweet, spicy herbs. You can use a spice mill or a coffee grinder reserved exclusively for the purpose.

    1 tablespoon freshly ground caraway seeds
    1 teaspoon freshly ground anise or fennel seeds
    ½ teaspoon hot red pepper flakes
    ½ teaspoon freshly ground pepper
    1 teaspoon freshly ground coriander seeds
    3 garlic cloves, minced
    ⅓ cup olive oil
    1½ to 2 pounds lamb shoulder chops

◉◉ Mix the caraway, anise, pepper flakes, pepper, coriander, garlic and olive oil in a baking dish. Add the chops and turn to coat well. Cover and refrigerate for 24 hours.

Prepare a hot wood or charcoal fire in a grill, or preheat a gas grill.

When the fire is ready, put the chops on an oiled rack and grill for about 4 minutes per side, or until the outside is nicely browned and the inside, faintly pink.

SERVES 4

Scenting the Smoke

To add complexity to your barbecue, add aromatics to the hot coals right before putting the food on the grill:

◉◉ Bunches of dried herbs such as bay leaves, thyme, rosemary, sage, fennel or lavender.

◉◉ Seaweed and kelp to impart the tang of the sea to seafood and fish.

◉◉ Cinnamon sticks, cloves and other sweet whole spices for an exotic, incense-like aroma.

◉◉ Grapevine cuttings— classic in the wine country here as well as in France and much of the Mediterranean.

◉◉ Aromatic wood chips, including mesquite and applewood; soak for 30 minutes before placing atop the coals.

Lamb Tagine with Dried Apricots

In this dish, Marlena Spieler pairs lamb and dried apricots with a sauce accented with meat juices and orange juice. It's ideal for those who adore fruity, slightly sweet components with meat.

25 dried apricots, preferably plump, sweet ones

3 to 4 tablespoons olive oil

4 pounds lamb shoulder, cut into pieces that will easily fit into the pan

Salt and freshly ground pepper, to taste

1 teaspoon ground ginger

1 to 1½ teaspoons cinnamon

Several large pinches of saffron threads

1 teaspoon cumin

2 medium-large onions, finely chopped

5 garlic cloves, chopped

½ cup coarsely chopped cilantro

1 cup beef or vegetable broth

1 cup fresh orange juice

1 tablespoon honey, or to taste

1 to 2 tablespoons lightly toasted sesame seeds

◉ Preheat the oven to 350 degrees.

Place the apricots in a heat-proof bowl and add boiling water to cover. Let soak while preparing the remaining ingredients.

Heat the olive oil in a Dutch oven over medium-high heat. Add the lamb in batches and sauté until lightly browned. Using a slotted spoon, remove each batch as it browns to a bowl. When all the meat has browned, return it to the pan, season with salt and pepper, then sprinkle in about three fourths of the ginger, cinnamon, saffron and cumin. Add the onions, garlic and cilantro. Stir well, then add the broth and enough water to barely cover the meat.

Cover tightly and bake for 1 hour. Remove from the oven and cut the meat into 2- to 3-inch chunks. Return to the oven and bake, uncovered, for 30 minutes to 1 hour longer, or until the lamb is tender and the liquid has reduced by about half. Remove from oven. Transfer the cooking liquid to a small bowl and carefully spoon off all the fat.

Bring the orange juice to a boil in a saucepan over high heat; boil until it has reduced to about one fourth. Add the degreased lamb-cooking liquid and the honey. Continue to boil, adjusting the seasonings with the remaining spices (especially the cinnamon), for about 10 minutes, or until the sauce is very flavorful and has reduced by about half.

Meanwhile, test the apricots. They should be very tender. If not, gently simmer them in their soaking liquid while the sauce is reducing.

Drain the apricots and add them to the lamb. Pour the sauce over all and sprinkle with the sesame seeds.

SERVES 4

Moroccan Lamb Shanks with Eggplant

Meaty lamb shanks are cooked in aromatic liquid before being roasted over slices of eggplant. To create a bold sauce for the lamb, Marlena Spieler reduces the cooking juices, then refreshes the flavor with lemon juice. Exotic garnishes add a decidedly Middle Eastern touch.

3 tablespoons extra virgin olive oil

6 small lamb shanks, or 3½ pounds lamb shoulder on the bone, cut into 12 chunks

2 medium-large onions, chopped

5 garlic cloves, chopped

1½ teaspoons cumin

1 teaspoon paprika

2 pinches of saffron threads

½ cup chopped cilantro

¼ teaspoon ground ginger

Pinch of cayenne pepper

Pinch of freshly ground black pepper

Salt, to taste

1 cup beef or vegetable broth

1 medium-large eggplant, cut crosswise into ¼-inch slices

Juice of ½ lemon, or to taste

Garnishes

4 tablespoons blanched skinless almonds

1 tablespoon butter

3 hard-cooked eggs, peeled and cut into wedges

2 tablespoons chopped cilantro

∞ Preheat the oven to 350 degrees.

Heat 2 tablespoons of the olive oil in a Dutch oven over medium-high heat. Add the lamb and sauté until browned on all sides. Add the onions, garlic, cumin, paprika, saffron, cilantro, ginger, cayenne, black pepper and salt. Cook for a moment or two, then pour in the broth and enough water to just about cover the ingredients.

Cover and bake for 2 to 3 hours, or until the meat is quite tender and the liquid has evaporated by about half. Transfer the cooking liquid to a saucepan and skim off the fat.

Brush the eggplant slices very lightly with the remaining 1 tablespoon oil; broil on both sides until almost tender.

Arrange the eggplant in a large, shallow baking dish and top with the lamb. Bake for about 30 minutes, or until the top has browned.

Meanwhile, boil the cooking liquid over high heat until reduced by half. Add the lemon juice and season with salt and pepper.

Sauté the almonds in the butter in a small skillet over medium heat until they are golden.

Remove lamb and eggplant from the oven, pour the sauce evenly over the top, then finish with the almonds, eggs and cilantro.

SERVES 6

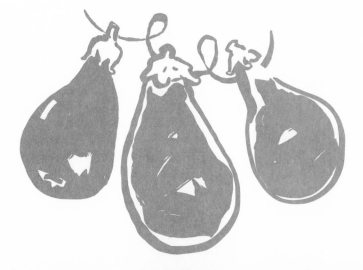

Lamb in Fragrant Korma Sauce

Homemade curry powder is far superior to store-bought blends, says Laxmi Hiremath. But if the recipe calls for just a little, as this one does, Madras curry powder is an acceptable substitute.

2 pounds boneless lamb, trimmed of all fat, cut into 2-inches pieces

1¾ cups water

5 bay leaves

½ teaspoon peppercorns

1 tablespoon fresh lemon juice

1-inch piece fresh ginger

2 shallots, coarsely chopped

½ to 1 teaspoon curry powder

2 tablespoons vegetable oil

½ cup plain yogurt, stirred

2 tablespoons sour cream (optional)

2 tablespoons Korma Masala (recipe follows)

Salt, to taste

Chopped green onions (white and most of the green part) for garnish

Put the lamb in a stockpot. Add 1½ cups of the water, the bay leaves, peppercorns and lemon juice. Bring to a boil over high heat, reduce heat to low and simmer for 20 minutes. Remove from heat.

Combine the ginger, shallots, curry powder and the remaining ¼ cup water in a blender and process until smoothly puréed.

Heat the oil in a heavy saucepan over medium heat. Add the puréed mixture and cook for 6 to 8 minutes, or until fragrant. Add the lamb and its cooking liquid, the yogurt, sour cream, if desired, the korma masala and salt. Simmer gently for 20 to 30 minutes, or until the meat is tender.

Transfer to a heated serving dish and garnish with the green onions.

SERVES 4

Korma Masala

2 tablespoons raw almonds

2 tablespoons shelled pistachios

2 tablespoons cashews

2 tablespoons pine nuts

Seeds from 20 green cardamom pods, ground

1 tablespoon cinnamon

½ tablespoon ground nutmeg

Combine the almonds, pistachios, cashews and pine nuts in a skillet over medium heat; toast, stirring frequently, for 5 to 6 minutes, or until lightly browned and fragrant. Transfer to a plate; let cool.

Reduce heat to low. Add the cardamom, cinnamon and nutmeg to the skillet and toast, stirring frequently, for 3 to 5 minutes, or until fragrant. Remove from heat.

Grind the nuts to a fine powder. Add to the spice mixture; blend well. Let cool, then transfer to an airtight glass jar. Store in the refrigerator for up to 2 months.

YIELDS ABOUT 1 CUP

Perking Up a Tired Sauce

Here's a quick way to invigorate a flat sauce: Mash a little anchovy in butter or olive oil and blend into the sauce. You won't be able to taste the fish, but it will enliven the sauce and give a rich depth of flavor.

To store unused anchovies: Cover with olive oil and refrigerate in an airtight container for up to 1 month.

Tagine of Meatballs and Peas

In this casserole from Marlena Spieler, sautéed meatballs are enhanced by a sweet tomato sauce studded with peas. The dish may be served with rice, pasta or couscous. It's also good with the addition of eggs—1 per person— poached in the tomato-pea sauce.

Meatballs

2 pounds lean ground lamb or beef

½ cup or so fresh breadcrumbs (see Note, page 192)

1 onion, grated

5 garlic cloves, chopped

4 tablespoons chopped Italian parsley

Salt and freshly ground black pepper, to taste

Cayenne pepper, to taste

½ teaspoon cumin

½ teaspoon paprika

¼ teaspoon cinnamon

¼ teaspoon powdered ginger

¼ teaspoon cardamom

Pinch of allspice

Flour for dusting meatballs

2 tablespoons extra virgin olive oil, or more as needed

Sauce

1 can (14 ounces) diced tomatoes; or 1½ pounds fresh tomatoes, peeled,
    cored and diced

1 cup water

2 tablespoons tomato paste

2 tablespoons extra virgin olive oil

1 onion, finely chopped

4 garlic cloves, coarsely chopped

4 tablespoons chopped Italian parsley

4 tablespoons chopped cilantro

1 teaspoon paprika

½ teaspoon cumin

½ teaspoon cinnamon

½ teaspoon ground ginger

Several pinches of saffron threads
Tiny pinch of sugar
Salt and cayenne pepper, to taste
1 to 2 cups shelled fresh peas, or frozen peas

To make the meatballs: Mix the ground meat in a bowl with the bread-crumbs, onion, garlic, parsley, salt, black and cayenne peppers, cumin, paprika, cinnamon, ginger, cardamom and allspice. Form into balls, about 1½ inches in diameter, and roll in flour.

Heat the olive oil in a large, heavy skillet over medium-high heat. Add the meatballs (work in batches, if necessary) and sauté until evenly browned. Add more olive oil, if necessary. Transfer meatballs to a plate.

To make the sauce: Combine the tomatoes, water and tomato paste in a saucepan. Stir in the olive oil, onion, garlic, parsley, cilantro, paprika, cumin, cinnamon, ginger, saffron, sugar, salt and cayenne pepper. Bring to a boil over high heat, then reduce heat to low and simmer for about 10 minutes. Taste and adjust seasonings as needed.

Combine the sauce and meatballs in a large sauté pan or Dutch oven. Add the peas and simmer over low heat for 8 to 10 minutes, or until the meatballs are cooked through and the sauce has thickened and developed a rich flavor. If the sauce is too thin in texture and flavor, pour it into a small saucepan and boil it down for a few minutes, then return it to the meatballs and peas.

SERVES 4 TO 6

Potée of Cabbage, Potatoes, Turnips, Carrots, Onions and Sausage

Potée is a hearty mountain dish from the alpine region of France. In its most rustic form, it's made with chunks of lard, uncured bacon and ham hocks. This version by Georgeanne Brennan is much lighter. Potée is especially appealing on a cold winter night, served with lots of bread for dipping into the sauce, bowls of mustard and horseradish for the sausages, and plates of pickled cucumbers and onions.

½ pound unsliced bacon, cut into ½-inch cubes

1 onion

4 turnips, peeled and quartered

6 boiling potatoes, quartered

4 carrots, cut into 2-inch lengths

4 or 5 thyme sprigs

2 fresh bay leaves, or 1 dried bay leaf

12 peppercorns

6 whole cloves

4 juniper berries

1½ teaspoons salt, or to taste

1 head cabbage, cored and cut into wedges

12 mild or spicy sausages

Combine the bacon, onion, turnips, potatoes, carrots, thyme, bay leaves, peppercorns, cloves and juniper berries in a heavy soup pot or large casserole. Add enough water to cover by 2 inches; sprinkle in 1½ teaspoons salt. Bring to a boil over medium heat and skim the foam that comes to the top. Reduce heat to low and simmer, uncovered, for 15 minutes. Add the cabbage and simmer for 15 minutes. Add the sausages and simmer for 30 minutes.

Using a slotted spoon, remove the bacon, sausages and vegetables and arrange them on a platter. Taste the broth and add more salt, if needed. Spoon a little of the cooking broth over the meat and vegetables and serve.

SERVES 6

Chapter 8

Poultry

Chicken is like an empty canvas with limitless possibilities. The current rage is to give it a burst of flavor with zesty marinades and to plump it up with brines.

At Chez Panisse, a whole chicken is soaked for 24 hours in a sugar-salt brine before being roasted. The chicken comes out moist and juicy. The results are so amazing, you may never go back to the traditional way. It's easy to do; you just have to plan ahead.

If you don't want to take the extra step of brining, you'll find several ways to roast a whole chicken to perfection: with a garlicky skin and walnuts (page 256) or stuffed with lemon and thyme (page 254).

Just about every country is represented by an array of international dishes: Spicy Vietnamese Chicken Curry (page 276); Pollo de Olla (page 280), a whole Mexican meal in a pot; and an Indian Tandoori Chicken (page 268). You'll also discover Tangerine-Bourbon Chicken Breasts (page 264) and Grilled Lavender Chicken on Arugula (page 261). For a more down-home taste, we have Southern-Fried Chicken (page 266) from Brad Levy of Firefly.

We also come to the rescue on how to cook the Thanksgiving turkey. The Food Department staff tried close to 40 different methods to find the best (page 294). And we also include recipes for leftovers, both in this chapter and several others. If you want to forego the whole bird, we have a great recipe for a honey-brined roast turkey breast (page 293).

In case you think we've forgotten other fine-feathered friends, you'll find Duck Breasts with Coriander-Cognac Sauce (page 286), Cornish Game Hen with Tomato-Olive Sauce (page 292) and Guinea Fowl with Gin and Juniper (page 300).

Lemon Thyme–Stuffed Chicken

For this recipe from Georgeanne Brennan, you need only a chicken, a generous bunch of fresh lemon thyme and a plump, juicy lemon. It's simple but one of the best roast chickens we've ever tasted.

1 chicken, about 3 pounds

1½ cups lemon thyme sprigs, or regular thyme sprigs

1 teaspoon salt

1 teaspoon freshly ground pepper

1 lemon

◉◉ Preheat the oven to 350 degrees.

Cut away any excess fat around the cavity of the chicken. Rub the outside of the chicken with the thyme sprigs. Rub the inside and the outside with the salt and pepper, then place the thyme sprigs in the cavity. Place the chicken breast-side up in a shallow roasting pan.

Roast, basting occasionally, for 1¼ to 1½ hours, or until the juices run clear when the thigh is pierced with a knife. Remove the chicken from the oven and immediately squeeze the juice of the lemon over it. Let stand for 5 to 10 minutes before carving and serving.

SERVES 3 OR 4

Super-Juicy Roasted Chicken with Garlic and Thyme

Brining is a great way to add flavor and moistness to today's commercial chickens. Janet Fletcher marinates chicken a half day in brine before roasting. If desired, brine overnight, then remove it from the brine in the morning but keep refrigerated until ready to roast.

Brine

1 gallon boiling water

1 cup kosher salt

½ bunch fresh thyme

4 garlic cloves, peeled and halved

1 tablespoon coarsely cracked peppercorns

1 chicken, 3½ to 4 pounds

1 lemon, halved

To make the brine: Combine the boiling water, salt, thyme, garlic and peppercorns in a bowl, small crock or heavy-duty plastic container just large enough to hold the chicken. Stir to dissolve the salt. Cool, then refrigerate until completely cold.

Place the chicken breast-side down in the brine. Weight with a plate if necessary to keep the chicken completely submerged. Refrigerate for 12 hours.

Preheat the oven to 425 degrees.

Remove the chicken from the brine and let air-dry at room temperature.

Squeeze 1 of the lemon halves in the cavity of the chicken, squeeze the other over the skin, then put both halves in the cavity. Truss the bird with string.

Place the chicken breast-side down on a rack in a roasting pan; roast for 30 minutes. Turn breast-side up and continue roasting for about 30 minutes longer, or until the juices run clear when the thigh is pierced with a knife.

Transfer the chicken breast-side down to a platter and let stand for 30 minutes. Remove the string and discard the lemons.

Carve the chicken into serving pieces and spoon any collected juices over them.

SERVES 3 OR 4

Roasted Chicken with Garlicky Skin and Walnuts

Garlic and walnuts are a natural combination in Georgeanne Brennan's Provence, where they're harvested shortly before the grapes. Fresh walnuts are considered a treat and are routinely incorporated into seasonal dishes such as this one, where chicken is stuffed under the skin with garlic, and toasted walnuts are sprinkled on at serving time. The combination is so simple, but so irresistible.

2 chickens, about 3 pounds each

2 tablespoons walnut oil

3 teaspoons salt

3 teaspoons freshly ground pepper

8 garlic cloves, thinly sliced lengthwise

1½ cups coarsely chopped walnuts

◉◉ Preheat the oven to 350 degrees.

Rub each chicken inside and out with half of the walnut oil, salt and pepper. Using your fingers, gently separate the breast skin from the flesh underneath, reaching as far as you can to the back of the chicken and down the thighs to create a pocket. Slip half of the garlic slices under the skin of each chicken.

Place the chickens on a rack in a roasting pan and roast, basting occasionally, for about 1 hour and 15 minutes, or until the juices run clear when the thigh is pierced with a knife. Remove from the oven and let stand for 10 minutes before carving.

Meanwhile, put the walnuts in a skillet over low heat and toast, shaking the skillet often, for about 10 minutes, or until the walnuts are golden brown when cut in half. Remove from the pan and set aside.

Carve the chickens, separating the thighs from the legs. Arrange the thighs, legs, wings and sliced breast meat on a platter, including any bits of garlic that slip from beneath the skin while carving. Sprinkle with the walnuts and serve.

SERVES 6

Roasted Chicken with Asparagus, Fennel and Potatoes

On his rare day off, Daniel Patterson, chef/owner of the stylish Elisabeth Daniel restaurant in San Francisco, loves to cook this homey, hearty dish. Try it and you'll discover why simple really is better.

1 chicken, 4 to 5 pounds

Salt and freshly ground pepper, to taste

1 pound small (creamer-size) Yukon Gold potatoes

2 fennel bulbs

5 tablespoons green (also called fall harvest) olive oil

1 pound asparagus

1 cup low-sodium chicken broth

1 tablespoon aged sherry vinegar

2 teaspoons minced chives for garnish

∞ Preheat the oven to 400 degrees.

Season the chicken generously, inside and out, with salt and pepper. Place the chicken breast-side up in a roasting pan. Roast for about 1 hour, or until the juices run clear when the thigh is pierced with a knife. Transfer the chicken to a platter and let rest for 10 minutes.

Meanwhile, put the potatoes in a saucepan and cover with water by 1 inch; add a generous amount of salt. Bring to a gentle boil over medium-high heat, then reduce heat to low and simmer for 5 to 10 minutes, or until the potatoes can easily be pierced with a sharp knife. Drain. When cool enough to handle, peel and quarter the potatoes. Set aside.

Quarter the fennel bulbs lengthwise. Cut out the core, then cut the fennel into ⅜-inch strips.

Heat 1 tablespoon of the olive oil in a large skillet over low heat. Add the fennel and gently sauté for about 30 minutes, or until tender. Season with salt and pepper. Remove from heat and set aside.

Trim the tough ends from the asparagus and cut the spears into 2-inch lengths.

Toss the asparagus with 2 tablespoons of the olive oil and a little salt in an ovenproof sauté pan. Place the pan in the oven and roast, tossing every few

Chicken Breasts with Pesto

Marlena Spieler suggests marinating boneless chicken breasts (with skin) in olive oil and dry white wine, plus salt and freshly ground pepper, to taste. Let stand for 1 hour. Mix several cloves of chopped garlic into a little pesto (jarred OK), and stuff beneath the skin. Cook over medium-hot coals for about 4 minutes per side, or until the chicken is just opaque and lightly marked from the grill.

minutes, for 10 to 15 minutes, or until the asparagus is tender. Remove from oven and set aside.

After the chicken is done, combine the asparagus and potatoes in the skillet with the fennel. Keep warm.

Pour off the fat from the roasting pan, reserving a few tablespoons. Add the reserved fat to the vegetables.

Add the chicken broth to the roasting pan and bring to a boil over high heat, stirring to scrape up the browned bits from the bottom of the pan. Boil until the liquid has reduced by one fourth. Strain the liquid into a bowl. Add the sherry vinegar and the remaining 2 tablespoons olive oil. Add any accumulated juices from the chicken. Season with salt and pepper.

Mound the vegetables in the center of a serving dish and pour the sauce over them. Place the chicken on top and garnish with the chives.

SERVES 4

Braised Chicken Maharaja

Don't be put off by the long list of ingredients; the result is well worth the effort. To speed up the preparation, you may substitute commercial garam masala for the peppercorns, cumin seeds, cinnamon stick, whole cloves and cardamom. To serve, Laxmi Hiremath suggests mounding the chicken on a heated platter over a bed of steaming basmati or wild rice.

¼ teaspoon peppercorns

½ teaspoon cumin seeds

1-inch piece cinnamon stick

8 whole cloves

5 green cardamom pods, husked

2 tablespoons mild vegetable oil, or unsalted butter

1 cup finely chopped onion

2 tablespoons minced garlic

1 tablespoon grated fresh ginger

2 large bay leaves

2 pounds skinless chicken breast halves with ribs

⅛ teaspoon turmeric

¼ teaspoon cayenne pepper

1 tablespoon sweet paprika

⅛ teaspoon nutmeg

½ teaspoon salt, or to taste

¾ cup plain yogurt

1 tablespoon sour cream

10 whole cashews

10 whole blanched almonds

½ cup water

Minced cilantro for garnish

👀 Combine the peppercorns, cumin, cinnamon, cloves and cardamom in a spice grinder and grind to a fine powder. Set aside.

Heat the oil in a large sauté pan over medium-high heat. Add the onion, garlic, ginger and bay leaves. Cook, stirring, for about 4 minutes, or until the onion is lightly browned. Reduce heat to medium.

Add the chicken and cook for 5 to 6 minutes, or until no longer pink. Add the ground spices, turmeric, cayenne, paprika, nutmeg and salt. Cook for 3 to 4 minutes, or until aromatic and the chicken is coated with the spices.

Combine the yogurt and sour cream in a small bowl; stir to blend. Add to the pan, a tablespoon at a time. Cook, stirring occasionally, for 3 minutes.

Combine the cashews, almonds and water in a blender; blend until smooth. Add to the pan. Reduce heat to low, cover and cook for about 30 minutes, or until the chicken is tender and the sauce is thick.

Transfer to a heated platter and garnish with cilantro.

SERVES 6

Pollo Diablo

Much to the delight of the rancho children, this "flattened" chicken grills under a cast-iron pan weighted with an adobe brick (or firebrick). It may look strange, but it's one of the most delicious ways to cook a chicken, according to Jacqueline McMahan. Leftovers are just as good the next day, so grill a few extra for weeknight dinners. The recipe may be doubled, tripled or quadrupled.

1 chicken, about 3 pounds, or a whole breast with bones

1 lemon

1 teaspoon salt

1 teaspoon freshly ground pepper, or to taste

2 garlic cloves, minced

1 tablespoon olive oil

Hot red pepper flakes, to taste (optional)

◉◉ Using poultry shears, cut out the backbone of the chicken. Remove and discard any excess fat. Place the bird skin-side up on a work surface and, using both hands, press down hard on the breastbone until you hear the cartilage break. (The chicken will flatten out a bit; if necessary, place a piece of wax paper over the bird and pound it with a mallet.)

Put the chicken in a nonaluminum pan (an 8- or 9-inch-diameter glass baking dish is perfect); squeeze the lemon juice over the bird, then rub all over with the salt, pepper, garlic and olive oil. If you want the chicken to really be "diablo," use lots of pepper or a few red pepper flakes, if desired. Let marinate at room temperature for 1 hour, turning a couple of times. (Or cover and refrigerate for up to 24 hours.)

Prepare a medium-hot fire in a grill. Place the chicken on the grill, reserving any leftover marinade. Put a 12-inch cast-iron pan on top of the chicken and place a heavy brick in the pan. Grill for 15 minutes. Baste with any leftover marinade. Turn the chicken, replace the pan with the brick on top, and grill for 15 to 20 minutes longer. The chicken will turn a deep brown but will remain juicy inside.

Eat with your fingers.

SERVES 2

Cooking Poultry on the Grill

To test poultry for doneness, stick a metal skewer or fork with long prongs into the deepest part of the flesh; the juices should run clear, not pink.

Mixed chicken parts: Sear pieces on both sides over hot coals, then cook over medium coals, turning occasionally. Dark meat takes about 30 minutes, white meat 15 minutes. To finish cooking simultaneously, put the dark meat on first, then add the breast meat.

Boneless chicken breasts: Cook quickly over medium-hot coals for 3 to 4 minutes per side, depending on their size.

Chicken halves: Cook, covered, over medium-hot coals for 30 minutes. It's not necessary to turn the meat.

Whole chicken: Cook, covered, over medium coals for about 1½ hours, or until an instant-read thermometer inserted into the fleshy part of a thigh, away from the bone, registers 170 degrees.

Chicken wings: Cook directly over medium-hot or hot coals for about

10 minutes per side. For the crispiest edges and most delectable eating, before cooking cut each wing into two pieces— the little wing part and the tiny drumette—and discard the third joint.

Spatchcocked chicken: Spatchcocking means splitting a whole bird down its backbone and flattening by pressing on it with the palm of your hand. This makes the chicken flat; it can be cooked directly on the barbecue as quickly and evenly as a half chicken.

Duck breasts: Sear for 1 minute per side, then cook over medium-hot coals for 3 to 4 minutes per side for rare, 5 to 6 minutes for medium and 6 to 8 minutes for well-done, depending on size. To serve, slice thinly across the grain; duck breasts can be chewy.

Duck halves: Cook, covered, if possible, over medium-hot coals for about 30 minutes. No need to turn the meat. Indirect heat is an excellent way to cook duck, and you have a nice little sauce for serving with the meat.

Grilled Lavender Chicken on Arugula

Lavender adds an unusual floral flavor to the chicken and lemon in this recipe by Robin Davis. Arugula works as a bitter counterpoint, creating a complex, satisfying dish that's easy to prepare.

1 tablespoon dried lavender blossoms

1½ teaspoons grated lemon zest

1 teaspoon coarse salt, plus more, to taste

1 teaspoon coarsely cracked black pepper, plus more, to taste

1 tablespoon plus ½ cup extra virgin olive oil

4 boneless chicken breast halves

¼ cup fresh lemon juice

1 tablespoon honey (preferably lavender honey)

1 tablespoon chopped fresh tarragon

1 teaspoon Dijon mustard

4 cups arugula

Combine the lavender, lemon zest, salt and pepper in a mortar and pestle and grind to a fine powder. Stir in the 1 tablespoon olive oil to form a paste. Smear the paste on both sides of the chicken, smearing some under the skin. Cover and refrigerate for at least 1 hour or up to 4 hours.

Prepare a fire in a barbecue (medium-high heat); alternatively, you may cook the chicken in a grill pan on the stovetop over medium-high heat.

Whisk together the lemon juice, honey, tarragon and mustard in a small bowl. Gradually whisk in the ½ cup olive oil. Season with salt and pepper.

Grill the chicken for about 4 minutes per side, or until cooked through. Transfer to a cutting board.

Toss the arugula with the dressing. Divide among serving plates. Slice the chicken crosswise into 1-inch strips. Arrange on the arugula.

SERVES 4

Roasted Chickens Stuffed with Orzo on a Bed of Rainbow Swiss Chard

Created by Julia McClaskey, the chef of Dine in San Francisco, this unusual chicken dish is perfect for a weekend dinner. The preparation can be time-consuming, but the end product is spectacular, and the presentation is impressive. Cutting the whole stuffed chickens in half during the roasting process is the trickiest part.

Chickens

6 garlic cloves, minced

½ bunch chives, chopped

½ bunch rosemary, chopped

½ bunch thyme, chopped

¼ cup olive oil

2 chickens, about 2 pounds each

Salt and freshly ground pepper, to taste

Parmesan Orzo

8 ounces orzo

¼ cup olive oil

2 tablespoons chopped fresh sage

½ cup plus 6 tablespoons freshly grated Parmigiano-Reggiano cheese

Salt and freshly ground pepper, to taste

Sauce

4 cups chicken stock

4 tablespoons butter (optional)

2 tablespoons fresh lemon juice

¼ cup chopped Italian parsley

Salt and freshly ground pepper, to taste

Chard

1 tablespoon butter

1 garlic clove, minced

1 shallot, minced

1 bunch rainbow Swiss chard, stems removed, leaves rinsed and chopped

◉◉ Preheat the oven to 350 degrees.

To make the chickens: Mix the garlic, chives, rosemary, thyme and olive oil in a large bowl. Coat the chickens with the mixture, then season with salt and pepper. Cover and refrigerate for at least 6 hours or as long as overnight.

To make the orzo: Cook the orzo according to the package directions, until al dente. Rinse with cold water and drain. Put in a bowl, toss with the olive oil, and combine with the sage and the ½ cup cheese. Season with salt and pepper.

Stuff the chickens with the orzo mixture, tie the legs together and place on a rack in a roasting pan. Roast for 1 hour, or until the juices run clear when the thighs are pierced with a knife.

Remove the chickens from the oven. Increase the oven temperature to 400 degrees.

Carefully cut each chicken in half. Place the halves stuffing-side up on a greased baking sheet. Top with the 6 tablespoons cheese. Bake for 10 minutes, or until the topping is browned.

While the chickens are roasting, prepare the sauce and chard.

To make the sauce: Pour the chicken stock into a saucepan and simmer over medium heat until reduced by half. Add the butter, if desired, the lemon juice and parsley. Season with salt and pepper. Keep warm.

To make the chard: Melt the butter in a large skillet over medium-high heat. Add the garlic and shallot and cook until slightly browned. Add the chard and cook, stirring, until wilted and tender.

To serve: Make a bed of the chard on a warmed serving platter. Arrange the chicken halves on the chard, then spoon the sauce over the chickens.

SERVES 4

Tangerine-Bourbon Chicken Breasts

Shirley Sarvis shows that the marriage of tangerine and bourbon is a natural when paired with chicken. It's a great main course for a romantic dinner for two.

2 boneless chicken breast halves, about 10 ounces total, trimmed of any excess fat

Salt, to taste

About ⅛ teaspoon hot red pepper flakes

1½ tablespoons bourbon

2 tablespoons unsalted butter

1 teaspoon grated tangerine zest

1 teaspoon fresh lemon juice

½ cup loosely packed watercress leaves

2 slender lemon wedges for garnish

∞ Gently pound each chicken breast half to an even ⅝-inch thickness. Rinse and dry. Season the skinless sides with salt, then turn the chicken over. Slip your fingers between skin and flesh at one side of each chicken breast half to loosen, then fold the skin back. Season the flesh with salt and sprinkle with red pepper flakes. Press the skin back in place.

Place a medium-size, heavy skillet over medium-high heat; sprinkle salt over the bottom. When the pan is hot, add the chicken skin-side down. Sauté until the skin is crisp and the chicken is well browned. Turn and sauté until browned on the other side and the flesh is opaque almost to the center. The total cooking time is about 6 minutes. Transfer the chicken to warmed plates.

Wipe out the pan, leaving the brown (not burned) particles in the pan. Add the bourbon and butter; cook, whisking, until the sauce has reduced to 2 tablespoons. Remove from heat and whisk in the tangerine zest and lemon juice. Season with salt.

Top each serving with a loose pile of watercress and spoon a portion of sauce under each breast half. Garnish with lemon wedges.

SERVES 2

Marinating Chicken Breasts

We marinated chicken breasts for 2 hours, 4 hours and overnight to find the optimum time to leave them in both salted and unsalted marinades. We found that 4 hours was the best amount of time. Salt helped to perk up the flavor and didn't dry out the flesh.

All-Purpose Marinade

2 tablespoons finely minced orange zest

1 cup fresh orange juice

⅔ cup hoisin sauce

¼ cup honey

6 garlic cloves, finely minced

¼ cup very finely minced fresh ginger

½ cup minced green onions (both white and green parts)

½ teaspoon salt

∞ Combine all ingredients in a nonreactive container. Add meat to the container, cover and refrigerate for 4 hours. Yields enough for 6 chicken breast halves.

Che's Havana-Style Chicken

The chicken has a rich, satisfying flavor in this exotic dish created by Johnny Alamilla, the chef of the now-closed Nuevo Latino restaurant, Che. Make sure the plantains are ripe, or they will not absorb enough flavor from the marinade. Alamilla recommends serving the chicken with sautéed greens such as spinach or chard.

Marinade

2 cups fresh orange juice (about 4 oranges)

2 cups fresh lime juice (about 9 limes)

1 tablespoon chopped fresh oregano

⅓ cup chopped Italian parsley

2 tablespoons chopped garlic

2 Fresno chiles, seeded and chopped

2 teaspoons ground coriander seeds

Chicken and Plantains

6 chicken breast halves, wing bone attached ("airline breast")

Salt and freshly ground pepper, to taste

Olive oil for frying

Juice of ½ lime

3 ripe plantains, peeled and sliced lengthwise, then halved

◉◉ To make the marinade: Combine the orange juice, lime juice, oregano, parsley, garlic, chiles and coriander in a bowl and let stand for 30 minutes.

To make the chicken and plantains: Rinse the chicken and pat dry, then add to the marinade. Let the chicken marinate overnight in the refrigerator for a bold citrus flavor, or for 1 hour at room temperature. (If marinating for only 1 hour, give the chicken a squeeze of lime before serving for extra zing.)

Preheat the oven to 375 degrees.

Remove the chicken from the marinade and pat dry. Season with salt and pepper.

Coat the bottom of a cast-iron skillet with olive oil. Place over medium heat. When hot, add the chicken skin-side down and sauté until browned. Turn the chicken breasts and transfer the skillet to the oven. Roast for 7 to 8 minutes, or until the chicken is three-fourths cooked (timing will depend on size of chicken breasts).

Remove the skillet from the oven and transfer the chicken to a plate.

Add the lime juice to the skillet. Add the plantains and toss them in the pan drippings until coated. Return the skillet to the oven and bake for 5 to 8 minutes.

Return the chicken breasts to the skillet and roast for 10 minutes longer.
SERVES 6

Southern-Fried Chicken

Brad Levy's version of Southern-fried chicken is absolutely delicious. From time to time, you can find it on the menu at Firefly, his eclectic Noe Valley restaurant in San Francisco that specializes in home cooking from around the world.

2 fryer chickens, about 3 pounds each

Spice Mixture

1 teaspoon paprika

1 teaspoon ground red chile (New Mexico or ancho)

2 teaspoons granulated garlic

1 teaspoon granulated or powdered onion

Pinch of celery salt

2 tablespoons kosher salt

2 teaspoons freshly ground pepper

Coating

2 cups all-purpose flour

1½ teaspoons salt

½ teaspoon freshly ground pepper

2 cups buttermilk

2 cups vegetable oil, or solid vegetable shortening, or as needed

Cut each chicken into 8 pieces.

To make the spice mixture: Mix together the paprika, chile, garlic, onion, celery salt, kosher salt and pepper in a bowl. Sprinkle the spice mixture on the chicken pieces heavily enough so the color of the skin barely shows through. Refrigerate for 5 to 10 minutes.

To make the coating: Combine the flour, salt and pepper in a medium-size shallow bowl. Pour the buttermilk into another medium-size shallow bowl.

Piece by piece, dip the chicken first into the buttermilk, then in the seasoned flour, coating well. Shake off any excess flour and place the pieces on a sheet of wax paper on a baking sheet; do not let them touch each other. Refrigerate for 15 to 30 minutes.

Pour ½ inch of vegetable oil or place the solid vegetable shortening in a large, heavy skillet over high heat. Heat the oil to 325 degrees.

Piece by piece, place the chicken skin-side down in the hot oil. Do not crowd the pan or the temperature of the oil will drop and the chicken will not cook properly. Fry, turning once or twice, for 10 to 20 minutes, or until the pieces are dark golden brown and cooked through. To test, cut into a piece or two. There should be no trace of pink near the bone.

Serve hot, at room temperature or cold.

SERVES 6 TO 8

Tandoori Chicken

Here's an easy at-home version of this famous Indian dish, perfected by Laxmi Hiremath. The chicken is marinated in a yogurt mixture for up to 36 hours and then grilled.

2½ pounds skinless, boneless chicken breast halves

2-inch piece fresh ginger, peeled and minced

6 large garlic cloves, minced

4 tablespoons fresh lime juice

2 teaspoons salt

2 teaspoons paprika

Marinade

1 large onion, coarsely chopped

⅔ cup plain yogurt

¼ teaspoon cinnamon

8 green cardamom pods, husked

10 whole cloves

1 teaspoon cumin seeds

½ teaspoon cayenne pepper

2 tablespoons mild vegetable oil

Garnishes

1 large red onion, peeled and cut into thin rings

1 lemon, cut into wedges

Rinse the chicken and pat dry. Place in a 3-quart casserole. Combine the ginger, garlic, lime juice, salt and paprika in a small bowl and mix well. Rub the mixture thoroughly onto the chicken. Cover and let stand at room temperature for 1 hour.

Combine the chopped onion, yogurt, cinnamon, cardamom, cloves, cumin, cayenne and oil in a blender; process until finely puréed. Pour over the chicken and rub in well, turning the pieces several times, pushing the marinade into crevices and crannies and coating the breasts evenly. Cover and refrigerate for 10 to 36 hours, turning occasionally.

Prepare a medium-hot fire in a charcoal grill or preheat a broiler. Place the chicken on the grill or on a broiler pan 6 inches from heat source.

Grill or broil for 6 to 8 minutes, turn and grill or broil for 6 to 8 minutes longer, or until tender and cooked through. Transfer to a platter. Surround with the onion slices and lemon wedges.

SERVES 2 TO 4

Jojo's Provençal Chicken

This earthy, Provençal-inspired dish was created by Curt Clingman, chef/owner of Jojo's in Oakland. It requires a minimum of preparation and tastes fabulous. Clingman specifies using quality green olives like Picholine or Lucques. They should not be pitted, Clingman says, because the pits add a wonderful nutty quality to the dish. Just be sure to warn your guests.

½ cup all-purpose flour

1 tablespoon salt, plus more, to taste

1 teaspoon pepper, plus more, to taste

6 chicken legs, drumsticks separated from thighs

¼ cup olive oil

6 spring onions, halved lengthwise

1½ cups dry white wine

4 thyme sprigs

4 savory sprigs

1½ cups chicken broth

6 small carrots, peeled and cut into small pieces

Peel from ½ organic orange (use a vegetable peeler)

½ cup Picholine or Lucques olives

2 tablespoons imported Dijon mustard

1 tablespoon chopped Italian parsley for garnish

◎ Preheat the oven to 350 degrees.

Mix together the flour, salt and pepper in a shallow bowl. Dredge the chicken pieces in the flour mixture, shaking off excess.

Heat the olive oil in an ovenproof skillet over medium-high heat. Add the chicken and fry, turning once, until lightly browned. Remove the chicken from the skillet and set aside. Add the onions cut-side down to the skillet and sauté for about 5 minutes, or until lightly browned; remove and set aside.

Drain the grease from the skillet. Add the wine and cook over high heat until reduced by one half. Tie the thyme and savory sprigs together with kitchen string. Add the chicken broth and the herb bundle. Season with salt and pepper. Bring to a boil, return the chicken and onions to the skillet, add the carrots and simmer for 5 minutes.

Loosely cover the skillet with a piece of parchment paper or aluminum foil and transfer to the oven. Bake for 45 minutes. Check after the first 15 minutes to be sure the liquid is simmering slowly. If not, adjust the heat as needed.

When the chicken is done, remove the skillet from the oven. Give the herb bundle a shake to free the leaves into the sauce. Discard the stems. Skim the fat from the sauce. Add the orange peel and olives, cover and let steep for 20 minutes. Stir in the mustard and bring to a simmer. Taste and adjust seasonings as needed. Garnish with the parsley.

SERVES 6

Kokkari's Grilled Chicken Souvlaki

Colorful and light, these Mediterranean skewers from chef Jean Alberti of Kokkari restaurant in San Francisco make a great grilling option on warm summer nights. The tangy lemon vinaigrette is designed to drizzle over the skewers.

Marinade

3 cups plain yogurt

1 tablespoon chopped fresh mint

1 tablespoon chopped fresh oregano

3 garlic cloves, minced

1 tablespoon fresh lemon juice

¼ cup fresh orange juice

1 tablespoon red wine vinegar

¼ teaspoon salt

⅛ teaspoon freshly ground pepper

6 skinless, boneless chicken breast halves

Marinades for Chicken

Here are three marinades from Marlena Spieler for perking up chicken and other poultry. Each is designed for about 2 pounds of meat. If chicken is marinated more than 30 minutes, be sure to refrigerate.

Olive Oil–Rosemary Marinade: Combine 3 to 5 tablespoons extra virgin olive oil, juice of ½ lemon, 3 to 5 coarsely chopped garlic cloves, 1 to 2 tablespoons chopped fresh rosemary, salt and freshly ground pepper, to taste. Marinate for 30 minutes or up to 2 days. Also good on zucchini, parboiled potatoes, peppers, artichokes, fish, pork and veal.

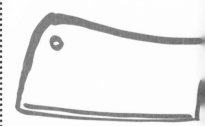

Teriyaki Marinade: Combine ¼ cup each dry sherry or rice wine, soy sauce, Asian sesame oil; 2 tablespoons sugar; 3 green onions, chopped; 3 garlic cloves, chopped; and 1 to 2 teaspoons grated fresh ginger. Marinate for up to 2 to 3 days. Also good on meats and fish.

Mexican Red Chile and Citrus Paste: Combine 5 chopped garlic cloves, 2 tablespoons ground red chile, 1 teaspoon cumin (or more, to taste), large pinch of dried oregano, juice of 1 orange and 1 lime or lemon, rind of ½ orange, 2 tablespoons olive oil, 2 tablespoons chopped cilantro, salt, freshly ground pepper and a pinch of sugar. Marinate for 1 hour or up to 2 days.

Vinaigrette

1 teaspoon chopped Italian parsley

1 teaspoon chopped fresh oregano

½ teaspoon dried oregano

1½ teaspoons minced shallot

1 garlic clove, minced

¼ cup fresh lemon juice

Salt and freshly ground pepper, to taste

¾ cup extra virgin olive oil

6 bamboo skewers

3 green bell peppers, seeded, deribbed and cut into 1-inch squares

3 red bell peppers, seeded, deribbed and cut into 1-inch squares

1 red onion, cut into 1-inch squares

¼ cup olive oil

Salt and freshly ground pepper, to taste

Oregano sprigs for garnish

◉◉ Mix together the yogurt, mint, oregano, garlic, lemon juice, orange juice, vinegar, salt and pepper in a glass container.

Cut each chicken breast half into 5 or 6 pieces and place in the marinade. Cover and refrigerate for 24 hours.

To make the vinaigrette: Mix together the parsley, fresh and dried oregano, the shallot, garlic and lemon juice in a bowl. Season with salt and pepper. Slowly whisk in the olive oil. Set aside.

Soak the bamboo skewers in warm water for 1 hour. Prepare a medium-hot fire in a grill.

Remove the chicken from the marinade. Thread the chicken, bell peppers and onion onto the skewers, alternating about 5 pieces of each per skewer. Brush each skewer with olive oil and season with salt and pepper.

Grill for 8 to 10 minutes per side, or until done.

Garnish with oregano sprigs and drizzle with the vinaigrette.

SERVES 6

Chicken Ragout

In Vietnam, this recipe also is made with pork ribs and beef tongue. Traditionally, the chicken version is made with whole chicken—bones, skin and all—for added flavor and richness, but Mai Pham updates it for the modern cook using either boneless thighs or breasts.

2 teaspoons minced garlic

½ teaspoon salt, plus more, to taste

2 tablespoons Asian fish sauce

2 tablespoons soy sauce

1 tablespoon sugar

1½ pounds skinless, boneless chicken thighs or breasts, cut into bite-size chunks

2 tablespoons vegetable oil

3 tablespoons butter

2 shallots, sliced

2 tablespoons tomato paste

2 plum tomatoes, cut into wedges

3 cups chicken broth

1 cup dry white wine, or vermouth

3 bay leaves

2 carrots, cut into 1-inch rounds (about 1½ cups)

3 red potatoes, cut into wedges (about 2 cups)

½ yellow onion, cut into wedges

1½ cups fresh or frozen peas, or lima beans

Cilantro leaves for garnish

◉ Combine the garlic, salt, fish sauce, soy sauce and sugar in a mixing bowl. Add the chicken and let marinate at room temperature for 30 minutes.

Heat the oil in a large skillet over medium heat. Add the chicken and sear until the sides are nicely browned. Remove from heat and set aside.

Heat the butter in a large saucepan over medium heat. Add the shallots and stir for about 30 seconds, or until fragrant. Add the tomato paste and the chicken and cook, stirring, for 3 minutes.

Add the tomatoes, chicken broth, wine and bay leaves; simmer for 5 minutes. Add the carrots, potatoes and onion; simmer for 10 minutes.

Add the peas, then simmer for about 5 minutes longer, or until the chicken and vegetables are done. Remove the bay leaf, season with salt and garnish with the cilantro leaves.

SERVES 6

Chicken with Lemon, Peppers and Olives

The combination of lemons and olives is a favorite in many cuisines, but in this Moroccan dish by Marlena Spieler, the combo is taken to new heights by the addition of a complex blend of spices.

1 chicken, 3½ to 4 pounds, cut into serving pieces, or 8 chicken thighs

Salt and freshly ground pepper, to taste

2 to 3 tablespoons olive oil

1 tablespoon cumin

2 teaspoons paprika

½ to 1 teaspoon powdered ginger

½ teaspoon turmeric

Large pinch of saffron threads

Pinch of cayenne pepper, or more, to taste

2 onions, chopped

5 to 8 garlic cloves, coarsely chopped

½ to ¾ cup chopped cilantro

1 red bell pepper, roasted, peeled, seeded, deribbed and cut into strips

1 cup diced tomatoes (canned OK)

Juice of 3 lemons (about ⅓ cup)

1 cup chicken broth

8 ounces Moroccan cracked green olives (see Note)

1 lemon, cut into wedges, for garnish

∞ Preheat the oven to 350 degrees.

Season the chicken with salt and pepper. Heat the olive oil in a sauté pan over medium-high heat. Add the chicken pieces and brown lightly. Sprinkle with the cumin, paprika, ginger, turmeric, saffron and cayenne. Add the onions, garlic and cilantro. Sauté for a moment or two, combining the spices with the chicken.

Arrange the chicken pieces in a single layer in a baking dish or casserole; add the roasted red pepper strips, tomatoes, half of the lemon juice and all of the broth.

Pour about 1 cup water into the sauté pan; stir to scrape up all the browned bits on the bottom of the pan, then pour over the chicken. You want the liquid to come about two thirds of the way up on the chicken.

Bake for 30 to 40 minutes, or until the chicken is tender and the liquid has evaporated slightly. Transfer the chicken to a platter and tent with aluminum foil.

Bring a saucepan of water to a boil over high heat. Add the olives and blanch for 1 minute. Drain, then arrange around the chicken.

Pour the cooking juices into a small saucepan and skim off the fat. Bring the juices to a boil over high heat and boil until reduced to a thick, flavorful sauce. Remove from heat, add the remaining lemon juice and pour the sauce over the chicken. Garnish with the lemon wedges.

SERVES 4

NOTE: Use good-quality olives, such as those available at Haig's Delicacies, 642 Clement St. (near 7th Avenue) in San Francisco.

Because various meats and vegetables cook at different rates, skewered foods are usually best with just one food per skewer, such as the classic Indian chicken tikka or Indonesian saté. A delicious exception, according to Marlena Spieler, is food that acts as a basting ingredient such as bacon. Thread a slice or two of bacon along with chunks of salmon or chicken livers, and you have self-basting kebabs. Pieces of spicy sausage are good with chicken or lamb.

Here are two more great combinations:
◉◉ Chicken (or pork) with sage leaves and prosciutto or bacon.
◉◉ Chunks of spicy Mexican or New Mexican sausage, chicken breast and onion.

Vanilla-Scented Chicken and Mushrooms Simmered in Coconut Milk

This recipe was inspired by a Paris bistro lunch enjoyed by Marlena Spieler. The bistro specialized in traditional dishes punctuated with unexpected flavors. For instance, a plate of scallops was brought to life with vanilla. Spieler thought, why not chicken? Why not, indeed. It's totally delicious. The sauce is simply the pan juices simmered with the shiitake-soaking liquid and coconut milk. The vanilla just adds a mysterious and alluring flavor note. Accompany with steamed rice or chunks of baguette.

20 to 25 dried shiitake mushrooms, or Chinese black mushrooms

2 cups boiling water

4 skinless, boneless chicken breast halves, sliced into ¾-inch-thick strips

8 garlic cloves, coarsely chopped

Grated zest of ½ orange

3 tablespoons strong spirits, such as rum, vodka or schnapps; or Chinese rice wine

1 teaspoon vanilla

2 tablespoons fresh lemon juice, plus more, to taste

Pinch or two of hot red pepper flakes, or more, to taste

Pinch or two of salt

½ teaspoon light soy sauce

1½ cups coconut milk

1 tablespoon vegetable oil

◉◉ Place the shiitakes in a bowl and add 2 cups of boiling water to cover. Cover and set aside until cool. Remove the mushrooms from the soaking water, reserving the water, and cut off and discard the stems. Strain the soaking water using a sieve lined with several thicknesses of cheesecloth or a paper coffee filter. Set aside.

Place the chicken strips in a bowl. Add the garlic, orange zest, spirits, vanilla, lemon juice, hot pepper flakes, salt, soy sauce and about ¼ cup of the coconut milk. Marinate for 30 minutes to 1 hour at room temperature or as long as overnight in the refrigerator.

Remove the chicken from the marinade, shaking off excess.

Place a wok over high heat; when it is very hot, add about half of the oil. Working in batches, add the chicken and stir-fry until it is lightly browned but not too firm. Transfer the chicken to a plate and keep warm.

Add the remaining oil, heat for 1 minute, then add the mushrooms and stir-fry for a minute or so. Spoon out any excess oil, then add about 1½ cups of the mushroom-soaking liquid. Bring to a boil over high heat and cook until the liquid is reduced by about one half. Pour in the remaining 1¼ cups coconut milk and continue to cook until the sauce is thickened.

Return the chicken and accumulated juices to the wok; stir and taste for seasoning, adding lemon juice to balance the richness of the sauce.

SERVES 4

Spicy Vietnamese Chicken Curry

In the winter, few foods can entice Mai Pham more than a bowl of this curry with steamed rice or a warm baguette. Traditionally, a whole cut-up chicken is preferred—bones, skin and all—to produce a rich-tasting sauce. However, if you'd rather not fuss with a whole bird, use chicken parts.

3 tablespoons vegetable oil

2 shallots, minced

3 garlic cloves, minced

4 tablespoons good-quality curry powder

1 teaspoon ground turmeric

2 teaspoons paprika

½ tablespoon hot red pepper flakes, or to taste

1 chicken, 3 to 4 pounds, trimmed of visible fat, cut into serving pieces and
    skin removed

2-inch piece fresh ginger, cut into ¼-inch-thick slices

1 stalk lemongrass (tender white part only), cut into 2-inch pieces

3 cups low-sodium chicken broth

5 bay leaves

3 tablespoons Asian fish sauce

2 tablespoons sugar

3 carrots, peeled and cut diagonally into 1-inch pieces

1½ cups coconut milk

1 pound new red potatoes, quartered

1 small yellow onion, cut into wedges

10 cilantro sprigs for garnish

Heat the oil in a large Dutch oven over medium heat. Add the shallots, garlic, 1 tablespoon of the curry powder, the turmeric, paprika and pepper flakes and stir for about 20 seconds, or until fragrant. Do not let the spices burn.

Add the chicken pieces and cook for about 3 minutes, or until lightly browned. Add the ginger, lemongrass, chicken broth, bay leaves, fish sauce, sugar and the remaining 3 tablespoons curry powder. Bring to a boil, reduce heat, cover and simmer for 15 minutes. Add the carrots and cook for 5 minutes. Add the coconut milk, potatoes and onion; simmer for 15 to 20 minutes longer, or until the chicken and vegetables are done.

Garnish with cilantro and serve.

SERVES 6

Ginger Chicken in a Clay Pot

In Vietnam, caramel sauce is used to enhance the color of this dish and to impart a sweet, smoky flavor, but Mai Pham has substituted brown sugar with no loss of flavor. A 2-quart Chinese sandy pot is best for this recipe, but you may also prepare it in a regular pot. Serve with lots of steamed rice.

1 tablespoon vegetable oil

1 shallot, minced

1 teaspoon minced garlic

1¼ pounds skinless, boneless chicken thighs, cut into large chunks

1½ tablespoons minced fresh ginger

½ teaspoon minced fresh chiles

2 teaspoons light brown sugar

2 tablespoons Asian fish sauce

½ cup chicken broth, or water

2 green onions (white and most of the green part), cut into 1-inch lengths

1 tablespoon chopped cilantro

¼ teaspoon freshly ground pepper, or to taste

◎◎ Heat the vegetable oil in a clay pot or other pot over medium heat. When it is hot, add the shallot and garlic and cook, stirring, for 2 to 3 minutes, or until fragrant.

Add the chicken, ginger and chiles and cook, stirring, for about 2 minutes, or until the chicken loses its raw look. Add the brown sugar and stir for 1 minute. Stir in the fish sauce and cook for 1 minute. Add the chicken broth and bring to a boil. Reduce heat to low and simmer for about 15 minutes, or until the chicken is done. The sauce should be slightly thick. (Add more water if necessary.)

Remove from heat. Top with the green onions and cilantro; season with the pepper. Serve right from the clay pot.

SERVES 4

Braised Chicken Wings with Tomato, Porcini and Sage

Inexpensive chicken wings soar to new culinary heights in this braise by Janet Fletcher. It's a great dish for a super-casual meal. Serve with steamed white rice or wild rice.

¼ ounce dried porcini mushrooms, soaked in ¾ cup water for 1 hour

2 tablespoons olive oil

2 pounds chicken wings, tips removed, each wing cut into 2 pieces

Salt and freshly ground pepper, to taste

½ cup dry white wine

4 garlic cloves, minced

⅔ cup chopped canned tomatoes

1 tablespoon chopped fresh sage

Lift the porcini out of the soaking liquid with a slotted spoon and chop coarsely. Strain the liquid through a double thickness of damp cheesecloth. Set aside.

Heat the olive oil in a large skillet over medium-high heat. Add the chicken wings, in batches, if necessary. Season with salt and pepper and brown on all sides, adjusting the heat so the wings brown without burning, for about 10 minutes.

Remove the wings from the skillet and pour off all the fat. Add the wine to the skillet and simmer until reduced by one half, stirring with a wooden spoon to scrape up the browned bits from the bottom of the skillet. Add the garlic and porcini and simmer for 30 seconds, then add ½ cup of the porcini soaking liquid, the tomatoes and sage. Simmer, stirring, for about 3 minutes to blend the flavors.

Return the chicken to the skillet. Cover, adjust heat to maintain a slow simmer, and braise for 1 hour.

Transfer the chicken wings to a warm platter. If the sauce seems a little thin, simmer it briefly to concentrate it. Spoon over the chicken.

SERVES 4

Pollo de Olla

Very rarely was anything cooked plain in the early California rancho kitchen. A paste of garlic and salt was a basic seasoning. To this the rancho cook might add cumin seed, red chile, oregano and black pepper. This lively paste—and it had numerous variations—was rubbed onto poultry, meat, fish and game before cooking. It was stirred into rice, as well, and almost any other savory dish. Here, it appears in a hearty chicken stew—a whole meal in a pot by Jacqueline McMahan.

Rancho Seasoning Paste

1½ teaspoons kosher salt

1 tablespoon minced garlic

1 teaspoon dried oregano

1 teaspoon mashed cumin seeds

1 teaspoon freshly ground pepper

2 teaspoons olive oil

Chicken and Vegetables

1 chicken, about 3½ pounds, cut into serving pieces, skin removed

1 tablespoon olive oil

8 cups water

1 onion, diced

1 can (15 ounces) stewed tomatoes

2 Anaheim chiles, charred, peeled, seeded and chopped

1 green or red bell pepper, seeded, deribbed and diced

4 carrots, peeled and cut into chunks

2 potatoes, peeled and cut into chunks

Rice

1 tablespoon olive oil

1 cup long-grain white rice

⊚⊚ To make the seasoning paste: Using a mortar and pestle, mash together the salt, garlic, oregano, cumin seeds and pepper. Drizzle in the olive oil to create a paste.

To make the chicken and vegetables: Rub the paste onto the chicken pieces. Heat the olive oil in a skillet over medium-high heat. Add the chicken, a few pieces at a time, and fry until barely golden. As the pieces finish browning, transfer them to a plate.

When all the pieces have been browned, return them to the skillet. Add the water and onion and simmer for 25 minutes, skimming frequently.

Add the stewed tomatoes, chiles, bell pepper, carrots and potatoes. Simmer for 20 minutes.

To make the rice: While the chicken and vegetables are cooking, heat the olive oil in a skillet over medium heat. Add the rice and sauté, stirring, for about 5 minutes, or until the grains are golden but not brown. Add to the chicken and vegetables. Simmer for about 20 minutes, or until the rice is tender.

Spoon into soup bowls and serve.

SERVES 6

Ponzu's Chicken Wings with Caramel–Black Pepper Glaze

These gooey chicken wings are addictive. They make an exciting appetizer or light entrée served with steamed jasmine rice. Because the dish is quick and easy to prepare, it's ideal for last-minute entertaining. It was created by John Beardsley, chef of the stylish fusion restaurant Ponzu in San Francisco.

    12 chicken wings

    1 quart vegetable oil for deep-frying

    ½ cup sugar

    1 tablespoon water

    ⅓ cup Asian fish sauce

    1 tablespoon freshly ground pepper

◉◉ Cut the chicken wings at the joint into 2 pieces. Remove the wing tips and reserve for stock, if desired.

Heat the oil in a large pot over high heat to 375 degrees.

Add the chicken wings and deep-fry for 10 to 15 minutes, or until golden brown and crispy. Remove the wings to paper towels to drain.

Combine the sugar and water in a small saucepan. Place over medium-high heat and let the sugar dissolve, then turn a light caramel color. Watch carefully so the sugar does not burn. Do not stir. The sugar should take about 7 minutes to caramelize. Remove from heat and add the fish sauce. The sauce will boil vigorously. Return to medium heat and cook for 30 seconds to 1 minute, or until slightly thickened. Stir in the pepper.

Toss the chicken wings with the sauce and serve.

SERVES 3

Mama's Tamale Pie

This is one of the first and best casseroles Jacqueline McMahan learned to make. A cornmeal batter is poured into a pan, topped with a spicy meat mixture, then crowned with a top layer of batter and a sprinkling of cheddar cheese. It's baked until firm and golden. The dish is ideal for a casual dinner party.

1 tablespoon olive oil

1 onion, chopped

2 garlic cloves, minced

1 red bell pepper, seeded, deribbed and chopped

1 can (7 ounces) green chiles, chopped

3 tomatoes, peeled, seeded and chopped

1 cup tomato sauce

1 tablespoon pure chile powder

1 teaspoon dried oregano

1 teaspoon crushed cumin seeds

1 teaspoon salt

½ teaspoon freshly ground pepper

2 cups cubed cooked chicken (poached, roasted or rotisseried)

1 cup corn kernels

1 cup pitted black olives

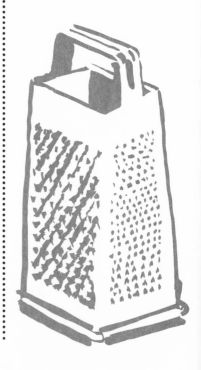

Smoky Mexican Chicken Legs

Coat chicken legs—skinless, if possible, so the marinade can sink in—with Mexican Red Chile and Citrus Paste (see recipe on page 271), and wrap each leg with a piece of bacon. Marinate in the refrigerator for 1 to 2 hours. Remove from refrigerator about 30 minutes before cooking. Grill over medium coals for 15 to 20 minutes, or until the bacon is crisply browned and the chicken is cooked through.

Cornmeal Crust

¾ cup stone-ground cornmeal

3 cups milk

½ teaspoon salt

1 tablespoon butter

2 eggs

1½ cups grated sharp cheddar cheese

Preheat the oven to 350 degrees. Grease a 2-quart casserole dish.

Heat the olive oil in a skillet over medium heat. Add the onion, garlic and bell pepper and sauté for about 10 minutes, or until softened. Add the green chiles, tomatoes, tomato sauce, chile powder, oregano, cumin, salt and pepper. Simmer for 10 minutes to blend the flavors. Add the chicken, corn and olives; simmer for 5 minutes. Set aside.

To make the crust: Blend the cornmeal with 1 cup of the milk in a bowl. Combine the remaining 2 cups milk, the salt and butter in a saucepan. Bring to a simmer over medium-high heat. Gradually add the cornmeal mixture, whisking constantly. Reduce heat to very low, cover and simmer for 5 minutes. Remove from heat.

Beat the eggs in a bowl. Stir a little of the hot mixture into the eggs, blending quickly, then stir this back into the cornmeal mixture. Blend in 1 cup of the grated cheese.

Spread half of the cornmeal on the bottom of the prepared casserole. Spoon in all the filling, then spread the remaining cornmeal over all, making sure it covers the filling. Sprinkle with the remaining ½ cup cheese.

Bake for 50 minutes. Remove from the oven and puncture the crust in a couple of places to release steam. Let cool for 15 minutes before serving.

SERVES 6

Mojo's Chicken and Dumplings

Donald Link, who is the executive chef of San Francisco's Elite Cafe and Palo Alto's Mojo, says this recipe was inspired by his grandfather. The level of heat can be adjusted by adding more—or less—cayenne pepper. For faster preparation, substitute a preroasted whole chicken, available at most grocery stores.

Chicken

1 lemon

4 fresh sage leaves

1 chicken, 2¼ to 3 pounds

Salt and freshly ground pepper, to taste

Cayenne pepper, to taste

Paprika, to taste

Sauce

4 tablespoons butter

1 cup diced onion

1 cup diced celery

1 cup diced carrot

1 teaspoon chopped garlic

1 teaspoon chopped fresh sage

1 teaspoon chopped fresh thyme

1 teaspoon Cajun seasoning, plus more, to taste (see Note)

2 teaspoons salt

4 tablespoons all-purpose flour

⅓ cup dry white wine

⅓ cup whipping cream

⅓ cup chicken broth

2 tablespoons fresh lemon juice

1 teaspoon hot sauce

Dumplings

2 tablespoons butter

2 tablespoons minced onion

1½ cups all-purpose flour

1 tablespoon chopped fresh sage

½ teaspoon dry mustard

1 teaspoon salt

1 teaspoon baking powder

½ teaspoon cayenne pepper

¼ cup milk

2 eggs

◎◎ To roast the chicken: Preheat the oven to 450 degrees.

Cut 2 thin slices from the lemon. Insert 1 lemon slice and 2 sage leaves under the skin on each chicken breast. Season the entire chicken with a generous amount of salt, pepper, cayenne pepper and paprika.

Roast the chicken for 35 to 40 minutes, or until the juices run clear when the thigh is pierced with a knife. Let the chicken cool, then remove the meat from the bones and cut the meat into bite-size pieces.

To make the sauce and assemble the dish: Melt 1 tablespoon of the butter in a skillet over medium heat. Add the onion, celery, carrot, garlic, sage, thyme, Cajun seasoning and salt. Cook for about 10 minutes, or until the vegetables are soft.

Add the remaining 3 tablespoons butter. When the butter melts, whisk in the flour. Cook, stirring constantly, for 2 minutes, or until the mixture takes on a "nutty" aroma. Slowly stir in the wine, cream, broth, lemon juice and hot sauce. Simmer for 10 minutes, stirring occasionally. Add the chicken and simmer for 10 minutes, stirring occasionally. Taste and adjust seasonings as needed.

To make the dumplings: Melt the butter in a small skillet over medium heat; add the onion and sauté for about 10 minutes, or until it softens and turns translucent. Set aside.

Combine the flour, sage, mustard, salt, baking powder and cayenne pepper in a mixing bowl; stir to blend.

Mix together the milk, eggs and sautéed onion in another bowl. Add to the dry ingredients and stir until just incorporated.

Transfer the chicken mixture to a 9-by-9-inch baking dish. Drop big spoonfuls of the dumpling batter about ½ inch apart on top. Cover and bake for 10 to 15 minutes. Uncover and bake for 5 minutes longer, or until the dumplings begin to brown.

SERVES 6 TO 8

NOTE: To make your own Cajun seasoning, mix together equal parts cayenne pepper, paprika, ground white and black pepper and ground allspice.

Duck Breasts with Coriander-Cognac Sauce

The preliminary step of salting the duck breasts and letting them stand gives the meat a delicacy and lushness it would not otherwise have, says Shirley Sarvis. Accompany with steamed white rice and let the sauce flow into the rice. For a special dinner, serve with a medium-weight California Cabernet Sauvignon, light on the wood.

4 boneless duck breast halves (from two 5-pound Petaluma or Long Island ducks)

Salt and freshly ground pepper, to taste

About 1½ tablespoons clarified butter (or half olive oil, half unsalted butter)

Coriander-Cognac Sauce

1 cup Cognac

3 tablespoons unsalted butter

1 teaspoon coarsely crushed toasted coriander seeds (see Note)

◉◉ Remove the skin from the duck breasts. Liberally season the meat with salt, cover loosely with wax paper and let stand at room temperature for 30 minutes to 1 hour.

Rinse and dry the duck breast halves; pound each between sheets of wax paper until it is an even ⅝ inch thick.

Heat the clarified butter in a large, heavy skillet over medium-high to high heat. When hot, add the duck and cook for 2 minutes. Turn the duck over and cook for 2 minutes longer, or until well browned on the outside and very rosy (near rare) on the inside (adjust heat if necessary).

Remove the duck from the pan, season with salt and pepper and let rest for 5 minutes.

To make the sauce: Boil the Cognac in a small saucepan over medium heat until reduced to ⅓ cup. Add the butter and simmer, whisking, until reduced to ¼ cup. Whisk in the coriander.

Carve the duck slightly diagonally across the grain into ⅜-inch-thick slices. Arrange, with juices, on serving plates. Spoon the sauce over the duck.

SERVES 2 TO 4

NOTE: To toast whole coriander seeds, place them in a small, heavy skillet over medium heat and toast, shaking the pan from time to time, until the seeds are fragrant. Transfer to a flat plate and let cool. Coarsely crush the seeds with a mortar and pestle, or place in a self-sealing plastic bag and crush with a rolling pin.

Spiced Duck with Couscous

The key to getting crispy skin on the duck is keeping the pan temperature hot enough to melt the fat but not burn the skin, says Robin Davis. This dish is great for a dinner party, served with a California Sangiovese.

Duck

½ cup crème de cassis

1 small onion, thinly sliced

2 garlic cloves, minced

1 teaspoon cracked pepper

1 teaspoon kosher or sea salt

1 teaspoon ground cumin

1 teaspoon cinnamon

½ teaspoon ground coriander

¼ teaspoon nutmeg

4 boneless duck breast halves

Couscous

1 tablespoon butter

1 onion, finely chopped

¼ cup currants

½ teaspoon kosher or sea salt

2 cups low-sodium chicken broth

1½ cups couscous

¼ cup pomegranate seeds (optional)

Chopped parsley for garnish

To make the duck: Combine the cassis, onion, garlic, pepper, salt, cumin, cinnamon, coriander and nutmeg in a shallow dish large enough to hold the duck breast halves in a single layer. Add the duck; turn to coat. Cover and refrigerate for 4 to 8 hours, turning occasionally.

To make the couscous: Melt the butter in a heavy saucepan over medium heat. Add the onion and sauté for about 5 minutes, or until translucent. Stir in the currants and salt. Add the chicken broth and bring to a boil. Stir in the couscous. Cover the pan and remove from heat.

Preheat the oven to 400 degrees.

Heat a large ovenproof sauté pan over medium heat. Remove the duck from the marinade. Using a sharp knife, score through the skin and fat on each duck breast half, being careful not to cut into the meat. Put the duck skin-side down in the pan. Cook for 6 to 8 minutes, or until the skin is crispy and golden brown and the fat underneath has melted, pouring off the fat as necessary. Turn the duck over. Transfer the pan to the oven and roast for about 8 minutes, or until the meat is medium-rare. Transfer the duck to a cutting board.

Fluff the couscous with a fork. Stir in the pomegranate seeds, if desired.

Place a spoonful of couscous in the center of each serving plate. Carve the duck crosswise into slices. Fan the slices around the couscous. Garnish with the parsley.

SERVES 4

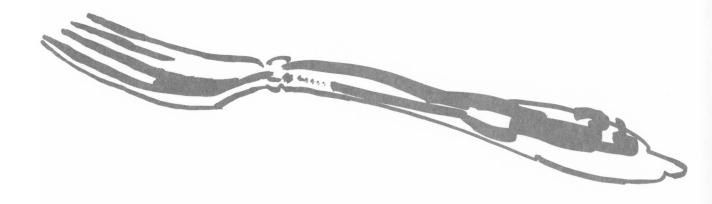

Mustard-Marinated Duck Breasts with Figs and Zinfandel

This recipe by Marlena Spieler is long, but the interplay of sweet and tangy ingredients brings out the best in duck. It's an ideal choice for an elegant dinner party. Begin the meal Italian-style, with a dish of gnocchi, ripe tomatoes and artichokes. End with a salad of delicate greens, frisee and chervil.

2 large duck breasts, halved, or 4 smallish duck breasts

10 garlic cloves, coarsely chopped

Juice of 1 to 1½ lemons

Sea salt, to taste

Large pinch of dried thyme

4 bay leaves

½ cup torn basil leaves, plus basil leaves for garnish

2 to 3 tablespoons extra virgin olive oil

3 to 4 tablespoons Dijon mustard

3 shallots, chopped

2 cups Zinfandel, or other fruity red wine

½ cup strong chicken broth, or ½ bouillon cube dissolved in ½ cup water

12 ripe figs, halved

1 to 2 teaspoons sugar

Dash of red wine vinegar

◑ Bone the duck breasts but leave the skin attached. Using a sharp knife, score the skin in a crosshatch pattern, cutting almost but not quite through to the flesh. Put the duck breasts in a shallow dish large enough to hold them in a single layer.

Combine about two thirds of the garlic with the lemon juice, salt, thyme, bay leaves, basil and olive oil in a bowl. Pour over the duck, cover and refrigerate for 1 hour or as long as overnight.

Add the mustard to the marinade and let the duck marinate for 1 hour at room temperature.

Remove the duck from the marinade and blot dry.

Heat a heavy pan over medium heat. Place the duck skin-side down in the pan and let it brown. Turn the duck and brown the other side for a few moments. Turn the duck skin-side down again, reduce heat to low and cook until the skin renders its fat and the duck is done to your liking. This should take 10 to 15 minutes, depending on the degree of rareness you prefer. This timing will give you duck that is only slightly pink.

Remove the duck to a plate and keep warm.

Pour out all but 1 tablespoon of the fat in the pan. Add the shallots and the remaining garlic and sauté for 7 to 10 minutes, or until softened. Add the wine and broth, increase the heat to high and boil the liquid until it is reduced to about one fourth of its volume and has thickened slightly.

Add the figs, sugar and vinegar; cook for 1 to 2 minutes. Return the duck to the sauce and simmer until heated through.

Remove the bay leaf, garnish with the basil leaves and serve.

SERVES 4

Tandoori Quail with Tropical Fruit Chaat

You don't have to go game hunting to make this dish from Laxmi Hiremath. Tender and juicy farm-raised quail are available in Bay Area markets. The garnish is a salsalike melange of fresh fruit, seasoned with ground cumin or chaat masala.

1 teaspoon garam masala

½ teaspoon salt

2-inch piece fresh ginger, peeled and minced

3 large garlic cloves, minced

4 tablespoons plain nonfat or low-fat yogurt

4 whole quail

5 cups loosely packed baby greens

¼ cup finely chopped red or white onion

4 cherry tomatoes, halved

2 tablespoons sherry vinegar

1 to 2 tablespoons walnut oil

Tropical Fruit Chaat for garnish (recipe follows)

oo   Combine the garam masala, salt, ginger, garlic and yogurt in a bowl. Mix well.

Using poultry shears or a sharp knife, cut out the backbone of each quail. Flatten each quail with the palm of your hand so it will lie flat on the grill.

Place the birds in a large glass dish. Pour the marinade over them, then rub the marinade into all sides. Cover and marinate in the refrigerator for 2 hours or overnight.

Prepare a medium-hot fire in an outdoor grill or preheat the broiler.

Combine the greens, onion, tomatoes, vinegar and oil in a bowl. Mix well and set aside.

Grill the quail for 6 to 8 minutes per side, or broil them for about 4 minutes per side, or until the juices run clear when the thigh is pierced with a knife.

Divide the greens among serving plates. Place a quail on each bed of greens. Garnish with spoonfuls of the chaat.

SERVES 4

Tropical Fruit Chaat

Chaats are Northern Indian snack-like salad dishes. They all are boldly flavored, and may be sweet and spicy at the same time, such as this bright combination of tropical and California-grown fruits. This also is good served with roast chicken, pork, lamb or sausages.

1 ripe pineapple, peeled, cored and cut into chunks

1 ripe mango, peeled, pitted and chopped

1 orange, peeled, halved, sliced and seeded

½ cup sliced strawberries

½ cup seedless grapes

2 teaspoons toasted ground cumin seed, or chaat masala (see Note)

oo   Combine the pineapple, mango, orange, strawberries and grapes in a bowl. Sprinkle in the cumin; toss gently to mix.

YIELDS ABOUT 6 CUPS

NOTE: Chaat masala is a spice blend used especially for chaats. It is available in Indian and some Middle Eastern markets.

Cornish Game Hen with Tomato-Olive Sauce

May Ditano, for many years the chef/owner of Columbus Ristorante in San Francisco, loves this fragrant dish on drizzly nights. The hens are infused with lush Mediterranean flavors, and they come out of the pan falling-off-the-bone tender. She suggests serving the hens with roasted potatoes, rice pilaf or soft polenta.

¼ cup plus 2 tablespoons olive oil

1 large Cornish game hen, quartered

2 garlic cloves, chopped

1 teaspoon chopped fresh rosemary

3 fresh sage leaves, chopped

Salt and freshly ground pepper, to taste

Paprika, to taste

1 ripe tomato, diced, or 1 cup drained canned diced tomatoes

½ cup (or more) dry red wine

10 black brine-cured olives, such as kalamata or niçoise

◉◉ Heat the ¼ cup olive oil in a large, heavy skillet over medium heat. Add the hen leg-thigh quarters and cook for 10 minutes. Add the breast pieces and cook, turning the quarters occasionally, for about 20 minutes, or until the meat is no longer pink. Transfer the quarters to paper towels to drain.

Heat the 2 tablespoons oil in a large, heavy saucepan over medium-high heat. Add the hen quarters, the garlic, rosemary and sage. Season with salt, pepper and paprika. Cook, stirring, for 1 minute. Add the tomato, wine and olives. Cover and simmer for about 15 minutes, or until the sauce thickens slightly and the hen quarters are cooked through.

SERVES 2

Boulevard's Staff Turkey Breast

This brined turkey breast occasionally is served at staff meals at Boulevard, one of San Francisco's most popular restaurants. If you're feeling flush, chef/owner Nancy Oakes suggests substituting apple juice or cider for the water, and reducing the honey to ½ cup. The turkey comes out moist and juicy, with just the right balance of sweet-spicy-salty. Leftovers are especially good in sandwiches, pasta dishes, potato gratins and chef's-style salads. The carcass makes wonderful soup, especially the Chinese rice porridge, jook.

Honey Brine

2 quarts water

¾ cup honey

½ cup kosher salt

2 tablespoons Dijon mustard

1½ teaspoons hot red pepper flakes

1 rosemary sprig, about 4 inches long

1 bone-in turkey breast half, 3 to 3½ pounds

1 tablespoon olive oil

ꙮ To make the brine: Bring the water to a boil in a large pot over high heat. Then pour the water into a container just large enough to hold the turkey breast; let cool for 5 minutes. Add the honey, salt, mustard and pepper flakes and whisk until the honey dissolves. Add the rosemary. Let cool to room temperature, then refrigerate until well chilled.

Add the turkey breast to the chilled brine. Weight with a plate if necessary to keep it completely submerged. Refrigerate for 1 to 2 days.

Remove the turkey breast from the brine, place in a roasting pan and bring to room temperature. Preheat the oven to 350 degrees.

Roast the turkey for 30 minutes, then brush with the olive oil. Continue roasting, basting occasionally with the drippings, for about 30 minutes longer, or until an instant-read thermometer inserted into the thickest part of the meat, away from the bone, registers 150 degrees. Remove from the oven and let rest for 30 minutes before carving.

SERVES 6

The Best Way Roast Turkey

After cooking nearly 40 turkeys in The Chronicle's *test kitchen, we found a brined turkey to be the best. It's cured overnight in a seasoned salt-sugar-water mixture created by Chez Panisse in Berkeley. To save space in the refrigerator, the turkey may be brined in a sealed garbage bag and packed in ice in a cooler. If you don't want to go to the extra effort to brine the bird, following the instructions for cooking and internal temperatures will still produce a superior result.*

Chez Panisse's Brine

2½ gallons cold water

2 cups kosher salt

1 cup sugar

2 bay leaves, torn into pieces

1 bunch fresh thyme, or 4 tablespoons dried thyme

1 head of garlic, cloves separated and peeled

5 allspice berries, crushed

4 juniper berries, smashed

Turkey

1 turkey, 12 to 16 pounds

2 tablespoons butter at room temperature

1½ teaspoons freshly ground pepper

½ to 1 cup turkey stock

To make the brine: Put the water in a large pot that can easily hold the liquid and the turkey you intend to brine. Add the salt, sugar, bay leaves, thyme, garlic, allspice and juniper berries and stir for 1 to 2 minutes, or until the salt and sugar dissolve.

Note: The recipe may be halved or doubled; the important thing is to have enough brine to completely cover the turkey.

Put the turkey into the brine and refrigerate for 12 to 24 hours. Use a plate or other weight if necessary to keep it completely submerged in the brine.

Remove the turkey from the brine, rinse and drain well. Pat dry.

Preheat the oven to 400 degrees.

Brining Times for Poultry

The thickness of the muscle, the strength of the brine and your own taste determine how long meat should soak. For a moderately strong brine (1 cup salt to 1 gallon water), the following brining times are rough guidelines. Always refrigerate meat during brining. If you aren't ready to cook at the end of the brining time, remove the meat from the brine, but keep the meat refrigerated.

Whole chicken (4 pounds): 8 to 12 hours

Chicken parts: 1½ hours

Cornish game hens: 2 hours

Turkey (12 to 14 pounds): 12 to 24 hours

Spread the butter over the skin of the turkey and season with pepper inside and out. Tuck the wing tips under, tie the legs together and place the turkey breast-side up on a V-shaped rack in a shallow roasting pan. Cover the breast tightly with aluminum foil and place in the oven.

Roast for 50 to 60 minutes, then baste with ½ cup turkey stock. Leave the foil off, return the turkey to the oven and continue roasting, basting with stock and pan drippings every 20 to 30 minutes, until an instant-read thermometer inserted into the thickest part of the thigh, away from the bone, registers 165 degrees. A 12- to 16-pound bird will cook in about 2 to 2¾ hours. Start checking the internal temperature after about 1½ hours of roasting time. If the legs begin to get too brown, cover loosely with foil.

Let the turkey rest at least 20 minutes before carving.

SERVES 12 TO 16

Turkey, Corn and Roasted Bell Pepper Enchiladas with Chipotle Sauce

Former Food Department intern Sean Forsha created this recipe as a way of using leftover turkey.

Chipotle Sauce

1 tablespoon canola oil

1 onion, diced

1½ tablespoons minced garlic

1 teaspoon ground cumin

¼ teaspoon dried Mexican oregano

1 can (28 ounces) diced tomatoes

1 canned chipotle chile en adobo, seeded

1 tablespoon adobo sauce from can of chipotles

1 cup water

½ teaspoon sugar

Salt and freshly ground pepper, to taste

Filling

3 red bell peppers

1 tablespoon canola oil

½ onion, finely diced

½ tablespoon minced garlic

2 cups diced roasted turkey

1 can (8¾ ounces) corn

¼ cup finely chopped cilantro

1 cup grated cheddar cheese

1 teaspoon fresh lime juice

1 teaspoon ground cumin

Salt and freshly ground pepper, to taste

Assembly

½ cup canola oil

12 corn tortillas

½ cup grated cheddar cheese

Black or green olive slices for garnish

❀ To make the chipotle sauce: Pour the oil into a medium pot and place over medium-high heat. When the oil is hot, add the onion and sauté for about 3 minutes, or until translucent. Add the garlic and sauté for 2 minutes. Add the cumin, oregano, tomatoes, chipotle, adobo sauce and water. Bring to a simmer, reduce heat to low and simmer for 10 minutes.

Working in small batches, purée the sauce in a blender and return to the pot. Add the sugar and season with salt and pepper. Set aside.

To make the filling: Preheat the broiler. Roast the bell peppers under the broiler, turning often, for about 5 minutes, or until the skins blister and blacken. Put the roasted peppers in a paper bag; fold over the top to seal and set aside for 15 minutes. Peel, seed, derib and dice the peppers and put in a bowl.

Reduce oven temperature to 375 degrees.

Heat the oil in a small skillet over medium-high heat. Add the onion and sauté for about 3 minutes, or until translucent. Add the garlic and sauté for 2 minutes, stirring frequently. Transfer the onions and garlic to the bowl with the roasted bell peppers. Add the turkey, corn, cilantro, 3 tablespoons of the chipotle sauce, the cheese and lime juice; stir to combine. Add the cumin and season with salt and pepper; set aside.

Assembling the enchiladas: Heat the oil in a heavy skillet over medium heat. Fry the tortillas, 1 at a time, for 2 to 3 seconds per side. Transfer to paper towels to drain.

Ladle a thin layer of chipotle sauce into an 11-by-7-inch ovenproof casserole dish. Dip a tortilla into the pot of chipotle sauce and place on a cutting board. Spoon 2 tablespoons of the filling down the center of the tortilla and roll it up. Place seam-side down in the casserole dish.

Repeat with the remaining tortillas, packing the enchiladas tightly in the dish. Pour the remaining sauce over the enchiladas and sprinkle with the cheese.

Bake for 20 minutes, or until heated through. Garnish with olives.

YIELDS 12 ENCHILADAS

Green Beans and Turkey in Asian Black Bean Sauce

Here's another way to use leftover turkey. This recipe, from Chronicle *staffer Lynne Bennett, cooks quickly, so the bulk of the time involves preparing the ingredients.*

8 ounces green beans, trimmed and cut into 1½-inch lengths

1 tablespoon vegetable or canola oil

2 tablespoons black bean paste, or dried fermented black beans, rinsed and crushed

2 teaspoons minced garlic

½ teaspoon minced fresh ginger

1 small yellow onion, peeled and cut lengthwise into ¼-inch-thick slices

1 tablespoon dry white wine

½ cup turkey or chicken stock

2 teaspoons soy sauce

2 teaspoons oyster sauce

½ can (6-ounce can) sliced water chestnuts, drained

1 cup roasted turkey, cut into 1½-inch lengths and similar in size to the beans

Pinch of sugar

◉◉ Bring a pot of salted water to a boil. Add the beans and boil for 2 to 3 minutes, until just crisp-tender. Drain and rinse under cold running water. Drain again. Set aside.

Place a nonstick sauté pan or wok over medium-high heat. When hot, add the oil, then add the black beans and garlic. Stir-fry for about 1 minute, or until aromatic, but do not let the garlic brown. Add the ginger, onion and white wine. Stir-fry for about 1 minute, or until the onion starts to lose its crispness. Add the stock, then the soy sauce and oyster sauce. Add the green beans, water chestnuts and turkey. Stir-fry until heated through. Stir in the sugar.

SERVES 2

What's Umami?

For years cooks have been talking about balancing four flavors: sweet, salty, sour and bitter. Increasingly they are now talking about a fifth flavor called umami. It's what makes the classic Caesar salad so good with Parmigiano-Reggiano cheese and the background hint of anchovies.

While umami is easy to taste, it's hard to describe: "It's that meaty, mouth-filling, savory sensation," says Marcia Pelchat, a sensory psychologist at Monell Chemical Senses Center in Philadelphia.

Much like the heat in a chile pepper, umami has an identifiable and measurable source. In 1908, a Japanese researcher at Tokyo Imperial University traced the savory taste primarily to L-glutamate, an amino acid found in high-protein foods such as meat, milk, mushrooms and seafood.

In consumer language, this chemical is the controversial monosodium glutamate (MSG), which occurs naturally in many foods. To produce the savory quality, the glutamate must be present in free form, not bound with other amino acids.

Here are some foods rich in umami:

◉◉ Cheeses: aged Danish blue cheese, Gruyère, Roquefort, Parmigiano-Reggiano

◉◉ Seafood: fresh clams, lobster, scallops

◉◉ Fish sauce (*nam pla* or *nuoc mam*)

◉◉ Shiitake mushrooms

◉◉ Dry-aged steak

◉◉ Fresh tomatoes

◉◉ Grapefruit

◉◉ Soy sauce

◉◉ Dried seaweed (*nori*)

◉◉ Cooked potatoes

◉◉ Green tea

◉◉ Aged balsamic vinegar

Spicy Asian-Style Cabbage and Turkey

The spiciness of this Asian-style dish may be adjusted by using more or less chile paste. The turkey adds a meaty texture, but the vegetables definitely are the main attraction, says staffer Lynne Bennett, who created this dish in The Chronicle's *test kitchen to use leftover roast turkey.*

1 tablespoon canola or vegetable oil

2 teaspoons minced garlic

1 teaspoon minced fresh ginger

½ yellow onion, thinly sliced lengthwise (about 1 cup)

¾ pound green cabbage, thinly sliced

2 tablespoons dry white wine

¼ cup turkey or chicken stock

2 carrots, peeled and julienned

½ large red bell pepper, stemmed, seeded, deribbed and julienned

1 cup julienned roasted turkey

2 teaspoons oyster sauce

2 teaspoons Asian fish sauce

1 tablespoon soy sauce

Salt, to taste

1 teaspoon Asian chile paste, or to taste

1 green onion (green part only), thinly sliced on the diagonal

◉◉ Place a nonstick skillet or wok over medium-high heat. When hot, add the oil. When the oil is hot, add the garlic and ginger. Stir-fry for about 1 minute, or until aromatic, but do not let the garlic brown. Add the onion and stir-fry for about 2 minutes, or until it starts to turn translucent.

Add the cabbage, wine and stock. Continue to cook, stirring occasionally, for about 2 minutes, or until the cabbage begins to soften.

Add the carrots, bell pepper and turkey, then the oyster sauce, fish sauce and soy sauce. Cook for 1 minute longer, or until the turkey is heated through and the carrots and pepper are still slightly crisp. Season with salt, then add the chile paste, stirring to combine well.

Sprinkle with the green onion.

SERVES 4

Guinea Fowl with Gin and Juniper

Shirley Sarvis uses traditional taste harmonies to flavor this dish. Guinea fowl is sautéed until crisp. A pan sauce begins with juniper berries, then it's smoothed with the sweetness of shallots and reduced cream and finished with gin. Guinea fowl is available at some specialty markets. In a pinch, chicken may be substituted.

2 boneless guinea fowl breast halves, about 5 ounces each

Salt and freshly ground pepper, to taste

1 tablespoon unsalted butter

3 tablespoons very thinly sliced shallots

1½ teaspoons minced juniper berries

¼ cup whipping cream

1½ teaspoons gin

Pound the guinea fowl to an even ⅝-inch thickness; rinse and pat dry. Slip your fingers between the skin and flesh on one side of each breast piece to loosen the skin. Fold back the skin and season the flesh with salt and pepper; replace the skin. Season the other side of the guinea fowl with salt and pepper. If possible, let stand for 30 minutes.

Heat a large, heavy pan over medium-high heat; sprinkle with salt. Add the guinea fowl skin-side down. Sauté until the skin is crisp and the breasts are well browned. Turn and brown the other side, cooking until the flesh is opaque almost to the center, about 7 minutes total. Transfer the guinea fowl to plates and let rest for 2 minutes.

Wipe out the pan, leaving the brown (not burned) particles. Let the pan cool slightly, then add the butter, shallots and juniper berries. Cook and stir over medium heat for a few moments until the shallots just wilt. Add the cream and cook, stirring, until the sauce reduces to 3 tablespoons. Stir in the gin. Season with salt and pepper, then spoon the sauce alongside the guinea fowl.

SERVES 2

Chapter 9

Fish and Shellfish

While fish fillets have become popular for a quick evening meal, savvy cooks are quickly discovering the unsung virtues of mussels. They're simple to prepare, they cook quickly and you always know when they're done. Like a well-timed magic trick, they open up when ready to eat.

The hardest part is figuring out which flavor to combine with them. In this chapter, we come to the rescue. You'll find Red Chile Mussels (page 322), Asian-style Mussels in Coconut Broth (page 323) and Mussels Steamed in Vouvray with Fennel and Leeks (page 324). We even offer a no-fuss way to roast them in the oven with a simple tarragon butter (page 325).

In fact, roasting is a great, effortless way to prepare most seafood, particularly salmon, as you'll discover in Roasted Salmon with Lentils (page 302) and Roasted Salmon Stuffed with Spinach (page 305). Swordfish never tasted better than when baked with a roasted red pepper vinaigrette (page 307), and Mexican snapper's delicate flavor is enhanced when cooked en papillote (page 313).

Seafood stew is ideal dinner-party fare, and we have five different variations, from a French-Vietnamese Bouillabaisse (page 328) to a Spanish Clam, Prawn and Chorizo Stew (page 330).

Shrimp is a universally loved ingredient, and we offer it grilled with tequila and chipotle (page 321) and combined with sweet potatoes in a coconut curry (page 318). Whether you're looking for a simple recipe for sand dabs or sea bass, you'll find it here.

Roasted Salmon with Lentils

The pairing of salmon and lentils has been showing up all over the Bay Area, but the version served at Pastis in San Francisco is one of the best.

Lentils

2 tablespoons olive oil

½ yellow onion, finely diced

1 thick bacon slice, chopped

1 garlic clove, chopped

1 carrot, peeled and halved

Bouquet garni (parsley sprig, thyme sprig and bay leaf, tied together with
    kitchen string)

3 cups French green lentils, washed and drained

7 cups chicken broth

Salt and freshly ground pepper, to taste

Salmon

2 tablespoons olive oil, or as needed

4 salmon fillets, 5 ounces each

Salt and freshly ground pepper, to taste

¼ cup finely diced shallots

¼ cup finely diced parsley

¼ cup finely diced chives

2 tablespoons balsamic vinegar

4 tablespoons unsalted butter

Fresh chervil for garnish

Removing Salmon Bones

Salmon fillets often have tiny pin bones that need to be removed. They run in a neat line in the thickest part of the fillet. If you run your hand down the length of the fish, you can feel them. Use tweezers or needle-nose pliers to pull them out.

◎◎ Preheat the oven to 450 degrees.

To make the lentils: Heat the olive oil in a deep, heavy pan over medium-high heat. Add the onion, bacon, garlic, carrot and bouquet garni. Sauté for 1 minute, stirring. Add the lentils, stir to coat and add the broth. Bring to a boil, then reduce heat and simmer, uncovered, for about 25 minutes, or until the lentils are tender. Season with salt and pepper; remove the bouquet garni and carrot halves. Transfer lentils to a bowl and set aside.

To make the salmon: Set 2 large, heavy ovenproof skillets over medium heat, and put 1 tablespoon olive oil in each. Season the salmon on both sides with salt and pepper. When the oil is very hot but not smoking, place the salmon skin-side up in the skillets. Sauté until browned on both sides, turning once. Transfer the skillets to the hot oven. Roast for 1 minute for rare, 2 minutes for medium, 3 to 4 minutes for well-done.

When the salmon is done to your liking, remove to a large plate and keep warm.

Return the lentils to a heavy pot. Stir in the shallots, parsley, chives, vinegar and butter; cook over medium heat until heated through.

Divide the lentils among shallow bowls, top each with a salmon fillet and garnish with chervil.

SERVES 4

Jardiniere's Wild Salmon with Olive Oil–Mashed Potatoes and Sauce Niçoise

Traci des Jardins, chef/owner at Jardiniere in San Francisco, pairs pan-roasted salmon with a simple tomato-niçoise olive sauce and her own version of mashed potatoes using Yukon Golds flavored with extra virgin olive oil. It's both rustic and elegant, and is bursting with flavor. A California Pinot Noir is the perfect accompaniment.

2½ pounds Yukon Gold potatoes

½ cup extra virgin olive oil

Salt and freshly ground pepper, to taste

1 dozen fava beans

8 garlic cloves, peeled

6 plum tomatoes, peeled, seeded and diced

4 sun-dried tomato halves, chopped

¼ cup roughly chopped niçoise olives

6 king salmon fillets, about 5 ounces each

4 green onions (white and most of the green part), thinly sliced

18 basil leaves, torn in half

Balsamic vinegar, to taste

👓 Peel and halve the potatoes, or quarter if large. Bring to a boil over high heat in salted water to cover. Reduce heat to low and simmer until potatoes are tender but not mushy. Drain well.

Using an electric mixer with a paddle attachment, beat the potatoes with 5 tablespoons of the olive oil until smooth. Season with salt and pepper. (For a more rustic result, mash potatoes by hand with a potato masher.) Set aside.

Preheat the oven to 400 degrees.

Shell the fava beans. Bring a saucepan of water to a boil over high heat. Add the beans and blanch for 1 minute, then remove with a slotted spoon to a bowl of ice water; drain when cool. Blanch the garlic in the boiling water for 30 seconds, then drain. Blanch the garlic 2 more times in fresh boiling water. Slice the garlic peel and the beans.

Combine the plum tomatoes and 1 tablespoon olive oil in a saucepan over medium heat. Season with salt. When the tomatoes begin to give off their juices, add the fava beans, garlic, sun-dried tomatoes and olives. Cook, stirring, until hot throughout. Reduce heat to very low and keep the sauce warm while you cook the salmon.

Heat 2 ovenproof skillets over medium-high heat. When very hot, put 1 tablespoon olive oil in each and swirl to coat the bottoms. Add 3 salmon fillets skin-side down to each skillet. Reduce heat to medium. Season the salmon with salt and pepper. Cook for 2 minutes, then transfer the skillets to the oven for 2 minutes.

Turn the salmon, return to the oven and cook for 1 minute longer. Transfer the salmon to a platter and let rest a few minutes before serving.

Reheat the mashed potatoes.

Add the green onions, basil and a dash of balsamic vinegar to the sauce.

Divide the mashed potatoes among warmed plates. Top with the salmon and surround with sauce.

SERVES 6

We tried various methods
to sauté salmon on the
stovetop, first using
different fats (canola oil,
olive oil, vegetable-oil
cooking spray and butter)
and then using different
pans and burner
temperatures to find how
those elements affected the
outcome. Finally, we tested
seasoning.

Here's what our research
uncovered: For moist and
rich-tasting salmon, melt
1 tablespoon butter in a
6-inch heavy-duty nonstick
skillet over medium heat.
Season both sides of a
5-ounce salmon fillet
with ⅛ teaspoon salt and
⅛ teaspoon freshly ground
pepper. Cook for 1½
minutes per side. Take
the salmon out of the pan
and let it rest for 1 minute
before serving; this allows
the fillet to arrive at
medium doneness. The
salmon is perfectly cooked
when the flesh is opaque,
firm and moist.

Roasted Salmon Stuffed with Spinach

This salmon roast, created by Georgeanne Brennan, actually is two fillets stacked one atop the other, with a thick layer of buttery cooked spinach in between.

1 teaspoon salt

3 bunches fresh spinach, washed and stemmed (about 6 cups)

2 bacon slices, finely chopped

3½ tablespoons butter

1 shallot, minced

2 tablespoons whipping cream

Freshly ground pepper, to taste

2 skinless salmon fillets, about ¾ pound each and ¾ inch thick

1 tablespoon olive oil

◎◎ Preheat the oven to 500 degrees.

Bring a large pot of water to a boil over high heat; add the salt. Add the spinach and cook for 45 seconds, or until it wilts and turns dark green. Drain, run under cold water, drain again and squeeze dry.

Fry the bacon in a skillet over medium heat until nearly crisp. Drain on paper towels and set aside.

Heat 2 tablespoons of the butter in a large skillet over medium heat. Add the shallot and sauté for 2 to 3 minutes, or until translucent.

Add the spinach, stirring to incorporate the shallot, then add the cream. Cook, stirring, until the butter and cream are nearly absorbed and the pan is nearly dry. Season with pepper and stir in all but a tablespoon or so of the fried bacon. Cover and set aside.

Place a piece of wax paper or aluminum foil on a work surface. Place several lengths of kitchen twine across the paper or foil. Place one of the salmon fillets across the twine. Spread the spinach mixture over the fillet. Top with the other fillet. Tie the fillets together with the twine.

Put the remaining 1½ tablespoons butter and the olive oil in a shallow baking dish and place in the oven. When the butter has melted, place the salmon "roast" in the pan. Roast for 8 to 10 minutes, then, using two spatulas and holding firmly, carefully turn the fish. Return to the oven and roast for 8 to 10 minutes longer, or until all but the innermost part of the fillets is opaque.

Transfer the fish to a platter. Cut away and discard the twine. Carve the roast into 4 portions, pour the pan juices over the pieces and finish with the reserved bacon.

SERVES 4

Ginger-Pepper Salmon

This preparation by Shirley Sarvis features salmon with a crackly, crisp topping of black pepper and fresh ginger.

4 skinless salmon fillets, 5 ounces each and ¾- to 1-inch thick

Salt, to taste

3 tablespoons very finely minced peeled fresh ginger

1 tablespoon coarsely cracked peppercorns (see Note)

4 tablespoons unsalted butter, melted just to creaminess

⊚ Preheat the broiler.

Wipe the salmon fillets dry. Arrange them in a single layer in a shallow buttered baking pan. Season the fish well with salt. Sprinkle the top evenly with ginger and pepper. Pour the butter evenly over the top.

Broil about 2½ inches from the heat source for 3 to 5 minutes, depending on the thickness of the fish, or until the ginger is deep golden and crisp and the fish is opaque almost to the center. Baste once or twice with pan juices. (If the topping is crisp but the salmon is not done, increase the distance between fish and heat source, or finish cooking in a 400-degree oven.)

Transfer to warmed plates and spoon juices over each serving.

SERVES 4

NOTE: To crack peppercorns, use a mortar and pestle and a pounding motion; or place peppercorns in a heavy plastic bag on a very firm surface and use a mallet or hammer; or cut the peppercorns on a board with a chef's knife. Whichever method you use, do not crush the peppercorns. Purchased black pepper labeled "cracked" is too finely cracked.

Baked Swordfish with Roasted Red Pepper Vinaigrette

This versatile and creamy vinaigrette could accompany any firm-fleshed white fish or grilled chicken breasts, says Janet Fletcher.

Vinaigrette

1 large red bell pepper, roasted, peeled, stemmed, seeded, deribbed and roughly chopped

1 tablespoon sherry vinegar

1 garlic clove, thinly sliced

About 7 tablespoons olive oil

Salt and cayenne pepper, or hot paprika, to taste

Fish

4 teaspoons olive oil

4 swordfish steaks, about 6 ounces each

Salt and freshly ground pepper, to taste

½ cup dry white wine

1 tablespoon minced Italian parsley for garnish

To make the vinaigrette: Combine the bell pepper, vinegar and garlic in a food processor. Process until puréed. With the motor running, add the olive oil through the feed tube, occasionally stopping to scrape down sides of bowl. You may need slightly more or less than 7 tablespoons oil, depending on the size of your bell pepper. Add just enough to leave the vinaigrette with an appealing tart edge. Transfer to a bowl and season with salt and cayenne pepper.

To make the fish: Preheat the oven to 375 degrees.

Put the olive oil in a heavy, low-sided baking dish large enough to hold all the fish. Add the swordfish and turn to coat both sides with oil. Season with salt and pepper. Pour the wine around the fish. Bake for 10 to 15 minutes, or until the fish just flakes.

Divide the vinaigrette among dinner plates. Top each portion with a swordfish steak and garnish with the parsley.

SERVES 4

Margarita-Style Fish with Mango Salsa

The intriguing name of this dish, created by Jacqueline McMahan, comes from the marinade, which includes lime juice, Cointreau and tequila. The combination gives a subtle lift to just about any fish. The garnish, a vibrant mango salsa, may be paired with most types of fish, as well as chicken or pork.

3 tablespoons fresh lime juice, plus more, to taste

1 tablespoon Cointreau

3 tablespoons silver tequila

½ teaspoon salt

Freshly ground pepper, to taste

2 tablespoons canola oil

4 fish fillets (halibut, red snapper or mahi mahi), about 5 ounces each

Lime wedges

Mango Salsa (recipe follows)

◉◉ Combine the 3 tablespoons lime juice, Cointreau, tequila, salt, pepper and oil in a bowl; blend well.

Place the fish fillets in a glass baking dish and pour the marinade over them. Refrigerate for 30 minutes, turning once.

Transfer the fish to a grill or preheated broiler. Grill or broil until done (10 minutes per inch of thickness using high heat).

Squeeze additional lime juice over the fish and serve immediately. Pass the salsa at the table.

SERVES 4

Mango Salsa

2 perfectly ripe mangoes

¼ cup diced red onion

Pinch of salt

Pinch of pure chile powder

1 jalapeño chile, seeded and minced

2 tablespoons fresh orange juice

1 tablespoon fresh lime juice

How to Grill Fish

Fish is fragile and can fall apart easily when cooked on the grill. A fish basket is great; it keeps the fish together and you simply turn the whole basket, cooking directly on the grill. Leaves such as vine, banana, unsprayed citrus leaves or corn husks are also good for wrapping up fish. They impart a lovely, subtle aroma and eliminate the need for a basket.

Whole fish and steaks: Make several large slashes on the outside of a whole fish to help it cook evenly and to let smoke permeate the flesh. Cook over hot coals for 10 minutes per inch of thickness. Whole or large pieces of fish should be cooked in a fish basket to keep them intact; turn halfway through cooking.

1 tablespoon silver tequila

½ cup diced peeled jicama

Peel the mangoes and cut the flesh from the large, flat pit in each. Dice the flesh, put in a bowl and add the onion, salt, chile powder, jalapeño, orange juice, lime juice and tequila; stir to combine. Fold in the jicama.

SERVES 4

Lemon-Dill Halibut

Halibut is an ideal fish for baking because its luxurious texture takes well to the gentle heat of a moderate oven. Watch carefully, however, because halibut can easily become dry with overcooking, says Shirley Sarvis. This dish also is good served at room temperature. Sarvis recommends serving the halibut with a Sauvignon Blanc from California or a Sancerre from France.

4 skinless halibut fillets, 5 ounces each

Salt and freshly ground pepper, to taste

⅓ cup minced green onion (white part only)

6 tablespoons finely chopped fresh dill feathers (not stems)

6 tablespoons finely chopped Italian parsley

6 tablespoons extra virgin olive oil

Slender lemon wedges for garnish

Preheat the oven to 350 degrees. Oil a shallow baking dish.

Wipe the halibut fillets dry. Season generously with salt and pepper. Arrange the fillets in a single layer in the prepared dish. Sprinkle with the onions, dill and parsley. Spoon the olive oil over the fish.

Bake, basting occasionally with pan juices, for about 10 minutes, or until the fish is just opaque in the center.

Transfer to serving plates. Spoon some of the juices over each fillet and garnish with lemon wedges.

SERVES 4

Fillets: Cook over medium-hot coals for 2 to 3 minutes per side (best in a hinged fish basket).

Kebabs: Cook over medium-hot coals for about 5 minutes per side.

Large shrimp: Skewer and cook over hot coals for 5 to 8 minutes per side.

Clams and mussels: Wrap mussels and clams loosely in foil or cover the grill so the heat can circulate and pop open the bivalves. Cook over hot coals for 8 to 10 minutes for mussels, slightly longer for clams.

Lobster and crab: Both need to be killed, then split and cleaned prior to grilling. Grill over hot coals for 3 to 4 minutes per side for crab and 6 to 8 minutes per side for lobster, or until shells turn bright red and flesh is opaque.

Sand Dabs with Lemon-Caper Vinaigrette

Sand dabs are a type of flatfish found only in the Bay Area. Rex sole or petrale sole also work well for this classic preparation from Janet Fletcher. You will need two large skillets to cook enough sand dabs for four people. Serve with tiny potatoes that have been steamed and buttered.

Vinaigrette

1 lemon

1½ tablespoons chopped capers

1 shallot, minced

1 tablespoon minced Italian parsley

2 teaspoons caper juice

6 tablespoons extra virgin olive oil

Salt and freshly ground pepper, to taste

Fish

2 tablespoons olive oil

2 pounds sand dabs, preferably about 4 ounces each

All-purpose flour seasoned with salt and freshly ground pepper

To make the vinaigrette: Cut off the ends of the lemon. Stand the lemon on one end and, with a small, sharp knife, remove all the peel and white pith by slicing from top to bottom all the way around the lemon, following the contour of the fruit. Cut the fruit sections away from the membranes and dice. Combine the diced lemon pulp, capers, shallot, parsley and caper juice in a small bowl. Gradually whisk in the olive oil. Season with salt and pepper.

To make the fish: Heat 2 large skillets over medium-high heat. When hot, put 1 tablespoon of the olive oil in each skillet and swirl to coat the bottom.

Coat the sand dabs with the seasoned flour, shaking off excess. Add to the skillets and reduce heat to medium. Panfry, turning once, for about 3 minutes per side, depending on thickness, or until sand dabs are done.

Divide the sand dabs among warmed dinner plates. Top with the vinaigrette.

SERVES 4

Substitutes for Popular Fish

If you're looking for a lean fish to subsit[sic] tute for Pacific snapper, choose cod, haddock or rockfish.

For sand dabs: Consider the sole family, including petrale and flounder.

For halibut: Turbot, red snapper, mahi mahi or shark.

For salmon: Tuna or mackerel.

When using acidic
ingredients and alcohol
with fish and shellfish,
marinate for no more than
about 4 hours. After that
time the acid toughens the
flesh and the alcohol
becomes too strong.

If you want to marinate
fish overnight, a mild white
wine and a touch of orange
juice with chile flakes,
tarragon and other spices
impart a subtle flavor
without changing the
texture.

Summertime Basil Bass

*This is a perfect dish for a warm summer night when you want something
light. The fish is baked with wine and tomatoes, then transferred to serving
plates. Mustard and wine are reduced with the pan juices to create a quick
sauce. For sheer simplicity, Shirley Sarvis recommends starting with a first
course of buttered fresh peas and new potatoes. Serve a butter-lettuce salad
after the fish, and for dessert, anything with fresh peaches. The dish goes
particularly well with a chilled crisp Sauvignon Blanc.*

2 ripe tomatoes, peeled, very thinly sliced and seeded

Pinch of sugar

Salt, to taste

4 skinless white-fleshed sea bass, true snapper, ling cod or mahi mahi fillets,
    5 ounces each, dark veining removed

Freshly ground white pepper, to taste

4 tablespoons unsalted butter

4 tablespoons finely slivered fresh basil leaves

1½ teaspoons Dijon mustard

⅔ cup dry white wine

⅜ teaspoon crumbled dried thyme

◎◎ Preheat the oven to 350 degrees.

Season the tomatoes well with sugar and salt. Wipe the fish dry, season
with pepper and arrange in a single layer in a well-buttered shallow
ovenproof skillet. Dot fish with butter.

Bake for 5 minutes, basting occasionally with the pan juices. Sprinkle
with the basil. Arrange the tomatoes, slightly overlapping, over the fish. Baste
again and return to the oven.

Bake, basting occasionally with pan juices, for about 8 minutes longer,
depending on the fish and its thickness, or until the fish is opaque almost to
the center. Transfer the fish to serving plates.

Add the mustard, wine and thyme to the juices in the skillet. Cook and
stir over high heat until blended and reduced to a generous ⅓ cup. Spoon the
sauce over the fish.

SERVES 4

Poached Sea Bass with Gremolata

Here, fish fillets are poached in wine and fennel, which impart a delicate flavor to this dish created by Robin Davis. Because of the simplicity and clean flavors, it's a perfect foil to a crisp Chardonnay without barrel fermentation.

Gremolata

2 tablespoons finely chopped lemon zest

¼ cup finely chopped Italian parsley

2 garlic cloves, minced

¼ cup dry white wine (preferably Chardonnay)

2 cups water

3 tablespoons fresh lemon juice

1 fennel bulb, trimmed and thinly sliced

1 onion, thinly sliced

2 garlic cloves, thinly sliced

1 bay leaf

1 fresh thyme sprig

4 sea bass fillets, 6 ounces each

Salt and freshly ground pepper, to taste

Kalamata olives for garnish

◉◉ To make the gremolata: Combine the lemon zest, parsley and minced garlic in a small bowl. Set aside.

Combine the wine, water, lemon juice, fennel, onion, sliced garlic, bay leaf and thyme sprig in a large, heavy skillet over medium-high heat. Bring to a boil, reduce heat to low and simmer for 15 minutes. Strain, then return the cooking liquid to the skillet.

Bring the cooking liquid to a low simmer. Season the fish on both sides with salt and pepper. Add to the skillet. Cover and simmer for 3 to 4 minutes, or until the fish is just cooked through. Using tongs, transfer the fish to serving bowls. Season the broth with salt and pepper, then spoon the broth around the fish. Top the fish with the gremolata and garnish with the olives.

SERVES 4

Mexican Snapper en Papillote

Steaming is an ideal cooking method for delicate fish. Sliced vine-ripened tomatoes, when in season, are a great addition to this dish, says Tara Duggan.

6 new red potatoes

1 small white onion

½ bunch cilantro

2 or 3 red snapper fillets, about 1½ pounds total

Salt and freshly ground pepper, to taste

2 tablespoons butter

4 tablespoons fresh lime juice

4 teaspoons dry white wine

Lime wedges for garnish (optional)

Preheat the oven to 450 degrees. Bring a medium pot of salted water to a boil over high heat.

Cut the potatoes into very thin slices. Add them to the boiling water and cook for about 4 minutes, or until just tender. Drain.

Thinly slice the onion; trim off the cilantro stems. Season the fish with salt and pepper.

Place 2 or 3 large sheets of aluminum foil (depending on the number of fillets), about 12 by 16 inches each, on a work surface. Rub some of the butter on each piece of foil, leaving a 1-inch border around the edges.

Place part of the potato slices, onion slices and cilantro sprigs on one half of each piece of foil. Season vegetables with salt and pepper. Place a fish fillet on each pile of vegetables. Drizzle with the lime juice and wine, then layer with the remaining vegetables and cilantro. Season again and dot with the remaining butter.

For each packet, bring the empty half of the foil over the fish, then starting at one corner, fold and crimp the edges to seal tightly.

Place the packets on a large baking sheet and bake for about 20 minutes, or until the fish flakes.

To serve, carefully cut open the foil packets. Divide the fish and vegetables among serving bowls and top with the juices. Garnish with lime wedges, if desired.

SERVES 4

Flavoring Steamed Fish

Place fish fillets on a bed of romaine lettuce, then steam them. This imparts a delicate, fresh flavor to the fish.

Fish in a Palace Way

The seasonings in this recipe were inspired by a dish Shirley Sarvis enjoyed at the Queluz Palace on the outskirts of Lisbon.

Red Bell Pepper–Onion Topping

2 red bell peppers

4 tablespoons extra virgin olive oil

1½ onions, cut into thin slices

Salt, to taste

Fish

4 skinless fillets of tender-fleshed fine sea fish (true snapper, lingcod, mahi mahi or
  sea bass), 6 ounces each

Salt, to taste

4 teaspoons dry white wine

2 teaspoons grated orange zest

To make the red bell pepper–onion topping: Preheat the broiler. Place the bell peppers on a foil-lined baking sheet and broil about 2 inches below the heat source until well blistered and charred on all sides, turning as needed. Transfer the peppers to a bowl and cover tightly. When peppers are cool enough to handle, peel them. Remove and discard stems, seeds and ribs. Cut the peppers into very thin julienne strips about 2½ inches long.

Heat the olive oil in a large, heavy skillet over medium-low heat. Add the onions and sauté for about 15 minutes, or until tender and golden (not browned). Season with salt. Stir in the pepper strips.

To make the fish: Preheat the oven to 350 degrees. Oil a shallow baking pan.

Wipe the fish fillets dry. Arrange them in the prepared pan. Season with salt, then sprinkle with the wine and orange zest. Spoon the red bell pepper–onion topping over the fish.

Bake, basting occasionally with pan juices, for 10 to 13 minutes, depending on the fish and its thickness, or until the fillets are almost opaque to the center.

Transfer to heated serving plates.

SERVES 4

Crab Cakes with Chile Mayonnaise

This slightly spicy version of crab cakes was created by Georgeanne Brennan. If you'd like them milder, omit the mustard and cayenne, and increase the mayonnaise by 1 teaspoon.

1 tablespoon Worcestershire sauce

1 teaspoon prepared Dijon-style mustard

½ teaspoon cayenne pepper, or hot paprika

1 teaspoon minced Italian parsley

1 tablespoon mayonnaise

½ teaspoon salt

1 egg

1 pound cooked crabmeat, picked over

Vegetable oil for frying

Lemon wedges

Chile Mayonnaise (recipe follows) (optional)

Selecting the Best Crab

Select live crabs that feel heavy for their size. Make sure the fishmonger lets the crab drain before weighing it—crabs can retain a fair amount of water.

The best crabs are dark in color. Light-colored legs mean the crab has recently molted and won't be as meaty.

If you can, pinch a leg to make sure it feels full of meat and not flimsy, another sign of a crab that has recently molted.

◉ Mix together the Worcestershire sauce, mustard, cayenne, parsley, mayonnaise, salt and egg in a bowl. Add the crabmeat and, with a fork or spoon, work just enough to hold the mixture together.

Shape the mixture into flat cakes about ½ inch thick and 2½ inches in diameter.

Pour the oil into a skillet to a depth of about ¼ inch. Heat over medium-high heat until a little piece of bread sizzles and browns when dropped into the oil. Remove the bread and fry the cakes about 2 minutes per side, or until golden brown. Place on paper towels to drain.

Serve with lemon wedges and chile mayonnaise, if desired.

YIELDS 8 OR 9 CAKES; SERVES 3 OR 4 AS A FIRST COURSE

Chile Mayonnaise

1 cup mayonnaise

2 tablespoons ketchup

1 tablespoon fresh lemon juice

½ teaspoon salt

2 teaspoons Worcestershire sauce

2 teaspoons cayenne pepper, or other dried red chile such as poblano, freshly ground, if possible

∞ Combine the mayonnaise, ketchup, lemon juice, salt, Worcestershire sauce and cayenne in a bowl. Taste and adjust seasonings as needed.

YIELDS ABOUT 1 CUP

Garlic-Roasted Crab

Garlic brings out the sweetness in Dungeness crab, as this recipe by Georgeanne Brennan demonstrates.

4 live Dungeness crabs, about 1¾ pounds each, or 4 cooked crabs

½ cup salt

1 large lemon, quartered

1 cup distilled white vinegar

2 gallons water

4 tablespoons butter

⅓ cup extra virgin olive oil

¼ cup minced garlic

Juice of 2 lemons

⅓ cup minced Italian parsley

Italian parsley sprigs for garnish

Lemon wedges for garnish

How to Cook Crab

Steaming: In a pan large enough to hold the crabs side by side, combine 1 cup white wine, 2 cups water, 1 bay leaf, black peppercorns and 1 lemon, cut into wedges. Bring to a boil and add the crabs, cover, reduce heat and simmer for 10 to 15 minutes, depending on the size of the crab.
Boiling: Drop crabs into a large pot of boiling water. Boil for about 10 minutes for a 1½-pound crab, 15 minutes for a 2-pound crab.

Cleaning and Cracking Cooked Crab

Twist the legs at the joint that connects them to the body. Pull legs off and set aside.

Place the crab on its back. Using the heel of your hand, press on either side of the shell until it cracks down the back. Pull off the shell halves. Pry up the tail flap, pull it back and twist it off.

Turn the crab over and clean out the guts, including the gray spongy, fingerlike lungs ("dead man's fingers"). Pinch the mouth and mandibles and pull them off. Rinse the body well.

To serve the crab: Break the body in half and crack each segment of leg and claw at the joint using a mallet, the side of a heavy knife or a nutcracker.

If you have bought live crabs, cook them: Combine the salt, lemon, vinegar and water in a large pot and bring to a boil over high heat. When the water is boiling, drop in 2 crabs, 1 at a time. When the water resumes boiling, reduce the heat to maintain a low boil, cover and cook the crabs for 10 minutes. Remove the crabs to a strainer in the sink. Repeat the cooking process with the remaining 2 crabs.

When the crabs are cool enough to handle, clean and crack them, reserving the crab butter, if desired.

Preheat the oven to 500 degrees.

Put the butter, olive oil and garlic in a roasting pan. Put the pan in the oven to melt the butter. Add the cooked crab pieces, turning them to coat with the butter-oil mixture. Roast for 10 to 15 minutes, or until the crab shells are shiny, the crab is hot all the way through and the garlic is golden.

Spoon the lemon juice and parsley over the crabs and turn to coat evenly. Spoon 1 or 2 tablespoons of the pan juices into the reserved crab butter (if using).

Arrange the crab pieces on serving platters, then pour the pan juices over them. Garnish with parsley sprigs and lemon wedges and serve with the crab butter, if desired.

SERVES 5 OR 6

Fijian Prawns with Sweet Potatoes in Coconut Curry

This dish from David Vera, a former student at the California Culinary Academy and a native Fijian, is a good example of the strong Indian influence prevalent in Fijian cooking. Serve with steamed white rice and garnish with lime wedges.

2 large sweet potatoes, peeled and cut into 1-inch cubes

2 tablespoons vegetable oil

2 onions, cut into medium dice

2 garlic cloves, minced

1 teaspoon minced fresh ginger

¼ teaspoon mustard seeds

¼ teaspoon cumin seeds

6 fenugreek seeds

1 cinnamon stick

2 whole cloves

2 hot chiles, seeded and finely diced

3 tablespoons curry powder

3 cups unsweetened coconut milk

1 pound medium prawns, shelled and deveined

Salt and freshly ground pepper, to taste

2 teaspoons chopped cilantro leaves for garnish

2 limes, cut into wedges, for garnish

◎◎ Boil the sweet potatoes in water to cover until they are just tender, not soft. Drain.

Heat the oil in a large skillet over medium heat. Add the onions, garlic and ginger and sauté for about 10 minutes, or until the onions are translucent. Stirring constantly, add the mustard, cumin and fenugreek seeds, the cinnamon, cloves, chiles and curry powder. Be careful the mixture doesn't burn.

Add the coconut milk and bring to a boil. Reduce heat and simmer for 10 minutes. Add the sweet potatoes and simmer for 5 minutes.

Stir in the prawns and bring to a boil, then remove from heat. Discard the cinnamon stick. Season with salt and pepper and garnish with the cilantro and lime.

SERVES 4

Angolan Prawns

This recipe is from Lisbon; the seasoning influences are from ancient Angola, says Shirley Sarvis. If you wish, accompany with sips of light dry rum on the rocks and delicate cornbread or steamed white rice.

About 1⅓ pounds large shrimp

Salt and freshly ground pepper, to taste

6 tablespoons unsalted butter

6 tablespoons minced green onions (white part only)

3 tablespoons minced green bell pepper

½ cup whipping cream

2 teaspoons Dijon mustard

1½ tablespoons peeled, seeded and finely diced fresh tomato

⅓ cup moist flaked or shredded coconut

2 tablespoons light dry rum

◉◉ Shell and devein the shrimp, then rinse and pat dry. Season with salt and pepper.

Melt the butter in a large, heavy skillet over medium heat. Add the shrimp, green onions and bell pepper; sauté, stirring the mixture in the butter, for about 3 minutes, or until the shrimp are pink outside and opaque about halfway through.

Stir together the cream, mustard, tomato and coconut in a bowl; add to the shrimp. Continue cooking the shrimp, turning them occasionally, for about 3 minutes longer, or until they are firm and just opaque throughout.

Heat the rum in a small pan just until warm, then ignite it, being careful to avert your face. When the flames die, add the rum to the shrimp and stir to blend. Season with salt and pepper. Divide among warmed plates.

SERVES 4

John Falcone's Grilled Prawns with Basil Baste

John Falcone, winemaker at Atlas Peak Vineyards in Napa, serves this dish with his winery's Sangiovese to show how wonderful red wine is with shellfish. The skewered jumbo prawns are placed on a hot grill and basted with olive oil and seasonings to bring out their sweetness.

24 jumbo prawns

1 cup extra virgin olive oil

2 garlic cloves, minced

12 basil leaves, chopped

1 teaspoon fresh lemon juice

½ teaspoon hot red pepper flakes (optional)

¼ teaspoon salt

¼ teaspoon freshly cracked pepper

Prepare a medium-hot charcoal fire or preheat a gas grill.

Shell and devein the prawns, leaving the tail intact. Rinse and pat dry.

Combine the olive oil, garlic, basil, lemon juice, pepper flakes, if desired, salt and pepper in a bowl.

Thread 6 prawns on each skewer, skewering them through the tail and the thickest part of the body in the shape of a "C." Lightly brush prawns with the basting mixture, using mostly oil.

Grill about 4 minutes on one side, then turn and baste, again mostly with oil. Cook for 3 to 4 minutes longer, or until the prawns turn white. Baste again, this time coating the prawns with some of the seasonings in the basting mixture. Serve immediately.

SERVES 4

Grilled Tequila-Chipotle Shrimp

In this recipe by Jacqueline McMahan, the shrimp are first marinated before being grilled. The marinade also works well with chicken. Any leftover shrimp are great added to a pasta salad or rice, or used as a garnish for a lightly dressed green salad.

2 tablespoons canned chipotle chiles en adobo

4 garlic cloves

2 tablespoons tequila

2 tablespoons fresh lime juice

2 tablespoons olive oil

½ teaspoon salt

Freshly ground pepper, to taste

2 tablespoons chopped cilantro leaves

1½ pounds large shrimp, shelled and deveined

Prepare a medium-hot fire in a grill or preheat the broiler.

Combine the chipotles, garlic, tequila, lime juice, olive oil, salt, pepper and cilantro in a food processor; process until the mixture is puréed.

Put the shrimp in a bowl or heavy-duty resealable plastic bag; add the marinade and let stand for 20 minutes.

Grill or broil the shrimp for 3 minutes, then turn and cook for 3 to 4 minutes longer.

SERVES 4

Red Chile Mussels

The mussel-cooking broth—slightly thickened and well-spiced with chiles—is great for sopping up with tortillas, says Georgeanne Brennan. You can, of course, adjust the number of chiles to your own taste.

1 to 2 tablespoons corn oil, or other light vegetable oil

3 garlic cloves, grated

1 tablespoon chopped onion

2 to 3 pounds mussels, scrubbed and debearded

1 tablespoon all-purpose flour

6 arbol or pequin chiles, seeded, stemmed and crushed into small pieces

1 cup chicken broth

½ cup dry white wine

¼ cup chopped cilantro

½ teaspoon freshly ground pepper

Heat the oil in a large, heavy pot over medium-high heat. When the oil is hot, add the garlic and onion and sauté for 1 to 2 minutes. Add the mussels and cook, stirring, for 1 to 2 minutes. Sprinkle in the flour and chiles. Cook, stirring, until the flour is no longer visible.

Slowly add the broth, stirring constantly. Stir in the wine, half of the cilantro and the pepper. Cover and cook for 10 to 12 minutes, or until the mussels open and a thin sauce has formed. Discard any mussels that do not open.

Spoon into bowls and sprinkle with the remaining cilantro.

SERVES 4

Buying and Cleaning Mussels

When buying mussels, choose ones that are tightly closed. If a mussel shell is open, tap on it and it will close if the mussel is alive. If the shell remains open, the mussel should be discarded. Always discard mussels with cracked or broken shells. Store mussels in the bottom of the refrigerator, covered with a damp towel, where they may keep two to three days.

To clean mussels: Scrub the mussel shells in cold water. Using needle-nose pliers, remove the brown fibers that stick out between the shells (the "beard").

After cooking, discard any mussels that do not open.

Mussels in Coconut Broth

A squeeze of lime juice added just before serving significantly brightens the flavors of this dish, created by Chronicle *staff writer/critic Robin Davis.*

1 can (14 ounces) unsweetened coconut milk
1 bottle (8 ounces) clam juice
1 small onion, thinly sliced
2 stalks lemongrass (tender white part only), thinly sliced
2 garlic cloves, thinly sliced
1-inch knob fresh ginger, cut into 4 slices
Salt and freshly ground white pepper, to taste
2 to 3 pounds mussels, scrubbed and debearded
Juice of 1 lime

∞ Combine the coconut milk, clam juice, onion, lemongrass, garlic and ginger in a heavy saucepan. Simmer over medium heat for 15 minutes to blend flavors. Strain, then return the broth to the saucepan. Season with salt and white pepper.

Bring the broth to a boil over high heat. Add the mussels, cover and simmer for about 5 minutes, or until the mussels open. Remove from heat. Discard any mussels that do not open.

Divide the mussels among serving bowls.

Add the lime juice to the broth. Adjust seasonings if needed. Pour the broth over the mussels and serve.

SERVES 4

Mussels Steamed in Vouvray with Fennel and Leeks

Vouvray, a light, fruity white wine, adds just a background note to the mussels in this recipe created by Tara Duggan. Serve with a baguette for soaking up the juices.

1 tablespoon olive oil

1 tablespoon butter

4 garlic cloves, thinly sliced

1 leek (white and light green parts only), well rinsed, halved lengthwise, then thinly
sliced crosswise

1 fennel bulb, quartered, cored and very thinly sliced

3 to 4 pounds mussels, scrubbed and debearded

2 cups Vouvray, or light-bodied Sauvignon Blanc

2 bay leaves

1 tablespoon minced Italian parsley for garnish

⊕⊕ Heat the olive oil and butter in a large, heavy stockpot over medium heat. Add the garlic, leek and fennel. Sauté, stirring occasionally, for 2 to 3 minutes, or until just softened.

Add the mussels, wine and bay leaves. Cover the pot and steam the mussels for about 2 minutes, or until they open. Uncover and cook 2 minutes longer, stirring once or twice. Discard any mussels that do not open.

Spoon the mussels and juices into bowls and garnish with the parsley.

SERVES 4

Oven-Roasted Mussels with Tarragon Butter

Oven-roasting is one of the easiest ways to prepare mussels. Dark shells glistening against crystalline salt make a glamorous oven-to-table presentation, says Georgeanne Brennan. Be careful, though, as the pan and salt get very hot. For a special occasion, serve with a number of sauces, such as roasted red pepper, aioli and lemon-parsley.

Rock salt

1 pound mussels, scrubbed and debearded

4 tablespoons butter

1 tablespoon chopped fresh tarragon

Preheat the oven to 500 degrees.

Make a bed of rock salt about 1½ inches deep in a heavy, ovenproof skillet or baking dish. Place it in the oven for 15 minutes, or until thoroughly heated.

Remove the dish from the oven and arrange the mussels in a single layer on top of the salt. Return to the oven and roast for 5 minutes, or just until the mussels open. Discard any mussels that do not open.

Serve the mussels on a platter, or bring the skillet to the table.

Melt the butter in a small skillet over medium heat. Remove from the heat and stir in the tarragon. Transfer the butter to a small bowl and serve alongside the mussels.

SERVES 2 OR 3

Miso in the Kitchen

Alison Richman, the former chef of the trendy XYZ restaurant in San Francisco's W Hotel, always has miso on hand. In addition to making a quick soup, miso enlivens sauces and adds flavor to fish, meat and vegetables. Coat fish with miso and broil or grill, then finish with butter and lemon, breadcrumbs and/or some fresh basil. Yellow miso is less yeasty than the red variety, but both are handy to have at your fingertips.

Cognac Scallops

This recipe by Shirley Sarvis is utterly simple, but the addition of Cognac gives it a sophisticated twist. Use finely minced parsley to give color if chervil is not available. Serve with a bone-dry Chenin Blanc.

8 ounces sea scallops, trimmed (see Note)

About 2½ tablespoons clarified unsalted butter

Salt and freshly ground white pepper, to taste

6 tablespoons Cognac

6 tablespoons whipping cream

A few small feathers of chervil

◉◉ Wipe the scallops dry. Heat the butter in a medium-large, heavy skillet over medium-high heat. Add the scallops (do not crowd in pan) and cook on one side until rich golden. Turn and cook until almost opaque throughout, very slightly less done than you wish. Remove to serving plates. Season well with salt and pepper.

Remove butter and any burned particles from the pan. Let the pan cool slightly, then add the Cognac and cook over high heat, stirring, until reduced by half.

Add the cream and cook, stirring, until the liquid has the consistency of whipping cream. Season with salt and pepper.

Spoon the sauce over the scallops. Sprinkle with the chervil.

SERVES 2

VARIATION: Add ½ teaspoon grated fresh lemon zest a few moments before the sauce has reduced to the desired consistency; omit the chervil.

NOTE: There is a small amount of meat attached to each scallop that has a different appearance and texture than the main muscle. Look on the shorter side of each scallop for a place where the grain of the muscle changes direction and density. This strip of meat is tougher than the main adductor muscle. Peel it off and discard.

Shrimp in Spicy Saffron Broth with Israeli Couscous

Israeli couscous grains are pearl-size balls that have a tapioca-like texture. They're great for soaking up the flavors of the saffron broth and shrimp. This recipe from Chronicle *staff writer Tara Duggan also works extremely well using mussels. However, mussels take longer to prepare as they need to be debearded. If you opt for mussels, scrub off any barnacles with a wire scrubber. Then use needle-nose pliers to pull off the fuzzy beards attached inside the shell. Rinse the mussels, place in a bowl and toss with the spice mixture.*

1 teaspoon ground coriander

1 teaspoon ground cumin

¼ teaspoon cayenne pepper

1 teaspoon paprika

1½ pounds medium shrimp, shelled and deveined

3 tablespoons olive oil

1 onion, diced

4 garlic cloves, minced

1 pound Israeli couscous (see Note)

Pinch of saffron threads

1 cup chicken broth

2 tablespoons minced cilantro for garnish (optional)

⊚⊚ Start bringing a large pot of salted water to a boil over high heat.

Combine the coriander, cumin, cayenne pepper and paprika in a bowl. Coat the shrimp with the spice mixture and marinate at room temperature.

Heat the olive oil in a large sauté pan over medium-low heat. Add the onion and sauté for 7 to 10 minutes, or until tender, then add the garlic and sauté for 1 minute longer.

While the onion sautés, add the couscous to the boiling water and cook according to package directions, just until al dente. Add a few tablespoons of the boiling water to the saffron in a separate bowl.

Mix the shrimp into the onion mixture and cook over medium-high heat for 2 to 3 minutes, or until the shrimp just turn pink. Add the broth and saffron and quickly bring to a boil. (If using mussels, add them now, cover the pan and cook until their shells open. Discard any that do not open.) Take care not to overcook the shrimp or they will become tough.

Spoon the couscous into shallow bowls and ladle the stew over each serving. Be sure to include plenty of the saffron broth. Garnish with the cilantro, if desired.

SERVES 4

NOTE: Israeli couscous is available at upscale supermarkets. If you can't find it, substitute orzo pasta or instant couscous.

French-Vietnamese Bouillabaisse

For interesting variations on this delicious recipe by Mai Pham, use different types of seafood and, perhaps, fortify the chicken broth by simmering shrimp shells or fish bones in it (strain before using in the recipe). Serve with warm garlic bread.

4 tablespoons butter

½ yellow onion, cut into 1-inch cubes

1 tablespoon minced garlic

1 teaspoon hot red pepper flakes, or to taste (optional)

1-inch piece fresh ginger, sliced

1 pound plum tomatoes, cut into large cubes

2 tablespoons Asian fish sauce

2 tablespoons sugar

3 cups chicken broth

2 cups dry white wine

¼ teaspoon saffron threads, softened in ¼ cup warm water

½ teaspoon chopped fresh rosemary

½ teaspoon chopped fresh thyme

⅔ pound red potatoes, cut into wedges

⅓ pound sea scallops

⅓ pound medium shrimp, shelled and deveined

1½ pounds clams and/or mussels, scrubbed and debearded

½ pound frozen cooked crab legs (optional)

2 celery stalks, sliced on the diagonal (about 1 cup)

1 tablespoon Pernod
Rosemary sprigs for garnish

Heat the butter in a soup pot over medium heat. Add the onion and garlic; cook, stirring, for about 2 minutes, or until fragrant. Add the pepper flakes, if desired, and give the mixture a quick stir. Add the ginger, tomatoes, fish sauce and sugar. Cook for about 3 minutes, or until slightly reduced.

Add the chicken broth, white wine, saffron, rosemary, thyme and potatoes. Cover and simmer for about 15 minutes. (The stock may be made in advance up to this point. Cool, cover and refrigerate.)

Bring a separate pot of water to a boil over high heat and blanch the scallops, shrimp, clams and crab legs, if desired, in it for 1 minute. Drain.

Add the seafood and celery to the soup pot. Stir in the Pernod and simmer for 2 to 3 minutes, or until the seafood is just done.

Ladle into bowls and garnish with rosemary sprigs.

SERVES 6

Quick Fish Stock

If you don't have time to make a fish stock, bottled clam juice mixed with equal parts water plus a squeeze of lemon juice will work just fine, especially if the rest of the dish is strongly flavored with tomato sauce, butter or herbs.

Spanish Clam, Prawn and Chorizo Stew

Jody Denton of LuLu in San Francisco created this lusty shellfish stew, made slightly spicy by the addition of chorizo. Great for easy entertaining.

1 pound yellow Finn potatoes, peeled and cut into 1-inch cubes

¼ cup extra virgin olive oil

1 onion, chopped

½ cup sliced garlic

1 teaspoon crushed fennel seeds

2 teaspoons paprika

1 teaspoon chopped fresh oregano

2 teaspoons salt, plus more, to taste

8 cups chicken or shellfish stock, canned low-salt chicken broth, or water

2 cups chopped seeded ripe tomatoes, or 1 can (14½ ounces) diced seeded tomatoes with juices

¾ pound chorizo sausage, casings removed

2 pounds small clams, scrubbed

1 pound large prawns, shelled and deveined

¼ cup chopped Italian parsley

Freshly ground pepper, to taste

Cook the potatoes in a large pot of boiling salted water until tender. Drain. Set aside.

Heat the olive oil in a large, heavy saucepan over medium heat. Add the onion, garlic, fennel seeds, paprika, oregano and salt. Cook, stirring, for about 8 minutes, or until the onion is translucent. Add the stock and tomatoes and their juices. Bring to a boil, reduce heat and simmer for 1 hour.

Cook the chorizo in a large skillet over high heat for about 10 minutes, breaking it into pieces with a spoon. Add the clams and cook, stirring, for 2 minutes. Add to the broth mixture. Bring to a boil, reduce heat, cover and simmer for about 2 minutes, or until the clams open. Discard any that do not open.

Add the prawns, potatoes and parsley. Simmer for about 2 minutes, or until the prawns are just cooked through. Season with salt and pepper.

SERVES 6

Seafood Kebabs

Here are a few suggestions from Marlena Spieler:
Three-color fish kebabs: Thread salmon, tuna and cod (or another white fish) on a skewer. Baste with teriyaki, soy or a lemon vinaigrette with fresh herbs.
Shrimp: Marinate the shrimp in their shells in olive oil, hot red pepper flakes, chopped garlic and coarse salt. Grill and serve with lemon wedges.

Basque-Style Fisherman's Stew

Loretta Keller, chef/owner of Bizou in San Francisco, likes to prepare this rustic stew on dark and stormy nights. Brimming with soul-satisfying flavors, it's so good you'll find it hard to stop eating. It's easy to put together, and all you need as an accompaniment is hearty country-style bread.

2 tablespoons extra virgin olive oil

2 onions, finely diced

3 russet potatoes, peeled and cut into 2-inch cubes

2 green bell peppers, stemmed, seeded, deribbed and chopped

2 garlic cloves, minced

Salt, to taste

8 cups fish stock, or bottled clam juice

1 cup dry white wine

6 ounces fresh tomatoes, peeled, seeded and diced; or ¾ cup diced canned tomatoes

2 pounds fatty fresh tuna (preferably from the belly), cut into large pieces

Freshly ground pepper, to taste

Chopped Italian parsley for garnish

◎◎ Heat the olive oil in a large, heavy saucepan over medium heat. Add the onions. Cover and cook, stirring occasionally, for about 10 minutes, or until onions are translucent but not colored.

Add the potatoes, bell peppers and garlic. Cook, stirring, for 10 minutes. Season lightly with salt.

Add the fish stock and wine. Simmer for about 10 minutes, or until the potatoes are tender and the stew has thickened slightly.

Add the tomatoes and simmer for 10 minutes.

Add the tuna, pushing it down into the stew with a spoon. Cover, remove from heat and let stand until tuna is cooked to desired doneness, about 5 minutes for medium-rare. Season with salt and pepper.

Ladle into bowls, garnish with parsley and serve.

SERVES 6

Seafood Klephtiko

Joanne Weir discovered that parchment works well for cooking not only lamb (see recipe, page 242) but also seafood.

3 tablespoons extra virgin olive oil

1 large yellow onion, thinly sliced

1 large red bell pepper, stemmed, seeded, deribbed and thinly sliced

1 large fennel bulb, trimmed and thinly sliced

6 garlic cloves, minced

⅓ cup dry white wine

1 jalapeño chile, seeded and minced

Coarse salt and freshly ground pepper, to taste

½ cup fresh lemon juice

18 Manila clams, scrubbed

18 mussels, scrubbed and debearded

12 ounces halibut or other firm white fish, cut into 6 pieces

18 medium prawns, shelled and deveined

1 cup basil leaves, thinly sliced

◉◉ Preheat the oven to 350 degrees. Have ready 6 lengths of parchment paper, each measuring 18 by 24 inches.

Heat the olive oil in a large skillet over medium heat. Add the onion, bell pepper and fennel and sauté for about 10 minutes, or until soft. Add the garlic and cook for 1 minute. Add the wine, chile, salt and pepper and cook for about 5 minutes, or until the liquid reduces and coats a spoon. Remove from the heat and add the lemon juice.

Fold each piece of parchment in half, then open it up again. Arrange equal amounts of cooked vegetables on one side of the fold, reserving the liquid. Arrange equal amounts of clams, mussels, halibut and prawns over the vegetables. Spoon the reserved liquid over the seafood, then sprinkle the basil over the top. Fold up the parchment packets and seal the edges securely so steam doesn't escape. Place the packets on a baking sheet and bake for 10 to 12 minutes, or until the parchment has puffed significantly and the clams and mussels open (if in doubt, slit open 1 packet and look).

Place the packets on heated serving plates and serve immediately.

SERVES 6

Chapter 10

Morning Repasts

Brunch is making a comeback in the Bay Area, both in restaurants and at home. When we published the first San Francisco Chronicle Cookbook, *we didn't include a breakfast and brunch chapter, but in the intervening years, more readers have told us that the morning repast is their favorite weekend meal.*

It's easy to see why this meal has become so popular for casual get-togethers. If you live outside San Francisco, where summer temperatures soar, mornings offer gentle breezes and natural air-conditioning, both of which wane as the sun gets higher. And if you live in San Francisco, summer's the time when the fog lifts for a few hours—at least in some neighborhoods—and the breezes are gentle. In the winter, having brunch or breakfast kick-starts the day.

The recipes in this chapter serve two purposes: There are choices for leisurely weekend family breakfasts, where you can enjoy dishes such as Wheat Berries with Ricotta, Almonds and Honey (page 334); plus selections for more festive occasions, such as Postrio's Lobster Scrambled Eggs (page 367) and Georgeanne Brennan's Wild Mushroom Omelet (page 354).

In this chapter, you'll find some interesting and creative recipes: Crisp Maple-Glazed Country Bacon (page 370), Pumpkin Pancakes with Toasted Pumpkin Seeds (page 336), delicate Birdseed Muffins (page 344) and Cranberry-Cream Scones (page 341), to name a few.

Eggs are still a mainstay, of course, and we'll tell you how to scramble (page 367) or hard-cook (page 362) the perfect egg. Beyond that, you'll find recipes from some of the best culinary minds in the country: Marion Cunningham's Featherbed Eggs (page 353); Marlena Spieler's Baked Eggs with Duxelles and Herbs (page 352), Jacqueline McMahan's Grandmama's Artichoke Frittatas (page 356) and Janet Fletcher's Butter-Steamed Asparagus with Egg (page 364).

Wheat Berries with Ricotta, Almonds and Honey

This dish by Robin Davis was inspired by a similar Sicilian recipe in Lynne Rosetto Kasper's The Italian Country Table *(Scribner, 1999). Serve it warm or at room temperature for breakfast or brunch. It's particularly good topped with sliced strawberries.*

1 cup wheat berries

3 cups water

2 tablespoons brown sugar

2 whole cinnamon sticks, broken in half

½ teaspoon salt

1½ cups whole-milk ricotta cheese

½ cup coarsely chopped toasted almonds

Honey, to taste

Ground cinnamon, to taste

@@ Put the wheat berries in a bowl and add water to cover by 2 inches. Let soak overnight.

Drain the wheat berries and transfer to a heavy saucepan. Add the 3 cups water, the brown sugar, cinnamon sticks and salt. Bring to a boil over medium-high heat, then reduce heat to low and simmer for about 1 hour, or until the berries are tender. Drain any excess liquid. Discard the cinnamon sticks.

Transfer the berries to a large bowl. Cool slightly, then stir in the ricotta and almonds. Sweeten with honey and sprinkle with cinnamon.

SERVES 4

BEST WAY:
Brewing Coffee

The best pot for brewing coffee is the press filter, but most people don't want to make the effort, at least on a daily basis. If using an electric pot, the best bet is one with a gold-screen cone filter. We use the Braun FlavorSelect drip coffeemaker, rated tops by *Consumer Reports* in November 1999.

Grinding the beans: Grinding the beans daily really does make a big difference. If you need to store whole beans for more than about a week, keep them in an airtight container, either at room temperature (away from light) or in the freezer. Stored ground beans rated the lowest in our tests.

Making the coffee: Although it sounds excessive, we brewed the richest, smoothest cup of coffee with a ratio of 2 tablespoons coffee for each 6 ounces (¾ cup) cold water. Using fewer grounds produced coffee with a bitter aftertaste.

Buttermilk-Cornmeal Pancakes

Here's a great pancake recipe from The Chronicle's *"Naturally" columnist, Sharon Cadwallader.*

2 eggs

1 cup buttermilk

4 tablespoons butter, melted

1 cup unbleached all-purpose flour

½ cup yellow cornmeal

1 tablespoon sugar

2 teaspoons baking powder

½ teaspoon baking soda

½ teaspoon salt

◉◉ Combine the eggs and buttermilk in a mixing bowl; whisk until blended. Stir in the butter.

Combine the flour, cornmeal, sugar, baking powder, baking soda and salt; whisk to blend.

Combine the wet and dry ingredients and stir until they are just mixed; do not overbeat.

Spoon the batter onto a hot, greased griddle and fry the pancakes until lightly browned on both sides, turning once.

YIELDS 10 TO 12 PANCAKES

Pumpkin Pancakes with Toasted Pumpkin Seeds

Alison Richman, the chef of Tantillo's in San Francisco, created this recipe. The pancakes get their distinctiveness from a smattering of toasted pumpkin seeds. Richman's pancakes are a simple, seasonal recipe that makes a lovely choice for brunch. Serve them with butter and a pitcher of real maple syrup.

3 cups all-purpose flour

1½ teaspoons salt

6 tablespoons sugar

1½ teaspoons baking soda

1 tablespoon baking powder

3 eggs

3 cups milk

3 tablespoons butter, melted

½ cup fresh or canned pumpkin purée

Vegetable oil for frying

½ cup toasted pumpkin seeds for garnish (see Note)

◉◉ Sift the flour, salt, sugar, baking soda and baking powder into a bowl.

Whisk the eggs in another bowl. Add the milk, butter and pumpkin purée and mix well. Mix the wet ingredients into the dry ingredients.

Heat a bit of oil on a griddle over medium-high heat. Spoon the batter onto the griddle and fry the pancakes until golden on both sides, turning once.

Garnish with the toasted pumpkin seeds and serve with maple syrup and butter.

SERVES 6

NOTE: Remove all stringy fibers from seeds, then rinse and blot seeds dry. Spread on a baking sheet. Roast in a 350-degree oven until light golden, stirring from time to time.

Strawberry Soufflé Pancake

This is a version of the popular soufflé pancakes served at Bette's Oceanview Diner in Berkeley. Anyone who can separate eggs can make it.

3 eggs
½ cup half-and-half
¼ cup all-purpose flour
½ teaspoon sugar
¼ teaspoon salt
1½ tablespoons butter, melted
1 tablespoon Grand Marnier (optional)
½ basket strawberries, washed, hulled and sliced
Powdered sugar for dusting

Place a rack 4 to 5 inches below the heating unit of a broiler and preheat.

Separate the eggs and reserve 1 of the yolks for another use. Beat together the remaining 2 egg yolks and the half-and-half in a bowl. Slowly stir in the flour, then the sugar, salt, butter and Grand Marnier, if desired.

Beat the egg whites in a large bowl to soft peaks. Fold the egg whites into the batter, then fold in 1 cup of the sliced strawberries.

Lightly grease a 10-inch nonstick skillet with an ovenproof handle, or a cast-iron skillet, and heat over high heat until almost smoking.

Pour the batter into the pan and reduce heat to medium. Cook for about 5 minutes, or until the bottom is nicely browned and the batter has begun to firm up.

Arrange a few berry slices over the top in a circular pattern. Place the pan on the broiler rack and broil for 3 to 4 minutes, or until the top of the pancake is brown and the center is just set but still a little soft.

Transfer the pancake to a warmed large plate and decorate with the remaining strawberries. Dust with powdered sugar and serve immediately.

SERVES 2

Kirk Webber's Waffles

Kirk Webber, chef/owner of Cafe Kati in San Francisco, says that when he was a boy, his father prepared these simple buttermilk waffles every Sunday morning. Serve them with additional melted butter, whipped butter, warmed real maple syrup, honey or fruit syrup as desired.

2 extra-large eggs at room temperature

1 cup all-purpose flour

½ teaspoon baking soda

1 teaspoon baking powder

¼ teaspoon salt

½ tablespoon sugar

1 cup buttermilk, or whole milk

2 tablespoons butter, melted and cooled

Vegetable oil for greasing waffle iron

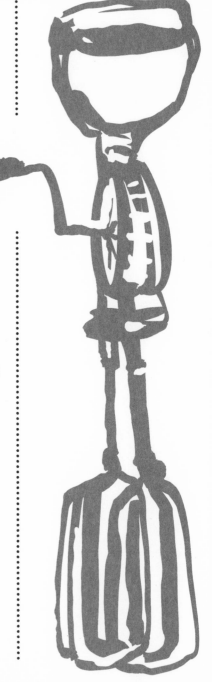

Separate the eggs. Combine the flour, baking soda, baking powder, salt and sugar in a bowl.

Beat the egg yolks with the buttermilk and butter in another bowl until well blended.

Fold the dry ingredients into the wet ingredients.

Beat the egg whites in a bowl to stiff peaks. Stir a small amount of the egg whites into the batter to lighten it, then fold in the remainder. Do not overmix.

Heat a waffle iron according to manufacturer's directions. Grease lightly. Spoon on enough batter to nearly cover the surface of the iron—it will spread to the edges once you close the lid. Cook until done.

YIELDS 6 WAFFLES

Rick & Ann's French Toast

This classic recipe is from Rick & Ann's restaurant in Berkeley.

Topping

1 cup mixed berries, such as blackberries, raspberries, sliced strawberries
    and/or blueberries

1 tablespoon sugar

½ teaspoon minced lemon zest

French Toast

2 eggs

1½ teaspoons sugar

¼ teaspoon cinnamon

Pinch of salt

¼ cup milk

¼ cup half-and-half

⅛ teaspoon vanilla

4 thick slices challah, cinnamon swirl or sturdy white bread

2 teaspoons unsalted butter

Extra sliced strawberries for garnish

⊛⊛ To make the topping: Crush the mixed berries in a bowl. Add the sugar and lemon zest; let stand for at least 5 minutes or up to 30 minutes.

To make the French toast: Whisk together the eggs, sugar, cinnamon and salt in a shallow bowl. Add the milk, half-and-half and vanilla and whisk to blend.

Dip the bread slices into the egg mixture, letting each soak for about 30 seconds.

Melt the butter in a nonstick skillet or on a griddle over medium-high heat. Fry the bread slices, in 2 batches if necessary, turning once, until well browned. Remove to warm plates.

Divide the berry mixture over the toast, letting it drip down the sides. Garnish each plate with the sliced strawberries.

SERVES 2

Blood Orange Mimosa

Georgeanne Brennan makes mimosas this way: Squeeze the juice from 2 blood oranges and strain. Mix 1 ounce juice with 3 ounces sparkling wine or Champagne.

Brown Scones

Traditionally, scones have been served with afternoon tea, but now they are in vogue on the breakfast table. Marion Cunningham likes them crisp and brown on top and rather dense inside. Scones are delicious when served warm, split and buttered, then spread with jam.

1½ cups all-purpose flour, plus flour for dusting

½ cup bran

2 teaspoons baking powder

½ teaspoon salt

1½ tablespoons sugar

4 tablespoons chilled butter

1 egg

½ cup milk

⊚⊚ Preheat the oven to 450 degrees.

Combine the flour, bran, baking powder, salt and sugar in a bowl and mix well. Cut the butter into bits and add to the flour mixture. Rub the butter into the flour using your fingertips or a pastry blender until the mixture resembles coarse breadcrumbs.

Beat the egg lightly in a bowl, add the milk and mix until well blended.

Stir the wet ingredients into the dry ingredients, stirring only until just blended.

Transfer the dough to a lightly floured work surface. Knead 12 times. Pat into a circle about ½ inch thick. Cut the dough into 12 wedges. Place the wedges ½ inch apart on an ungreased baking sheet.

Bake for 10 to 12 minutes, or until the tops are golden. Serve hot or warm.

YIELDS 12 SCONES

Cranberry-Cream Scones

These scones by Flo Braker have an exceptionally rich flavor and a tender, feather-light crumb because of a surprise ingredient—whipped cream.

2 cups all-purpose flour, plus flour for dusting

⅓ cup sugar

3 teaspoons baking powder

¼ teaspoon salt

½ cup fresh cranberries

1⅓ cups whipping cream

1 tablespoon butter, melted

1 tablespoon powdered sugar

◉◉ Position the rack in the lower third of the oven; preheat to 375 degrees. Line a baking sheet with parchment paper.

Sift together the flour, sugar, baking powder and salt into a large bowl. Mix the cranberries into the flour mixture. Whip the cream in a bowl until soft peaks form.

Fold the whipped cream into the dry ingredients just until it forms a rough semicohesive mass. (It's OK that some parts are moister than others.)

Transfer the dough to a lightly floured work surface and knead only a few times until the dough holds together. Lightly flour your hands and pat the dough into an 8-inch circle; place on the baking sheet. Brush the surface with the butter and sprinkle with the powdered sugar.

Cut the circle into 10 wedges without detaching them.

Bake for 30 to 35 minutes, or until golden brown. Cut into the premarked wedges. Serve hot or at room temperature.

YIELDS 10 SCONES

Delicate Cornmeal Muffins

These unusual muffins by Marion Cunningham are both fine-textured and rich. The special texture comes from a simple substitution of cake flour for all-purpose flour.

1 egg at room temperature

½ cup butter, melted

¼ cup vegetable oil

1 cup milk, warmed

1 cup cake flour

⅔ cup yellow cornmeal

1 tablespoon baking powder

½ teaspoon salt

1 tablespoon sugar

Preheat the oven to 400 degrees. Grease 12 muffin cups.

Beat the egg, butter and oil in a mixing bowl until well blended. Stir in the milk.

Combine the flour, cornmeal, baking powder, salt and sugar in a bowl; stir with a fork until well mixed. Add the dry ingredients to the wet ingredients and stir until blended.

Spoon the batter into the muffin pan, filling each cup at least three fourths full.

Bake for 15 to 20 minutes, or until the edges of the muffins are slightly golden and a cake tester comes out clean when inserted into the center of a muffin.

Remove the muffins from the pan and let cool a little before serving.

YIELDS 12 MUFFINS

Santa Fe Cooking School Blue Corn Muffins

Many chefs have taught classes at the Santa Fe Cooking School and have added their personal touch to these muffins. They can no longer be improved upon; these are the best, says Jacqueline McMahan. Serve warm with butter or honey butter.

¾ cup butter at room temperature

½ cup sugar

5 eggs

½ cup milk

4 tablespoons minced jalapeño chile (canned OK)

1 cup corn kernels (canned or blanched fresh corn)

1 cup grated Monterey Jack cheese

1 cup grated cheddar cheese

1 cup all-purpose flour

1 cup blue cornmeal

2 teaspoons baking powder

1 teaspoon salt

⊚⊚ Preheat the oven to 375 degrees. Grease 12 muffin cups.

Combine the butter and sugar in a bowl and beat with an electric mixer until fluffy. Combine the eggs and milk in another bowl and slowly stir into the butter-sugar mixture. Blend well. Stir in the jalapeño, corn, Monterey Jack and cheddar cheeses.

Combine the flour, cornmeal, baking powder and salt in a bowl.

Slowly add the dry ingredients to the wet ingredients, blending well. Pour the batter into the muffin cups.

Bake for about 20 minutes, or until a cake tester comes out clean when inserted into the center of a muffin.

Serve warm.

YIELDS 12 LARGE MUFFINS

Birdseed Muffins

These nubby golden-brown muffins are light, moist and delicious, and have a slight crunch from the millet. Although 2 cups of sugar may seem like a lot, it's just the right amount, says Marion Cunningham. The oats "absorb" much of the sweetness. The muffins are great served warm or at room temperature, and they freeze well.

1¼ cups boiling water

1 cup uncooked rolled oats

½ cup butter at room temperature

1 cup granulated sugar

1 cup light brown sugar

2 teaspoons vanilla

2 eggs

1½ cups all-purpose flour

1 teaspoon baking soda

½ teaspoon salt

½ cup millet (see Note)

◉◉ Preheat the oven to 350 degrees. Grease 12 muffin cups.

Combine the boiling water and oats in a bowl; stir to mix. Cover and let stand for about 20 minutes.

Put the butter in a mixing bowl and beat with an electric mixer until creamy. Slowly add the granulated and brown sugars, beating until the mixture is smooth and creamy. Add the vanilla and eggs and beat until well mixed.

Add the oats to the butter mixture; blend well.

Sift together the flour, baking soda and salt in a bowl. Stir into the batter and mix well. Add the millet and mix well.

Spoon the batter into the muffin cups, filling them to the top.

Bake for about 20 minutes, or until a cake tester comes out clean when inserted into the center of a muffin.

BEST WAY:

Cooking Instant Oatmeal

The Food Department tested multiple batches of instant oatmeal to find out which method—stovetop or microwave—produced the best texture and whether nonfat, low-fat or whole milk or water provided the best flavor.

We preferred the stovetop method using low-fat milk, which produced a loose, creamy and slightly sweet cereal with a bold oat flavor.

The results in the microwave were inferior to the stovetop method, although the low-fat milk was better than either water, nonfat or whole milk.

Run a table knife around the edge of each muffin and lift out of the pan. Place on a rack and let cool for 5 to 10 minutes.

Serve warm or at room temperature.

YIELDS 12 LARGE MUFFINS

NOTE: Millet may be found in natural-food and health-food stores.

Irish Soda Bread

True Irish soda bread contains no baking powder; it is leavened by the reaction of buttermilk (acid) and baking soda (alkali). Because the leavening begins as soon as the ingredients are mixed, prepare the dough quickly and pop it into the oven. This traditional recipe is from Marion Cunningham.

4 cups all-purpose flour

1½ teaspoons salt

1 teaspoon baking soda

2 cups buttermilk

◉ Preheat the oven to 375 degrees. Grease a baking sheet or an 8-inch round cake pan.

Combine the flour, salt and baking soda in a large mixing bowl; stir and toss until well blended. Add the buttermilk and stir briskly with a fork until the dough holds together in a rough mass.

Knead the dough on a lightly floured surface for about 30 seconds, then pat into an 8-inch round about 1½ inches thick. Using a sharp knife, slash a large ¼-inch-deep "X" across the top.

Place the dough round on the prepared baking sheet or in the cake pan and bake for 45 to 50 minutes, or until the bread is nicely browned and the "X" has spread open.

Transfer to a rack to cool (if using a cake pan, remove bread from pan), then wrap bread in a slightly damp towel and let rest on the rack for at least 8 hours. The soda bread should be completely cool before serving.

SERVES 8

Hot Grilled Blue Cheese Toasts

In Burgundy, these toasts are served as a casse-croute, *a midmorning break from the rigors of work. Marlena Spieler thinks they also make fine brunch or lunch fare.*

1 baguette, preferably sourdough, split lengthwise

2 to 3 tablespoons dry red or white wine

3 or 4 garlic cloves, finely chopped

6 to 8 ounces Roquefort cheese, or other blue sheep's milk cheese that is not too fatty
 and has a good, strong flavor, crumbled or sliced

6 ounces Emmentaler, shredded

1 to 2 tablespoons extra virgin olive oil (optional)

The Condiments (optional)

2 or 3 cooked beets, peeled and sliced or diced

Handful of mixed baby greens or watercress

Vinaigrette (your favorite recipe)

◉ Preheat the broiler.

Sprinkle the cut sides of the baguette with the wine, then rub on the chopped garlic. Top with a layer of blue cheese, then a layer of Emmentaler, and finally a sprinkling of the olive oil, if desired.

Broil until the baguette lightly browns at the edges and the cheeses melt.

Serve immediately, either on its own or with cooked beets and baby greens tossed with vinaigrette.

SERVES 4

Apple–Sour Cream Coffee Cake

This homey cake from Kerry Heffernan at Autumn Moon Cafe in Oakland is moist, rich and oh, so satisfying. Enjoy it for breakfast, brunch, teatime or as a midnight snack. Instead of apples, try using any not-too-juicy fruit, such as pears, pineapple, papaya, mango, blackberries or raspberries.

Crumb Topping

½ cup light brown sugar

½ cup unbleached all-purpose flour

½ teaspoon cinnamon

4 tablespoons chilled butter

¼ cup finely chopped walnuts (optional)

Cake

1 cup butter, at room temperature

2 cups sugar

6 eggs

Grated zest of 2 lemons

4 cups unbleached all-purpose flour

2 teaspoons baking powder

2 teaspoons baking soda

½ teaspoon salt

2 cups sour cream

2 cups diced Granny Smith and/or Fuji apples (1-inch dice) (peeled, if desired)

◶ To make the topping: Combine the sugar, flour and cinnamon in a small bowl. Using a pastry blender, cut in the butter until the texture is coarse. Stir in the walnuts, if desired. Set aside.

To make the cake: Preheat the oven to 350 degrees. Grease a 10-inch angel food cake pan.

Put the butter in a large bowl and beat with an electric mixer until soft and creamy. Add the sugar and beat until light in color and fluffy. Beat in the eggs, 1 at a time. Add the lemon zest and beat again.

Combine the flour, baking powder, baking soda and salt in a mixing bowl. Stir to mix. Add the flour mixture to the butter mixture, alternately with the sour cream. Beat until smooth.

Spoon half of the batter into the prepared pan. Spread the apples evenly over the batter, then spoon the remaining batter over the apples, spreading it evenly.

Sprinkle the topping evenly over the batter. Bake for 1 hour and 15 minutes, or until a cake tester comes out clean when inserted into the center of the cake.

Let the cake cool on a rack for 45 minutes before removing it from the pan.

SERVES 8 TO 10

Fig and Chocolate Coffee Cake

Jacqueline McMahan loves the combination of warm, oozy chocolate and figs. This cake is best when served slightly warm (it's a wonderful addition to a special holiday breakfast) but also is delicious at room temperature. Its texture is more like a pound cake than a traditional coffee cake. Even though the recipe calls for dried figs, be sure to use ones that are plump and supple; avoid those that are hard and very, very dry.

Filling

2 tablespoons unsalted butter at room temperature

4 tablespoons light brown sugar

3 ounces bittersweet chocolate, chopped

½ cup chopped dried figs

Cake

2 cups all-purpose flour

½ teaspoon salt

2 teaspoons baking powder

1 teaspoon baking soda

1 cup unsalted butter at room temperature

1½ cups sugar

2 eggs

1 cup sour cream

3 teaspoons vanilla

⊚⊚   To make the filling: Combine the butter, brown sugar, chocolate and figs in a bowl. Set aside.

Pan-Fried Breakfast Tomatoes

Georgeanne Brennan suggests choosing meaty beefsteak tomatoes, such as Striped Marvel, Mortgage Lifter or Brandywine. Cut them into ½-inch-thick slices. Heat a little olive oil in a skillet. Add the sliced tomatoes and fry for 1 to 2 minutes per side, just to soften. Season with salt and freshly ground pepper. Serve with bacon and eggs.

To make the cake: Preheat the oven to 375 degrees. Liberally grease a 1½-quart tube or bundt pan with butter.

Whisk together the flour, salt, baking powder and baking soda in a bowl.

Using an electric mixer, beat the butter in a bowl until light. Beat in the sugar, a little at a time, scraping the sides of the bowl as necessary. Add the eggs, 1 at a time, beating for 2 minutes. Blend in the sour cream and vanilla. Add the dry ingredients to the butter mixture and blend quickly; do not overmix.

Pour half of the batter into the prepared pan. Spoon in the filling, keeping it away from the edges of the pan, then top with the remaining batter.

Bake for 1 hour, or until the cake begins to pull away from the sides of the pan and a cake tester comes out clean when inserted into the center of the cake (some of the filling may cling to the tester). Let cool on a rack for 20 minutes.

Run a thin knife between the cake and the pan to loosen the edges. Unmold, then let cake stand at least 10 minutes before slicing.

SERVES 8

Pumpkin Cinnamon Rolls

Once Jacqueline McMahan had baked Beth Hensperger's Pumpkin Cinnamon Rolls, which she adapted from her Breads of the Southwest *(Chronicle Books, 1998), she vowed never to return to the more traditional versions. These are moister, with a faint pumpkin color. After the recipe appeared in* The Chronicle, *we received mail from satisfied readers saying that, indeed, these were absolutely the best cinnamon rolls around.*

Dough

5 teaspoons active dry yeast

¼ cup warm water

1 teaspoon granulated sugar

½ cup slightly warm buttermilk

2 teaspoons vanilla

1 egg

1½ cups fresh or canned pumpkin purée

½ cup light brown sugar

1 tablespoon salt

1 teaspoon cinnamon

¼ cup canola oil

About 7 cups unbleached all-purpose flour, or bread flour

½ cup butter, melted

Cinnamon Filling

½ cup granulated sugar

½ cup light brown sugar

2 tablespoons cinnamon

½ cup currants

Glaze

1 tablespoon butter

1 tablespoon milk

1½ cups powdered sugar

About 2 tablespoons boiling water

1 teaspoon vanilla

⊛⊛ To make the dough: Combine the yeast, warm water and granulated sugar in a bowl; set aside until foamy, about 5 minutes.

Blend together the buttermilk, vanilla, egg, pumpkin purée, brown sugar, salt, cinnamon and oil in a large bowl. Stir in the yeast mixture, then the flour, ½ cup at a time, until a soft dough forms and cleans the side of the bowl as you mix.

Transfer the dough to a floured work surface and knead for about 5 minutes, or until springy and smooth. Add 1 tablespoon of flour at a time to keep the dough from sticking.

Transfer the dough to an oiled mixing bowl, cover with plastic wrap and let rise in a warm place for 1½ to 2 hours, or until doubled in bulk. The rising time is longer than normal due to the heaviness of the pumpkin.

Divide the dough into 2 equal portions. Pat or roll each portion into a thick rectangle, about 8 by 12 inches. Spread each rectangle with half of the melted butter.

To make the filling: Combine the granulated sugar, brown sugar, cinnamon and currants; sprinkle half over each rectangle. Press the currants into the dough. Roll up each rectangle into a cylinder, then cut each cylinder into about 9 thick rolls. Place the rolls on parchment-covered or greased baking sheets. Cover loosely with plastic wrap and set aside to rise for about 45 minutes, or until doubled.

Preheat the oven to 350 degrees.

Bake the rolls for 22 to 25 minutes. Remove from oven and let cool for 20 minutes before glazing.

To make the glaze: Combine the butter and milk in a bowl and warm in a microwave for 30 seconds. Or combine the butter and milk in a saucepan and warm over low heat just until the butter melts. Stir in the powdered sugar. Add the boiling water and vanilla, whisking until smooth.

Pour the glaze over just-barely-warm cinnamon rolls. (If you add the glaze to hot rolls, it will not stick to them.)

YIELDS ABOUT 18 ROLLS

Baked Eggs with Duxelles and Herbs

Each little baking dish holds a layer of rich, earthy mushroom duxelles, topped with a baked egg and glistened with cream. Marlena Spieler says leftover duxelles are delicious the next day, added to pasta, sauce or soup. Duxelles also freeze well.

4 to 6 tablespoons butter

1 pound mushrooms, finely diced

Several tablespoons (about ½ ounce) dried porcini mushrooms, broken into
   small pieces

2 to 3 garlic cloves, finely chopped

4 to 6 tablespoons brandy

Salt, to taste

Tiny pinch of freshly ground pepper

Freshly ground nutmeg, to taste

¾ to 1 cup whipping cream, or crème fraîche

Drizzle of truffle oil (optional)

6 or 12 eggs

1 tablespoon chopped Italian parsley, or chives

◉◉ Melt the butter in a sauté pan over high heat. Add the mushrooms and sauté until they are lightly browned. Work in batches, if necessary, so the mushrooms brown rather than steam. Add the porcini and garlic, then pour in the brandy and step out of the way in case the flames flare up. Cover the pan to extinguish any flames. Season the mushrooms with salt, pepper and nutmeg. Pour in half of the cream, reduce heat to medium-low and simmer for a few minutes, or until the porcini are soft. Increase heat to medium and cook until the liquid evaporates and the mushrooms become a delicious brown mush. Taste, adjust seasonings as needed and remove from the heat. Add the truffle oil, if desired. This mixture may be made up to 2 days ahead of time (add the truffle oil at the last minute); cover and refrigerate until ready to use.

Preheat the oven to 400 degrees.

Spoon a few tablespoons of the mushroom duxelles into each ramekin or custard cup, making an indentation for the eggs. Break each egg into a saucer

How to Store Eggs

Store eggs in their carton in the refrigerator as far away as possible from anything with a strong odor. With their porous shells, eggs are prone to picking up odors and acquiring off-flavors. Well-closed egg cartons offer a measure of protection, especially the heavy paper cartons, which absorb moisture and a certain amount of odors.

or cup, then slide it onto the mushroom mixture, using either 1 or 2 eggs per person depending on whom you're feeding and the size of the ramekins. Top the egg(s) with 1 or 2 tablespoons of cream.

Place the ramekins in a roasting pan and pour boiling water in the pan to come halfway up the sides of the ramekins. Cover with foil and bake for about 10 minutes, or until the whites are opaque and firm but the yolks are still soft.

Sprinkle with the parsley and serve.

SERVES 6

Marion Cunningham's Featherbed Eggs

This light strata is perfect for an easy brunch. The layers of bread, cheese and eggs are assembled the night before and refrigerated. When ready to serve, start baking the casserole in a cold oven. Serve with sautéed ham slices or bacon and a fresh fruit compote. The recipe may be doubled or tripled.

6 slices white bread

Salt and freshly ground pepper, to taste

1½ cups grated sharp cheddar, Gouda, provolone or Monterey Jack cheese, or
    a combination

1½ cups milk

6 eggs

◉◉ Butter the sides and bottom of a 9-by-13-inch baking dish. Arrange the slices of bread in a single layer in the dish, trimming the edges, if necessary. Season the bread with a little salt and pepper. Sprinkle the grated cheese evenly over the bread.

Combine the milk and eggs in a bowl and briskly stir until the mixture is completely blended. Pour the milk mixture over the bread and cheese. Cover and refrigerate for at least 6 hours or as long as overnight.

Place the baking dish in a cold oven and turn the thermostat to 350 degrees. Bake for 45 minutes to 1 hour, or until the bread custard is puffy and lightly golden.

SERVES 4

Wild Mushroom Omelet

There's hardly a better venue for showing off wild mushrooms than this omelet, created by Georgeanne Brennan.

10 eggs

¾ teaspoon salt

¾ teaspoon freshly ground pepper

1 tablespoon minced parsley

1 tablespoon minced chives

1 tablespoon olive oil

¾ pound mixed wild mushrooms, or a mixture of cultivated and wild, sliced or
    coarsely chopped

3 tablespoons butter

Chopped parsley or chives for garnish

Combine the eggs, ½ teaspoon each of the salt and pepper, the parsley and chives in a bowl. Mix well. Set aside.

Heat the olive oil in a skillet over medium-high heat. When it is hot, add the mushrooms and sauté for 2 to 3 minutes, sprinkling them with the remaining ¼ teaspoon salt and ¼ teaspoon pepper. When the mushrooms begin to release their juices and look shiny, remove them from the skillet, draining the liquid. Set aside.

Melt the butter in a large skillet over medium heat. When it is foamy, add the egg mixture and reduce the heat to low. Cook for about 6 minutes, lifting the edges of the eggs as they set, tilting the pan and letting the uncooked egg run underneath. When the eggs are almost set, spoon the mushrooms over half of the omelet, then flip the other half over them. Cook 1 minute longer.

To serve, transfer to a heated platter and garnish with parsley.

SERVES 6

Pumpkin and Goat Cheese Omelet with Glazed Pumpkin Wedges

One of the most unusual omelets we've encountered is the creation of Mark Zeitouni, former chef of Bistro Viola in Berkeley. Pumpkin purée adds a soft texture and delicate flavor to the omelet. The dish also is served with a sweet wedge of baked pumpkin, an extra touch that makes it an ideal fall brunch dish for entertaining. The recipe yields 4 large, rather rich omelets. If you are cooking for dainty eaters, each omelet could easily serve 2.

1 small Sugar Pie pumpkin

½ cup butter at room temperature

1 teaspoon cinnamon

2 tablespoons light brown sugar

Olive oil as needed

Salt and freshly ground pepper, to taste

12 eggs, beaten and strained

1 cup fresh goat cheese at room temperature

½ cup chopped toasted pecans

8 fresh sage leaves, cut into chiffonade (thin strips)

Garnishes

1 tablespoon olive oil

1 large potato, peeled and cut into large dice

4 parsley sprigs for garnish

⊚⊚ Preheat the oven to 350 degrees.

Cut the pumpkin in half and scoop out the seeds. Cut one of the halves into 4 wedges. Rub a little of the butter on the pumpkin wedges, place on a baking sheet, and sprinkle with cinnamon and brown sugar. Rub the remaining pumpkin half with olive oil, season with salt and pepper and place cut-side down on the baking sheet. Bake for 25 to 30 minutes, or until the pumpkin wedges are soft and golden brown and the pumpkin half is soft.

Remove the pumpkin from the oven but leave the oven on. Set the wedges aside. Rewarm when assembling the dish. Scoop out the flesh from the pumpkin half and purée in a food processor or by hand with a potato masher.

Melt one fourth of the remaining butter in a 10-inch nonstick ovenproof skillet over medium heat. Add one fourth of the eggs. Stir with a rubber spatula, season with salt and pepper, and cook until the eggs start to solidify. Remove from heat. Top with 2 tablespoons of the pumpkin purée and one fourth of the cheese, pecans and sage. Place in the oven for 45 seconds to 1 minute, or until the cheese is warm and the eggs finish setting. Tip the omelet onto a warmed plate, folding the sides over the middle. Cover loosely and keep warm while preparing the remaining 3 omelets.

To make the garnish: Heat the olive oil in a small sauté pan over medium-high heat. Add the diced potato and sauté until crisp.

To serve: Scatter the fried potato cubes over the omelets and garnish each with a parsley sprig. Serve with the roasted pumpkin wedges.

SERVES 4

Grandmama's Artichoke Frittatas

These unusual frittatas look almost like little pancakes. Jacqueline McMahan mixes together eggs, bread and cooked artichokes, then drops the mixture by spoonfuls into a pan, where they are immediately flattened and browned on both sides.

Juice of 1 lemon

4 artichokes, or 1 can (15 ounces) artichoke hearts, minced (about 2 cups)

2 garlic cloves, minced

3 tablespoons minced Italian parsley

1 tablespoon minced fresh basil

4 slices French or Italian bread, crusts removed, soaked in ½ cup milk

½ teaspoon salt

Freshly ground pepper, to taste

4 eggs

⅓ cup grated Parmigiano-Reggiano cheese

4 tablespoons olive oil, or basil oil (see Note)

Basil leaves

¼ cup crumbled queso fresco

Aioli (see recipe, page 389) (optional)

◎◎ If using fresh artichokes, bring a heavy pot filled with 3 inches of water to a boil over high heat. Add the lemon juice and artichokes and cook for 35 minutes, or until tender when pierced with a knife. Drain. Pull off the tough outer leaves. Remove the pale center leaves; cut off the tender part and place in a bowl. Cut out the fuzzy chokes, then roughly chop the hearts. Add to the bowl.

Stir in the garlic, parsley and basil. Squeeze the milk from the bread, discard the milk and crumble the bread into the bowl. Add the salt and season with pepper. Beat the eggs, 1 at a time, into the mixture, then stir in the cheese. Set aside for 10 minutes.

Heat 2 tablespoons of the olive oil in a 10-inch skillet over medium-high heat. Drop the artichoke mixture by large spoonfuls into the hot oil (do not crowd the pan; cook about 4 at a time). Flatten each frittata with the back of the spoon. Fry, turning once, for 2 to 3 minutes total, or until golden on both sides. When the frittatas are done, remove them with a slotted spoon and set on paper towels to drain.

Continue cooking, adding more oil to the pan as needed, until all the artichoke mixture has been used.

Stack 3 frittatas on each plate, sandwiching a few basil leaves and the queso fresco between the frittatas. Top with a dab of aioli, if desired.

YIELDS ABOUT 12 FRITTATAS; SERVES 4

NOTE: To make basil oil, combine ¾ cup light olive oil and ¼ cup extra virgin olive oil in a food processor; add ½ cup lightly packed basil leaves and process until blended. Store in the freezer. Use for sautéing, in tomato sauces and for drizzling over vegetables.

Asparagus & Goat Cheese Frittata

In a small, nonstick skillet, Marlena Spieler sautés small pieces of asparagus with some chopped shallot and garlic. She then pours in 1 beaten egg, tops it with nuggets of goat cheese and cooks it as she would a frittata or flat omelet.

Frittata with Prosciutto and Plum Tomatoes

A frittata is a great dish to make for a company brunch or for a light supper served with country-style bread and a salad. It takes only 20 minutes to create Tara Duggan's dish: a gorgeous combination of fluffy eggs, salty prosciutto, ripe tomato and soft, creamy cheese. Looking something like a pizza, it may be cut into wedges for serving.

10 eggs

Freshly ground pepper, to taste

2 tablespoons olive oil

¾ cup grated fontina cheese

2 ripe plum tomatoes, sliced into very thin rounds

4 to 6 slices prosciutto (about ¼ pound), cut into bite-size pieces

◉ Preheat the broiler.

Beat the eggs in a bowl, seasoning them with pepper.

Heat the olive oil in a nonstick ovenproof skillet over medium heat. Pour in the eggs. As the eggs cook, lift the bottom with a rubber spatula to prevent them from sticking and to let the uncooked egg run underneath. Cook for 5 to 6 minutes, or until the bottom is set and the top still runny.

Remove the eggs from the heat. Sprinkle most of the cheese on top, then arrange the tomatoes in a layer over the cheese, leaving a 1-inch border around the perimeter. Sprinkle the prosciutto over the tomatoes, then top with the remaining cheese.

Place the pan directly under the broiler and broil for about 3 minutes, or until the cheese is melted, the eggs are cooked through and the edges are puffy and golden brown.

SERVES 4

Chorizo Quiche in a Cornmeal Crust

This quiche by Jacqueline McMahan makes a perfect companion dish to the Cazuela de Huevos Rancheros (see page 360). All you need to complete a rancho-inspired buffet is a pitcher of fresh orange juice, some warm rolls and a big bowl of sliced tropical fruit. Finish with dark coffee laced with steamed milk.

Cornmeal Crust

¾ cup all-purpose flour

½ cup cornmeal

½ teaspoon salt

⅓ cup shortening

2 tablespoons butter

4 tablespoons cold water

Filling

1 cup grated Monterey Jack or Italian fontina cheese

½ pound chorizo sausage, crumbled, cooked and drained

½ cup minced green onions (white and most of the green part)

3 eggs

1½ cups half-and-half

Pinch of salt

⚭ To make the cornmeal crust: Sift together the flour, cornmeal and salt into a mixing bowl. Using a pastry blender or 2 table knives, cut in the shortening and butter until coarse crumbs form. Add the water, a little at a time, stirring gently with a fork, until the pastry barely clings together but is not sticky.

Transfer the pastry to a lightly floured surface, press it into a flat round and roll it out into a 12-inch round. Fit the pastry into a 10-inch quiche pan.

Preheat the oven to 400 degrees.

To make the filling: Sprinkle the cheese in the cornmeal crust. Cover the cheese with the chorizo, then sprinkle with the green onions.

Beat together the eggs and half-and-half in a bowl. Season with salt. Carefully pour into the crust.

Bake for 10 minutes. Reduce oven temperature to 350 degrees and bake for 30 to 35 minutes longer. Remove from oven and let stand for 10 minutes before cutting into wedges.

SERVES 6 TO 8

Cazuela de Huevos Rancheros

Making traditional huevos rancheros for more than four people can be time-consuming if each is made separately, so Jacqueline McMahan simplified the dish. She layers softened corn tortillas, ranchero sauce, cheese and eggs in a casserole, then bakes it. It's a great concoction for a brunch.

Ranchero Sauce

1 can (28 ounces) diced tomatoes with juices

2 ripe tomatoes, cored and diced

1 cup diced onion

1 jalapeño chile, seeded and minced

2 garlic cloves, minced

1 cup water

2 tablespoons pure chile powder

½ teaspoon salt

½ teaspoon ground cumin

1 teaspoon dried oregano

1 teaspoon sugar

1 tablespoon cider vinegar

2 tablespoons canola oil

10 corn tortillas

2 cups grated cheddar cheese

8 eggs

¾ cup crumbled cotija cheese (see Note)

How to Heat Store-Bought Flour Tortillas

The flour tortillas sold in supermarkets are about 90 percent cooked. To make them taste more like homemade, Jacqueline McMahan suggests heating them on a comal (a round, flat griddle on which tortillas are cooked), griddle or large skillet just until they puff a little and their freckles begin to turn golden brown. This is a much better method than wrapping them in foil and placing them in the oven to steam. Wrap the heated tortillas in a clean dish towel, then in foil. They'll stay warm for about 20 minutes.

To make the ranchero sauce: Combine the canned tomatoes and their juices, the ripe tomatoes, onion, jalapeño, garlic, water, chile powder, salt, cumin, oregano, sugar and vinegar in a 2-quart saucepan. Bring to a boil over high heat. Reduce heat to low and simmer for 15 to 20 minutes.

Meanwhile, preheat the oven to 350 degrees. Heat the oil in a skillet over medium-high heat. Place a tortilla in the hot oil and fry, turning once, until just softened. As each tortilla is done, place it on a plate. Repeat with remaining tortillas.

Oil a 9-by-13-inch baking dish. Spoon half of the sauce over the bottom, then arrange the tortillas over the sauce. Top the tortillas with more sauce. Sprinkle with half of the grated cheddar cheese.

Break the eggs onto the cheese layer, spacing them a few inches apart. Spoon the remaining sauce over the eggs and sprinkle with the remaining cheddar cheese.

Bake for about 15 minutes. Pierce one of the egg yolks with a sharp paring knife to check the degree of doneness. (Do not bake longer than 20 minutes, or the eggs will be hard-cooked.) Remove the pan from the oven and let cool for 10 minutes before serving.

Cut into squares and sprinkle with the cotija cheese.

SERVES 6 TO 8

NOTE: Sold in small rounds, cotija cheese is available in the dairy case of many supermarkets. It is easily crumbled. You may substitute feta cheese.

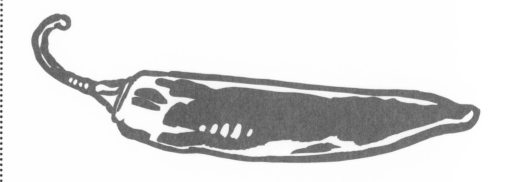

Huevos a la Flamenca

This spicy Spanish breakfast dish was created by Marlena Spieler. Eggs are garnished with fresh asparagus, peas and strips of roasted red bell pepper, then baked in a lively tomato and sausage mixture.

2 tablespoons olive oil

2 onions, chopped

6 garlic cloves, chopped

1 green bell pepper, seeded, deribbed and chopped

1 spicy sausage (such as chorizo, luganega or smoked green peppercorn duck sausage), about 4 ounces, cut into rounds

8 vine-ripened tomatoes, cored, peeled and diced; or 2 cans (28 ounces each) good-quality canned tomatoes

8 eggs

⅓ cup peas, fresh and blanched, or frozen

1 roasted red bell pepper, peeled, seeded, deribbed and cut into strips

12 thin asparagus spears, trimmed and cut into 1-inch lengths

2 to 3 tablespoons dry sherry

◎◎ Preheat the oven to 375 degrees.

Heat the olive oil in a sauté pan over medium-high heat. Add the onions, garlic and green bell pepper and sauté for about 10 minutes, or until the onions soften. Add the sausage and sauté until lightly browned in spots. Add the tomatoes and cook until it becomes a saucelike mixture.

Divide about two thirds of the sauce evenly among 4 individual ramekins, or spoon into 1 large one. Break the eggs into this mixture, either 2 in each individual ramekin or all 8 in the large one. Top with the remaining sauce, spooned around the eggs, as well as the peas, pepper strips and asparagus. Sprinkle with the sherry.

Cover and bake for 10 to 15 minutes, until the eggs are set.

SERVES 4

BEST WAY:
Hard-Cooking Eggs

When hard-cooking eggs, overcooking is one of the most common mistakes. The result can be rubbery egg whites, chalky centers or a dark-greenish halo surrounding the yolks.

After trying a dozen ways, here's the fail-proof method: Place extra-large eggs in a pot large enough to hold them in a single layer. Add cold water to cover by 1 inch. Bring the water to a rolling boil and cook for 8 minutes. Remove from the heat. Drain and rinse the eggs. Crack and peel under cold running water. Note: Eggs that are a few days or up to a week old are much easier to peel.

Sour Cream and Avocado Omelet

Marion Cunningham created this dish using one of California's favorite products: the avocado. The rich, mild flavor adds an exciting texture to the eggs, and sour cream lends just the right accent. An 8-inch-diameter nonstick skillet is perfect for a 3-egg omelet.

3 eggs

¼ teaspoon salt

Freshly ground pepper, to taste

1 tablespoon butter

4 tablespoons sour cream

⅓ avocado, peeled, pitted and cut into ¼-inch slices; lightly salt the slices

◉ Break the eggs into a small bowl, add the salt and season with pepper; whisk briskly with a fork until yolks and whites are thoroughly blended.

Place an 8-inch nonstick skillet over high heat. When it is hot, add the butter and tilt the skillet so the butter coats the bottom. Pour in the eggs. Let them set about 5 seconds. Using a spatula, pull the cooked egg from the edges of the pan toward the center, allowing the uncooked egg to run underneath.

After about 15 seconds, while the eggs are still moist, push the omelet toward the side of the pan. Spread the sour cream on half of the omelet, then cover with the avocado slices.

Using a spatula, fold the other half of the omelet over the sour cream. Let the omelet cook 5 seconds longer, then quickly tilt the pan upside down over a plate so the omelet lands bottom-side up. (You can pat the omelet into shape with your hands, if needed.)

If desired, spread a little butter over the top to make it shiny.

SERVES 1

Butter-Steamed Asparagus with Egg

Fresh, sweet asparagus, glistening with butter, is topped with a fried egg in this recipe by Janet Fletcher. The yolk should still be runny so it coats the vegetable. It's ideal for a quick home-alone brunch with toast. If you're feeling more social, you can multiply the recipe to feed a crowd.

½ pound trimmed asparagus spears

1 tablespoon plus 1 teaspoon butter

Salt and freshly ground pepper, to taste

1 egg

Soak the asparagus in a bowl of cold water for 15 minutes.

Melt 1 tablespoon butter in a small skillet over medium heat. Add the asparagus spears with just the water clinging to them. Season with salt and pepper. Cover and adjust heat so the asparagus steams without burning. Cook for 5 to 10 minutes, depending on thickness, or until crisp-tender. Check often.

Melt 1 teaspoon butter in a small, nonstick skillet over medium-low heat.

Carefully break the egg into a bowl, then slide it into the skillet. Season with salt and pepper. Cook until the egg white is set, then turn and cook briefly. The yolk should still be runny.

Transfer the asparagus and any pan juices to a warm plate. Top with the fried egg.

SERVES 1

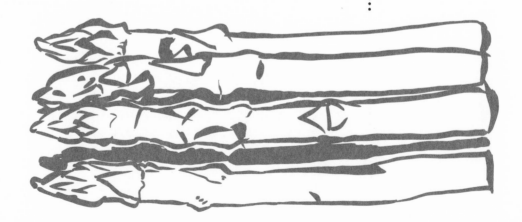

Asparagus Tart

Serve for a late breakfast or brunch, accompanied by baby greens dressed in vinaigrette, which work as a fresh counterpoint to the rich tart, says Marlena Spieler.

One 9-inch unbaked pie shell

2 tablespoons butter

6 shallots, chopped

Salt and freshly ground pepper, to taste

Freshly grated nutmeg, to taste

1 to 1½ pounds medium asparagus, tough ends snapped off; reserve about 10 long
   spears for garnish

1 cup whipping cream

½ cup milk

4 eggs, lightly beaten

◉◉ Preheat the oven to 400 degrees.

Gently fit a piece of foil into the pie shell and fill with dry beans or pie weights. Bake for 10 minutes, or until the dough is set but not browned. Carefully remove the foil and weights from the shell.

Melt the butter in a sauté pan over medium heat. Add the shallots and sauté for about 5 minutes, or until they are softened. Season with salt, pepper and nutmeg; set aside.

Bring a saucepan of salted water to a boil over high heat.

Meanwhile, cut the trimmed asparagus spears into 1-inch pieces. Add the asparagus—both the small pieces and reserved spears—to the boiling water and cook for about 5 minutes, or until just tender. Drain. Set aside the whole spears.

Combine the small pieces of asparagus with the cream, milk and eggs in a blender or food processor and purée. Season with salt, pepper and nutmeg.

Spread the sautéed shallots in the crust, then pour in the custard mixture. Top with the reserved asparagus spears.

Bake for 30 to 35 minutes, or until the custard is set and the top is golden brown.

SERVES 6 TO 8

Crab Soufflé with Green Onion and Lemon

Here's one of the best ways to use crab, suspended in a puffy soufflé with lemon and green onions. It's from Lauren Elizabeth Lyle, former chef of Bay Wolf restaurant in Oakland.

1 Dungeness crab, or 6 ounces crabmeat

4 tablespoons butter

½ small red onion, diced

1 leek (both white and light green parts), well rinsed and diced

1 thyme sprig

1 bay leaf

5 tablespoons all-purpose flour

1 cup milk, heated

5 eggs

¼ cup grated Parmigiano-Reggiano cheese

2½ tablespoons chopped green onions (white and most of the green part)

1 teaspoon grated lemon zest

1 teaspoon chopped chives

Pinch of cayenne pepper

Pinch of paprika

Salt and freshly ground white pepper, to taste

1 teaspoon fresh lemon juice, or to taste

⊚⊚ If using a live crab, bring a large pot of salted water to a boil over high heat and add the crab. Cook for 15 to 25 minutes, depending on its size, or until it turns bright red. Crack, clean and pick out the meat. Save the liver (crab butter), if desired.

Heat the butter in a large saucepan over medium heat. Add the red onion, leek, thyme and bay leaf. Cook, stirring occasionally, for about 10 minutes, or until the vegetables are soft. Stir in the flour and cook 1 minute longer. Remove from heat and whisk in the milk. Return to heat and cook, stirring, until thickened. Transfer the mixture to a blender or food processor and purée.

Separate the eggs. Beat the yolks in a bowl until well blended, then stir them into the puréed vegetables. Reserve the egg whites in a medium bowl.

Preheat the oven to 425 degrees. Liberally grease a 1-quart soufflé dish with butter, then sprinkle with the cheese.

Fold the green onions, lemon zest, chives, cayenne, paprika, crabmeat and crab butter, if desired, into the puréed vegetables. Adjust seasonings with salt, pepper and lemon juice.

Beat the egg whites with a pinch of salt to stiff peaks. Fold one third of the egg whites into the soufflé mixture to lighten it, then fold in the remainder. Transfer to the prepared soufflé dish. Bake for about 15 minutes, or until lightly browned on top. Reduce oven temperature to 375 degrees and bake for 3 to 5 minutes longer, or until the soufflé is set in the center.

Serve immediately.

SERVES 4 TO 6

BEST WAY:
Scrambling Eggs

After scrambling dozens of eggs and doing side-by-side tests, we found the following method produced the creamiest eggs.

For 2 extra-large eggs: Beat with a wire whisk with a dash of salt and freshly ground pepper and 2 tablespoons half-and-half. Cook in a nonstick skillet over medium-high heat for about 1½ minutes, stirring occasionally. Add a little more salt and freshly ground pepper at the end of cooking, and serve immediately.

If you want an even lighter and richer texture, increase the half-and-half to 3 tablespoons, although the egg flavor will be a little mellower.

Lobster Scrambled Eggs

This is a favorite dish at Postrio restaurant in San Francisco, where Mitchell and Steven Rosenthal serve some of the best brunches in town. The combination of creamy eggs lightened with mascarpone and sweet seafood is unbeatable. It's easy to prepare, but it's about as elegant a combination as you'll find.

2 ounces cooked lobster meat

1 tablespoon clarified butter (see page 443), or 2 teaspoons butter plus 1 teaspoon
    flavorless vegetable oil

3 medium-size eggs, lightly beaten

Salt and freshly ground white pepper, to taste

1 heaping tablespoon mascarpone cheese

1 teaspoon minced chives

∞ Pick over the lobster meat and remove any bits of shell. Heat the clarified butter in a 6-inch nonstick skillet over medium heat until hot but not smoking. Add the lobster meat and sauté, stirring, for about 2 minutes, or until warm.

Add the eggs and season with salt and pepper. Scramble loosely, stirring constantly with a wooden spoon; do not overcook.

Turn out onto a warmed plate. Top with the mascarpone and sprinkle with the chives.

SERVES 1

Fiery Breakfast Potatoes with Eggs

Any of Jacqueline McMahan's leftover red chile sauce is like having money in the bank. Use it for little inspirations, such as huevos rancheros or this eye-opening breakfast dish. If you don't happen to have any chile sauce on hand, we've included the recipe for a quick red sauce.

1½ pounds tiny new red potatoes

1 tablespoon mild olive oil, or canola oil

4 eggs

¼ cup Quick Red Sauce, warmed, plus extra sauce for passing at the table
   (recipe follows)

2 cups grated Monterey Jack cheese

½ cup minced green onions (white and most of the green part)

Bring a pot of water to a boil over high heat. Add the potatoes and boil for 10 minutes. Drain. Set aside to cool for at least 10 minutes, or cover and refrigerate overnight.

Halve the potatoes. Heat the oil in a heavy nonstick skillet over medium-high heat. Add the potatoes and fry, turning occasionally, until golden.

When the potatoes are almost done, fry the eggs in a medium-size nonstick skillet over medium heat until done to your liking.

Divide the potatoes among 4 deep serving bowls, drizzle 1 tablespoon warm red sauce over each serving, then sprinkle with the cheese and green onions. Top each with a fried egg. Pass extra sauce at the table.

SERVES 4

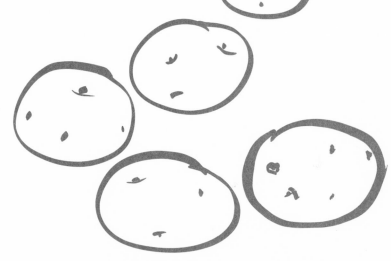

Quick Red Sauce

2 tablespoons mild olive oil, or canola oil

1 tablespoon butter

2 tablespoons all-purpose flour

¼ teaspoon crushed cumin seeds

3 cups cold water

½ cup ground red chile (a blend of California and New Mexican, or pure Dixon)

1 teaspoon to 1 tablespoon ground chipotle chile (optional)

1 garlic clove, minced

1 teaspoon salt

Pinch of garlic salt

Heat the oil and butter in a wide, heavy skillet over medium heat; whisk in the flour. Cook the roux for about 2 minutes, or until light golden—do not let it turn brown. Add the cumin and remove from heat.

Whisk 2 cups of the cold water into the roux. Whisk the red chile and chipotle chile, if desired, into the remaining 1 cup water until very smooth. Add the chile-water to the skillet. Place over medium heat, whisking constantly to keep the sauce velvety. Stir in the garlic, salt and garlic salt. Simmer gently for 20 minutes; watch carefully so it doesn't burn. Remove from heat and let cool. If the sauce is too thick, whisk in 1 to 2 tablespoons of water or mild broth. Set aside for a few hours to mellow, or let cool, then cover and refrigerate overnight.

YIELDS ABOUT 3½ CUPS

Crisp Maple-Glazed Country Bacon

This recipe by Marlena Spieler may be made with any kind of bacon you like: pork, turkey, even soy. But whatever you do, be sure to use real maple syrup. The bacon may be made ahead and reheated in a 350-degree oven. Served on the side, it makes even the simplest scrambled eggs taste special.

2 pounds thick-cut country-style bacon
¼ to ⅓ cup maple syrup

∞ Place the bacon slices in a cold large skillet, laying them flat so they will brown evenly. Turn the heat to medium. Cook the bacon, turning the slices, until they are browned and crisp in places, removing each slice from the pan as it is finished. Adjust the heat as needed so they do not burn. Continue, adding more slices until all the bacon is browned.

Pour off all fat in the pan, then return all of the bacon to the pan over medium heat. Add the maple syrup and toss the bacon in it as it bubbles and cooks down to a thick syrup. Do not let it burn, which it can do very easily. It should heat for only a few minutes at the most. Remove to a baking dish and serve immediately.

SERVES 8 TO 10

MAPLE-GLAZED SAUSAGE SLICES: Substitute an interesting smoked sausage such as duck and green peppercorn for the bacon. Cut the sausages into thick slices and brown lightly, then add the maple syrup as above. Serve with toothpicks for spearing, or alongside waffles or pancakes.

BEST WAY:
Cooking Bacon

We tried five methods of cooking bacon: on the stovetop in a nonstick skillet and in a cast-iron skillet, baked on a wire rack, baked on a rimmed baking sheet and microwaved.

In a side-by-side blind tasting, the bacon baked in the oven on a baking sheet was deemed the best. Here's how it's done:

Preheat the oven to 500 degrees. Arrange the bacon on a rimmed baking sheet and place on the middle rack in the oven. Bake for 7 to 10 minutes, or until cooked to the desired crispness. Transfer the bacon to paper towels to drain.

Chapter 11

Relishes, Sauces and Chutneys

One of the quickest ways to perk up a simple meal is by adding a little dollop of Backward Spanish Aioli (page 389), Fresh Pineapple Salsa (page 386) or a Cauliflower and Green Olive Relish (page 375) to a plate. Suddenly those steamed vegetables, sautéed fish or grilled chicken breasts don't seem so dull.

Having a repertoire of quick relishes, sauces and chutneys is a cook's best defense against tedium. Sweet, savory or hot, you'll find dozens of ideas in this chapter from some of the best chefs and home cooks in the United States: There is Kumquat-Cranberry-Lime Sauce (page 376) created by Gary Danko of Gary Danko restaurant; Bell Pepper and Almond Relish (page 380) from Carlo Middione of Vivande; Fuyu Persimmon Relish (page 379) perfected by Traci des Jardins of Jardiniere; and a Killer Red Sauce (page 391) from our "South to North" columnist, Jacqueline McMahan.

None of these taste-teasers is retiring and subtle. They're designed to grab the spotlight and make the palate sing.

Pickled Yellow Wax Beans

*We love yellow wax beans, and Alice Waters of Chez Panisse in Berkeley
has come up with one of the best ways to preserve their color and flavor.
These are great as an accent on the holiday table, at a cocktail party or as
an accompaniment to a sandwich for lunch.*

¾ pound yellow wax beans

2 garlic cloves

1 dried cayenne chile, or other red chile

½ teaspoon coriander seeds

⅛ teaspoon peppercorns

1 bay leaf

¾ cup white wine vinegar, or cider vinegar

¾ cup dry white wine

¾ cup water

1 tablespoon kosher salt

2 tablespoons sugar

Top and tail the beans; peel and halve the garlic cloves. Halve the chile
lengthwise and remove the seeds. Place the beans upright in a nonreactive
container with a tight-fitting lid. Place the garlic, chile, coriander, peppercorns
and bay leaf between the beans.

Combine the vinegar, wine, water, salt and sugar in a small pan over high
heat. Bring to a boil over high heat and boil for 1 minute. Pour the liquid over
the beans; let cool.

Cover and refrigerate for 3 days to 2 weeks.

SERVES 8

BEST WAY:
Cooking with Wine

Does the variety and the
quality of wine really
make that much difference
in cooking? To find out,
we reduced seven wine
varietals—Chenin Blanc,
Sauvignon Blanc,
Chardonnay, California
Burgundy, Pinot Noir,
Zinfandel and Cabernet
Sauvignon—and used them
in a traditional beurre
blanc (or beurre rouge) and
in a classic coq au vin.

We also tried some
more expensive wines
to see if the individual
characteristics of each wine
came through. We found
that generally the more
expensive wines tasted
better. What varietal you
choose depends on the
dish. For a cool-night
coq au vin, for example,
Zinfandel lends a deep
fruitiness to the stew. For
a fresher, lighter version, a
Sauvignon Blanc is perfect.

If you're creating a sauce
where the wine is standing
pretty much alone, use a
varietal that is mellow and
rounded such as a good
Pinot Noir or Sauvignon
Blanc.

Roasted Beet and Tomato Relish with Chermoula Flavors

This relish by Marlena Spieler was inspired by North African flavors combined with the French affection for beets. She serves it alongside macaroni and cheese, but it will enhance almost anything, especially foods such as couscous, kebabs, country-style breads, soft-cooked eggs and soups.

4 to 6 small to medium beets

2 garlic cloves, chopped

Pinch of sugar

2 shallots, chopped

1 tablespoon balsamic vinegar

Juice of 1 lime

3 ripe tomatoes, cored and coarsely chopped

Pinch of curry powder

Pinch of ground turmeric

¼ teaspoon ground cumin

Salt and cayenne pepper, to taste

⅓ red bell pepper, stemmed, seeded, deribbed and chopped

2 to 3 tablespoons extra virgin olive oil

3 tablespoons chopped cilantro

◉◉ Preheat the oven to 350 degrees.

Place the whole beets in a shallow baking pan and roast for about 30 minutes, or until they are just tender when pierced with a knife. Young beets will take less time than older ones.

Let the beets cool until you can handle them, then slip off the skins. Dice the beets and place them in a bowl.

Add the garlic, sugar, shallots, balsamic vinegar, lime juice, tomatoes, curry powder, turmeric, cumin, salt, cayenne pepper, bell pepper, olive oil and cilantro. Gently fold and stir to combine.

Taste and adjust seasonings as needed before serving.

SERVES 4

Roasted Corn and Chanterelle Relish

This multitextured relish is so good, you may want to serve it as a salad instead of a condiment. It's from Steven Levine of the Cosmopolitan Cafe in San Francisco.

10 ears of corn, husked

¼ cup olive oil

½ pound chanterelle mushrooms, cleaned and sliced

2 red bell peppers, stemmed, seeded, deribbed and cut into small dice

1 red onion, cut into small dice

3 celery stalks, cut into small dice

2 cucumbers, peeled, seeded and cut into small dice

Leaves from 1 bunch thyme, roughly chopped

⅓ cup cider vinegar

1 cup extra virgin olive oil, or to taste

Salt and freshly ground pepper, to taste

ꝏ Preheat the broiler.

Rub the corn with some of the olive oil, then broil until the ears have roasted on all sides, turning as necessary. Watch them carefully as they have a high sugar content and will burn easily. Let cool, then cut the kernels from the cobs.

Heat the remaining olive oil in a nonstick pan over high heat. Add the mushrooms and sauté for 1 to 2 minutes. Transfer to a bowl and refrigerate.

Combine the bell peppers, red onion, celery and cucumbers in a large mixing bowl. Add the thyme, vinegar and extra virgin olive oil (use less, if desired); toss to combine. Fold in the corn and the cooled mushrooms. Season with salt and pepper. Refrigerate until ready to serve.

YIELDS ABOUT 1 QUART; SERVES 8 TO 10

Cauliflower and Green Olive Relish

Crunchy white cauliflower pairs with tender green olives in this colorful relish from John Caputo of the now-closed Socca restaurant in San Francisco. It's designed to accompany turkey or any fowl.

Olive oil as needed

1 head cauliflower, broken into small florets

1 large onion, diced

2 carrots, peeled and diced

2 celery stalks, diced

3 garlic cloves, minced

2½ cups white wine vinegar

½ cup water

½ cup honey

1 bay leaf

1 teaspoon crushed hot red pepper flakes

1 tablespoon mustard seeds

½ teaspoon dried oregano

12 basil leaves

2 cups green olives, pitted and chopped

◉◉ Heat a small amount of olive oil in a large saucepan over low to medium heat. Add the cauliflower, onion, carrots, celery and garlic; lightly sauté for 2 to 3 minutes. Add the vinegar, water and honey.

Place the bay leaf, pepper flakes, mustard seeds, oregano and basil in a 2-inch square of cheesecloth; tie closed. Add to the saucepan and bring to a boil. Reduce heat and simmer for 2 to 3 minutes, or until the vegetables are crisp-tender. Remove from heat and let cool.

Remove the spice bag, squeezing excess liquid back into the relish. Fold the olives into the relish.

Using a slotted spoon, transfer the relish to a serving bowl.

YIELDS ABOUT 1 QUART; SERVES 8 TO 10

NOTE: The relish may be made up to 1 week ahead. Store in a tightly covered container in the refrigerator.

Kumquat-Cranberry-Lime Sauce

In this variation on the traditional cooked cranberry-orange relish, sweet-tart kumquats and tangy lime zest and juice add intrigue to the citrus flavor, while Grand Marnier liqueur, splashed in at the last moment, gives a rich complexity to the finished product. This is so good, in fact, you could almost eat it over ice cream. The sauce is the creation of Gary Danko of his self-named restaurant in San Francisco.

2 bags (12 ounces each) cranberries

⅓ pound kumquats

2 cups sugar

½ cup apple cider, or apple juice

4 tablespoons fresh orange juice

4 tablespoons fresh lime juice

Grated zest of 2 limes

Pinch of salt

6 tablespoons Grand Marnier

◉◉ Pick over the cranberries, discarding any stems or rotten, shriveled or "petrified" berries. Halve the kumquats and discard seeds. Put the kumquats in a food processor and grind to a medium-fine texture.

Combine the cranberries, ground kumquats, the sugar, cider, orange and lime juices, lime zest and salt in a large, heavy saucepan. Bring to a gentle boil over medium-high heat and cook for 5 to 10 minutes, or until the cranberries pop. Remove from heat and add the Grand Marnier.

YIELDS ABOUT 5½ CUPS

NOTE: The relish may be made up to 1 week ahead. Store in a tightly covered container in the refrigerator.

Zesting Citrus

The best tool, of course, is a good-quality zester with multiple holes at the top. By stroking down from top to bottom, you can zest an entire fruit in seconds. The zest is then ready to be gathered together and chopped, if needed.

If you don't have a zester, use a vegetable peeler to remove the zest, starting at the end and pulling the peeler toward the tip. Use just enough pressure to remove the skin but not the bitter white pith. The zest is ready to be chopped and slivered. Stack the pieces on top of each other and cut into thin strips, then chop into desired consistency.

Gingered Cranberry and Pear Relish

Sweet and tart combine in this seasonal relish from Daniel Patterson, who owns the chic Elisabeth Daniel restaurant in San Francisco. Served warm or at room temperature, it's sure to please those who like a little sweet with their savory.

    1½ cups sugar
    1½ cups water
    6 ripe Bosc pears
    1 bag (12 ounces) cranberries
    1½ teaspoons grated fresh ginger
    2 tablespoons pear vinegar, or cider vinegar
    2 tablespoons fresh lemon juice
    1½ cups pear juice
    ¼ teaspoon cinnamon
    Salt and freshly ground pepper, to taste

◎ Combine the sugar and water in a small saucepan over high heat and boil for about 5 minutes, or until the mixture is clear. Cook for 1 minute longer, then remove the syrup from the heat.

Peel, core and quarter 2 of the pears. Add to the syrup in the saucepan and cook over medium heat until tender. (Pears must be completely submerged in the syrup. Use a small plate to weight them down.) Using a slotted spoon, remove the pears to a plate and let cool.

Pick over the cranberries, discarding any stems or rotten, shriveled or "petrified" berries. Cook the cranberries in the same syrup over medium heat for 5 to 10 minutes, or until they soften. Remove with a slotted spoon and spread out on a plate to cool.

Strain the syrup into a stainless-steel bowl. Add the ginger, vinegar, half of the lemon juice, the poached pears and the pear juice. Purée the mixture in a blender, then strain through a fine sieve. Transfer the purée to a saucepan and place over low heat.

Peel, core and dice the remaining 4 pears; add to the saucepan and simmer until just tender. Using a slotted spoon, remove the pear pieces from the liquid and spread out on a plate to cool.

Cook the liquid over low heat, stirring frequently, until it is reduced to an applesauce consistency. Remove from heat and let cool to room temperature.

Whisk the cinnamon, salt and pepper into the reduced liquid.

Combine the pear pieces, cranberries and reduced liquid. Taste and add the remaining lemon juice, if desired.

SERVES 6

Scorpion Tomato Relish

One of the finest things in life is a good hamburger. When Jacqueline McMahan grills burgers at home, she slathers them with this relish, tops them with a thick slice of red onion, and tucks them into toasted onion buns.

2 pounds plum tomatoes, peeled and diced

1 cup diced onion

½ green bell pepper, stemmed, seeded, deribbed and diced

½ cup thinly sliced jalapeño chiles, seeded if you like

5 garlic cloves, minced

½ cup apple cider vinegar

⅓ to ½ cup light brown sugar

1 teaspoon salt

∞ Combine the tomatoes, onion and bell pepper in a 3-quart pot. Simmer over medium-low heat for 10 minutes to reduce some of the liquid the tomatoes will exude.

Add the chiles, garlic, vinegar, brown sugar and salt. Simmer for 10 to 15 minutes, or until thickened.

YIELDS ABOUT 3 CUPS

Fuyu Persimmon Relish

Chef Traci des Jardins of Jardiniere in San Francisco uses the short, squat Fuyu persimmon for this relish because of its firm texture and not-too-sweet flavor. This relish is perfect with the Thanksgiving turkey or even grilled chicken. When selecting persimmons, look for brightly colored fruit that show no signs of bruising.

How to Ripen Persimmons

Ripening times of store-bought Hachiya persimmons may vary from a few days to a month or more, which can be quite frustrating. To hasten the ripening process, Marion Cunningham puts the persimmons in a plastic bag with an apple, then she ties the bag shut. The ethylene gas produced by the apple acts as a ripening agent for the persimmons.

½ tablespoon olive oil

1 cup diced onion

1 tablespoon mustard seeds

½ cup sherry

¼ cup sherry vinegar

5 Fuyu persimmons, stemmed, seeded (if necessary) and diced

1 cup water

¼ cup currants

Salt and freshly ground pepper, to taste

Heat the olive oil in a large saucepan over medium heat. Add the onion and sauté for about 10 minutes, or until soft. Add the mustard seeds and sherry, and cook until all the liquid has evaporated.

Add the sherry vinegar, persimmons and water. Cook until most of the liquid has evaporated. Sprinkle in the currants and cook a few minutes longer, or until there is just a small amount of liquid remaining. Remove from heat and season with salt and pepper.

Let cool, cover and refrigerate for 24 hours before serving.

SERVES 12

Mandorlata di Peperoni
(Bell Pepper and Almond Relish)

This Southern Italian relish looks good, tastes good and is easy to prepare. Carlo Middione of Vivande in San Francisco says he particularly likes this on turkey or chicken sandwiches. It's also terrific with roast pork or lamb. And, you can serve the relish cold as an antipasto spread on bruschetta or stuffed into hollowed-out tomato halves.

½ cup slivered or coarsely chopped almonds

3 red bell peppers, stemmed, seeded and deribbed

1 green bell pepper, stemmed, seeded and deribbed

3 tablespoons olive oil

⅓ cup currants or raisins (dark or golden)

1½ teaspoons sugar

¼ cup red wine vinegar

½ teaspoon sea salt, or to taste

ꙮ Preheat the oven to 350 degrees.

Spread the almonds on a baking sheet and bake, stirring from time to time, for 10 to 15 minutes, or until golden brown. Let cool; set aside.

Cut the bell peppers lengthwise into ¼-inch-wide strips.

Heat the olive oil in a large sauté pan over medium-high heat. Add the bell peppers and sauté, stirring constantly, for 5 to 7 minutes, or until they begin to soften and develop small burn marks on the skin.

Reduce heat to medium and add the currants. Stir and cook for 1 minute. Stir in the sugar and almonds, then add the vinegar and salt. Cook, stirring, for 5 minutes, allowing most of the liquid to cook off. It should not be too wet.

Serve hot, at room temperature or cold.

SERVES 10 TO 12

NOTE: The relish may be made up to 4 days ahead. Store in a tightly covered container in the refrigerator.

How to Blanch Almonds

Drop whole almonds into boiling water for a few seconds, rinse in cold water and gently slip the nuts from the skins.

Pomegranate and Persimmon Relish

Pomegranate molasses, found in Middle Eastern food stores, gives this jewel-toned condiment a haunting sweet/sour note. It's from Julia Drori and Daniel Martes of Garibaldi's On College in Oakland. This relish is perfect with roasted or grilled birds of many persuasions: turkey, chicken, pheasant, duck, quail, guinea fowl and Cornish hens.

8 Fuyu persimmons, stemmed, peeled, seeded (if necessary) and finely diced
(about 4 cups)

2 cups pomegranate seeds (about 1½ pomegranates)

1 red bell pepper, stemmed, seeded, deribbed and finely diced

1½ cups walnuts, toasted and finely chopped

5 tablespoons chopped fresh mint

1 teaspoon hot red pepper flakes, or to taste

Pinch of salt and freshly ground pepper

10 tablespoons pomegranate molasses

Combine the persimmons, pomegranate seeds, bell pepper and walnuts in a large bowl. Add the mint, pepper flakes, salt and pepper; toss lightly to mix.

Drizzle the pomegranate molasses over the top and toss again until the ingredients are well mixed.

Serve at room temperature.

YIELDS ABOUT 7 CUPS

Toasting Nuts

Nuts can be toasted in a skillet on the stovetop over medium heat, but the oven method is the easiest. Spread nuts on a baking sheet and place in a 350-degree oven for 10 to 15 minutes, or until they start to color and are fragrant.

Rancho Sarsa

The early Californios called salsa "sarsa." It accompanied everything but was especially good with barbecued meats, and was a favorite topping for rancho beans, says Jacqueline McMahan.

4 perfectly ripe large tomatoes

4 green Anaheim chiles

1 sweet red onion, diced

1 garlic clove, minced

1 to 2 teaspoons salt

1 tablespoon red wine vinegar

1 tablespoon olive oil

Handful of finely snipped cilantro

½ to 1 teaspoon chopped fresh oregano leaves

๑๑ Briefly char the tomatoes over a gas burner or on a grill. Set aside.

Char the chiles in the same way (they will take a bit longer). Cover the chiles with a clean dishcloth to steam for 10 minutes.

While the chiles are steaming, peel, core and halve the tomatoes, then remove the seeds. Dice the flesh.

Peel the chiles, then remove the stems and seeds (reserve the seeds). Dice the chiles.

Combine the tomatoes, chiles, onion, garlic, salt, vinegar, olive oil and cilantro in a bowl, along with enough of the reserved chile seeds to add authority to your sarsa. Stir in the oregano.

Serve immediately, or let stand at cool room temperature for up to 1 hour.

YIELDS ABOUT 1½ QUARTS; SERVES 6 TO 8

NOTE: If you have any leftover sarsa, you can simmer it (with its juices) for about 5 minutes, then spoon over huevos rancheros.

Chimichurri Sauce

Jacqueline McMahan says this sauce originated in Argentina and was used to complement roasted meats. Sometimes she varies the recipe by using New Mexican red chile powder or Spanish red pepper flakes instead of cayenne.

¼ cup red wine vinegar

½ cup extra virgin olive oil

1 teaspoon salt

2 teaspoons mild dried oregano

3 garlic cloves, minced

3 tablespoons minced mild onion

1 cup finely minced Italian parsley

1 cup finely minced cilantro, including some stems

Freshly ground black pepper, to taste

Pinch of cayenne pepper

Combine the vinegar, olive oil, salt, oregano and garlic in a bowl. Whisk until it thickens into a dressing.

Stir in the onion, parsley and cilantro. Season with black pepper and cayenne.

Let stand for several hours before serving.

YIELDS ABOUT 1 CUP

Sunset Salsa

The colors of this salsa remind Jacqueline McMahan of a golden autumn sunset. It's particularly good with broiled halibut or red snapper.

4 tomatoes (preferably heirloom varieties such as Pineapple, Russian Persimmon or
    Zapotec Pleated)

1 mango (not too ripe), peeled and pitted

1 papaya (not too ripe), peeled and seeded

¼ red bell pepper, stemmed, seeded and deribbed

1 teaspoon salt

½ teaspoon ground cumin

Juice of 1 lime

1 tablespoon rice vinegar

2 serrano chiles (red if available), minced, seeds reserved

2 tablespoons minced cilantro

◕ Halve the tomatoes and, using your finger or a small spoon, flick out some of the seeds. Cut the tomatoes into ½-inch dice.

Cut the mango, papaya and bell pepper into ½-inch dice.

Combine the tomatoes, mango, papaya and bell pepper in a bowl; add the salt, cumin, lime juice, rice vinegar, serrano chiles (and as many of their seeds as you like) and cilantro. Toss to combine.

YIELDS ABOUT 5½ CUPS

Salsa Fresca al Fresco

This salsa is a basic in Jacqueline McMahan's kitchen during tomato season. Serve with black beans or as a topping for rice or baked potatoes. You can also spoon it over thick slices of toasted sourdough bread for bruschetta.

5 tomatoes (preferably a mixture of heirloom varieties)

½ cup diced red onion (¼-inch dice)

2 jalapeño chiles, seeded and minced

2 heirloom chiles (such as Bolivian, Hungarian Black or serrano), seeded and minced

1 garlic clove, minced

About ½ teaspoon salt (optional)

3 tablespoons coarsely chopped cilantro leaves

1 tablespoon fresh lime juice, or a dash of pepper vinegar

Core the tomatoes, then halve them horizontally. Use your fingertip or small spoon to scoop out most of the seeds. Cut the tomatoes into small dice.

Combine the tomatoes, onion, jalapeño chiles, heirloom chiles, garlic, salt, if desired, cilantro and lime juice in a bowl. Stir to combine.

YIELDS ABOUT 1 QUART

NOTE: This is best the day it is made. If you wish to keep it longer, heat the salsa briefly (3 minutes on top of the stove; 2 minutes in a microwave). Store in a tightly covered bowl in the refrigerator for up to 3 days.

Painless Way to Seed Jalapeños

Jacqueline McMahan has come up with this easy way to prepare jalapeño chiles. Cut ¼ inch off the tip of the chile. Stand the jalapeño on end and hold by the stem. Using a sharp paring knife, slice from top to bottom. Slice only enough to remove the chile flesh and not the seeds. This saves you from the messy seeding. Cut the chile strips into dice and use as desired.

Fresh Pineapple Salsa

Jacqueline McMahan has a salsa for every occasion. This one is perfect with barbecued or grilled fish or chicken.

2 cups peeled and diced fresh pineapple

½ cup peeled and diced jicama

⅓ cup minced red onion

½ cup diced red bell pepper

1 serrano or jalapeño chile, seeded (if desired) and minced

2 teaspoons minced fresh ginger

¼ to ½ teaspoon crushed dried japonés or arbol chile

1 tablespoon unseasoned rice vinegar

Minced cilantro, to taste (optional)

◉◉ Combine all ingredients in a bowl and mix lightly. Taste for seasoning and, if desired, add a little more crushed red chile.

Keeps for 2 days in a covered container in the refrigerator.

YIELDS ABOUT 3 CUPS

John Caputo's Anchoiade

At his now-closed San Francisco restaurant, Socca, John Caputo made this recipe in volume in a food processor. To make the small quantity described below, use a minifood processor or a mortar and pestle. Use as a spread for toasted baguette slices and sprinkle with parsley for a quick hors d'oeuvre, or to accompany a soup or salad. It also may be used to flavor a romaine lettuce salad or to garnish a fish-based soup.

2 ounces canned anchovy fillets

1 hard-cooked egg yolk

½ garlic clove, minced

1 tablespoon extra virgin olive oil

A few drops of Champagne vinegar

Freshly ground white pepper, to taste

Mixed Melon Salsa

This salsa from Georgeanne Brennan is great for grilled or sautéed chicken, fish or pork. Chop several varieties of melons and place in a bowl. Add chopped tomatillo, minced Anaheim chile, chopped jicama, chopped cilantro leaves, fresh lime juice, and salt and freshly ground pepper, to taste. Mix well. Fold in diced avocado. Sprinkle with pasilla or other ground dried red chile.

Using a mini-food processor or a mortar and pestle, purée the anchovies, egg yolk and garlic to a paste. Stir in the olive oil. Add the vinegar and season with white pepper.

YIELDS ABOUT ⅓ CUP, ENOUGH FOR 12 TO 15 TOASTS

"It's Not Guacamole" Avocado Salsa

Unlike guacamole, which is made with soft avocados, this salsa requires avocados that have just become ripe—tender to the touch but not mushy or squishy. Olive oil brings out the nuttiness of the avocado. The salsa is delicious in soft tacos as well as in salads, says Jacqueline McMahan.

2 firm-ripe avocados

2 tablespoons fresh lemon juice

2 tablespoons flavorful olive oil

2 tablespoons minced red onion

2 garlic cloves, minced

¼ teaspoon salt

2 red or green jalapeño chiles, charred, peeled, seeded and minced

2 tablespoons minced cilantro

Halve and pit the avocados. Using a large spoon, lift out the flesh in one piece. Cut into long strips, then dice. Put avocados in a bowl.

Whisk together the lemon juice, olive oil, onion, garlic and salt in a bowl. Pour over the avocados. Gently fold in the jalapeños and cilantro.

Serve immediately.

YIELDS ABOUT 2 CUPS

Zchug

Zchug, the Yemenite chile sauce that has become Israel's national seasoning, is one of Marlena Spieler's favorite condiments. It is hot with chiles, pungent with garlic and fragrant with exotic cardamom. Eat it with rice, couscous, soup, chicken or other meats. You also can add a little to a tomato sauce for spaghetti, or dunk french fries into it, or stir it into a coleslaw that will knock your socks off.

6 or more garlic cloves, chopped

2 or 3 jalapeño chiles, stemmed, seeded and chopped

5 ripe tomatoes, diced (canned OK)

1 cup coarsely chopped cilantro

1 cup coarsely chopped Italian parsley

2 tablespoons extra virgin olive oil

2 teaspoons cumin

½ teaspoon turmeric

½ teaspoon curry powder

Seeds from 3 to 5 cardamom pods, crushed

Juice of ½ lemon, or to taste

Pinch of sugar

Salt, to taste

Combine all the ingredients in a food processor or blender. Process to a chunky consistency.

YIELDS ABOUT 2 CUPS

Backward Spanish Aioli

Jacqueline McMahan calls this garlicky mayonnaise "backward" because she adds garlic at the last second instead of at the beginning. This way, she says, the garlic doesn't become completely liquidized and bitter. Serve with steamed asparagus, artichokes or on sandwiches.

3 garlic cloves

½ teaspoon sea salt

2 teaspoons Dijon mustard

1 tablespoon fresh lemon juice

2 egg yolks

1 cup olive oil

3 tablespoons boiling water

Place the garlic cloves on a cutting board and smash them with the flat side of a chef's knife. Sprinkle the salt over the garlic and mince finely. Transfer to a small bowl and mash with a spoon. Set aside.

Combine the mustard, lemon juice and egg yolks in a food processor. Process until blended, then, with the motor running, begin very slowly drizzling the olive oil through the feed tube. Stop every few seconds to make sure the sauce is emulsifying into a mayonnaise.

When all the oil has been added, incorporate the boiling water, 1 tablespoon at a time. (The boiling water smooths out the mayonnaise and sets it.)

To finish the mayonnaise, add the garlic-salt mixture. Pulse twice just to barely blend in the garlic. Do not add garlic with the machine running. You want the texture to remain.

YIELDS 1¼ CUPS

NOTE: Add any additional flavorings you like, such as minced fresh basil, cilantro or Italian parsley; puréed chipotle chile; puréed charred and skinned red bell peppers; or charred and skinned Anaheim chiles.

Green Herb Sauce

This sauce by Marion Cunningham is lovely on baked potatoes, scrambled eggs and hearty fish like salmon. It also can be stirred into a soup or salad dressing. To give the sauce a peppy edge, omit the lemon and add 2 tablespoons capers. This variation is good on steak or beef roast.

5 garlic cloves, finely chopped

Grated zest and juice of 2 lemons

1 cup chopped cilantro leaves

1 cup chopped basil leaves

½ cup chopped Italian parsley leaves

1 cup olive oil

1 teaspoon salt

½ teaspoon freshly ground pepper

Combine the garlic, lemon zest and lemon juice in a bowl. Stir in the cilantro, basil and parsley, then add the olive oil. Stir until well blended. Add the salt and pepper; stir to blend, then taste the sauce. Add more salt, if desired.

YIELDS ABOUT 1 CUP

For this test, we made a basic tomato sauce three ways: using a food mill, a food processor and a blender.

We discovered the sauce passed through the food mill had the most texture of the three and was the Food Department's favorite. The food mill produces a multidimensional, slightly rustic texture. In addition, the tiny pieces of tomato add little bursts of flavor.

As for salting, if you salt throughout the cooking process, you will need less salt and the sauce will have a homogenous, long-simmered flavor. Adding salt at the end produces both a sweet and salty effect.

Killer Red Sauce

Cooking dried chiles with tomato, onion and garlic sweetens and intensifies the chiles' flavor in this versatile sauce by Jacqueline McMahan. It freezes beautifully, so you can always have it on hand for saucing meats, grilled foods or casseroles, or using on enchiladas and in burritos.

12 dried red chiles (New Mexican, California or ancho), about 3 ounces total

½ cup chopped onion

3 whole unpeeled garlic cloves

1½ cups chopped tomatoes, about 8 ounces

¼ teaspoon salt

½ teaspoon sugar

4 cups water

◉◉ Preheat the oven to 250 degrees.

Place the chiles on a baking sheet and toast in the oven for 8 minutes. Do not toast them too long or they will become bitter.

Cool quickly by plunging them into a basin of cold water. Rinse the chiles, then remove the stems and seeds.

Combine all the ingredients in a saucepan. Bring to a boil over high heat. Reduce the heat to low, cover and simmer for 30 minutes, pushing the chiles down into the liquid every 5 minutes. The chiles will absorb a lot of the liquid.

Purée the mixture in a food processor in 2 batches, then push through a fine sieve to remove the skins.

Transfer the sauce to a skillet and simmer over medium heat for at least 5 minutes to concentrate the flavors.

YIELDS ABOUT 2½ CUPS SAUCE, ENOUGH FOR 10 ENCHILADAS OR BURRITOS (¼ CUP PER SERVING)

Bagna Cauda

Bagna cauda—literally, hot bath—is a highly aromatic sauce from the Piedmont region of Italy. Raw or blanched vegetables are dipped into the sauce, which usually is served in a pot with a flame underneath. It also can be passed communally around the table or offered in small, individual bowls. In Italy, bagna cauda vegetables usually include fennel, cauliflower, cabbage and bell peppers, but any vegetable that is good raw will work fine.

Marion Cunningham says that, like all good sauces, bagna cauda may be used in other ways: to add tang to a potato salad, to pep up pasta or to highlight the mealy sweetness of steamed tiny new red potatoes.

1½ cups olive oil

6 garlic cloves, finely chopped

½ cup butter, melted

10 anchovy fillets, drained and finely chopped

Salt, to taste

◉ Put ¼ cup of the olive oil in a 1-quart pan. Add the garlic and cook, stirring, over medium heat for about 2 minutes, or until slightly softened but not browned. Remove the pan from the heat. Add the remaining 1¼ cups olive oil, the butter and anchovies. Cook, stirring constantly, over medium heat until the anchovies are incorporated into the sauce and the sauce is warm. Season with salt, if needed.

Serve immediately, or pour into a quart container. Let cool, then cover and refrigerate until needed.

YIELDS ABOUT 2 CUPS

Asian-Style Peanut Barbecue Sauce

In this recipe by Robin Davis, the peanut butter predominates, but hoisin sauce gives sweetness, the chile paste and chile peppers lend heat, and soy sauce adds the salty component. It's great for satés with chicken or beef.

¼ cup creamy peanut butter

6 tablespoons rice vinegar

¼ cup soy sauce

2 tablespoons hoisin sauce

2 tablespoons light brown sugar

1 tablespoon Asian sesame oil

1 tablespoon chile paste

1 tablespoon grated fresh ginger

1 serrano chile, minced

1 teaspoon chile oil

ఴ Spoon the peanut butter into a blender or food processor. Add the vinegar, soy sauce, hoisin sauce, brown sugar, sesame oil, chile paste, ginger, minced chile and chile oil.

Process until the sauce is smooth.

YIELDS ABOUT 1½ CUPS

Quick Plum Sauce

This sweet sauce from Georgeanne Brennan is designed for grilled items. The sweet flavors in the sauce will be balanced by the smoky flavors in the meat. It's also a good accompaniment to spicy food. Cook pitted, soft plums with a little water, sugar and lemon for 10 to 15 minutes, or until thickened and slightly jammy. Strain through a sieve.

Spicy Tomato Barbecue Sauce

This recipe from Robin Davis is ideal for ribs because it is hearty and robust with just a hint of sweetness. Marinate the ribs in the sauce for up to 8 hours, or just brush it on while they're cooking.

1 can (14½ ounces) chopped peeled tomatoes with juices

¼ cup distilled white vinegar

3 tablespoons olive oil

4 garlic cloves, minced

2 tablespoons dark molasses

1 tablespoon canned chipotle chiles en adobo

1 tablespoon grated orange zest

1 tablespoon kosher or sea salt

1 teaspoon freshly ground pepper

◉ Put the tomatoes and their juices in a blender or food processor. Add the vinegar, olive oil, garlic, molasses, chipotle chiles, orange zest, salt and pepper. Process until the sauce is smooth.

YIELDS ABOUT 2½ CUPS

Honey-Mustard Barbecue Sauce

This sauce from Robin Davis is particularly pungent but tastes great when brushed on ribs while they're cooking. The mustard is quite strong but as the honey caramelizes, the sauce mellows.

1 cup Dijon mustard

½ cup honey

4 garlic cloves, minced

2 tablespoons soy sauce

2 tablespoons fresh lemon juice

◉ Combine all the ingredients in a blender or food processor. Process until the sauce is smooth.

YIELDS ABOUT 1¾ CUPS

Egyptian Haroset

This thick, jamlike haroset is unusual—it contains no wine. It's served at the Passover dinner at Saul's Deli in Berkeley, but it also is great as a topping for bagels, toasted English muffins or crumpets.

½ pound raisins

½ pound pitted dates

¼ cup fresh lemon juice

¼ cup fresh orange juice

2 tablespoons sugar

¾ cup chopped toasted walnuts

Soak the raisins and dates in the lemon and orange juices for 1 hour. Combine the raisins, dates, lemon and orange juices and sugar in a food processor; pulse to chop. Transfer to a saucepan and simmer over low heat for 20 minutes. Let cool, then stir in the walnuts.

YIELDS ABOUT 4 CUPS

Fresh Mint and Cilantro Chutney

This Indian condiment is super with barbecued chicken, any curry or thinly sliced steak, says Marlena Spieler. It will keep in the refrigerator for up to 2 days but tends to pale with age. If you've stored it, you'll need to zip up the heat with a little additional chile, or add more fresh mint and/or cilantro.

2 garlic cloves, chopped

2 green jalapeño chiles, stemmed, seeded and chopped

1 cup mint leaves

½ cup cilantro leaves

½ teaspoon cumin, or to taste

1 teaspoon chopped fresh ginger, or to taste

2 tablespoons fresh lime juice

½ teaspoon salt, or to taste

🌀 Combine all ingredients in a blender or food processor and process, adding just enough water to make a smooth mixture.

Taste for seasoning. If a hotter sauce is desired, add more chile.

YIELDS ABOUT 2 CUPS

Red Pepper Jelly

Here's a wonderful sweet-and-hot jelly from Marion Cunningham. Serve with cornbread, muffins or as an accompaniment to roasted meats, or any way you would use mint jelly.

2 red bell peppers, stemmed, seeded, deribbed and finely chopped like confetti

1 green bell pepper, stemmed, seeded, deribbed and finely chopped like confetti

3 jalapeño chiles, seeded and finely chopped

6 cups sugar

1½ cups apple cider vinegar

½ cup fresh lemon juice

2 teaspoons salt

6 ounces liquid pectin (2 pouches of Certo)

🌀 Combine the bell peppers, chiles, sugar, vinegar, lemon juice and salt in a large stainless-steel or enameled-iron saucepan. Bring the mixture to a hard boil over high heat and cook for 5 minutes, stirring constantly and making sure the mixture continues to boil while you are stirring. Add the liquid pectin and continue to stir and boil for exactly 1 minute. Remove from the heat and pour into hot, sterilized jars. Seal according to manufacturer's directions.

YIELDS 7 EIGHT-OUNCE JARS

How to Fix Unjelled Jelly

This is an old Nebraska remedy from Marion Cunningham for soft jelly that was made with liquid pectin.

Measure the jelly to be recooked. For each quart of jelly, have ready ¾ cup sugar, 2 tablespoons fresh lemon juice and 2 tablespoons liquid pectin.

Bring the jelly to a boil over high heat. Quickly add the sugar, lemon juice and pectin; bring to a full rolling boil, stirring constantly, and boil hard for 1 minute. Remove the jelly from the heat, skim, pour into hot, sterilized jars and seal.

English Country-House Lemon Curd

Jackie Mallorca uses this tart-sweet mixture to fill tiny tart shells, or as a spread for toasted English muffins or scones. It's also good folded into whipped cream and served in individual dessert glasses (garnish with slivers of candied lemon peel or a small sprig of mint).

6 tablespoons unsalted butter, cut into pieces

6 tablespoons sugar

3 egg yolks

3 tablespoons fresh lemon juice

◉◉ Combine all the ingredients in the top of a double boiler, or in an earthenware bowl placed over (but not touching) simmering water. Cook, stirring, for 6 to 7 minutes, or until the mixture thickens and coats the back of a spoon.

Pour through a fine sieve into a sterilized glass jar. Cover airtight and refrigerate. The curd will thicken as it cools.

Use within 4 weeks.

YIELDS ABOUT 1 CUP

Quick Preserved Lemons

Preserved lemons are absolutely delicious but take weeks to prepare. Faced with a Meyer lemon tree bearing too much fruit, Michael Bauer remembered seeing a quick method of preserving them. The recipe stuck with him, but the name of the cookbook didn't.

The intense flavor adds a pleasant note when the lemons are stuffed under the skin or into the cavity of a chicken before roasting it. They're great finely chopped in vinaigrettes or stirred into pasta, and also add wonderful flavor to mayonnaise for dips and sandwiches.

◎◎ To prepare preserved lemons in a week, quarter each fresh Meyer or Eureka lemon lengthwise. Place in a stainless-steel or glass bowl and freeze for 8 hours. (A heavy-duty freezer bag may also be used.) Remove the lemons from the freezer and sprinkle on 1 tablespoon kosher salt for each lemon. Toss to coat. Cover and let stand at room temperature for 6 days, stirring once a day. At the end of 1 week, refrigerate. The lemons will keep for several months in the refrigerator. If the lemons begin to feel slimy, rinse well, cut away the pulp and use only the rind.

Chapter 12

Desserts

Puddings and pies, cookies and cakes seem to have captured the San Francisco palate. We talk a sophisticated game, but when it comes to sweets, we like comfort.

Blessed with some of the best dessert makers in the country, it's little wonder this chapter is filled with the creamiest puddings and richest cakes we've ever eaten. There is creamy Mexican Chocolate Bread Pudding (page 404) by Jacqueline McMahan, cooling Italian Panna Cotta with Citrus-Strawberry Salad (page 402) from Farallon and a wonderful Almond Cake (page 419) from Left Bank in Menlo Park.

From Flo Braker, you'll get Velvet Pound Cake (page 421) and Lavender Shortbread (page 429), to name a couple. Marion Cunningham offers many favorites, as well: Cranberry Upside-Down Cake (page 417), Christmas Nut Chews (page 428) and Oatmeal Cake with Walnut Topping (page 416).

Fruit also plays a major role here—in pies, cobblers, cakes and other creations. Many of our fruit-based desserts are easy to toss together, such as Oven-Roasted Figs with Crème Fraîche (page 437), Peaches and Berries in Herbed Red Wine (page 438) and Strawberries with Whipped Ricotta (page 438).

And for something cool, try Gin and Tonic Granita (page 440) and Watermelon Sherbet (page 439).

Zuni Cafe's Chocolate Pots de Crème

This rich dessert has been served at Zuni since the early 1980s, well before the San Francisco restaurant's famous hamburger or roast chicken found legions of followers.

6 ounces bittersweet chocolate, chopped

1½ cups whipping cream

1½ cups milk

¼ cup sugar

8 egg yolks

Preheat the oven to 300 degrees.

Melt the chocolate with ½ cup of the cream in a 2-quart saucepan over low heat or in a bowl set over a pan of simmering water. Remove from heat.

Combine the remaining 1 cup cream, the milk and sugar in a saucepan and warm over medium-low heat until the sugar dissolves.

Whisk the egg yolks in a bowl, then slowly stir in the warm cream mixture. Pour the resulting custard mixture through a fine sieve into the melted chocolate and stir to combine.

Divide the mixture among 6 custard cups and place them at least 1 inch apart in a baking pan. Add enough hot water to the pan to reach just under the lip of the cups.

Bake for about 45 minutes, or until the custards are just set at the edges. They will continue to cook after you remove them from the oven, and the chocolate will harden as it cools. Take care not to overcook; this custard is best when slightly soft. Loosely cover and refrigerate until cold, at least 4 hours or overnight.

SERVES 6

Tips for a Perfect Custard

Have all ingredients at warm room temperature to ensure even cooking. If eggs are refrigerator cold, place them in a large bowl of lukewarm water for 10 minutes before cracking them.

Strain uncooked egg-milk mixtures through a fine sieve to insure a smooth, silky texture.

Never cook custards at more than medium heat. Oven temperatures more than 350 degrees will toughen the protein in the eggs, resulting in tough curds and a watery texture.

To test for doneness, insert a sharp knife or skewer near the edge of the dish. If the custard is done, the knife will come out clean. The residual heat will finish cooking the center of the custard as the dish cools.

Butterscotch Pots de Crème

Nicole Plue made these pots de crème when she was at Hawthorne Lane in San Francisco. Even those who aren't wild about butterscotch came back for more when we prepared them in The Chronicle's *kitchen.*

3 cups whipping cream
Zest of ½ orange
2 tablespoons rum
Pinch of salt
½ vanilla bean, split lengthwise
½ cup light brown sugar
2 tablespoons water
8 egg yolks
2 tablespoons granulated sugar
Lightly sweetened whipped cream for garnish

Preheat the oven to 300 degrees.

Combine the cream, orange zest, rum and salt in a small, heavy saucepan. Scrape in seeds from the vanilla bean; add the bean. Bring to a simmer over medium heat. Remove from heat and cover.

Combine the brown sugar and water in a small, heavy saucepan. Cook over medium heat, swirling the pan occasionally, until the mixture reaches 300 degrees on a candy thermometer. Remove from heat.

Carefully add the cream mixture to the hot brown sugar (it will bubble vigorously). Stir until smooth.

Whisk the yolks with the granulated sugar in a large bowl. Whisk 1 cup of the hot cream mixture into the yolks. Add the yolk mixture to the remaining cream mixture; stir to blend. Strain through a fine sieve into a bowl.

Divide the mixture among eight 6-ounce custard cups and place them in a large baking pan. Add enough hot water to the pan to come halfway up the sides of the cups.

Bake for about 45 minutes, or until the custards are softly set. Cool, then refrigerate until cold, at least 4 hours or overnight.

Garnish with a dollop of whipped cream.

SERVES 8

Panna Cotta with Citrus-Strawberry Salad

This cool and creamy Italian dessert, paired with a sprightly "salad," is from Mark Franz, the chef/owner of Farallon in San Francisco.

1 cup milk

1 envelope unflavored gelatin

2 cups whipping cream

½ cup sugar

1 vanilla bean, split and seeds scraped, or 1 tablespoon vanilla extract

Citrus-Strawberry Salad (recipe follows)

◉ Pour the milk into a small bowl and sprinkle the gelatin over the surface. Let stand for 5 minutes, or until the gelatin absorbs the milk and softens.

Combine the cream, sugar, vanilla seeds and vanilla bean in a saucepan. Bring to a simmer over medium heat. Remove from heat and cover. Let steep for 30 minutes.

Reheat the cream mixture over medium heat to about 100 degrees (just warm to the touch). Stir in the softened gelatin. Continue to stir until the gelatin has dissolved. If using vanilla extract, stir it in now. Strain into a 2-quart plastic container with a tight-fitting lid. Refrigerate for at least 4 hours. May be made 1 day ahead.

To serve, divide the panna cotta among individual bowls and spoon the Citrus-Strawberry Salad over each serving.

SERVES 6

Citrus-Strawberry Salad

¼ cup water

¼ cup fresh orange juice

½ cup sugar

3 tangerines or oranges

1 pint strawberries, hulled and quartered

Combine the water, orange juice and sugar in a saucepan. Bring to a boil over high heat, then remove from heat and let cool to room temperature. Chill in the refrigerator.

Peel the tangerines, removing as much pith and skin as possible, then cut the segments from the membranes.

Toss the tangerine segments and strawberries in the chilled syrup. Spoon into a plastic container with a tight-fitting lid. Refrigerate until ready to serve.

SERVES 6

Rose-Accented Rice Pudding

This pudding from Laxmi Hiremath is delicious served warm or chilled. Its unique flavor comes from rose essence, which is available in Middle Eastern, specialty and Indian markets.

¼ cup basmati, jasmine or other long-grain white rice

1 quart whole or low-fat milk

½ cup sugar

2 tablespoons chopped pistachios

1 tablespoon chopped dates (optional)

⅛ teaspoon rose essence, or ½ teaspoon rose water

Wash the rice in several changes of water; drain well. Combine rice and milk in a Dutch oven. Bring to a boil over medium-high heat, stirring constantly. Reduce heat to medium and cook, uncovered, stirring occasionally, for about 15 minutes, or until the rice is tender.

Stir in the sugar, pistachios and dates, if desired. Continue to simmer, stirring occasionally, for 20 to 25 minutes, or until the pudding is thick and reduced by half. Remove from heat and stir in the rose essence.

Keeps well for up to 5 days in a covered container in the refrigerator.

SERVES 4

Mexican Chocolate Bread Pudding

This creamy pudding, featuring chocolate and caramelized sugar, is from Jacqueline McMahan.

1¼ cups sugar

1 cup milk

1 can (14 ounces) evaporated milk

3 cups finely diced crustless bread, dried out in oven

4 ounces semisweet chocolate, melted

1 tablespoon vanilla

1 teaspoon instant espresso powder

2 eggs

2 egg yolks

Topping

1 cup whipping cream

1 teaspoon instant espresso powder

1 teaspoon vanilla

1 tablespoon powdered sugar

⊚⊚ Place an ovenproof 2-quart baking dish or deep metal pan near the stove.

Put ¾ cup of the sugar in a saucepan over medium heat. After 3 to 4 minutes, begin swirling the pan. Do not stir. Cook for 8 to 10 minutes (again, do not stir), or until the sugar caramelizes. Immediately pour into the baking dish.

In the same pan, heat the milk and evaporated milk over medium heat, stirring in the remaining ½ cup sugar. Cook, stirring, until the sugar dissolves. Remove from heat and add the dry bread. Push the bread into the milk and let it soak for 30 minutes.

Preheat the oven to 350 degrees. Place a roasting pan filled with 1 inch of water in the oven.

Stir the chocolate, vanilla and espresso powder into the mushy bread.

Beat together the eggs and egg yolks in a bowl; add to the bread mixture. Pour into the prepared baking dish, cover with aluminum foil and place in the roasting pan in the oven.

Bake for 35 minutes; uncover and bake for 20 minutes longer.

Transfer the pudding to a rack and let cool for 30 minutes. Refrigerate for 1 hour before serving.

To serve, loosen the edges with a knife, then unmold the pudding onto a rimmed platter.

Just before serving, make the topping: Whip the cream to very soft peaks. Stir in the espresso powder, vanilla and powdered sugar. Spoon a dollop on each serving.

SERVES 10

A Cheese Treat

Here's a quick and easy dessert using cheese from Georgeanne Brennan. It's particularly good after a big dinner with the last of the red wine or with a glass of dessert wine. Thin fromage blanc with a little cream so it can be easily spooned into individual dishes. Drizzle with lavender or eucalyptus honey. Serve with thin slices of walnut bread, toasted if desired.

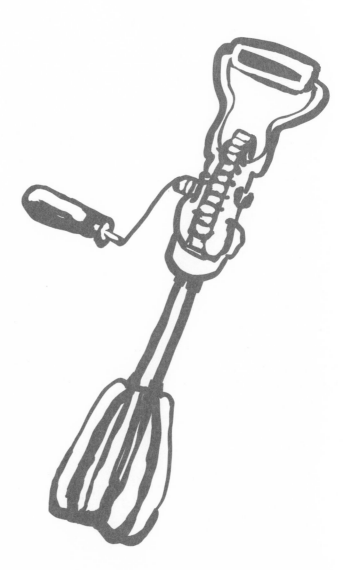

The Ultimate Lemon Meringue Pie

Jacqueline McMahan's mother, Marie Chavarria, often topped off her rancho feasts with this dessert.

Lemon Filling

1½ cups sugar

1½ cups plus ⅓ cup water

½ teaspoon salt

½ cup cornstarch

4 egg yolks, lightly beaten

2 tablespoons minced lemon zest (preferably from Meyer lemons)

½ cup fresh lemon juice (preferably from Meyer lemons)

1 tablespoon butter

Meringue

4 egg whites

Pinch of salt

½ cup sugar

1 baked 9-inch pie shell

ଏ Preheat the oven to 325 degrees.

To make the filling: Combine the sugar, 1½ cups water and the salt in a saucepan. Bring to a boil over high heat. Mix the cornstarch and ⅓ cup water to a smooth paste in a bowl. Whisking constantly, add the cornstarch mixture to the sugar-water mixture, cooking until very thick and clear. Remove from heat.

Combine the egg yolks, lemon zest and juice in a bowl. Whisk into the hot mixture; return to medium heat for 1 minute, then remove from heat and stir in the butter. Set aside.

To make the meringue: Place a metal mixing bowl over a pot of hot water. Add the egg whites, salt and sugar; whisk just until blended and the mixture is warm to the touch. Using a handheld mixer, beat to soft peaks.

Fold 2 heaping tablespoons of the meringue into the warm lemon filling, then spread the filling into the pie shell. Gently spoon little mountains of

BEST WAY:
Beating Egg Whites

Is the centuries-old tradition that says a copper bowl is imperative for making meringues really true? Do egg whites beat higher when they're at room temperature rather than straight from the refrigerator? Does cream of tartar do any good?

We tested these premises using a handheld mixer with a standard beater attachment at low speed for 1 minute, before switching to high. Here's what we found:

For best results, follow tradition. This produces a finer texture and a lighter, fluffier mound than any other method. If you don't have a copper bowl, use stainless steel.

Adding a pinch of cream of tartar to the eggs as they foam during the initial beating improves the results dramatically. When egg whites are overbeaten, they separate and the cream of tartar mimics copper in helping stabilize the foam, allowing leeway for overzealous beaters. The whites stay at full volume nearly twice as long as the whites beaten in the stainless-steel bowl without the cream of tartar.

meringue on top. Use a spatula to spread the meringue right up to the edges of the pastry so there will be a seal between the crust and the meringue. Make billowy swirls in the meringue with the spatula.

Bake for 15 minutes. Let cool to room temperature before serving. Refrigerate any leftovers.

SERVES 6 TO 8

John Carroll's Peach Pie

This peach pie from cookbook author John Carroll is one of the best we've tasted.

Dough

3 cups all-purpose flour

1 teaspoon salt

1 cup vegetable shortening

About 9 tablespoons cold water

Filling

7 cups peeled and sliced peaches (from about 3 pounds fruit)

⅔ cup sugar

⅓ cup all-purpose flour

¼ teaspoon freshly grated nutmeg

¼ teaspoon salt

3 tablespoons fresh lemon juice

2 tablespoons butter (optional)

1 tablespoon sugar

◎ Preheat the oven to 425 degrees. Line a baking sheet with aluminum foil.

To make the dough: Sift the flour and salt into a large bowl. Add the shortening, then briskly massage it into the flour with your fingertips until the mixture looks like fine breadcrumbs with just a few pea-size pieces. Add the water gradually, tossing the mixture with a fork until it is damp enough to come together into a ball.

Divide the ball into 2 pieces, 1 slightly larger than the other. On a lightly floured surface, pat the larger piece by hand into a disk about 1 inch thick

The Perfect Pie Pan?

Cookbook author John Carroll and *Chronicle* columnist Marion Cunningham prefer a glass pie dish. They believe it makes a crisper crust, and they like being able to see the bottom cook.

Carolyn Weil, owner of the Bakeshop in Berkeley, likes aluminum pie tins, preferably thin ones. Because metal conducts heat better than glass, an aluminum tin produces a crisper, better-cooked bottom crust, she argues.

So, the perfect pan may be in the eye of the pie baker.

and 5 inches in diameter. Then roll out into a round about ⅛ inch thick and at least 1 inch larger in diameter than your pie pan. If the dough threatens to stick, slide a long stainless-steel spatula underneath it to release it and then lightly flour the work surface.

Transfer the dough to a 9-inch pie pan. Gently press it into the pan.

Roll out the second piece of dough into a round about ⅛ inch thick and at least 1 inch larger in diameter than the pie pan. Let rest while you make the filling.

To make the filling: Place the peaches in a large bowl. Combine ⅔ cup sugar, the flour, nutmeg and salt in another bowl; stir to blend. Add to the peaches and stir to coat them evenly. Stir in the lemon juice.

Transfer the filling to the pie shell, mounding it slightly. Dot with the butter, if desired. Using a damp paper towel, moisten the dough all around the rim of the pan. Place the second dough round over the filling. Firmly press the dough rounds together at the pan edge. Cut off extra dough, leaving a ¾-inch overhang. Fold the overhang under to make a neat ridge. Flute the ridge as desired. Using a small, sharp knife, cut about a dozen small slits in the top to allow steam to escape.

Place the pie on the foil-lined baking sheet; bake for 25 minutes. Reduce oven temperature to 350 degrees and bake for 20 to 25 minutes longer, or until the filling is bubbling up through the slits and the crust is golden brown. About 15 minutes before the pie is done, sprinkle 1 tablespoon sugar over the top.

Let cool at least 1 hour before serving.

SERVES 6

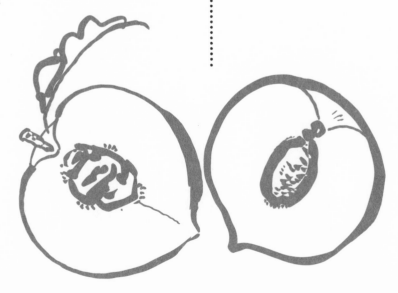

Mary Risley's Fresh Fig and Plum Tart

Mary Risley of Tante Marie's Cooking School combines fresh plums and figs into one spectacular tart.

Crust

1 cup all-purpose flour

½ cup butter, cut into 1-inch pieces

1 tablespoon sugar

⅛ teaspoon salt

1 tablespoon water mixed with a few drops of vanilla

Filling

⅓ cup unpeeled almonds

⅓ cup sugar

1 egg

3 tablespoons butter

3 teaspoons raspberry or cherry eau-de-vie (framboise or kirsch)

1 pound fresh unpeeled figs, halved

1 pound dark plums, halved and pitted

½ cup red currant jelly

◉ To make the crust: Put the flour, butter, sugar and salt in a food processor. Process until the butter is the size of oatmeal flakes. With the machine running, add the water mixture. Process until the dough comes together in a ball.

Press the dough into a 9-inch tart pan with a removable bottom. Refrigerate for at least 2 hours, or until chilled.

Preheat the oven to 375 degrees.

Bake the crust for 10 to 12 minutes, or until lightly browned. Transfer to a rack and let cool for 30 minutes, or until the crust is at room temperature.

To make the filling: Maintain the oven temperature of 375 degrees.

Put the almonds and sugar in a food processor and process until the almonds are finely ground. Add the egg, butter and 2 teaspoons of the eau-de-vie. Process for 1 minute.

Spread the almond mixture in the cooled pastry shell. Arrange the figs and plums cut-sides up, in alternating concentric circles, over the almond

If fresh black Mission figs are out of season, you can substitute dried black Mission figs in many recipes, says Flo Braker.

To soften dried figs, combine ½ cup fresh orange juice and 2 table-spoons sugar in a small saucepan. Bring to a boil and cook for about 3 minutes, or until the liquid is reduced by almost one third. Reduce the heat; add 8 stemmed and quartered dried figs and simmer for about 3 minutes, stirring occasionally. Remove the pan from the heat and set aside until the figs are cool. There's no need to drain them before using.

mixture. The almond mixture should be completely covered with fruit. Bake for 30 minutes. Let cool for 20 minutes before brushing with the melted jelly.

Combine the jelly and the remaining 1 teaspoon eau-de-vie in a small saucepan and melt over low heat.

Unmold the tart onto a serving plate. Using a pastry brush, lightly coat the figs and plums with the melted jelly.

SERVES 6

Rick and Ann's Black 'n' Blue Pie

Baker Kimberley Case provided this recipe for an incredible blackberry and blueberry pie that's served at Rick & Ann's in Berkeley. The crust is unusual because it contains cake flour.

Dough

2 cups all-purpose flour

½ cup cake flour

1½ tablespoons sugar

¾ teaspoon salt

¼ teaspoon almond extract

10 tablespoons chilled unsalted butter

4 tablespoons chilled lard, or vegetable shortening

¾ teaspoon vanilla mixed with ¼ cup water, preferably in a squeeze bottle

Filling

2 pints blueberries

2 to 3 baskets (6 ounces each) blackberries

1 cup sugar, or more, to taste

5½ tablespoons cornstarch

Pinch of salt

2 tablespoons fresh lemon juice

2 teaspoons lemon zest

1 teaspoon orange zest

2 tablespoons unsalted butter, melted

Tips for a Tender Crust

Here are Flo Braker's tips for making a perfect crust:

The fats (butter and vegetable shortening) should be firm and cold. The goal is to coat the flour, not let the flour absorb warm fat.

Incorporate the butter first, since it is the firmer of the two fats. If both fats were cut in simultaneously, the softer fat would be overworked into the flour, resulting in a mealier dough that cracks and tears and has a crumbly texture.

Refrigerate the dough for at least 2 hours before rolling. This gives the flour time to absorb any liquid and the gluten time to relax. The dough will be easier to roll and less susceptible to shrinkage.

Keep the work surface lightly floured while rolling out the dough. Rolling over dough that sticks will stretch it and increase its chances of becoming tough.

To roll a circle, begin with a flat round of dough. Roll from the center upward or away from you; lift the pin, begin in the center of the dough and roll downward or toward you. To keep the dough round, gently lift the dough and give it an eighth turn. Repeat rolling and turning until the dough is the diameter you desire. Avoid rolling over the edges of the dough; this helps eliminate cracking or creating too thin of an edge.

◌◌ Preheat the oven to 425 degrees. Line a baking sheet with aluminum foil.

To make the dough: Combine the flours, sugar, salt and almond extract in a food processor; process to blend. Cut the butter and lard into small pieces. Add about two thirds of the fat to the dry ingredients, poking the fat down into the flour. (Be careful of the blade.) Pulse until the mixture looks like dry breadcrumbs with some small pea-size pieces. Add the remaining fat and pulse to a small pea-size texture. Transfer to a large bowl.

Gradually add a little vanilla-water from the squeeze bottle while tossing with a fork. Add just enough water—about 4 tablespoons—to form a dough. Divide the dough into 2 pieces and form each into a ball. Wrap each ball in plastic, then pat and press into a thick disk. Refrigerate if desired, or roll out immediately. If refrigerated, let the dough come to near room temperature before rolling out.

Roll out 1 of the disks on a floured work surface to a round about ⅛ inch thick and 11 inches in diameter. Transfer to a 10-inch pie pan and press it gently into the pan. Trim the dough even with the edge of the pan.

Roll out the second piece of dough into a round about ⅛ inch thick and 11 inches in diameter. Let rest while you make the filling.

To make the filling: Carefully pick over the berries, discarding leaves, stems and berries with any sign of mold. Place the berries in a large bowl; toss with 1 cup sugar, the cornstarch and salt. Then add the lemon juice, lemon and orange zests and butter, crushing some of the berries if the mixture seems dry. Taste and add more sugar, if needed.

Spoon the filling into the pie shell. Place the second dough round over the filling. Lift up the edge of the bottom dough and fold the top dough underneath it to make a seal. Flute edge as desired. Using a small, sharp knife, cut 8 small slits in the top to allow steam to escape.

Place the pie on the foil-lined baking sheet and place in the oven. Immediately reduce the oven temperature to 350 degrees. Bake for 1 to 1½ hours, or until the crust is golden and the filling is thick and bubbly.

SERVES 8

Plums 'n' Spice Shortcakes

Flo Braker has created one of the most delicious variations on the traditional strawberry shortcake. Plums, seasoned with orange zest, are sautéed in butter, then spooned over a shortcake with the intriguing flavor of Chinese five-spice powder.

Fruit

10 ripe plums, about 4 ounces each, pitted and cut into ½-inch slices

6 tablespoons granulated sugar

1 tablespoon finely grated orange zest

2 tablespoons unsalted butter

Shortcake Dough

2 cups all-purpose flour

¼ cup light brown sugar

2½ teaspoons baking powder

1 teaspoon Chinese five-spice powder

¼ teaspoon salt

1 egg, lightly beaten

⅓ cup plus 1 tablespoon half-and-half, or whipping cream

½ cup unsalted butter, cut into ⅛-inch slices

2 tablespoons granulated sugar

Whipped Cream

1 cup whipping cream

1 tablespoon granulated sugar

1 teaspoon vanilla

✆ To make the fruit: Put the plums, sugar and orange zest in a large skillet; set aside for 10 minutes, stirring occasionally. Cook over medium heat for 4 minutes, stirring occasionally. Add the butter; cook for 3 to 5 minutes, or until the plum slices are just soft. Using a rubber spatula, gently stir from time to time without crushing the fruit.

To make the shortcakes: Adjust the rack to the lower third of the oven and preheat to 400 degrees. Line a large baking sheet with parchment paper.

Sift the flour, brown sugar, baking powder, five-spice powder and salt into a large bowl. Mix the egg with the half-and-half in a small bowl. Cut the butter into the dry ingredients until the mixture resembles coarse meal. Make a well in the center of the dry ingredients and pour in the egg mixture. Gently stir with a fork until moistened and the dough just comes together and pulls away from the sides of the bowl.

Transfer the dough to a lightly floured work surface and, using your fingertips, pat it out into a 7½-inch square, about ¾ to 1 inch thick. Using a floured knife, cut into nine 2½-inch squares. Set the squares about 1 inch apart on the prepared baking sheet. Sprinkle the sugar over the tops.

Bake for 20 to 25 minutes, or until golden. Cool the shortcakes on a wire rack.

To make the whipped cream: Combine the cream, sugar and vanilla in a bowl. Whip to soft peaks.

To assemble: Split the shortcakes in half horizontally, preferably with the tines of a fork. Place the bottom halves of the shortcakes on dessert plates, top each with plum slices, then whipped cream, then the shortcake tops.

SERVES 9

Alsatian Apple Cake

This cake, by Maria Helm of Sinskey Winery in the Napa Valley's Carneros region, has a crumbly texture and rich taste. It's particularly good served with warm caramel sauce and French vanilla ice cream.

8 to 10 Fuji or other firm apples, about 3½ pounds total, peeled, cored and sliced

¼ cup granulated sugar

¾ cup water

1 tablespoon fresh lemon juice

1 cinnamon stick

1 teaspoon vanilla

½ cup butter

2 cups panko or other dry breadcrumbs

½ teaspoon ground cinnamon

¾ cup light brown sugar

◉◉ Preheat the oven to 325 degrees. Grease (or coat with vegetable-oil cooking spray) an 8-inch springform pan.

Combine the apples, sugar, water, lemon juice and cinnamon stick in a saucepan. Bring to a boil over high heat, then reduce heat to low, cover and simmer until the apples are soft but not mushy. Uncover the pan during the last few minutes of cooking until the liquid evaporates. Discard the cinnamon stick. Stir in the vanilla.

Melt the butter in a saucepan over medium-low heat. Add the breadcrumbs, stirring until well mixed. Add the ground cinnamon and brown sugar; heat, stirring, for 2 minutes. Remove from heat and cool slightly.

Sprinkle one third of the crumb mixture over the bottom of the springform pan. Top with half of the apples, then sprinkle with half of the remaining crumbs. Make a final layer of apples and top with the remaining crumbs. Pat smooth.

Bake for about 45 minutes, or until the crumbs are golden.

Cool on a rack, then loosen the edges of the pan and remove the rim. Cut the cake into wedges (it will be crumbly) and serve.

SERVES 6 TO 8

Tequila Carrot Cake

Tequila is a great enhancer: It brings out the fruit and spice in this lavish carrot cake, created by Jacqueline McMahan.

Cake

½ cup golden raisins

3 tablespoons tequila anejo

2 tablespoons sweet orange marmalade

2 cups all-purpose flour

2 teaspoons baking powder

½ teaspoon baking soda

1 teaspoon salt

2 teaspoons cinnamon

¼ teaspoon nutmeg

4 eggs

2 cups sugar

1 cup canola oil

1 tablespoon vanilla

3 cups grated carrots

1 can (8 ounces) crushed pineapple, drained

Icing

11 ounces cream cheese

2 tablespoons unsalted butter

2 cups powdered sugar

2 tablespoons tequila anejo

1 tablespoon Grand Marnier, or other orange-flavored liqueur

◉◉ To make the cake: Preheat the oven to 350 degrees. Line three 9-inch cake pans with rounds of parchment paper. Oil the parchment.

Soak the golden raisins in the tequila in a bowl until they are plump and have soaked up all the tequila. (To speed the process, you can heat them in the microwave for 30 seconds.) Stir in the orange marmalade.

Sift together the flour, baking powder, baking soda, salt, cinnamon and nutmeg in a bowl. Set aside.

Combine the eggs and sugar in a bowl and beat with an electric mixer until well blended and light in color. Slowly add the oil, then the vanilla.

Add the flour mixture along with the carrots and pineapple. Stir in the raisins. Divide among the prepared pans.

Bake for 30 to 35 minutes, or until a cake tester comes out clean when inserted into the center of the cake. Let cool for 10 minutes, then unmold. Let cool to room temperature.

To make the icing: Using an electric mixer, beat together the cream cheese, butter and sugar in a bowl, then add the tequila and Grand Marnier. Use as filling and frosting for the carrot cake.

SERVES 8 TO 10

Oatmeal Cake with Walnut Topping

Marion Cunningham is the doyenne of American home cooking, and she fondly remembers this cake, which was one of her mother's favorites.

Cake

1½ cups quick-cooking oatmeal

½ cup butter

1½ cups boiling water

¾ cup granulated sugar

1 cup light brown sugar

2 eggs

2 teaspoons vanilla

½ teaspoon maple flavoring

1½ cups all-purpose flour

1 teaspoon baking soda

1 teaspoon salt

Topping

6 tablespoons butter, melted

½ cup chopped walnuts

½ cup light brown sugar

½ teaspoon vanilla

¼ cup milk

1 cup coconut

To make the cake: Preheat the oven to 350 degrees. Butter a 9-by-13-inch baking pan.

Place 1 cup of the oatmeal and the butter in a large bowl; pour in the boiling water and stir. Let stand for 15 minutes.

Stir the oatmeal mixture, then add the granulated sugar, brown sugar, eggs, vanilla, maple flavoring, flour, the remaining ½ cup oatmeal, the baking soda and salt. Stir briskly until well blended. Pour the batter into the prepared baking pan.

Bake for 20 to 30 minutes, or until a cake tester comes out clean when inserted into the center of the cake.

While the cake is baking, prepare the topping.

To make the topping: Combine the melted butter, walnuts, brown sugar, vanilla, milk and coconut in a bowl; stir to blend.

When the cake is done, remove from the oven. Turn on the broiler.

Spread the topping with a spatula over the top of the cake. Put the cake under the broiler and stand right there watching. When the topping bubbles all over, remove the cake from the broiler.

Serve warm or at room temperature.

SERVES 14

Cranberry Upside-Down Cake

Marion Cunningham created this wonderful upside-down cake using cranberries in place of pineapple. It makes a spectacular presentation, too, with the deep-red berries glistening like rubies.

Topping

2½ cups fresh cranberries

4 tablespoons butter

¾ cup light brown sugar

Cake

⅓ cup vegetable shortening

⅔ cup granulated sugar

1 teaspoon vanilla

2 eggs

1⅔ cups all-purpose flour

2 teaspoons baking powder

¼ teaspoon salt

⅔ cup milk

Whipped Cream

1 cup whipping cream

3 or 4 tablespoons granulated sugar

∞ Preheat the oven to 350 degrees.

To make the topping: Rinse the cranberries in a colander under cold running water. Remove any soft or shriveled cranberries and discard. Shake the colander to get rid of excess water. Set aside.

Melt the butter in a 2-quart ovenproof skillet over medium heat. Stir in the brown sugar. Continue to cook, stirring, until the sugar melts and is bubbling a little. Remove from heat and add the cranberries, spreading them in a single layer in the sauce. Set aside.

To make the cake: Combine the shortening and sugar in a mixing bowl. Using the back of a large spoon, press and smooth the shortening and sugar together until they are a single mass. (If you have an electric mixer, this can be done quickly.) Add the vanilla and eggs. Beat the mixture until it is all one color and smooth (again, an electric mixer does this quickly, or a hand rotary beater will smooth out lumps).

Combine the flour, baking powder and salt in a bowl. Stir with a fork to blend. Add the flour mixture to the creamed mixture along with the milk, beating with a large spoon or a hand rotary beater until the batter is smooth and free of lumps.

Spread the batter evenly over the cranberries.

Bake for 25 to 30 minutes, or until a cake tester comes out clean when inserted into the center of the cake.

Remove from the oven and let sit for 10 minutes, then put a large serving plate over the skillet and turn the skillet upside down. The cake will drop onto the platter.

To make the whipped cream: Combine the cream and 3 tablespoons of the sugar in a bowl. Beat, using a hand rotary beater or electric mixer, to soft peaks. Taste, and add more sugar if you like.

Serve the cake slightly warm with the whipped cream.

SERVES 6 TO 8

Quick Marinated Strawberries

Here's a quick recipe for strawberries. Wash and slice strawberries. Pour enough fruity red wine over them to moisten. Add a little sugar and a pinch of freshly ground black pepper or finely chopped fresh rosemary. Cover and refrigerate for 4 to 6 hours. Serve with whipped cream or ice cream.

Left Bank Almond Cake

This deceptively plain-looking cake is rich, moist and buttery, with a heavenly tender texture. It was created by Amy Whitelaw, pastry chef of Left Bank in Menlo Park. Serve it with lightly sweetened sliced strawberries and vanilla ice cream or whipped cream.

1 cup (8 ounces) almond paste (preferably Blue Diamond)

1¼ cups sugar

1¼ cups butter at room temperature

1 teaspoon vanilla

6 eggs

1 cup all-purpose flour

1½ teaspoons baking powder

¼ teaspoon salt

◉◉ Preheat the oven to 325 degrees. Grease and flour a 9-inch springform pan.

Combine the almond paste and sugar in a food processor and pulse until well blended. Add the butter and vanilla; pulse until well combined. Add the eggs, 1 at a time, and pulse until just combined (do not overmix).

Sift together the flour, baking powder and salt into a bowl. Add the dry ingredients to the processor and pulse to blend.

Transfer the batter to the prepared pan. Place the pan on a baking sheet and bake for 1 to 1½ hours, or until the cake is golden on top and has started to pull away from the sides of the pan.

Place on a rack and let cool to room temperature. Remove the cake from the pan.

SERVES 8 TO 10

Sweet Polenta-Orange Cake

This light and delicate cake from Joanne Weir has a very polenta-like taste.
She suggests serving it with a strawberry-rhubarb compote.

2 oranges

4 cups milk

½ cup sugar

1 cup fine yellow cornmeal

1 egg

4 egg yolks

4 tablespoons unsalted butter at room temperature

Grated rind of 1 large orange

Powdered sugar for dusting

⊚⊚ Peel the oranges with a vegetable peeler. Reserve oranges for another use. Combine the peels, milk and sugar in a saucepan. Bring to a boil over medium-high heat, then remove from heat. Let steep for 1 hour so the milk acquires a pronounced orange flavor. Strain and discard the peels.

Bring the milk to a boil over medium-high heat; gradually add the cornmeal, whisking constantly. Reduce heat to low and simmer for about 25 minutes, or until very thick. Let cool to lukewarm.

Preheat the oven to 375 degrees. Butter a 9-inch cake pan.

When the polenta has cooled, stir in the whole egg, the yolks, butter and orange rind.

Spread the mixture in the prepared pan and bake for 30 to 35 minutes, or until a cake tester comes out clean when inserted into the center of the cake and the top just begins to turn golden.

Turn out onto a cooling rack and let cool for 15 minutes. Dust with powdered sugar.

SERVES 10

Velvet Pound Cake

The name is a good clue to the wonderful texture of this cake by Flo Braker.
For optimum flavor and texture, make it 1 day ahead.

3 cups all-purpose flour

½ teaspoon salt

¼ teaspoon baking powder

¼ teaspoon baking soda

1 cup unsalted butter

3 cups sugar

6 eggs

1 teaspoon vanilla

1 cup sour cream

◉◉ Have all ingredients at room temperature. Adjust the rack to the lower third of the oven and preheat to 325 degrees. Grease and flour a 10-inch Bundt or tube pan.

Sift together the flour, salt, baking powder and baking soda into a bowl. Beat the butter with an electric mixer until soft and smooth. Gradually add the sugar, beating until the mixture is light and fluffy. Add the eggs, 1 at a time, beating well after each addition. Add the vanilla.

Stir in the dry ingredients alternately with the sour cream, beginning and ending with the dry ingredients. Spoon the batter into the prepared pan.

Bake for 1 hour and 20 minutes, or until a cake tester comes out clean when inserted into the center of the cake. Cool for 10 minutes, then remove the cake from the pan.

To serve, cut into thin slices.

SERVES 16 TO 20

Perfect Poppy Seed Cake

The black poppy seeds that dot this cake by Marion Cunningham add an interesting texture. The cake needs no frosting and is best served warm.

¾ cup butter at room temperature

1⅔ cups sugar

3 eggs

Zest of 1 lemon

2 tablespoons fresh lemon juice

1½ teaspoons vanilla

2⅔ cups cake flour

1½ teaspoons baking powder

½ teaspoon baking soda

½ teaspoon salt

1½ tablespoons poppy seeds

¾ cup buttermilk

◎◎ Preheat the oven to 350 degrees. Butter and flour a 9-by-13-inch cake pan.

Combine the butter and sugar in a medium-size bowl and beat with an electric mixer until well blended and smooth, occasionally scraping down the sides of the bowl with a rubber spatula.

Add the eggs, 1 at a time, beating well after each addition; continue beating until the batter is smooth. Add the lemon zest, lemon juice and vanilla and mix well.

Mix together the cake flour, baking powder, baking soda, salt and poppy seeds in another bowl. Stir with a fork, mixing well. Add the dry ingredients to the butter-sugar mixture alternately with the buttermilk in three additions, scraping down the sides of the bowl with a rubber spatula after each addition and beating until the batter is smooth.

Pour the batter into the prepared pan, using a spatula to spread the batter evenly.

Bake for about 30 minutes, or until a cake tester comes out clean when inserted into the center of the cake.

Remove the cake from the oven and let cool in the pan for 10 minutes before serving.

SERVES 12

Preserving Summer's Bounty

When fresh fruit and berries are plentiful, a good way to preserve their flavor is to purée the fruit with sugar and freeze the purée. For best results, mix equal parts of purée and sugar. Blend until the sugar dissolves, then transfer to freezer containers and freeze for up to six months. Fruit purée is great as a sauce for plain cakes and ice cream.

Chocolate Buttermilk Cake

It's the buttermilk that makes this cake light and tender, says Flo Braker.

2 cups sifted cake flour

1 teaspoon baking soda

¼ teaspoon salt

½ cup unsalted butter

1 cup sugar

2 eggs

1 teaspoon vanilla

2 ounces unsweetened chocolate, melted and cooled

1 cup buttermilk

Chocolate Buttermilk Frosting (recipe follows)

◉◉ Have all ingredients at room temperature. Adjust the rack to the lower third of the oven and preheat to 350 degrees. Grease and flour two 9-inch cake pans.

Sift the flour, baking soda and salt into a bowl; set aside.

Using an electric mixer, preferably with a paddle attachment, beat the butter until smooth. Add the sugar and continue to beat until light and fluffy. Add the eggs, 1 at a time, beating well after each addition. Beat in the vanilla, then the chocolate. Beat in the dry ingredients alternately with the buttermilk, beginning and ending with the dry ingredients.

Spoon equal amounts of batter into each cake pan, spreading it to level the top.

Bake for 22 to 25 minutes, or until a cake tester comes out clean when inserted into the center of the cakes. Cool in the pans on a wire rack for 10 minutes. Invert and remove pans; cool the cakes completely on racks before frosting. Spread the frosting between the layers, around the sides and on top of the cake.

SERVES 10

Chocolate Buttermilk Frosting

2 cups powdered sugar

⅛ teaspoon salt

2 tablespoons unsalted butter at room temperature

3 tablespoons buttermilk

4 ounces unsweetened chocolate, melted and cooled

1 teaspoon vanilla

◉◉   Using an electric mixer, beat together the sugar, salt and butter in a bowl. Slowly add the buttermilk, mixing until well blended and smooth. Blend in the chocolate and vanilla.

If the frosting is too runny, add more powdered sugar, 1 tablespoon at a time; if too thick, add more buttermilk, 1 teaspoon at a time, to achieve a spreading consistency.

FROSTS TWO 8- OR 9-INCH CAKE LAYERS

Raised Cheesecake

Even if you don't like cheesecake, you'll make an exception for this version by Marion Cunningham. A buttery pastry crust is filled with cream cheese, sour cream and eggs, which puff into a light, airy cloud during baking.

Pastry

1 cup all-purpose flour

½ cup butter at room temperature

1 egg yolk

2 tablespoons sugar

Filling

1 pound cream cheese

1 tablespoon all-purpose flour

½ cup sugar

4 eggs, separated

¼ cup whipping cream

¼ cup sour cream

2 teaspoons vanilla

¼ teaspoon salt

Before you begin making
a cheesecake, have the
cream cheese at room
temperature. Soft cheese
will blend more smoothly
with the other ingredients.
Don't worry if some very
tiny bits of cream cheese
remain. They will
magically melt while the
cheesecake bakes.

◉◉ Preheat the oven to 400 degrees.

To make the pastry: Combine the flour and butter in a bowl. Using an electric mixer, beat until well blended. Add the egg yolk and sugar and beat until well blended. Take apart a 9-inch springform pan with a removable bottom and press about half of the pastry into the bottom. Bake for about 8 minutes. Let cool. Attach the springform rim to the bottom of the pan, then press the remaining pastry all around the inside of the rim about halfway up. Don't worry if it is not even.

Reduce the oven temperature to 350 degrees.

To make the filling: Using an electric mixer, beat the cream cheese in a large bowl until soft. Add the flour and sugar and mix well. Add the egg yolks, whipping cream, sour cream and vanilla; beat well.

Combine the egg whites and salt in a bowl and beat to soft peaks. Fold the egg whites into the cheese mixture.

Pour the filling into the pastry-lined pan. Bake for about 45 minutes. Let cool.

Serve at room temperature.

SERVES 10

Tequila–Fresh Pineapple Cheese Pie

In this rich and creamy dessert by Jacqueline McMahan, tequila intensifies the flavor of fresh pineapple.

Crust
1¼ cups graham cracker crumbs

⅓ cup light brown sugar

4 tablespoons butter, melted

Filling
1 cup peeled and diced fresh pineapple

2 tablespoons plus ¾ cup sugar

2 tablespoons tequila

1 tablespoon Grand Marnier (optional)

1 teaspoon vanilla

1 pound cream cheese at room temperature

¾ cup sour cream, or Mexican crema

3 eggs

Topping

1 cup sour cream

Juice of ½ lime

1 tablespoon sugar

∞ To make the crust: Lightly butter a 10-inch-diameter glass pie dish. Combine the cracker crumbs, brown sugar and butter in a bowl. Pat the mixture firmly onto the bottom and up the sides of the pie dish.

Preheat the oven to 350 degrees.

To make the filling: Combine the pineapple and 2 tablespoons sugar in a saucepan. Cook over medium heat until the pineapple begins to release its juices. Add the tequila and Grand Marnier, if desired. Simmer for about 2 minutes, or until the tequila is just absorbed. Remove from heat and add the vanilla. Let cool to room temperature.

Blend together the cream cheese, sour cream and ¾ cup sugar in a large mixing bowl. Do not whip air into the mixture. Too much air makes the filling rise in the oven—and then fall.

Add the eggs, 1 at a time, blending slowly without whipping. Finally, add the cooled pineapple mixture.

Pour the filling into the crust, spreading it evenly. (There may be some leftover filling.) Bake for 30 to 35 minutes, or until the center is still a little wiggly.

To make the topping: While the pie is baking, combine the sour cream, lime juice and sugar in a bowl and blend well.

Spread the topping evenly over the cheese pie, return to the oven and bake for 5 minutes longer. The pie will continue to cook after it has been removed from the oven.

Cool, then refrigerate for at least 4 hours but preferably overnight before serving.

SERVES 10 TO 12

Is It Done Yet?

Many times, the first hint that a baked item is almost done is when its aroma fills the kitchen. But there are much better and more accurate ways to judge, says baking expert Flo Braker.

Cookies are finished baking when they're no longer shiny on top; the bottoms should be light brown. For crisp cookies, whether dropped, rolled or molded, bake until firm to the touch and pale gold in color. Bake most drop cookies, such as chocolate chip or oatmeal, just until pale gold yet still a bit soft in the center. As the cookies cool, their residual heat continues the baking process, so the end result is a tender-crisp cookie rather than an overbaked, tasteless one.

Oatmeal-Walnut–Chocolate Chip Cookies

David Chesarek of Black Cat restaurant in San Francisco was looking to create a cookie with the taste of a Toll House but the crispy, light character of a French tuile. The ratio of butter to flour is so high, we had calls questioning whether the recipe was correct. "Yes," says Chesarek, "the recipe is right." There is a trick to assure the cookies come out as intended: Pat the dough once it's on the baking sheet, just lightly pressing with your thumb. That will assure a more uniform but still delicate cookie. Watch the cookies carefully as they bake. They burn easily.

1¼ cups all-purpose flour

½ teaspoon baking powder

¼ teaspoon salt

1½ cups butter at room temperature

¾ cup granulated sugar

1 cup dark brown sugar

1 egg

1 teaspoon vanilla

3 tablespoons milk

1¼ cups instant oatmeal

14 ounces semisweet chocolate chips

1 cup chopped toasted walnuts

Sift together the flour, baking powder and salt into a bowl.

Using an electric mixer on low speed, beat the butter, granulated sugar and brown sugar until creamy. Blend in the egg, vanilla and milk. Add the sifted dry ingredients; mix on medium speed until just incorporated. Using a spatula, fold in the oatmeal, chocolate chips and walnuts.

Wrap the dough in plastic wrap and refrigerate for 4 hours, or until chilled.

Preheat the oven to 325 degrees. Line 2 baking sheets with parchment paper.

Drop generously rounded tablespoonfuls of dough onto the prepared baking sheets, spacing the cookies about 2 inches apart. Flatten the dough with your thumb into round disks.

Bake cookies for 15 to 18 minutes, or until lightly browned.

YIELDS 60 TO 70 COOKIES

Cakes are done when they spring back slightly when lightly touched in the center, the sides contract from the pan (especially butter cakes), and a toothpick inserted and then removed from the center comes out clean.

Flaky pie crusts and puff pastries are finished baking when golden in color; when stuck with a metal skewer, the pastry sounds crispy, not soft.

Brownies, chocolate butter cakes and dense chocolate cakes must not be overbaked, because the chocolate firms as it cools. Brownies and dense chocolate cakes should be slightly soft in the center when removed from the oven.

Christmas Nut Chews

Because these are soft, chewy cookies, often called "bar" cookies, you can also cut them into large pieces and serve them as dessert with a little whipped cream on top, says Marion Cunningham.

2 tablespoons butter

2 eggs

1 cup light brown sugar

⅓ cup all-purpose flour

⅛ teaspoon baking soda

¼ teaspoon salt

½ teaspoon vanilla

1 cup walnuts, coarsely chopped

👁 Preheat the oven to 350 degrees. Have ready an 8-inch-diameter pie plate or an 8-inch square baking pan.

Put the butter into a small saucepan over low heat. Tilt the pan as the butter begins to melt so it will melt evenly. Pour the melted butter into the pie plate and tilt and turn the plate until the bottom is completely covered with butter.

Using a fork, beat the eggs in a mixing bowl until well blended. Add the sugar, flour, baking soda, salt and vanilla. Using a large spoon, beat the batter until it is completely blended and smooth. Stir in the walnuts. Pour the batter into the prepared pan.

Bake for 12 to 15 minutes. After 10 minutes, check the dough by touching the center gently. If it feels firm, insert a toothpick into the center; if it comes out clean, the cookies are done. If in doubt, bake an extra 1 to 2 minutes.

Remove pan from oven and place on a wire rack to cool. Cut cookies into wedges or squares.

These freeze well if wrapped in 2 or 3 layers of plastic wrap.

YIELDS 12 TO 14 COOKIES

Lavender Shortbread

In the kitchen, lavender packs a triple sensory punch: color, aroma and flavor. Unlike its pungent presence in soaps, lavender benefits from restraint when used in making desserts, says Flo Braker. Cookies, such as these simple shortbreads, need only a hint of dried lavender—a bit more when you're using fresh blossoms. Subtlety is what you're after.

1 cup all-purpose flour

2 tablespoons white rice flour (see Note), or cornstarch

1 teaspoon dried lavender flowers (preferably English or French lavender)

⅛ teaspoon salt

½ cup unsalted butter at room temperature

¼ cup sugar, plus more for garnish

½ teaspoon lemon zest

½ teaspoon vanilla

◎ Adjust the rack to the lower third of the oven and preheat to 325 degrees.

Combine the all-purpose flour, rice flour, dried lavender and salt in a bowl; mix with a fork to blend. Mix the butter with ¼ cup sugar in a bowl until well blended, then add the lemon zest, vanilla and the dry ingredients, mixing just until incorporated. Press the dough with your fingertips into a 9-inch-diameter quiche pan, preferably with a removable bottom, and score 12 wedges with the tines of a fork. Sprinkle with sugar.

Bake for about 25 minutes, or until the shortbread appears set when lightly touched and is lightly colored.

Cool on a rack for 10 minutes, then cut into wedges. When cooler, remove from pan with the aid of a small metal spatula.

YIELDS 12 SHORTBREADS

NOTE: White rice flour is available in some supermarkets (check bins) and health-food stores.

Orange-Polenta Shortbread

These little golden triangles, inspired by the Italian countryside, were created by Shanna Masters, who was a culinary intern at The Chronicle *and now is editor of* Veggie Life.

½ cup butter

½ cup plus 2 teaspoons sugar

Zest of 1 orange

1 egg, lightly beaten

2 tablespoons orange juice concentrate

¾ cup yellow cornmeal

1 cup unbleached all-purpose flour

¼ teaspoon salt

∞ Preheat the oven to 325 degrees. Line a baking sheet with parchment paper.

Using an electric mixer, beat the butter with the ½ cup sugar and the orange zest until creamy. With the mixer running, add all but 1 teaspoon of the beaten egg and 1 teaspoon of the orange juice concentrate (combine the remaining egg and juice in a bowl and set aside). With the mixer still running, add the cornmeal, flour and salt, blending until incorporated.

Transfer the dough to a lightly floured surface and knead a few times, just until smooth. Pat and roll the dough into a 6-by-8-inch rectangle, about ¾ inch thick. Cut into small triangles and place about 1 inch apart on the prepared baking sheet. Brush with the reserved egg–orange juice mixture and sprinkle with the 2 teaspoons sugar.

Bake for 25 to 30 minutes, or until the edges are lightly browned. Remove to a rack to cool.

YIELDS ABOUT 2 DOZEN COOKIES

How to Grill Fruit

Some fruit is marvelous cooked over the coals, although because of the strong smell of the smoke, the fruit is generally better for savory rather than sweet dishes. But as long as the coals are going, experiment, says Marlena Spieler. The fruit can be grilled over either hot or medium-hot coals.

Peaches, nectarines, apricots and figs: Halve and pit stone fruit. Figs may be halved or left whole. Baste with a little honey mixed with white wine and grill, turning once, until just warmed through. Serve with ice cream or goat cheese and a sprinkling of sweet basil.

Walnut Wonder Bars

These easy but truly delicious cookies, made with a pastry crust and topped with a drizzle of sugar frosting, are from Marion Cunningham.

Crust

½ cup butter at room temperature

⅓ cup light brown sugar

1 egg

1¼ cups all-purpose flour

¼ teaspoon salt

1 teaspoon vanilla

Filling

2 eggs

1¼ cups light brown sugar

1½ cups chopped walnuts

2 tablespoons all-purpose flour

¾ teaspoon baking powder

½ teaspoon salt

2 teaspoons vanilla

Icing

1½ cups powdered sugar, sifted

1 to 2 tablespoons cold water, or as needed to make the icing spreadable

◉◉ Preheat the oven to 350 degrees. Grease a 9-by-13-inch baking pan.

To make the crust: Combine the butter and sugar in a mixing bowl and beat with an electric mixer until smooth and blended. Stir in the egg and mix well. Add the flour, salt and vanilla and mix well. Pat the dough evenly over the bottom of the prepared baking pan. Set aside.

To make the filling: Lightly beat the eggs in a mixing bowl until blended. Stir in the brown sugar and mix well. Add the walnuts, flour, baking powder, salt and vanilla. Stir until well mixed. Spread over the crust.

Bake for 20 to 25 minutes, or until the sides shrink away from the baking pan. Remove from the oven.

To make the icing: Mix together the sugar and water in a bowl until spreadable.

Pineapple: Before grilling, baste slices with brown sugar mixed with lime juice and butter. Serve with anything spicy, especially Mexican or Southeast Asian dishes. For a fire-and-ice ending, serve with pineapple sorbet.
Bananas: Grill alongside anything Mexican or marinated in Mexican-style seasoning paste.
Assorted fruits: Grill a mix of apples, pears, peaches, nectarines, figs and pieces of pineapple; remove from grill and splash fruit with liqueur, then serve with sorbet or ice cream and a big spoon.

Spread the icing on the bars while they are still hot. Cool completely and cut into squares.

YIELDS 12 LARGE SQUARES

Ginger Date Bars

The gooey-delicious combination of dates, crystallized ginger and walnuts gives these traditional confections by Flo Braker a sophisticated twist. For convenience, use chopped dates right from the package.

¾ cup all-purpose flour

¼ teaspoon baking powder

4 tablespoons unsalted butter

1 cup sugar

2 eggs

1 cup chopped walnuts

1 cup chopped dates

¼ cup chopped crystallized ginger

⊚⊚ Adjust the rack to the lower third of the oven and preheat to 350 degrees. Grease and flour a 9-inch square baking pan; line the pan with parchment paper or wax paper.

Sift or whisk the flour and baking powder in a small bowl to combine.

Using an electric mixer, beat the butter with the sugar in a bowl until creamy. Add the eggs and beat until just blended. Stir in the flour mixture, then the nuts, dates and crystallized ginger. Transfer to the prepared pan, spreading the batter evenly.

Bake for 30 minutes, or until light golden on top. Let cool in the pan for 5 minutes, then invert immediately onto a sheet of parchment or wax paper. Lift off the paper lining.

While warm, cut into 1½-inch squares with a sharp knife.

YIELDS ABOUT 3 DOZEN BARS

Chile Tranquilizers (Brownies with Chocolate Salsa)

These simple brownies often get more raves from Jacqueline McMahan's guests than complicated, fancy desserts. She calls them "chile tranquilizers" because they soothe the palate after a spicy meal.

½ cup butter

1 ounce semisweet chocolate

2 ounces unsweetened chocolate

½ cup light brown sugar

½ cup granulated sugar

2 tablespoons corn syrup

2 eggs

¾ cup all-purpose flour

¼ teaspoon baking powder

Pinch of salt

1 tablespoon vanilla

1 cup chopped walnuts

Chocolate Salsa (recipe follows)

◉◉ Preheat the oven to 350 degrees. Grease an 8-inch square baking pan.

Melt the butter, semisweet and unsweetened chocolate in a 2-quart saucepan over medium-low heat. Remove from heat and stir in the brown and granulated sugars and the corn syrup, blending until the sugars dissolve.

Beat in the eggs, 1 at a time. Add the flour, baking powder, salt, vanilla and walnuts. Pour into the prepared pan.

Bake for 30 minutes, or until a cake tester inserted into the center comes out with just a thin film of chocolate clinging to it.

Cut into squares while still warm. Serve napped with a couple tablespoons of Chocolate Salsa. (Beware: Diners will want more of the salsa, but let them help themselves to this particular sin.)

YIELDS 9 BROWNIES

Chocolate Salsa

3 ounces sweet chocolate (such as German's or Mexican Ibarra), roughly chopped

1 cup evaporated milk

Pinch of cinnamon

¼ cup sugar

2 tablespoons unsalted butter

1 teaspoon vanilla

◐◑ Combine the chocolate, milk, cinnamon, sugar and butter in a saucepan. Bring to a simmer over low heat, whisking until blended. Remove from heat and stir in the vanilla. Serve warm.

YIELDS 1½ CUPS

Fresh Apricot Cobbler

Fresh apricots make the best cobbler, as this recipe from Jacqueline McMahan demonstrates.

8 cups halved and pitted fresh apricots (you may also use peaches or cherries)

1 cup water

½ cup granulated sugar

½ cup light brown sugar

2 tablespoons cornstarch

2 tablespoons fresh lemon juice

½ teaspoon almond extract

Crust

2 cups all-purpose flour

2 tablespoons granulated sugar

½ teaspoon salt

½ cup shortening, cut into tablespoon-size pieces

⅓ cup unsalted butter, cut into tablespoon-size pieces

5 tablespoons ice water

1 tablespoon cider vinegar

1 teaspoon vanilla

1 tablespoon sugar mixed with ½ teaspoon cinnamon

Quick Fruit Dessert

Here are some easy ways to end the meal, from Marion Cunningham:

Persimmons: An old and beloved California recipe for persimmons (preferably Hachiya) is to freeze them, and then slice them. Sprinkle slices with brown sugar, and serve with a dollop of yogurt.

Papaya: Cut the papaya in half and seed it. Save 1 tablespoon of the seeds, rinse them and sprinkle over the fruit. Squeeze the juice of ½ lime over the top. This is very beguiling, especially with the surprising peppery crunch of the seeds.

Dates and figs: These are luscious stuffed with a little soft cheese and served with walnuts.

Combine 2 cups of the apricots with ½ cup of the water and the granulated and brown sugars in a blender or food processor and puree.

Combine the remaining ½ cup water, the cornstarch, lemon juice and almond extract in a bowl and stir to make a paste.

Combine the apricot purée and the cornstarch paste in a 4-quart saucepan. Bring to a simmer over medium-low heat. Simmer for about 5 minutes, or until the mixture is thick and clear. Stir in the remaining apricots. Spoon into a deep 9-by-12-inch baking dish. Let cool to room temperature.

To make the crust: Using a pastry blender or food processor, blend together the flour, sugar and salt. Add the shortening and butter and cut in to make a coarse, crumbly mixture. (Use short, on-and-off pulses if using a processor.) Combine the ice water, vinegar and vanilla in a bowl and drizzle over the flour mixture in 3 additions, stirring or pulsing in just enough liquid so the pastry holds together but is not wet.

Transfer the pastry to a floured work surface and push it together. Lightly form into a disk, wrap in plastic wrap and refrigerate for 20 to 30 minutes.

Preheat the oven to 375 degrees.

Roll out the pastry on a floured surface into a ¼-inch-thick rectangle. Place over the fruit, prick with a fork in several places, then sprinkle with the cinnamon sugar.

Bake for 35 minutes, or until the crust is golden and the fruit is bubbling and tender.

SERVES 8 TO 10

Oranges: Peel 4 or 5 oranges. Cut the sections into bite-size cubes or, to be a little fancier, remove the sections individually from the orange by cutting each one vertically between the white membrane. Stir ½ cup orange marmalade into the orange pieces; refrigerate until time to serve.

Strawberries: When strawberries are sweet and ripe, try serving them with their stems on with a bowl of sour cream and one of brown sugar, so you can dip the berries into the cream and sugar, then pop them right into your mouth.

Trio Fruit Crumble

Flo Braker uses strawberries, rhubarb and pineapple in this crunchy crumble that relies on granola for texture. Serve it warm or at room temperature with a few spoonfuls of heavy cream, crème anglaise or a scoop of vanilla ice cream.

Crumble Topping

1 cup plus 2 tablespoons all-purpose flour

2 cups granola

½ cup light brown sugar

½ cup granulated sugar

1 teaspoon baking powder

½ teaspoon ground ginger

⅛ teaspoon salt

¾ cup butter at room temperature

Fruit

1 pint strawberries, hulled and sliced

1½ cups rhubarb (stalks without leaves weighing about 9 ounces),
     cut into ½-inch slices

8 ounces peeled fresh pineapple, cut into small wedges (1 cup)

2 teaspoons finely grated orange zest

3 tablespoons fresh orange juice

⅓ cup granulated sugar

1½ tablespoons cornstarch

To make the topping: Combine the flour, granola, brown and granulated sugars, baking powder, ginger and salt in the large bowl of an electric mixer, preferably with a paddle attachment; mix on low speed. Add the butter and blend until the mixture has a crumbly consistency similar to a coarse streusel; set aside.

Adjust the rack to the lower third of the oven and preheat to 350 degrees. Set six 8-ounce ramekins on a baking sheet.

To make the fruit: Toss the strawberries, rhubarb, pineapple, orange zest and juice in a large bowl to combine. Pour the sugar and cornstarch into a small sieve and sprinkle over the fruit mixture; toss again to combine.

Divide the fruit mixture among the ramekins. Top each ramekin with about ½ cup crumble topping. Don't pat the topping to pack it down.

Bake for 30 minutes, or until the topping is light golden.

SERVES 6

Oven-Roasted Figs with Crème Fraîche

When figs are roasted, their natural sugars begin to caramelize and the flavors deepen and intensify. Georgeanne Brennan says they are wonderful with the addition of crème fraîche.

8 soft, ripe figs

2 tablespoons sugar

½ cup crème fraîche, or 6 tablespoons sour cream mixed with 2 tablespoons
    whipping cream

4 mint sprigs for garnish

◉ Preheat the oven to 400 degrees.

Butter a shallow roasting pan just large enough to hold the figs. Place the figs in the pan and turn them once or twice. Sprinkle with the sugar.

Bake for 10 to 12 minutes, or until the figs are warmed through and just beginning to caramelize. Remove the pan from the oven and let stand for 5 minutes.

Place 2 figs on each plate and drizzle 2 tablespoons crème fraîche over each serving. Garnish with the mint sprigs.

SERVES 4

Peaches and Berries in Herbed Red Wine

This easy-to-toss-together recipe by Marlena Spieler is based on the Italian tradition of slicing peaches into a glass of lusty red wine. Spieler uses a California Zinfandel with a splash of cassis and a few fresh basil leaves. The sweet fragrance of the herb has a real affinity for peaches. If you find cinnamon basil in the farmers' market or your local nursery, this recipe is a great place to use it.

6 perfectly ripe peaches or nectarines

1 cup fruity red wine, such as Zinfandel

Sugar, to taste (a small amount; the cassis is quite sweet)

1 to 2 tablespoons cassis

6 to 8 fresh basil leaves, slivered

1 basket berries: blackberries, olallieberries, raspberries, strawberries or blueberries

1 pint sorbet, such as peach and/or raspberry, or a sorbet/ice cream mix

◉◉ Slice the peaches into a bowl and add the wine, sugar, cassis and basil; toss to combine. Fold in the berries. Refrigerate until ready to serve.

Serve each portion with a scoop or so of sorbet.

SERVES 4

Strawberries with Whipped Ricotta

Janet Fletcher recommends this easy fruit dessert for a picnic. Whipped sweetened ricotta makes a luscious dipping sauce for whole strawberries.

15 ounces whole-milk ricotta cheese

¼ cup honey

¼ Tahitian vanilla bean (cut 1 whole bean crosswise to halve, then halve 1 piece lengthwise)

2 pounds strawberries

Grilled Peaches

For a quick dessert during peach season, halve and pit peaches and sprinkle with lemon juice. Place cut-side down on a hot grill or indoor grill pan. Cook for 1 to 2 minutes, or until grill marks form and peaches are warm. Serve grilled-side up with a dollop of mascarpone, whipped cream or ice cream. This same technique also works well with thick slices of fresh pineapple.

oo   Put the ricotta in a food processor and purée until it is completely smooth. Add the honey and blend again. Scrape the tiny seeds from the vanilla pod into the whipped cheese. Blend again. The mixture should be soft and creamy.

Spoon the mixture into a plastic container, cover with a lid and refrigerate.

To serve, put a dollop of whipped ricotta and a few strawberries on each plate.

SERVES 8

Watermelon Sherbet

This pale-pink dessert looks as good as it tastes. It's the creation of Shanna Masters, who was a Food Department intern and now is editor of Veggie Life.

2 cups chilled watermelon juice (see Note)
⅔ cup whipping cream
⅓ cup sugar, or to taste
1 tablespoon Triple Sec, or other orange-flavored liqueur

oo   Combine all ingredients in a bowl; stir until the sugar dissolves. Freeze according to the manufacturer's directions.

Or, pour into a freezer container, cover tightly and freeze solid. Break the frozen sherbet into chunks and process in a food processor. Return to the freezer to firm up for about 1 hour before serving.

YIELDS ABOUT 1 QUART

NOTE: A 3-pound piece of watermelon should yield about 1 quart of juice. Cut the flesh into chunks, discard seeds, then purée the flesh in a blender or food processor. Strain the juice and refrigerate until chilled before using.

Gin and Tonic Granita

One summer evening in London when Marlena Spieler was totally deflated by the heat, she decided to whip up a gin and tonic granita. Since alcohol doesn't freeze solid, this comes out icy and cool—perfect for a sizzling evening. It probably will take all day to freeze, so start it either in the morning or the night before.

1½ cups tonic water

2 to 3 tablespoons sugar

⅔ cup gin

1 large or 2 smallish lemons, thinly sliced

Combine the tonic and sugar in small saucepan. Cook over medium heat, stirring, for about 5 minutes, or until the sugar dissolves. Remove from heat and let cool to room temperature.

Stir in the gin, then pour the mixture into a shallow bowl or pan. Freeze for about 2 hours, or until partially frozen; check at 1 hour to mark its progress. When the mixture starts to freeze around the edges, scrape a fork over the ice, then stir those icy crystals back into the mixture. Repeat freezing and scraping until the granita has an icy-soft, sorbet-like consistency.

To serve, spoon the mixture into glasses, layering it with lemon slices as you go. Serve immediately since the gin makes the mixture defrost.

SERVES 4

Cool Melons

During melon season, here's one of the best desserts. Halve and seed a cantaloupe or other melon and refrigerate. When ready to serve, pour about 2 ounces of port into the center of each half.

Coconut Ice Cream

Flo Braker makes this wonderful ice cream with the singular flavor of coconut. It's great by itself, with chocolate sauce or as an accompaniment to a thick slice of Velvet Pound Cake (see recipe, page 421).

1½ cups milk

1 cup medium-shred unsweetened coconut

¾ cup sugar

5 egg yolks

1 can (14 ounces) pure unsweetened coconut milk

½ cup whipping cream

◈ Combine the milk, coconut and ¼ cup of the sugar in a large saucepan and bring to a boil over medium-low heat.

Beat the yolks in a large bowl, gradually beating in the remaining ½ cup sugar.

As the milk comes to a boil, strain a small amount into the yolks and mix well. Strain the remaining milk into the yolks, blending thoroughly. Be sure to press as much milk from the coconut as you can. Discard the coconut (its flavor is now infused into the milk).

Return the custard to the saucepan and bring just to a boil over medium heat, stirring constantly. Remove from heat and stir in the coconut milk.

Refrigerate for about 4 hours, or until cold.

Stir in the whipping cream and freeze according to the manufacturer's directions.

YIELDS ABOUT 1 QUART

Spearmint Custard Ice Cream

Shanna Masters' mint ice cream is the best we've tasted, with an intense mint flavor. The secret? Fresh mint leaves and crème de menthe in a rich custard base. Unlike fresh (uncooked) ice creams, this version has a dense texture, closer to that of store-bought ice cream. It's the perfect filling for ice-cream sandwiches made with chewy chocolate cookies. Or, serve alongside a deep chocolate brownie, still warm from the oven.

1 cup milk

1 egg

½ cup sugar

1 tablespoon minced fresh mint leaves

1 tablespoon crème de menthe

1 cup whipping cream

◉◉ Combine the milk, egg, sugar and mint in the top of a double boiler; whisk to blend. Place over simmering water and cook, stirring, for about 15 minutes, or until the mixture thickens slightly and coats the back of the spoon. Remove from heat and stir in the crème de menthe and cream. Refrigerate for about 4 hours, or until cold.

Freeze according to the manufacturer's directions.

Or, pour into a freezer container, cover tightly and freeze solid. Break the frozen ice cream into chunks and process in a food processor. Return to the freezer to firm up for about 1 hour before serving.

YIELDS ABOUT 3½ CUPS

Glossary of Ingredients

Anaheim pepper: This fresh, slender chile is bright green, shiny and about 7 inches long. It is gently spicy and has a pleasant flavor. Available in many supermarkets and produce markets.

Arborio rice: A short-grain Italian rice traditionally used for risotto.

Arugula (rocket): A bitterish salad green with a peppery mustard flavor. A great addition to mixed green salads, or use instead of lettuce on sandwiches; add it to soups and sautés, or use as a bed for roasted meats and poultry.

Asadero cheese: Mexican melting cheese with a buttery, slightly tangy flavor.

Asian fish sauce (nuoc mam): A salty fish extract used to season Southeast Asian foods and make dipping sauces. Available in Asian markets and some supermarkets.

Balsamic vinegar: A pungent sweet-sour Italian vinegar made from Trebbiano grapes. It is aged in barrels made of different woods and of gradually diminishing sizes until it becomes dark, thick, complex and richly flavored. The oldest vinegars will be the best and the most expensive.

Basmati rice: A long-grain rice with a perfumed, nutlike flavor and a fine texture. Traditionally used in Indian and Middle Eastern cuisines.

Cannellini beans (white kidney beans): Used mainly in Italian cooking, these beans are similar to great Northerns, but they retain a firmer texture when cooked. Available dried and canned.

Cardamom: Related to ginger, this aromatic Indian spice is an essential ingredient in curries. Three main varieties are available: white (tan), black and green. The pods range in size from ¼ to ½ inch long; the seeds inside are tiny and black, with a pungent, almost lemony flavor and aroma. Cardamom is available ground or in the pod.

Cellophane noodles (bean thread noodles): These very thin, translucent noodles are made from the starch of green mung beans. They add an intriguing silky-slippery texture to soups and stir-fries. When deep-fried, they puff up into a white, crispy mass. Available in Asian markets and the ethnic section of some supermarkets.

Chile paste: A Chinese/Southeast Asian product containing chile peppers, salt, oil and often garlic. Available in Asian markets and some supermarkets.

Chipotle chiles: These are smoked jalapeño chiles. They're sold both dried and canned in adobo, a spicy brick-red marinade. Once opened, transfer the canned chiles and their marinade to a clean glass jar with a tight-fitting lid and store in the refrigerator. They will keep for several months. Available in Latin markets and some supermarkets.

Clarified butter (desi ghee): When butter is melted over low heat, the milk solids will settle to the bottom of the pan, leaving the clear (clarified) butter on top. See also ghee.

Coconut milk, coconut cream: Made from the grated and steeped meat of coconuts, this pearly white liquid is sold in cans. When coconut milk stands, it separates, with the thick coconut cream rising to the top. Available in Asian markets and most supermarkets.

Crème fraîche: A lightly soured cream used in both sweet and savory dishes. Although it is somewhat like sour cream, it does not curdle when used in hot preparations. Available in many supermarkets.

Curry leaves: See kari leaves.

Daikon: A giant white Japanese radish. Ranging from 6 inches to over 2 feet long, daikon has a peppery flavor and juicy, crisp texture. May be used like other radishes, or added to stir-fries or braises.

Desi ghee: See clarified butter.

Escarole: A bitter green with broad, pale-green leaves. It is related to endive, but the flavor is milder. Used mainly in salads, it may also be added to stir-fries or braises. Available year-round.

Fava beans (broad beans, horse beans): Available fresh or dried, these legumes resemble large lima beans. The fresh beans must be shelled and peeled before using. Favas are a popular ingredient in Mediterranean and Middle Eastern cuisines, and were used by the early California rancho cooks.

Fenugreek: An ocher yellow, square and somewhat flat seed with a bittersweet flavor. Available whole or ground, it is commonly used in Indian cooking: spice blends (notably curry powder), soups, stews and beverages.

Five-spice powder (also called Chinese five-spice powder): A blend of spices used in Chinese cooking. Usually includes equal parts of ground cinnamon, star anise, fennel seeds, cloves and Sichuan peppercorns. Available in Asian markets and some supermarkets.

Galangal (Siamese or Thai ginger, laos): Related to ginger, this thin-skinned rhizome is pale yellow with zebralike markings and pink shoots. It is available fresh or dried. When dried, it is generally called *laos*. It is used extensively in Thai cooking.

Garam masala: An Indian spice blend that may contain any number of spices but commonly includes cinnamon, cloves, chile pepper, black pepper, coriander, cumin, cardamom, fennel, mace and nutmeg. Usually added to a dish just before it is finished, or sprinkled over it just before serving. Available in Indian, Middle Eastern and some gourmet stores.

Ghee: Clarified butter that has been simmered until all the moisture has evaporated and the milk solids have "caramelized," giving the butter a nutty flavor, a higher smoking point (375 degrees) and a longer shelf life than regular clarified butter. Used extensively in Indian cooking, it is available in Indian, Middle Eastern and some gourmet stores.

Jaggery (palm sugar): A dark, coarse, unrefined sugar made from the sap of various palm trees or from sugarcane juice. Used primarily in India, it comes in a soft form or solid blocks. Available in Indian markets.

Jicama: A Latin American root vegetable with a tan skin and white flesh. It has a crisp, somewhat juicy texture and sweet-starchy flavor. This bulbous root may be used raw in salads or as a garnish, or it may be cooked in soups, stews or stuffings. It is a good substitute for fresh water chestnuts in Asian stir-fries.

Kaffir lime leaves: These jade-green leaves are shaped like a figure eight. Used in Asian curries, soups and stir-fries, the leaves impart a lemony aroma. Fresh leaves are difficult to find, but dried and frozen ones are carried in many Southeast Asian markets.

Kari leaves (curry leaves): Small, shiny, dark-green leaves of the curry bush (not related to curry powder) that are often used in Indian cooking. The flavor enhances lentil and rice dishes, soups, stews and raitas. The fresh and dried leaves are carried in Indian markets, although supplies of fresh leaves are erratic.

Lemongrass: This lemon-flavored herb resembles a long, somewhat dried-out green onion with thin, gray-green leaves and an off-white base. It is a common ingredient in Thai cooking. Available in Asian markets, specialty produce markets and some supermarkets.

Lily buds (tiger lily buds, golden needles): These are the dried buds of the day lily plant. Used in Chinese cooking, these 2- to 3-inch-long light golden buds have a delicate musky-sweet flavor. They must be rehydrated in warm water before using. Available in Asian markets.

Mexican crema: A thick, slightly sour cream used in Mexican dishes. Similar to sour cream, it is available in Latin markets and some supermarkets.

Mirin (sweetened rice wine): This Japanese low-alcohol cooking wine, made from glutinous rice, is used in a multitude of dishes, including sauces, glazes, soups and dips. It is available in Asian markets and most supermarkets.

Nuoc mam: See Asian fish sauce.

Orzo: A small rice-shaped pasta.

Palm sugar: See jaggery.

Pancetta: Italian unsmoked bacon cured with pepper, salt and spices. It is used much like bacon to flavor vegetable dishes, sauces, soups, stews, meats and pastas.

Panko: These Japanese breadcrumbs look like white flakes and are usually found in cellophane packages. Available in Asian supermarkets and ethnic section of some supermarkets. Regular breadcrumbs may be substituted.

Pecorino romano: An Italian sheep's milk cheese with a sharp flavor and hard, granular texture. It is used much like Parmigiano-Reggiano.

Polenta: A Northern Italian mushlike dish made from coarsely ground yellow cornmeal. Soft polenta often is used as a base for braised meats or stews; firm polenta can be cut into shapes and baked, or fried in butter or olive oil.

Portobello mushroom: A common brown mushroom that has been allowed to grow, reaching 6 to 7 inches in diameter.

Queso anejo: Any aged Mexican cheese. It has a hard texture and pungent aroma and is used as a grating cheese.

Queso cotija: Similar to queso fresco, this cheese is a bit drier and saltier. It is firm enough to be grated.

Glossary of Grains

Arborio rice: Shorter and fatter than any other rice, this high-starch rice is used primarily in risotto because the starchiness gives the Italian rice dish its creamy quality.

To cook: Gradually add hot stock or water to the rice, stirring constantly over medium-high heat. Add the hot liquid about ½ cup at a time, and when the liquid is absorbed, add ½ cup more. Continue to add, stir and reduce until all the liquid is absorbed and the grains are creamy outside, with just a touch of resistance inside. One cup of rice will absorb approximately 4 cups liquid, and takes 20 to 25 minutes to cook. One cup of uncooked rice yields about 3 cups cooked.

Barley: This round, ivory-colored grain dates back to the Stone Age. Today, much of it is used for animal feed or is malted to make beer or whiskey. Pearl barley has the husk and bran removed and has been steamed and polished. Hulled or whole-grain barley has just the outer hull removed and is more nutritious but not as readily available.

To cook: Cook 1 cup barley in 3 cups boiling water, uncovered, for 40 to 50 minutes, or until tender but still firm to the bite. Drain any excess liquid. One cup of raw barley yields about 3 cups cooked.

Bulgur wheat: Also called cracked wheat, bulgur is the whole kernel of wheat that has been steamed, dried and crushed. It is a staple of Middle Eastern cooking.

To cook: Pour 2 cups boiling water over 1 cup bulgur, cover and let stand for about 30 minutes, or until the liquid is absorbed. Uncover and fluff with a fork.

For a slightly more tender grain, cook 1 cup bulgur in 2½ cups boiling water for 15 minutes. Cover the pan, remove from the heat and let bulgur steam for 10 minutes, or until all the liquid is absorbed.

One cup of uncooked bulgur yields about 2¾ cups cooked.

Kasha: In this country, kasha refers to toasted buckwheat groats. In Russia, it means any cooked grain. Don't confuse kasha with kashi, a cereal mixture available in some health-food stores.

To cook: The traditional method starts with dry-toasting 1 cup kasha with 1 beaten egg in a skillet over medium heat, stirring with a fork until the mixture is dry. This step keeps the grains from sticking together, but it isn't necessary. Cook 1 cup kasha in 2½ cups boiling liquid, covered, for about 20 minutes, or until all the liquid is absorbed. Fluff with a fork. One cup of uncooked kasha yields 2½ to 3 cups cooked.

Millet: In the United States, millet is cultivated almost exclusively for bird and animal feed, but serves as a food staple for about one third of the world, including much of Africa.

To cook: Cook 1 cup millet in 4 cups simmering water, uncovered, for about 30 minutes, or until the water is absorbed and grains are tender. One cup of uncooked millet yields about 4 cups cooked.

Quinoa: Many people consider this a "super grain" because it's so high in protein. It was a staple for the Incas in Peru but is fairly new to the United States.

To cook: Rinse the grains before cooking. Cook 1 cup quinoa in 3 cups simmering liquid, uncovered, for about 30 minutes, or until the grains are tender and the liquid is absorbed. One cup of uncooked quinoa yields about 3 cups cooked.

Wheat berries: These are whole, unprocessed wheat kernels that have a rich, nutty flavor and chewy texture. They can be used in pilafs, breakfast cereals, soups and vegetable gratins.

To cook: Soak wheat berries in water overnight. Drain, then cook 1 cup wheat berries in 3 cups simmering liquid, uncovered, for about 1 hour, or until tender. Drain any excess liquid. One cup of uncooked wheat berries yields about 3 cups cooked.

Wild rice: This nutty, firm-textured grain isn't a rice at all but rather a marsh grass indigenous to the Great Lakes region. Now it's cultivated in many parts of the country.

To cook: Cook 1 cup wild rice in 4 to 5 cups boiling water, uncovered, for about 45 minutes, or until most of the grains split. Drain any excess liquid. One cup of uncooked wild rice yields about 4 cups cooked.

Queso fresco: A crumbly fresh cheese similar to feta, used in Mexican cooking. It has a delicate, slightly acid flavor. Available in Latin markets and some supermarkets.

Sesame oil, Asian: Pressed from toasted sesame seeds, this dark amber oil has a rich, nutty taste and is used as an accent flavor for Asian or Asian-style dishes. Once opened, it should be refrigerated. Available in Asian markets and many supermarkets.

Seven-spice pepper: See shichimi.

Shaoxing wine: Chinese wine made of glutinous rice, rice millet and a special yeast. Golden in color, it is similar to dry sherry in flavor and aroma. Available in Asian markets and some supermarkets.

Shichimi (seven-spice pepper): A spicy Japanese seasoning containing chile peppers, black pepper, sesame seeds, poppy seeds, hemp seeds, ground orange peel and powdered nori. Available in Japanese markets and some supermarkets.

Soba: A taupe-colored Japanese noodle made of wheat flour and buckwheat flour. Available fresh or dried in Japanese markets and many supermarkets.

Soy sauce: This fermented soybean product comes in two forms: light and dark. Light soy sauce (also called thin soy sauce) has a more delicate flavor and is used mainly in seafood and vegetable dishes, soups and dipping sauces. Dark soy sauce (also called black soy sauce) is darker, thicker and has a stronger flavor; it is generally used for more robust dishes.

Tahini: Sesame seed paste. This Middle Eastern ingredient resembles peanut butter and is used to flavor dishes such as hummus and baba ghanoush. Available in Middle Eastern markets and some supermarkets.

Tamarind: Also known as "Indian dates," tamarind seeds have a sweet-sour flavor and are used much like lemon juice. Unlike lemon juice, however, tamarind's sourness does not dissipate with prolonged cooking. Tamarind is available in Indian, Middle Eastern and some Asian and Latin markets in various forms: jars of liquid concentrate, cellophane-wrapped blocks of pulp with seeds, canned paste and whole dried pods.

Tomatillos (Mexican green tomatoes): Except for its papery husk, this fruit— a member of the nightshade family— resembles a small green tomato. It has a clean flavor with hints of lemon and herbs. Tomatillos can be used raw or cooked. Available fresh in Latin markets, farmers' markets, specialty produce markets and some supermarkets. They're also available canned.

Truffle oil: Olive oil scented with shavings of French black or Italian white truffles. Used sparingly to add an earthy aroma and flavor to dishes such as pastas, risottos, salads, soups and vegetable terrines. Sold in small bottles, this product is fairly expensive, but a little goes a long way.

Udon: A Japanese noodle made of white flour, salt and water. May be flat or round. Available fresh or dried in Japanese markets and many supermarkets.

Wood ear mushrooms (tree ear, cloud ear, black fungus): A variety of dried mushroom used in Asian cuisines. Sold in cellophane packages, these mushrooms must be rehydrated in warm water before using. They have little flavor but add a pleasant rubbery-crunchy texture to dishes. Available in Asian markets and some supermarkets.

Zest: The outermost skin of a citrus fruit. The easiest way to "zest" is with a round-holed zester. A vegetable peeler can also be used to take off only the colored outer skin, leaving the bitter white pith behind. Zest, primarily from lemon, lime and orange, is used in both savory and sweet dishes to intensify the citrus flavor.

Mail-Order and Online Sources

Asian, Pacific Rim and Latino Ingredients

The Chile Shop

109 E. Water St.
Santa Fe, NM 87501
(505) 983-6080
Fax: (505) 984-0737
Catalog available. No online ordering yet, but check out their Web site: www.thechileshop.com.

Chile powders and pods, including Dixon chile powder and some hard-to-find heirloom varieties, salsas, sauces and more.

Mo Hotta-Mo Betta

P.O. Box 4136
San Luis Obispo, CA 93403
(800) 462-3220
Fax: (800) 618-4454 or (805) 545-8389
Online ordering: www.mohotta@ mohotta.com

African, Asian, Caribbean, Indian, Latin American and regional American ingredients. A variety of dried chile peppers, spices, hot sauces, seasoning mixes, curry pastes, spicy condiments, salsas and more.

Santa Fe School of Cooking

116½ West San Francisco St.
Santa Fe, NM 87501
(505) 983-4511
Fax: (505) 983-7540
E-mail: cooking@net.com
Web site/online ordering: www.santafeschoolof cooking.com

Specializing in New Mexican and other Southwestern ingredients, such as sauces, condiments, beans, herbs, spices and dried chiles, as well as corn and blue corn products.

Spice Merchant

P.O. Box 524
Jackson Hole, WY 83001
(800) 551-5999
Fax: (307) 733-6343
E-mail: stirfry@compuserve.com
Online ordering: www.emall.com/Spice/ Spice1.html

Wide selection of Chinese, Thai, Indonesian, Japanese and Indian specialties, including noodles, rice, flours and grains, teas, spices, herbs, sauces, vinegars, oils, pastes and condiments.

Cheeses and Charcuterie

Dean and DeLuca

2526 East 36th St.
North Circle
Wichita, KS 67219
(800) 221-7714 or (212) 226-7714
Fax: (800) 781-4050
E-mail: atyourservice@ deandeluca.com
Online ordering: www.deandeluca.com

Selection of gourmet and specialty foods, with a large variety of domestic and imported cheeses, smoked items, caviar, truffles, foie gras, sausages and wursts, herbs, spices, honeys, oils and vinegars.

Specialty Cheese Co.

455 South River Street
Lowell, WI 53557
(800) 367-1711
Fax: (920) 927-3200
E-mail: specialcheese@ globaldialog.com
Online ordering: www.specialcheese.com

Ethnic cheeses from around the world, including Mexican queso blanco, queso fresco, panela, asadero, cotija and anejo, as well as crema Mexicana and crema agria. Also Indian paneer, jibneh and ackawi.

Vella Cheese Company of California
315 Second Street East
P.O. Box 191
Sonoma, CA 95476
(800) 848-0505 or
(707) 938-3232
Fax: (707) 938-4307
Online ordering:
www.vellacheese.com
  A variety of domestic cheeses, plain and flavored.

Flours and Baking Needs

King Arthur Flour
Route 5 South
Norwich, VT 05055
(800) 827-6836
E-mail: Bakers@
KingArthurFlour.com
Online ordering:
www.kingarthurflour.com
  Wide selection of baking needs, including specialty flours and grains; tools and equipment; yeasts and starters; cookie, cake, pie and pastry ingredients and more.

Specialty Produce

Frieda's
Online ordering:
www.friedas.com
  Selection of specialty produce, including fresh and dried chiles and mushrooms. Web site also supplies information on stores in your state that carry Frieda's products.

Contributors' Notes

Flo Braker has written "The Baker" column for *The Chronicle* since 1986. She lives in Palo Alto and for the past 24 years has taught baking techniques all across the United States. She is the author of *The Simple Art of Perfect Baking* (William Morrow) and *Sweet Miniatures* (Chronicle Books).

Georgeanne Brennan, a cookbook author and *Chronicle* food columnist, divides her time between her small Northern California farm and Provence, where she runs a cooking school. She is the author of many cookbooks, including *Potager: Fresh Garden Cooking in the French Style* (Chronicle Books), *The Glass Pantry* (Chronicle Books) and *The New American Vegetable Cookbook* (Aris Books).

Marion Cunningham, the "Learning to Cook" columnist for *The Chronicle*, lives in Walnut Creek and is known as the modern-day Fannie Farmer. She is the author of two revisions of *The Fannie Farmer Cookbook*. She also has written *The Fannie Farmer Baking Book*, *The Supper Book*, *Cooking with Children* and *Learning to Cook with Marion Cunningham* (all Alfred A. Knopf).

Robin Davis has been a staff writer and restaurant reviewer at *The Chronicle* since 1996, and is the recipient of the 2000 James Beard feature writing award for journalism. A graduate of the California Culinary Academy, she worked as an assistant editor at *Bon Appétit* in Los Angeles before moving back to San Francisco. She is the author of *The Star Wars Cookbook: Wookiee Cookies and other Galactic Recipes* and *Infusions* (Chronicle Books).

Tara Duggan is a staff writer for *The Chronicle*'s Food Section, where she has been writing "The Working Cook" column since 1999. She is a graduate of the California Culinary Academy and a former writer and editor for *Fodor*'s travel guides.

Janet Fletcher, a former cook at Chez Panisse, has been a *Chronicle* staff writer since 1995 and lives in the Napa Valley. Her many honors include the James Beard journalism award for wine writing in 1999 and the Bert Green award for food writing in 2000. She is the author of *Fresh from the Farmers' Market*, *Pasta Harvest* and *The Cheese Course* (all Chronicle Books).

Laxmi Hiremath is an East Bay cooking teacher and food writer. She grew up in Bombay and is the author of *Laxmi's Vegetarian Kitchen* (Harlow and Ratner).

Jacqueline Higuera McMahan, who was raised on one of the last Bay Area ranchos, is the "South to North" columnist for *The Chronicle*. She is the author of numerous books, including *California Rancho Cooking*, *The Salsa Book*, *The Chipotle Chile Cook Book*, *The Red and Green Chile Book*, *Healthy Fiesta* and *The Mexican Breakfast Cookbook* (all Olive Press).

Mai Pham, *The Chronicle*'s "East to West" columnist, is the chef/owner of Lemon Grass Restaurant in Sacramento. Originally from Saigon, Pham worked as a television reporter and anchor in Washington, D.C., and Sacramento. She is the author of *The Best of Vietnamese and Thai Cooking* (Prima Publishing).

Shirley Sarvis lives in San Francisco and is one of the pioneers in food and wine matching. She consults with wineries and restaurants and writes for many national publications. She is the author of more than a dozen cookbooks, including *The Best of Scandinavian Cooking: Danish, Norwegian and Swedish* (Hippocrene Books).

Marlena Spieler divides her time between San Francisco and London, where she makes regular appearances on the BBC. She is the author of more than 35 cookbooks, including *The Vegetarian Bistro* (Chronicle Books), *Beggars' Banquet* (Piatkus Books) and *101 Essential Tips: Barbecuing* (DK Publishers).

Joanne Weir wrote the "Mediterranean Express" column for *The Chronicle*, and is currently starring in the PBS cooking show "Weir Cooking in the Wine Country"; she also wrote the companion book, *Weir Cooking: Recipes from the Wine Country* (Time-Life Books). Weir travels and teaches cooking all over the world. She is the author of *From Tapas to Meze* (Crown Publishers) and *You Say Tomato* (Broadway Books).

Permissions

The recipes on page 30 and 243 are from *Savoring France* by Georgeanne Brennan. Copyright © 1999 by Georgeanne Brennan. Reprinted by permission of Weldon Owen, Inc. ◉◉ The recipe on page 345 is from *The Fannie Farmer Baking Book* by Marion Cunningham. Copyright © 1984 by Marion Cunningham. Reprinted by permission of Alfred A. Knopf, Inc. ◉◉ The recipe on page 353 is from *The Breakfast Book* by Marion Cunningham. Copyright © 1987 by Marion Cunningham. Reprinted by permission of Alfred A. Knopf, Inc. ◉◉ The recipe on page 154–155 is from *Rancho Cooking: Mexican and Californian Recipes* by Jacqueline Higuera McMahan. Copyright © 2001 by Jacqueline Higuera McMahan. Reprinted by permission of Sasquatch Books.

Index

A

Aioli, Backward Spanish, 389
All-American Spaghetti Sauce, 127
All-Purpose Marinade, 264
Almonds
 blanching, 380
 Iron Horse Party Mix, 4
 Left Bank Almond Cake, 419
 Mandorlata di Peperoni (Bell Pepper and Almond Relish), 380
 Oven-Baked Quinoa Pilaf, 130
 Tomato and Almond Pesto, 128
 Wheat Berries with Ricotta, Almonds and Honey, 334
Alsatian Apple Cake, 414
Anchovies
 Bagna Cauda, 392
 John Caputo's Anchoiade, 386–87
 Perciatelli with Anchovies and Breadcrumbs, 107–8
Angolan Prawns, 319
Anne Gingrass's Green Olive Risotto, 140
Apples
 Alsatian Apple Cake, 414
 Apple–Sour Cream Coffee Cake, 347–48
 Curried Turkey Salad with Apple and Walnuts, 87
 Zucchini with Apple and Mint, 210
Apricots
 Fresh Apricot Cobbler, 434–35
 grilling, 430
 Lamb Tagine with Dried Apricots, 245–46

Arroz Caldo (Filipino Rice Porridge), 54–55
Arroz con Rajas y Crema, 159
Arroz Rojo, 131–32
Artichokes
 Artichoke Heart Pâté, 21
 Asparagus, Artichokes and Peas, 186
 Grandmama's Artichoke Frittatas, 356–57
 grilling, 212
Arugula
 French-Style Cobb Salad, 79
 Grilled Lavender Chicken on Arugula, 261
 Pappardelle with Arugula, Cherry Tomatoes and Breadcrumbs, 101
 Three-Cheese Pizza with Arugula, 176–77
Asian Greens with Garlic, 198
Asian Marinade, 213
Asian-Style Peanut Barbecue Sauce, 393
Asian-Style Pork Burgers, 241
Asian vegetables, 196–97
Asparagus
 Asparagus and Goat Cheese, 74
 Asparagus and Goat Cheese Frittata, 357
 Asparagus, Artichokes and Peas, 186
 Asparagus Risotto, 138
 Asparagus Tart, 365
 Asparagus with Pesto, 186
 Asparagus with Tarragon Mayonnaise, 209
 Butter-Steamed Asparagus with Egg, 364
 Huevos a la Flamenca, 362

Lemon-Asparagus Rice Pilaf, 132–33
 Potato Gnocchi with Asparagus and Tomatoes, 181
 Potato Salad with Asparagus and Pesto Vinaigrette, 85
 Roasted Asparagus, 209
 Roasted Chicken with Asparagus, Fennel and Potatoes, 257–58
Avocados
 Avocado-Tarragon Dip, 23
 with balsamic vinegar, 78
 Guacamole Soup, 36
 "It's Not Guacamole" Avocado Salsa, 387
 preparing, 79
 ripe, 79
 Sour Cream and Avocado Omelet, 363

B

Backward Spanish Aioli, 389
Bacon
 cooking, 370
 Crisp Maple-Glazed Country Bacon, 370
 Gordon's Warm Brussels Sprout Salad with Bacon and Eggs, 68–69
 Grilled Plums with Bacon and Goat Cheese, 21
 Wilted Cabbage Salad with Bacon and Cashel Blue Cheese, 90
Bagna Cauda, 392
Baked Eggs with Duxelles and Herbs, 352–53
Baked Swordfish with Roasted Red Pepper Vinaigrette, 307

Bamee Haeng, 118–19
Barbecue Sauce, 239
Barley, 446
Basic Bruschetta, 10
Basil. *See also* Pesto
 Basil Vinegar, 85
 Fresh Shelling Bean and Basil Soup, 39–40
Basque-Style Fisherman's Stew, 331
Beans. *See also* Black beans; Chickpeas; Green beans; Long beans
 Braised Oxtails with White Beans and Salsa Verde, 228–29
 cooking, 149, 182
 Fresh Cranberry Bean Sambar, 50–51
 Fresh Shelling Bean and Basil Soup, 39–40
 Lamb Shank Soup with Lima Beans, 62–63
 Mexican Minestrone with Cilantro Pesto, 42–43
 Orecchiette with Fava Beans and Frisee, 102–3
 Pickled Yellow Wax Beans, 372
 soaking and salting dried, 148–49
 White Bean and Pesto Dip, 4
 White Bean and Roasted Garlic Soup, 41–42
Béchamel Sauce, 184
Beef
 Beef and Shiitake Skewers, 223
 Beef with Green Beans, Lime Leaves and Chiles (Nua Pad Ki Mow), 224

Braised Oxtails with White
  Beans and Salsa Verde,
  228–29
Cognac-Pepper Steaks, 217
Daube of Beef Auberge
  d'Aillaine, 222–23
grilling times for, 216
Hamburgers with Portobellos
  and Pink Peppercorn–Tarragon
  Butter, 227–28
marinade for, 226
Pan-Grilled Steaks with Toasted
  Walnuts and Roquefort-
  Shallot Butter, 216
Pot Roast with Caramelized
  Onion Sauce and Roasted
  Winter Vegetables, 220–21
Roast Beef and Yorkshire
  Pudding, 219–20
Roasted Beef Tenderloin with
  Red Pepper–Goat Cheese
  Sauce, 218
Stir-Fried Flank Steak with Bok
  Choy, 226–27
Tagine of Meatballs and Peas,
  250–51
Thai Red Curry with Beef and
  Kabocha Squash, 225
Vietnamese "Shaking" Beef
  Salad, 88–89
Beets
French-Style Cobb Salad, 79
grilling, 212
Mediterranean-Style Marinated
  Red Beets, 188
Roasted Beet and Tomato
  Relish with Chermoula
  Flavors, 373
Belgian endive
Belgian Endive with Prosciutto,
  190–91
Escarole and Endive Salad with
  Bosc Pears, 66
Quick Endive Appetizer, 6

Berries. *See also* Cranberries;
  Strawberries
Peaches and Berries in Herbed
  Red Wine, 438
Rick and Ann's Black 'n' Blue
  Pie, 410–11
Rick and Ann's French Toast,
  339
Best Way Roast Turkey, 294–95
Birdseed Muffins, 344–45
Biryani, Vegetarian Corn,
  156–57
Bitter melon, 196
Black beans
Black Bean and Corn Salad,
  80–81
Black Bean and Sweet Potato
  Stew, 148–49
Green Beans and Turkey in
  Asian Black Bean Sauce, 298
Black Olive Tapenade, 3
Blood Orange Mimosa, 339
Bok choy
Cellophane Noodles with Black
  Mushrooms, 100
Grilled Tuna Salad with Bok
  Choy and Papaya, 91
Stir-Fried Flank Steak with Bok
  Choy, 226–27
Bottle gourd, 196
Bouillabaisse, French-
  Vietnamese, 328–29
Boulevard's Staff Turkey Breast,
  293
Braised Chicken Maharaja,
  258–59
Braised Chicken Wings with
  Tomato, Porcini and Sage,
  279
Braised Cucumbers in Dill, 189
Braised Garden Spinach, 206
Braised Oxtails with White Beans
  and Salsa Verde, 228–29
Brandade, Creamy, of Salt Cod
  and Potatoes with Garlic
  Croutons, 8–9

Bread. *See also* Bruschetta;
  Crostini; French toast;
  Muffins; Pancakes; Scones;
  Waffles
Hot Grilled Blue Cheese Toasts,
  346
Irish Soda Bread, 345
Mexican Chocolate Bread
  Pudding, 404–5
Morels in Brandy Cream on
  Toast, 165–66
Pumpkin Cinnamon Rolls,
  350–51
toast points, 166
Wild Mushroom Bread
  Pudding, 167
Breadcrumbs
making coarse, 192
making fine, 108
toasting, 192
Brines
Chez Panisse's Brine, 294
Honey Brine, 293
Nancy Oakes' Vanilla Brine,
  235
Brining
pork, 235
poultry, 295
tips, 234–35
Broccoli
cooking, 190
grilling, 213
Broccoli Rabe, Orecchiette with
  Turnips and, 103–4
Brown Derby French Dressing,
  78
Brownies with Chocolate Salsa,
  433–34
Brown Scones, 340
Bruce Cost's Beijing Noodles
  with Meat Sauce, 119–20
Bruschetta
Basic Bruschetta, 10
Bruschetta with Prosciutto and
  Teleme, 12
Piatti's Bruschetta with Spinach
  and Lemon, 11

Brussels sprouts
Brussels Sprouts with Toasted
  Hazelnut Butter, 189
Gordon's Warm Brussels Sprout
  Salad with Bacon and Eggs,
  68–69
Bulgur wheat, 446
Buttermilk-Cornmeal Pancakes,
  335
Butterscotch Pots de Crème, 401
Butter-Steamed Asparagus with
  Egg, 364

C
Cabbage
Cabbage Soup with Roquefort,
  37
Grilled Tuna Salad with Bok
  Choy and Papaya, 91
Mexican Coleslaw, 70
Minty Thai Chicken Salad, 86
Spicy Asian-Style Cabbage and
  Turkey, 299
Wilted Cabbage Salad with
  Bacon and Cashel Blue
  Cheese, 90
Cajun Dry Rub, 239
Cakes
Alsatian Apple Cake, 414
Chocolate Buttermilk Cake,
  423
Cranberry Upside-Down Cake,
  417–18
Left Bank Almond Cake, 419
Oatmeal Cake with Walnut
  Topping, 416–17
Perfect Poppy Seed Cake, 422
Sweet Polenta-Orange Cake,
  420
Tequila Carrot Cake, 415–16
testing for doneness, 426
Velvet Pound Cake, 421
Calamari Salad, Hot-and-Spicy,
  92
Caldo de Tlalpeno, 57–58

Carol Field's Creamy Pumpkin-Flavored Risotto, 141
Carrots
  grilling, 213
  Roasted Onions, Potatoes, Carrots and Fennel, 214
  Tequila Carrot Cake, 415–16
Cauliflower
  Cauliflower and Green Olive Relish, 375
  Cauliflower in the Style of Puebla, 191–92
  Quick Vegetable Appetizer, 24
Cazuela de Huevos Rancheros, 360–61
Celery root
  Celery Root, Mache and Blood Orange Salad, 73
  Tarte Tatin of Celery Root, Leek and Potato, 173
Cellophane Noodles with Black Mushrooms, 100
Chaat, Tropical Fruit, 291
Charred Corn with Chile Butter, 194
Chayote, 196
Cheese. See also Cheesecakes; Feta cheese; Goat cheese; Ricotta cheese
  Bruschetta with Prosciutto and Teleme, 12
  Cabbage Soup with Roquefort, 37
  Cazuela de Huevos Rancheros, 360–61
  Charred Corn with Chile Butter, 194
  Cheese Treat, 405
  Chile Relleno Casserole, 162
  Chorizo Quiche in a Cornmeal Crust, 359–60
  Cream of Leek Soup with Stilton, 46–47
  Duck Bolognese, 123–24
  Fiery Breakfast Potatoes with Eggs, 368–69

Formaggio alla Griglia con Limone (Grilled Cheese on a Lemon Leaf), 18
Fresh Corn Tamales, 151–52
Green Garlic Pizza, 179–80
Hot Grilled Blue Cheese Toasts, 346
Jalapeño Macaroni, 109
Lentil and Squash Lasagna with Caramelized Onions, 182–83
Light-as-a-Cloud Gnocchi with Gorgonzola Cream, 111–12
Mama's Tamale Pie, 282–83
Marion Cunningham's Featherbed Eggs, 353
Michelle Anna Jordan's Soft Polenta with Walnuts, 144–45
Millet and Kale Gratin, 161–62
Morel Quesadillas with Mild Red Chile, 16–17
  pairing wine and, 18
Pan-Grilled Steaks with Toasted Walnuts and Roquefort-Shallot Butter, 216
  queso cotija, 194
Red Enchiladas, 154
Santa Fe Cooking School Blue Corn Muffins, 343
  storing and serving, 19
Tequila–Fresh Pineapple Cheese Pie, 425–26
Three-Cheese Pizza with Arugula, 176–77
Turkey, Corn and Roasted Bell Pepper Enchiladas with Chipotle Sauce, 296–97
Wilted Cabbage Salad with Bacon and Cashel Blue Cheese, 90
Cheesecakes
  making, 425
  Raised Cheesecake, 424–25
Che's Havana-Style Chicken, 265–66
Chez Panisse's Brine, 294

Chicken
  Arroz Caldo (Filipino Rice Porridge), 54–55
  Braised Chicken Maharaja, 258–59
  Braised Chicken Wings with Tomato, Porcini and Sage, 279
  brining, 295
  Caldo de Tlalpeno, 57–58
  Che's Havana-Style Chicken, 265–66
  Chicken Breasts with Pesto, 257
  Chicken Ragout, 272–73
  Chicken with Lemon, Peppers and Olives, 273–74
  Chipotle Chicken Wings, 29
  Clay-Pot Rice with Chicken and Black Mushrooms, 136–37
  Cobb Salad Brown Derby, 78–79
  French-Style Cobb Salad, 79
  Garlic Chicken Wings with Garam Masala, 28
  Ginger Chicken in a Clay Pot, 278
  Grilled Lavender Chicken on Arugula, 261
  grilling, 260–61
  Guacamole Soup, 36
  Jojo's Provençal Chicken, 269–70
  Kokkari's Grilled Chicken Souvlaki, 270–71
  Lemon Thyme–Stuffed Chicken, 254
  Mama's Tamale Pie, 282–83
  marinating, 264, 270–71
  Minty Thai Chicken Salad, 86
  Mojo's Chicken and Dumplings, 284–85
  Pollo de Olla, 280–81
  Pollo Diablo, 260
  Ponzu's Chicken Wings with Caramel–Black Pepper Glaze, 281–82

Roasted Chickens Stuffed with Orzo on a Bed of Rainbow Swiss Chard, 262–63
Roasted Chicken with Asparagus, Fennel and Potatoes, 257–58
Roasted Chicken with Garlicky Skin and Walnuts, 256
Smoky Mexican Chicken Legs, 283
Southern-Fried Chicken, 266–67
Spicy Vietnamese Chicken Curry, 276–77
Super-Juicy Roasted Chicken with Garlic and Thyme, 255
Tandoori Chicken, 268–69
Tangerine-Bourbon Chicken Breasts, 264
Thai Chicken Soup with Coconut Milk and Galangal, 56
Vanilla-Scented Chicken and Mushrooms Simmered in Coconut Milk, 275–76
Chickpeas
  Chickpea Salad with Provençal Herbs and Olives, 82
  Chickpea Soup with Kale and Diavolicchio, 45–46
  Egyptian Chickpea and Orzo Soup, 44
Chiffonade, 94
Chiles. See also Chipotle chiles; Jalapeño chiles
  Arroz con Rajas y Crema, 159
  Charred Corn with Chile Butter, 194
  charring Anaheim, 162
  Chile Mayonnaise, 316
  Chile Relleno Casserole, 162
  Chile Sauce, 197
  Diavolicchio, 45
  Fresh Corn Tamales, 151–52
  Killer Red Sauce, 391
  Mama's Tamale Pie, 282–83
  purée, 155

Quick Red Sauce, 369
Rancho Sarsa, 382
Red Chile Mussels, 322
Red Chile Sauce, 155
Super-Rica Rajas, 158–59
Tecomate and Poblano Chile
Crostini, 13
Tomato and Hot Pepper Relish,
6
Chile Tranquilizers (Brownies
with Chocolate Salsa), 433–34
Chimichurri Sauce, 383
Chinese mustard, 196
Chinese Noodles with Five-Spice
Shiitake Mushrooms, 98–99
Chinese Spicy Red Pepper
Dipping Sauce, 7
Chipotle chiles
Chipotle Chicken Wings, 29
Chipotle Oil, 21
Chipotle Sauce, 296–97
Grilled Tequila-Chipotle
Shrimp, 321
storing, 443
Sweet Potato Gratin with
Chipotles, 205
Chocolate
Chile Tranquilizers (Brownies
with Chocolate Salsa), 433–34
Chocolate Buttermilk Cake,
423
Chocolate Buttermilk Frosting,
424
Fig and Chocolate Coffee Cake,
348–49
Mexican Chocolate Bread
Pudding, 404–5
Oatmeal-Walnut–Chocolate
Chip Cookies, 427
Zuni Cafe's Chocolate Pots de
Crème, 400
Chorizo
Chorizo Quiche in a Cornmeal
Crust, 359–60
Pork, Chorizo and Hominy
Stew, 237–38

Spanish Clam, Prawn and
Chorizo Stew, 330
Christmas Nut Chews, 428
Chrysanthemum, 196
Chutney, Fresh Mint and
Cilantro, 395–96
Cianfotto Lucana (Eggplant,
Tomato, Pepper and Potato
Stew), 149–50
Cilantro Pesto, 42–43
Cinnamon Rolls, Pumpkin,
350–51
Citrus-Strawberry Salad, 402
Clams
grilling, 309
Spanish Clam, Prawn and
Chorizo Stew, 330
Clay-Pot Rice with Chicken and
Black Mushrooms, 136–37
Cobbler, Fresh Apricot, 434–35
Cobb Salad Brown Derby, 78–79
Coconut and coconut milk
Coconut Ice Cream, 441
Fijian Prawns with Sweet
Potatoes in Coconut Curry,
318–19
Malabar Coconut Rice, 133–34
Malaysian Coconut Curry of
Autumn Vegetables, 175–76
Mussels in Coconut Broth, 323
Spicy Vietnamese Chicken
Curry, 276–77
Thai Chicken Soup with
Coconut Milk and Galangal,
56
Vanilla-Scented Chicken and
Mushrooms Simmered in
Coconut Milk, 275–76
Yellow Curry with Mixed
Vegetables, Tofu and Thai
Basil, 174
Coffee, brewing, 334
Coffee cakes
Apple–Sour Cream Coffee
Cake, 347–48
Fig and Chocolate Coffee Cake,
348–49

Cognac
Cognac-Pepper Steaks, 217
Cognac Scallops, 326
Coriander-Cognac Sauce, 286
Veal Braised with Cognac, 230
Cold Cucumber Soup with
Cilantro, 32
Cold Udon Noodles with Morels
and Fresh Peas, 97
Coleslaw, Mexican, 70
Colleen McGlynn's Marinated
Dry-Cured Olives, 2
Cookies
Chile Tranquilizers (Brownies
with Chocolate Salsa), 433–34
Christmas Nut Chews, 428
Ginger Date Bars, 432
Lavender Shortbread, 429
Oatmeal-Walnut–Chocolate
Chip Cookies, 427
Orange-Polenta Shortbread,
430
testing for doneness, 426
Walnut Wonder Bars, 431–32
Cool Melons, 440
Coriander-Cognac Sauce, 286
Corn
Arroz con Rajas y Crema, 159
Black Bean and Corn Salad,
80–81
Charred Corn with Chile
Butter, 194
cooking, 194–95
Corn and Jalapeño Polenta,
145–46
Corn-Basil Sauce, 211
Corn Pudding, 195
Fresh Corn Tamales, 151–52
Frisee and Corn Salad with
Fried Tomatoes, 75–76
grilling, 213
Heavenly Corn Soup, 34–35
Mama's Tamale Pie, 282–83
Mexican Zucchini and Corn
Gratin, 211
Roasted Corn and Chanterelle
Relish, 374

Santa Fe Cooking School Blue
Corn Muffins, 343
Turkey, Corn and Roasted Bell
Pepper Enchiladas with
Chipotle Sauce, 296–97
Vegetarian Corn Biryani,
156–57
Cornish Game Hen with
Tomato-Olive Sauce, 292
Cornmeal. See also Polenta
Buttermilk-Cornmeal Pancakes,
335
Chorizo Quiche in a Cornmeal
Crust, 359–60
Delicate Cornmeal Muffins,
342
Fresh Corn Tamales, 151–52
Mama's Tamale Pie, 282–83
Santa Fe Cooking School Blue
Corn Muffins, 343
Couscous
Saffron and Raisin Couscous
with Fresh Mint, 146
Shrimp in Spicy Saffron Broth
with Israeli Couscous, 327–28
Spiced Duck with Couscous,
287–88
Spicy Citrus Couscous
Tabbouleh, 83
Crab
cleaning and cracking cooked,
317
cooking, 316
Crab Cakes with Chile
Mayonnaise, 315
Crab Pasta, 112
Crab Soufflé with Green Onion
and Lemon, 366–67
Garlic-Roasted Crab, 316–17
grilling, 309
selecting, 315
Cranberries
Cranberry-Cream Scones, 341
Cranberry Upside-Down Cake,
417–18
Gingered Cranberry and Pear
Relish, 377–78

Kumquat-Cranberry-Lime
Sauce, 376
Cream of Leek Soup with Stilton,
46–47
Creamy Brandade of Salt Cod
and Potatoes with Garlic
Croutons, 8–9
Creamy Lemon Spaghetti with
Olives and Basil, 94
Crisp Maple-Glazed Country
Bacon, 370
Crostini
Easy Fig Crostini, 13
making, 14–15
Shrimp Crostini with Thai Basil
and Kaffir Lime Sauce, 14
Smoked Trout, Asian Pear and
Horseradish Cream Crostini,
15
Tecomate and Poblano Chile
Crostini, 13
Cucumbers
Braised Cucumbers in Dill, 189
Cold Cucumber Soup with
Cilantro, 32
Cucumber Vodka, 30
Minted North African
Cucumber Salad, 68
Plaka Greek Salad, 72
Tofu, Cucumber and Chive
Soup, 33
Tzatziki, 17
Curried Turkey Salad with Apple
and Walnuts, 87
Curries
Fijian Prawns with Sweet
Potatoes in Coconut Curry,
318–19
Malaysian Coconut Curry of
Autumn Vegetables, 175–76
Spicy Vietnamese Chicken
Curry, 276–77
Thai Red Curry with Beef and
Kabocha Squash, 225
Yellow Curry with Mixed
Vegetables, Tofu and Thai
Basil, 174

Custard, tips for, 401

D
Dates
Egyptian Haroset, 395
Ginger Date Bars, 432
quick dessert, 434
Daube of Beef Auberge
d'Aillaine, 222–23
Delfina's Spaghetti, 95–96
Delicate Cornmeal Muffins, 342
Diavolicchio, 45
Dips
Avocado-Tarragon Dip, 23
Chinese Spicy Red Pepper
Dipping Sauce, 7
East-West Pesto Dip, 5
Libyan Spicy Pumpkin Dip,
9–10
Russian Dilled Spinach Dip,
6–7
Spiced Cheese, 19
Tzatziki, 17
White Bean and Pesto Dip, 4
Drinks
Blood Orange Mimosa, 339
Cucumber Vodka, 30
Margarita, 15–16
Martini, 3
Sangria, 26
Duck
Duck Bolognese, 123–24
Duck Breasts with Coriander-
Cognac Sauce, 286–87
French-Style Cobb Salad, 79
grilling, 261
Mustard-Marinated Duck
Breasts with Figs and
Zinfandel, 289–90
Spiced Duck with Couscous,
287–88
Dumplings, Mojo's Chicken and,
284–85

E
East-West Pesto Dip, 5
Easy Fig Crostini, 13
Easy Pad Thai, 114–15
Eggplant
Asian, 196
Cianfotto Lucana (Eggplant,
Tomato, Pepper and Potato
Stew), 149–50
Eggplant Caviar with Chipotle
Oil, 20–21
Grilled Asian Eggplant with
Chile-Lime Sauce and Scallion
Oil, 197
Moroccan Lamb Shanks with
Eggplant, 246–47
Roasted Eggplant Bisque,
38–39
Eggs. *See also* Frittatas; Omelets
Baked Eggs with Duxelles and
Herbs, 352–53
beating whites, 406
Butter-Steamed Asparagus with
Egg, 364
Cazuela de Huevos Rancheros,
360–61
Chorizo Quiche in a Cornmeal
Crust, 359–60
Crab Soufflé with Green Onion
and Lemon, 366–67
Fiery Breakfast Potatoes with
Eggs, 368–69
Gordon's Warm Brussels Sprout
Salad with Bacon and Eggs,
68–69
hard-cooking, 362
Huevos a la Flamenca, 362
Lobster Scrambled Eggs, 367
Marion Cunningham's
Featherbed Eggs, 353
scrambling, 367
storing, 352
Egyptian Chickpea and Orzo
Soup, 44
Egyptian Haroset, 395
Emerald Fire Noodles, 115
Enchiladas

Red Enchiladas, 154
Turkey, Corn and Roasted Bell
Pepper Enchiladas with
Chipotle Sauce, 296–97
English Country-House Lemon
Curd, 397
Escarole
Escarole and Endive Salad with
Bosc Pears, 66
Turkey Soup with Wild Rice
and Escarole, 58–59

F
Fallen Butternut Squash Gratin,
207
Fennel
Fennel and Dry Goat Cheese
Salad with Lemon Vinaigrette,
74
Fennel Choucroute, 193
Mussels Steamed in Vouvray
with Fennel and Leeks, 324
Roasted Chicken with
Asparagus, Fennel and
Potatoes, 257–58
Roasted Onions, Potatoes,
Carrots and Fennel, 214
Spaghetti with Marinated
Fennel, Tomato and Olives,
96
Feta cheese
Plaka Greek Salad, 72
Spiced Cheese, 19
Summer Fruit Salad with Feta
and Cilantro, 77
Fiery Breakfast Potatoes with
Eggs, 368–69
Figs
Easy Fig Crostini, 13
Fig and Chocolate Coffee Cake,
348–49
grilling, 430
Mary Risley's Fresh Fig and
Plum Tart, 409–10
Mustard-Marinated Duck
Breasts with Figs and
Zinfandel, 289–90

Oven-Roasted Figs with Crème Fraîche, 437
quick dessert, 434
rehydrating, 409
Fijian Prawns with Sweet Potatoes in Coconut Curry, 318–19
Filipino Rice Porridge (Arroz Caldo), 54–55
Fine Fruit Salad, 77
Fish. *See also* Anchovies; Salmon; Salt cod; Tuna
Baked Swordfish with Roasted Red Pepper Vinaigrette, 307
Fish in a Palace Way, 314
flavoring steamed, 313
grilling, 308–9
kebabs, 330
Lemon-Dill Halibut, 309
Lucas' Sardinas en Escabeche (Marinated Sardines), 26–27
Margarita-Style Fish with Mango Salsa, 308
marinating, 311
Mexican Snapper en Papillote, 313
Nan Yang's Burmese Fish Noodle Soup (Mohingar), 60–61
Poached Sea Bass with Gremolata, 312
Quick Fish Stock, 329
Sand Dabs with Lemon-Caper Vinaigrette, 310
substitutes for popular, 310
Summertime Basil Bass, 311
Foie Gras, Sautéed, with Grapes, 30
Foothill Cafe Ribs, 238–39
Formaggio alla Griglia con Limone (Grilled Cheese on a Lemon Leaf), 18
42 Degrees' Cider-Cured Pork Chops, 234
French-Style Cobb Salad, 79
French Toast, Rick and Ann's, 339

French-Vietnamese Bouillabaisse, 328–29
Fresh Apricot Cobbler, 434–35
Fresh Corn Tamales, 151–52
Fresh Cranberry Bean Sambar, 50–51
Fresh Mint and Cilantro Chutney, 395–96
Fresh Pineapple Salsa, 386
Fresh Shelling Bean and Basil Soup, 39–40
Frisee
Frisee and Corn Salad with Fried Tomatoes, 75–76
Orecchiette with Fava Beans and Frisee, 102–3
Frittatas
Asparagus and Goat Cheese Frittata, 357
Frittatas with Prosciutto and Plum Tomatoes, 358
Grandmama's Artichoke Frittatas, 356–57
Frosting, Chocolate Buttermilk, 424
Fruit. *See also* specific fruits
Fine Fruit Salad, 77
grilling, 430–31
preserving, 422
quick desserts, 434–35
Summer Fruit Salad with Feta and Cilantro, 77
Trio Fruit Crumble, 436–37
Tropical Fruit Chaat, 291
Fuyu Persimmon Relish, 379

G
Galette, Potato and Goat Cheese, 172
Garlic. *See also* Green garlic
Asian Greens with Garlic, 198
Backward Spanish Aioli, 389
Bagna Cauda, 392
Garlic Chicken Wings with Garam Masala, 28
Garlicky Shrimp from a Tapas Bar, 24

Garlic-Roasted Crab, 316–17
grilling, 213
Kasma Loha-unchit's Garlic Noodles (Bamee Haeng), 118–19
mincing, 106
Roasted Chicken with Garlicky Skin and Walnuts, 256
Roasted Winter Roots with Whole Garlic Heads, 150–51
White Bean and Roasted Garlic Soup, 41–42
Zarzuela's Patatas al Ajillo (Potatoes with Garlic), 202
Gin
Gin and Tonic Granita, 440
Guinea Fowl with Gin and Juniper, 300
Ginger
Ginger Chicken in a Clay Pot, 278
Ginger Date Bars, 432
Gingered Cranberry and Pear Relish, 377–78
Ginger-Orange Glaze, 233
Ginger-Pepper Salmon, 306
Ginger-Tomato Rasam, 51–52
Glass noodles, Asian, 98
Glazes
Ginger-Orange Glaze, 233
Mango Chutney–Mustard Glaze, 239
using, 238
Gnocchi
Judy Rodgers' Ricotta Gnocchi, 110
Light-as-a-Cloud Gnocchi with Gorgonzola Cream, 111–12
Potato Gnocchi with Asparagus and Tomatoes, 181
Goat cheese
Asparagus and Goat Cheese, 74
Asparagus and Goat Cheese Frittata, 357
Fennel and Dry Goat Cheese Salad with Lemon Vinaigrette, 74

French-Style Cobb Salad, 79
Grilled Plums with Bacon and Goat Cheese, 21
Potato and Chèvre Salad, 68
Potato and Goat Cheese Galette, 172
Pumpkin and Goat Cheese Omelet with Glazed Pumpkin Wedges, 355–56
Roasted Beef Tenderloin with Red Pepper–Goat Cheese Sauce, 218
Gordon's Warm Brussels Sprout Salad with Bacon and Eggs, 68–69
Grandmama's Artichoke Frittatas, 356–57
Granita, Gin and Tonic, 440
Grapes, Sautéed Foie Gras with, 30
Greek Taverna-Style Zucchini with Lemon, 209
Green beans
Beef with Green Beans, Lime Leaves and Chiles (Nua Pad Ki Mow), 224
Green Bean Gremolata, 186–87
Green Beans and Turkey in Asian Black Bean Sauce, 298
Green garlic
Green Garlic and Spinach Risotto, 139
Green Garlic Pizza, 179–80
storing, 139
Green, Green Dressing, 73
Green Herb Sauce, 390
Green Papaya Salad, 76
Greens. *See also* Salads; *specific greens*
Asian Greens with Garlic, 198
Sauté of Summer Greens, 199
storing, 75
Gremolata, 312
Grilled Asian Eggplant with Chile-Lime Sauce and Scallion Oil, 197

Grilled Lavender Chicken on Arugula, 261
Grilled Plums with Bacon and Goat Cheese, 21
Grilled Tequila-Chipotle Shrimp, 321
Grilled Tuna Salad with Bok Choy and Papaya, 91
Grilled Winter Squash with Cumin, 207
Guacamole Soup, 36
Guinea Fowl with Gin and Juniper, 300

H

Halibut, Lemon-Dill, 309
Hamburgers
  Asian-Style Pork Burgers, 241
  grilling time for, 216
  Hamburgers with Portobellos and Pink Peppercorn–Tarragon Butter, 227–28
Ham Hock and "Peppercorn" Pasta Soup, 63–64
Haroset, Egyptian, 395
Heavenly Corn Soup, 34–35
Herb-Rubbed Oven Fries, 203
Hominy, Pork and Chorizo Stew, 237–38
Honey Brine, 293
Honey-Mustard Barbecue Sauce, 394
Hot-and-Spicy Calamari Salad, 92
Hot Grilled Blue Cheese Toasts, 346
Huevos a la Flamenca, 362

I

Ice cream
  Coconut Ice Cream, 441
  Spearmint Custard Ice Cream, 442
Irish Soda Bread, 345
Iron Horse Party Mix, 4

Italian Marinade, 213
Italian-Style Tomato Sauce, 125
"It's Not Guacamole" Avocado Salsa, 387

J

Jalapeño chiles
  Corn and Jalapeño Polenta, 145–46
  Jalapeño Macaroni, 109
  Salsa Fresca al Fresco, 385
  Scorpion Tomato Relish, 378
  seeding, 385
  Zchug, 388
Jardiniere's Wild Salmon with Olive Oil–Mashed Potatoes and Sauce Niçoise, 303–4
Jelly
  fixing unjelled, 396
  Red Pepper Jelly, 396
Jicama Appetizer, Juicy, 11
John Caputo's Anchoiade, 386–87
John Carroll's Peach Pie, 407–8
John Falcone's Grilled Prawns with Basil Baste, 320
Jojo's Provençal Chicken, 269–70
Judy Rodgers' Ricotta Gnocchi, 110
Juicy Jicama Appetizer, 11

K

Kale
  Chickpea Soup with Kale and Diavolicchio, 45–46
  Millet and Kale Gratin, 161–62
Kasha
  cooking, 446
  Kasha and Vegetable Casserole, 153
  Kasma Loha-unchit's Garlic Noodles (Bamee Haeng), 118–19
Kebabs. See also Skewers
  beef, 216

fish, 309
pork, 231
seafood, 330
Killer Red Sauce, 391
Kirk Webber's Waffles, 338
Kiwi Antipasto, 9
Kokkari's Grilled Chicken Souvlaki, 270–71
Korma Masala, 249
Kumquat-Cranberry-Lime Sauce, 376

L

Lamb
  grilling times for, 242
  Lamb in Fragrant Korma Sauce, 248
  Lamb Klephtiko, 241
  Lamb Ravioli with Yogurt, Garlic and Mint, 120–21
  Lamb Shank Soup with Lima Beans, 62–63
  Lamb Tagine with Dried Apricots, 245–46
  marinade for, 226
  Moroccan Lamb Shanks with Eggplant, 246–47
  Roasted Leg of Lamb with Potatoes and Onions, 243–44
  Tagine of Meatballs and Peas, 250–51
  Tunisian-Style Grilled Lamb Chops, 244
Lasagna, Lentil and Squash, with Caramelized Onions, 182–83
Lavender Shortbread, 429
Lavender, Thyme and Rosemary Pork Chops, 236
Leeks
  Cream of Leek Soup with Stilton, 46–47
  grilling, 213
Left Bank Almond Cake, 419
Lemons
  English Country-House Lemon Curd, 397

Lemon-Asparagus Rice Pilaf, 132–33
Lemon-Dill Halibut, 309
Quick Preserved Lemons, 398
Ultimate Lemon Meringue Pie, 406–7
Lemon Thyme–Stuffed Chicken, 254
Lentils
  cooking, 182
  Lentil and Squash Lasagna with Caramelized Onions, 182–83
  Puy Lentil Soup, 53–54
  Rice with French Green Lentils, 135–36
  Roasted Salmon with Lentils, 302–3
  Short Rice with Long Beans, 160–61
Lettuce, 75. See also Salads
Libyan Spicy Pumpkin Dip, 9–10
Light-as-a-Cloud Gnocchi with Gorgonzola Cream, 111–12
Lobster
  grilling, 309
  Lobster Scrambled Eggs, 367
Long beans
  preparing, 196
  Short Rice with Long Beans, 160–61
Lucas' Sardinas en Escabeche (Marinated Sardines), 26–27
Luffa squash, 196
Lush Yogurt Rice, 84

M

Macadamia Nuts, Mango Rice with, 134–35
Malabar Coconut Rice, 133–34
Malaysian Coconut Curry of Autumn Vegetables, 175–76
Mama's Tamale Pie, 282–83
Mandorlata di Peperoni (Bell Pepper and Almond Relish), 380

Mangoes
  Mango Chutney–Mustard
    Glaze, 239
  Mango Rice with Macadamia
    Nuts, 134–35
  Mango Salsa, 308–9
  Sunset Salsa, 384
Maple syrup
  Crisp Maple-Glazed Country
    Bacon, 370
  Maple-Glazed Sausage Slices,
    370
Margaritas, 15–16
Margarita-Style Fish with Mango
  Salsa, 308
Marinades. *See also* Pastes; Rubs
  All-Purpose Marinade, 264
  Asian Marinade, 213
  for beef and lamb, 226
  for chicken, 264, 270–71
  for fish, 311
  Italian Marinade, 213
  Olive Oil–Rosemary Marinade,
    270
  Red Wine Marinade, 226
  Teriyaki Marinade, 271
Marinara Sauce, 168–69
Marinated Vegetables in a Grill
  Pan, 212
Marion Cunningham's
  Featherbed Eggs, 353
Martini, 3
Mary Risley's Fresh Fig and Plum
  Tart, 409–10
Masa, 152
Mashed Potatoes, 202–3
Mayonnaise
  Backward Spanish Aioli, 389
  Chile Mayonnaise, 316
Meatballs and Peas, Tagine of,
  250–51
Mediterranean Sage Paste, 239
Mediterranean-Style Marinated
  Red Beets, 188
Melons
  Cool Melons, 440
  Mixed Melon Salsa, 386

Mexican Chili Paste, 239
Mexican Chocolate Bread
  Pudding, 404–5
Mexican Coleslaw, 70
Mexican Minestrone with
  Cilantro Pesto, 42–43
Mexican Red Chile and Citrus
  Paste, 271
Mexican Snapper en Papillote,
  313
Mexican Zucchini and Corn
  Gratin, 211
Michelle Anna Jordan's Soft
  Polenta with Walnuts, 144–45
Millet
  Birdseed Muffins, 344–45
  cooking, 446
  Millet and Kale Gratin, 161–62
Mimosa, Blood Orange, 339
Minestrone, Mexican, with
  Cilantro Pesto, 42–43
Mint
  Fresh Mint and Cilantro
    Chutney, 395–96
  Minted North African
    Cucumber Salad, 68
  Minty Thai Chicken Salad, 86
  Spearmint Custard Ice Cream,
    442
Miso, 325
Mixed Melon Salsa, 386
Mohingar, 60–61
Mojo's Chicken and Dumplings,
  284–85
Morels. See Mushrooms
Moroccan Lamb Shanks with
  Eggplant, 246–47
Muffins
  Birdseed Muffins, 344–45
  Delicate Cornmeal Muffins,
    342
  Santa Fe Cooking School Blue
    Corn Muffins, 343
Mushrooms
  Baked Eggs with Duxelles and
    Herbs, 352–53
  Beef and Shiitake Skewers, 223

Cellophane Noodles with Black
  Mushrooms, 100
Chinese Noodles with Five-
  Spice Shiitake Mushrooms,
  98–99
Clay-Pot Rice with Chicken and
  Black Mushrooms, 136–37
Cold Udon Noodles with
  Morels and Fresh Peas, 97
Hamburgers with Portobellos
  and Pink Peppercorn–Tarragon
  Butter, 227–28
Morel Quesadillas with Mild
  Red Chile, 16–17
Morels in Brandy Cream on
  Toast, 165–66
Portobello-Polenta Pie, 168–69
Potato and Portobello
  Mushroom Casserole, 164–65
Potato and Wild Mushroom
  Gratin, 201–2
Roasted Corn and Chanterelle
  Relish, 374
Roasted Portobellos with Pink
  Peppercorns, 163
Tecomate and Poblano Chile
  Crostini, 13
Vanilla-Scented Chicken and
  Mushrooms Simmered in
  Coconut Milk, 275–76
Wild Mushroom Bread
  Pudding, 167
Wild Mushroom Omelet, 354
Wild Mushroom Soup, 47
Winter Wild Mushroom
  Risotto, 143–44
Mussels
  buying and cleaning, 322
  grilling, 309
  Mussel Risotto, 142
  Mussels in Coconut Broth, 323
  Mussels Steamed in Vouvray
    with Fennel and Leeks, 324
  Oven-Roasted Mussels with
    Tarragon Butter, 325
  Red Chile Mussels, 322
  Stuffed Mussels, 25

Mustard-Marinated Duck
  Breasts with Figs and
  Zinfandel, 289–90

N
Nancy Oakes' Vanilla Brine, 235
Nan Yang's Burmese Fish Noodle
  Soup (Mohingar), 60–61
Noodles. *See* Pasta and noodles
Nuts, toasting, 381

O
Oatmeal
  Birdseed Muffins, 344–45
  cooking instant, 344
  Oatmeal Cake with Walnut
    Topping, 416–17
  Oatmeal-Walnut–Chocolate
    Chip Cookies, 427
O Chame's Soba with Salmon
  and Bean Sprouts, 116–17
Okra, Spicy Asian Pan-Fried,
  200–201
Olive Oil–Rosemary Marinade,
  270
Olives
  Anne Gingrass's Green Olive
    Risotto, 140
  Black Olive Tapenade, 3
  Cauliflower and Green Olive
    Relish, 375
  Chicken with Lemon, Peppers
    and Olives, 273–74
  Chickpea Salad with Provençal
    Herbs and Olives, 82
  Colleen McGlynn's Marinated
    Dry-Cured Olives, 2
  Cornish Game Hen with
    Tomato-Olive Sauce, 292
  Creamy Lemon Spaghetti with
    Olives and Basil, 94
  Iron Horse Party Mix, 4
  Jardiniere's Wild Salmon with
    Olive Oil–Mashed Potatoes
    and Sauce Niçoise, 303–4

Plaka Greek Salad, 72
Spaghetti with Marinated
    Fennel, Tomato and Olives,
    96
Tomato, Lemon, Green Olive
    and Onion Salad, 71
Omelets. *See also* Frittatas
    Pumpkin and Goat Cheese
        Omelet with Glazed Pumpkin
        Wedges, 355–56
    Sour Cream and Avocado
        Omelet, 363
    Wild Mushroom Omelet, 354
Onions
    caramelizing, 220–21
    Roasted Onions, Potatoes,
        Carrots and Fennel, 214
    Super-Rica Rajas, 158–59
Oranges
    Blood Orange Mimosa, 339
    Celery Root, Mache and Blood
        Orange Salad, 73
    Ginger-Orange Glaze, 233
    Orange-Polenta Shortbread,
        430
    quick dessert, 435
    Sweet Polenta-Orange Cake,
        420
Orecchiette. *See* Pasta and
    noodles
Oven-Baked Quinoa Pilaf, 130
Oven-Roasted Figs with Crème
    Fraîche, 437
Oven-Roasted Mussels with
    Tarragon Butter, 325
Oxtails, Braised, with White
    Beans and Salsa Verde,
    228–29

P

Pad Thai, Easy, 114–15
Pancakes
    Buttermilk-Cornmeal Pancakes,
        335
    Pumpkin Pancakes with
        Toasted Pumpkin Seeds, 336

Strawberry Soufflé Pancake,
    337
Pancetta and Tomato Sauce, 126
Pan-Fried Breakfast Tomatoes,
    349
Pan-Grilled Steaks with Toasted
    Walnuts and Roquefort-
    Shallot Butter, 216
Panna Cotta with Citrus-
    Strawberry Salad, 402
Papayas
    Green Papaya Salad, 76
    Grilled Tuna Salad with Bok
        Choy and Papaya, 91
    quick dessert, 434
    Sunset Salsa, 384
Pappardelle with Arugula,
    Cherry Tomatoes and
    Breadcrumbs, 101
Party Mix, Iron Horse, 4
Pasta and noodles. *See also*
    Gnocchi
    Asian glass noodles, 98
    Bruce Cost's Beijing Noodles
        with Meat Sauce, 119–20
    Cellophane Noodles with Black
        Mushrooms, 100
    Chinese Noodles with Five-
        Spice Shiitake Mushrooms,
        98–99
    Cold Udon Noodles with
        Morels and Fresh Peas, 97
    Crab Pasta, 112
    Creamy Lemon Spaghetti with
        Olives and Basil, 94
    Delfina's Spaghetti, 95–96
    Duck Bolognese, 123–24
    Easy Pad Thai, 114–15
    Egyptian Chickpea and Orzo
        Soup, 44
    Emerald Fire Noodles, 115
    Ham Hock and "Peppercorn"
        Pasta Soup, 63–64
    Jalapeño Macaroni, 109
    Kasma Loha-unchit's Garlic
        Noodles (Bamee Haeng),
        118–19

Lamb Ravioli with Yogurt,
    Garlic and Mint, 120–21
Lentil and Squash Lasagna with
    Caramelized Onions, 182–83
Mexican Minestrone with
    Cilantro Pesto, 42–43
Nan Yang's Burmese Fish
    Noodle Soup (Mohingar),
    60–61
O Chame's Soba with Salmon
    and Bean Sprouts, 116–17
Orecchiette with Broccoli Rabe
    and Turnips, 103–4
Orecchiette with Fava Beans
    and Frisee, 102–3
Pappardelle with Arugula,
    Cherry Tomatoes and
    Breadcrumbs, 101
Pasta with Saffron-Scented
    Cream, Peas and Prosciutto,
    122
Penne with Butternut Squash,
    Turkey, Currants and Spinach,
    105–6
Penne with Three Herbs,
    Capers and Tuna, 89
Perciatelli with Anchovies and
    Breadcrumbs, 107–8
precooking, 102
Rice Stick Noodles with Grilled
    Pork and Lime Vinaigrette,
    113
Roasted Chickens Stuffed with
    Orzo on a Bed of Rainbow
    Swiss Chard, 262–63
Sicilian Tomato Pesto with
    Linguine, 104
Southeast Asian Summer Salad
    of Cellophane Noodles and
    Herbs, 67–68
Whole-Wheat Spaghetti with
    Chard, 106–7
Pastes
    Mediterranean Sage Paste, 239
    Mexican Chili Paste, 239
    Mexican Red Chile and Citrus
        Paste, 271

Rancho Seasoning Paste, 280
Seasoning Paste, 131–32
Pâté, Artichoke Heart, 21
Peaches
    grilling, 430, 438
    John Carroll's Peach Pie, 407–8
    Peaches and Berries in Herbed
        Red Wine, 438
Peanut Barbecue Sauce, Asian-
    Style, 393
Pears
    Escarole and Endive Salad with
        Bosc Pears, 66
    Gingered Cranberry and Pear
        Relish, 377–78
Peas
    Asparagus, Artichokes and
        Peas, 186
    Cold Udon Noodles with
        Morels and Fresh Peas, 97
    Ginger-Tomato Rasam, 51–52
    Huevos a la Flamenca, 362
    Pasta with Saffron-Scented
        Cream, Peas and Prosciutto,
        122
    Tagine of Meatballs and Peas,
        250–51
Penne. *See* Pasta and noodles
Peppercorns, cracking, 306
Peppers. *See also* Chiles
    Baked Swordfish with Roasted
        Red Pepper Vinaigrette, 307
    Chicken with Lemon, Peppers
        and Olives, 273–74
    Chinese Spicy Red Pepper
        Dipping Sauce, 7
    Cianfotto Lucana (Eggplant,
        Tomato, Pepper and Potato
        Stew), 149–50
    Mandorlata di Peperoni (Bell
        Pepper and Almond Relish),
        380
    Red Pepper Jelly, 396
    Roasted Beef Tenderloin with
        Red Pepper–Goat Cheese
        Sauce, 218

Swiss Chard with Peppers and
Walnuts, 187
Turkey, Corn and Roasted Bell
Pepper Enchiladas with
Chipotle Sauce, 296–97
Perciatelli with Anchovies and
Breadcrumbs, 107–8
Perfect Poppy Seed Cake, 422
Persimmons
Fuyu Persimmon Relish, 379
Pomegranate and Persimmon
Relish, 381
quick dessert, 434
ripening, 379
Pesto
Asparagus with Pesto, 186
Chicken Breasts with Pesto, 257
Cilantro Pesto, 42–43
East-West Pesto Dip, 5
Potato Salad with Asparagus
and Pesto Vinaigrette, 85
Sicilian Tomato Pesto with
Linguine, 104
Tomato and Almond Pesto, 128
White Bean and Pesto Dip, 4
Piatti's Bruschetta with Spinach
and Lemon, 11
Pickled Yellow Wax Beans, 372
Pies
crusts, tender, 410–11
John Carroll's Peach Pie, 407–8
Mama's Tamale Pie, 282–83
pans for, 407
Polenta Pie with Pork in Salsa
Verde, 240–41
Portobello-Polenta Pie, 168–69
Rick and Ann's Black 'n' Blue
Pie, 410–11
Tequila–Fresh Pineapple Cheese
Pie, 425–26
testing for doneness, 426
Ultimate Lemon Meringue Pie,
406–7
Pilaf
Lemon-Asparagus Rice Pilaf,
132–33
Oven-Baked Quinoa Pilaf, 130

Pineapple
Fresh Pineapple Salsa, 386
grilling, 431
Tequila–Fresh Pineapple Cheese
Pie, 425–26
Pinzimonio, 82
Pizzas
Green Garlic Pizza, 179–80
Pizza Crust Dough, 178
Three-Cheese Pizza with
Arugula, 176–77
Plaka Greek Salad, 72
Plums
Grilled Plums with Bacon and
Goat Cheese, 21
Mary Risley's Fresh Fig and
Plum Tart, 409–10
Plums 'n' Spice Shortcakes,
412–13
Quick Plum Sauce, 393
Poached Sea Bass with
Gremolata, 312
Polenta. See also Cornmeal
Corn and Jalapeño Polenta,
145–46
Michelle Anna Jordan's Soft
Polenta with Walnuts, 144–45
Orange-Polenta Shortbread,
430
Polenta Baked with Vegetables,
170–71
Polenta Pie with Pork in Salsa
Verde, 240–41
Portobello-Polenta Pie, 168–69
Quick Oven Polenta, 145
Sweet Polenta-Orange Cake,
420
Pollo de Olla, 280–81
Pollo Diablo, 260
Pomegranate and Persimmon
Relish, 381
Ponzu's Chicken Wings with
Caramel–Black Pepper Glaze,
281–82
Poppy Seed Cake, Perfect, 422
Pork
Asian-Style Pork Burgers, 241

Bruce Cost's Beijing Noodles
with Meat Sauce, 119–20
chops, cooking times for, 236
Duck Bolognese, 123–24
Foothill Cafe Ribs, 238–39
42 Degrees' Cider-Cured Pork
Chops, 234
grilling times for, 231
Lavender, Thyme and
Rosemary Pork Chops, 236
Polenta Pie with Pork in Salsa
Verde, 240–41
Pork, Chorizo and Hominy
Stew, 237–38
Pork Loin Roast with Ginger-
Orange Glaze, 232–33
Pork Loin Stuffed with Chile-
Glazed Prunes, 231–32
quick sauce for, 233
Rice Stick Noodles with Grilled
Pork and Lime Vinaigrette,
113
Portobellos. See Mushrooms
Potatoes
baking, 172
Best Mashed Potatoes, 202–3
Cianfotto Lucana (Eggplant,
Tomato, Pepper and Potato
Stew), 149–50
Fiery Breakfast Potatoes with
Eggs, 368–69
Green Garlic Pizza, 179–80
grilling, 213
Herb-Rubbed Oven Fries, 203
Jardiniere's Wild Salmon with
Olive Oil–Mashed Potatoes
and Sauce Niçoise, 303–4
Potato and Chèvre Salad, 68
Potato and Goat Cheese
Galette, 172
Potato and Portobello
Mushroom Casserole, 164–65
Potato and Wild Mushroom
Gratin, 201–2
Potato Gnocchi with Asparagus
and Tomatoes, 181

Potato Salad with Asparagus
and Pesto Vinaigrette, 85
Roasted Chicken with
Asparagus, Fennel and
Potatoes, 257–58
Roasted Leg of Lamb with
Potatoes and Onions, 243–44
Roasted New Potatoes with
Sage, 205
Roasted Onions, Potatoes,
Carrots and Fennel, 214
Steamed New Potatoes with
Lemon-Caper Sauce, 205
Tarte Tatin of Celery Root,
Leek and Potato, 173
Zarzuela's Patatas al Ajillo
(Potatoes with Garlic), 202
Potée of Cabbage, Potatoes,
Turnips, Carrots, Onions and
Sausage, 252
Pot Roast with Caramelized
Onion Sauce and Roasted
Winter Vegetables, 220–21
Pots de crème
Butterscotch Pots de Crème,
401
Zuni Cafe's Chocolate Pots de
Crème, 400
Poultry. See also specific types of
poultry
brining, 295
grilling, 260–61
Prawns. See Shrimp and prawns
Prosciutto
Belgian Endive with Prosciutto,
190–91
Bruschetta with Prosciutto and
Teleme, 12
Frittatas with Prosciutto and
Plum Tomatoes, 358
Pasta with Saffron-Scented
Cream, Peas and Prosciutto,
122
Prunes, Chile-Glazed, Pork Loin
Stuffed with, 231–32
Puddings
Corn Pudding, 195

Mexican Chocolate Bread
  Pudding, 404–5
Rose-Accented Rice Pudding,
  403
Wild Mushroom Bread
  Pudding, 167
Yorkshire Pudding, 219–20
Pumpkin
  Carol Field's Creamy Pumpkin-
    Flavored Risotto, 141
  Libyan Spicy Pumpkin Dip,
    9–10
  Pumpkin and Goat Cheese
    Omelet with Glazed Pumpkin
    Wedges, 355–56
  Pumpkin Cinnamon Rolls,
    350–51
  Pumpkin Pancakes with
    Toasted Pumpkin Seeds, 336
  Pumpkin Soup with Leeks and
    Chervil, 49
Puy Lentil Soup, 53–54

Q

Quail, Tandoori, with Tropical
  Fruit Chaat, 290–91
Quesadillas, Morel, with Mild
  Red Chile, 16–17
Queso cotija, 194
Quiche, Chorizo, in a Cornmeal
  Crust, 359–60
Quick Chinese Soup, 56
Quick Endive Appetizer, 6
Quick Fish Stock, 329
Quick Marinated Strawberries,
  418
Quick Oven Polenta, 145
Quick Plum Sauce, 393
Quick Preserved Lemons, 398
Quick Red Sauce, 369
Quick Vegetable Appetizer, 24
Quinoa
  cooking, 447
  Oven-Baked Quinoa Pilaf, 130

R

Raised Cheesecake, 424–25
Raisins
  Egyptian Haroset, 395
  Iron Horse Party Mix, 4
  Saffron and Raisin Couscous
    with Fresh Mint, 146
Rajas, Super-Rica, 158–59
Ranchero Sauce, 360–61
Rancho Sarsa, 382
Rancho Seasoning Paste, 280
Rasams
  cooking legumes for, 182
  Ginger-Tomato Rasam, 51–52
  Rasam Powder, 52
Ravioli, Lamb, with Yogurt,
  Garlic and Mint, 120–21
Red Chile Mussels, 322
Red Chile Sauce, 155
Red Enchiladas, 154
Red Pepper Jelly, 396
Red Wine Marinade, 226
Red Wine Vinaigrette, 72
Relishes
  Cauliflower and Green Olive
    Relish, 375
  Fuyu Persimmon Relish, 379
  Gingered Cranberry and Pear
    Relish, 377–78
  Mandorlata di Peperoni (Bell
    Pepper and Almond Relish),
    380
  Pomegranate and Persimmon
    Relish, 381
  Roasted Beet and Tomato
    Relish with Chermoula
    Flavors, 373
  Roasted Corn and Chanterelle
    Relish, 374
  Scorpion Tomato Relish, 378
  Tomato and Hot Pepper Relish,
    6
Rice
  adding pizzazz to white,
    136–37
  Anne Gingrass's Green Olive
    Risotto, 140

Arroz Caldo (Filipino Rice
  Porridge), 54–55
Arroz con Rajas y Crema, 159
Arroz Rojo, 131–32
Asparagus Risotto, 138
basmati, 134–35
Carol Field's Creamy Pumpkin-
  Flavored Risotto, 141
Clay-Pot Rice with Chicken and
  Black Mushrooms, 136–37
cooking, 131, 134–35, 158–59,
  446
Green Garlic and Spinach
  Risotto, 139
Lemon-Asparagus Rice Pilaf,
  132–33
Lush Yogurt Rice, 84
Malabar Coconut Rice, 133–34
Mango Rice with Macadamia
  Nuts, 134–35
Mussel Risotto, 142
Pollo de Olla, 280–81
precooking steps for, 129
Rice with French Green Lentils,
  135–36
Rose-Accented Rice Pudding,
  403
Short Rice with Long Beans,
  160–61
Stir-Fried Black, White and Red
  Rice, 129–30
Vegetarian Corn Biryani,
  156–57
Winter Wild Mushroom
  Risotto, 143–44
Rice Stick Noodles with Grilled
  Pork and Lime Vinaigrette,
  113
Rick and Ann's Black 'n' Blue
  Pie, 410–11
Rick and Ann's French Toast,
  339
Ricotta cheese
  Judy Rodgers' Ricotta Gnocchi,
    110
  Kasha and Vegetable Casserole,
    153

Strawberries with Whipped
  Ricotta, 438–39
Wheat Berries with Ricotta,
  Almonds and Honey, 334
Risotto. See Rice
Roast Beef and Yorkshire
  Pudding, 219–20
Roasted Asparagus, 209
Roasted Beef Tenderloin with
  Red Pepper–Goat Cheese
  Sauce, 218
Roasted Beet and Tomato Relish
  with Chermoula Flavors, 373
Roasted Chickens Stuffed with
  Orzo on a Bed of Rainbow
  Swiss Chard, 262–63
Roasted Chicken with
  Asparagus, Fennel and
  Potatoes, 257–58
Roasted Chicken with Garlicky
  Skin and Walnuts, 256
Roasted Corn and Chanterelle
  Relish, 374
Roasted Eggplant Bisque, 38–39
Roasted Leg of Lamb with
  Potatoes and Onions, 243–44
Roasted New Potatoes with Sage,
  205
Roasted Onions, Potatoes,
  Carrots and Fennel, 214
Roasted Portobellos with Pink
  Peppercorns, 163
Roasted Salmon Stuffed with
  Spinach, 305–6
Roasted Salmon with Lentils,
  302–3
Roasted Sweet Potatoes with Red
  Pepper–Chile-Lime Butter, 204
Roasted Winter Roots with
  Whole Garlic Heads, 150–51
Rose-Accented Rice Pudding, 403
Rose Pistola's Cured Salmon
  with Green Peppercorns, 27
Rubs. See also Pastes
  Cajun Dry Rub, 239
  using, 238
Russian Dilled Spinach Dip, 6–7

S

Saffron and Raisin Couscous with Fresh Mint, 146

Salad dressings
  Brown Derby French Dressing, 78
  Green, Green Dressing, 73
  Red Wine Vinaigrette, 72

Salads
  Black Bean and Corn Salad, 80–81
  Celery Root, Mache and Blood Orange Salad, 73
  Cobb Salad Brown Derby, 78–79
  Curried Turkey Salad with Apple and Walnuts, 87
  dressing, 67
  Escarole and Endive Salad with Bosc Pears, 66
  Fennel and Dry Goat Cheese Salad with Lemon Vinaigrette, 74
  Fine Fruit Salad, 77
  French-Style Cobb Salad, 79
  Frisee and Corn Salad with Fried Tomatoes, 75–76
  Gordon's Warm Brussels Sprout Salad with Bacon and Eggs, 68–69
  Green Papaya Salad, 76
  Grilled Tuna Salad with Bok Choy and Papaya, 91
  Hot-and-Spicy Calamari Salad, 92
  Lush Yogurt Rice, 84
  Mexican Coleslaw, 70
  Minted North African Cucumber Salad, 68
  Minty Thai Chicken Salad, 86
  Penne with Three Herbs, Capers and Tuna, 89
  pinzimonio, 82
  Plaka Greek Salad, 72
  Potato and Chèvre Salad, 68
  Potato Salad with Asparagus and Pesto Vinaigrette, 85
  Southeast Asian Summer Salad of Cellophane Noodles and Herbs, 67–68
  Spicy Citrus Couscous Tabbouleh, 83
  Summer Fruit Salad with Feta and Cilantro, 77
  tips for, 88
  Tomato, Lemon, Green Olive and Onion Salad, 71
  Vietnamese "Shaking" Beef Salad, 88–89
  Wilted Cabbage Salad with Bacon and Cashel Blue Cheese, 90

Salmon
  Ginger-Pepper Salmon, 306
  Jardiniere's Wild Salmon with Olive Oil–Mashed Potatoes and Sauce Niçoise, 303–4
  O Chame's Soba with Salmon and Bean Sprouts, 116–17
  removing bones from, 302
  Roasted Salmon Stuffed with Spinach, 305–6
  Roasted Salmon with Lentils, 302–3
  Rose Pistola's Cured Salmon with Green Peppercorns, 27
  sautéing, 305

Salsas
  Fresh Pineapple Salsa, 386
  "It's Not Guacamole" Avocado Salsa, 387
  Mango Salsa, 308–9
  Mixed Melon Salsa, 386
  Rancho Sarsa, 382
  Salsa Fresca al Fresco, 385
  Salsa Verde, 228–29
  Sunset Salsa, 384

Salt cod
  Creamy Brandade of Salt Cod and Potatoes with Garlic Croutons, 8–9
  preparing, 318

Sambars
  cooking legumes for, 182
  Fresh Cranberry Bean Sambar, 50–51

Sand Dabs with Lemon-Caper Vinaigrette, 310

Sangria, 26

Santa Fe Cooking School Blue Corn Muffins, 343

Sardines, Marinated, 26–27

Sauces. See also Pesto; Salsas
  All-American Spaghetti Sauce, 127
  Asian-Style Peanut Barbecue Sauce, 393
  Bagna Cauda, 392
  Barbecue Sauce, 239
  Béchamel Sauce, 184
  Chile Sauce, 197
  Chimichurri Sauce, 383
  Chinese Spicy Red Pepper Dipping Sauce, 7
  Chipotle Sauce, 296–97
  Coriander-Cognac Sauce, 286
  Corn-Basil Sauce, 211
  Green Herb Sauce, 390
  Honey-Mustard Barbecue Sauce, 394
  Italian-Style Tomato Sauce, 125
  Killer Red Sauce, 391
  Kumquat-Cranberry-Lime Sauce, 376
  Marinara Sauce, 168–69
  perking up, 249
  for pork, quick, 233
  Quick Plum Sauce, 393
  Quick Red Sauce, 369
  Ranchero Sauce, 360–61
  Red Chile Sauce, 155
  Spicy Tomato Barbecue Sauce, 394
  Tomato and Pancetta Sauce, 126
  Tomato Sauce, 391
  Zchug, 388

Sausage. See also Chorizo
  All-American Spaghetti Sauce, 127
  grilling times for, 231
  Huevos a la Flamenca, 362
  Maple-Glazed Sausage Slices, 370
  Potée of Cabbage, Potatoes, Turnips, Carrots, Onions and Sausage, 252

Sautéed Foie Gras with Grapes, 30

Sauté of Summer Greens, 199

Scallion Oil, 197

Scallops
  Cognac Scallops, 326
  French-Vietnamese Bouillabaisse, 328–29
  trimming, 326

Scones
  Brown Scones, 340
  Cranberry-Cream Scones, 341

Scorpion Tomato Relish, 378

Seafood. See also specific types of seafood
  French-Vietnamese Bouillabaisse, 328–29
  Seafood Klephtiko, 332

Seasoning Paste, 131–32

Sherbet, Watermelon, 439

Shortbread
  Lavender Shortbread, 429
  Orange-Polenta Shortbread, 430

Shortcakes, Plums 'n' Spice, 412–13

Short Rice with Long Beans, 160–61

Shrimp and prawns
  Angolan Prawns, 319
  Easy Pad Thai, 114–15
  Fijian Prawns with Sweet Potatoes in Coconut Curry, 318–19
  Garlicky Shrimp from a Tapas Bar, 24
  Grilled Tequila-Chipotle Shrimp, 321
  grilling, 309
  John Falcone's Grilled Prawns with Basil Baste, 320

kebabs, 330
Shrimp Crostini with Thai Basil and Kaffir Lime Sauce, 14
Shrimp in Spicy Saffron Broth with Israeli Couscous, 327–28
Spanish Clam, Prawn and Chorizo Stew, 330
Spicy Hot-and-Sour Prawn Soup, 59–60
Vanilla Shrimp with Avocado-Tarragon Dip, 22–23
Sicilian Tomato Pesto with Linguine, 104
Skewers. *See also* Kebabs
Beef and Shiitake Skewers, 223
ideas for, 274
Kokkari's Grilled Chicken Souvlaki, 270–71
Smoked Trout, Asian Pear and Horseradish Cream Crostini, 15
Smoky Mexican Chicken Legs, 283
Soups
Arroz Caldo (Filipino Rice Porridge), 54–55
Cabbage Soup with Roquefort, 37
Caldo de Tlalpeno, 57–58
Chickpea Soup with Kale and Diavolicchio, 45–46
Cold Cucumber Soup with Cilantro, 32
Cream of Leek Soup with Stilton, 46–47
Egyptian Chickpea and Orzo Soup, 44
Fresh Cranberry Bean Sambar, 50–51
Fresh Shelling Bean and Basil Soup, 39–40
Ginger-Tomato Rasam, 51–52
Guacamole Soup, 36
Ham Hock and "Peppercorn" Pasta Soup, 63–64
Heavenly Corn Soup, 34–35

Mexican Minestrone with Cilantro Pesto, 42–43
Nan Yang's Burmese Fish Noodle Soup (Mohingar), 60–61
Pumpkin Soup with Leeks and Chervil, 49
Puy Lentil Soup, 53–54
Quick Chinese Soup, 56
Roasted Eggplant Bisque, 38–39
Spicy Hot-and-Sour Prawn Soup, 59–60
Spicy Sweet Potato Soup, 48
Thai Chicken Soup with Coconut Milk and Galangal, 56
Tofu, Cucumber and Chive Soup, 33
Tomato-Lime Soup with Tapenade, 35–36
Turkey Soup with Wild Rice and Escarole, 58–59
White Bean and Roasted Garlic Soup, 41–42
Wild Mushroom Soup, 47
Sour Cream and Avocado Omelet, 363
Southeast Asian Summer Salad of Cellophane Noodles and Herbs, 67–68
Southern-Fried Chicken, 266–67
Souvlaki, Kokkari's Grilled Chicken, 270–71
Spaghetti. See Pasta and noodles
Spanish Clam, Prawn and Chorizo Stew, 330
Spearmint Custard Ice Cream, 442
Spice blends. *See also* Pastes; Rubs
Korma Masala, 249
Rasam Powder, 52
Spiced Cheese, 19
Spiced Duck with Couscous, 287–88

Spicy Asian Pan-Fried Okra, 200–201
Spicy Asian-Style Cabbage and Turkey, 299
Spicy Citrus Couscous Tabbouleh, 83
Spicy Hot-and-Sour Prawn Soup, 59–60
Spicy Sweet Potato Soup, 48
Spicy Tomato Barbecue Sauce, 394
Spicy Vietnamese Chicken Curry, 276–77
Spinach
Braised Garden Spinach, 206
Cold Udon Noodles with Morels and Fresh Peas, 97
Green Garlic and Spinach Risotto, 139
Green, Green Dressing, 73
Penne with Butternut Squash, Turkey, Currants and Spinach, 105–6
Piatti's Bruschetta with Spinach and Lemon, 11
Polenta Baked with Vegetables, 170–71
Roasted Salmon Stuffed with Spinach, 305–6
Russian Dilled Spinach Dip, 6–7
Spreads
Black Olive Tapenade, 3
Eggplant Caviar with Chipotle Oil, 20–21
John Caputo's Anchoiade, 386–87
Spiced Cheese, 19
Squash. *See also* Pumpkin; Zucchini
Fallen Butternut Squash Gratin, 207
Grilled Winter Squash with Cumin, 207
Lentil and Squash Lasagna with Caramelized Onions, 182–83

luffa, 196
Penne with Butternut Squash, Turkey, Currants and Spinach, 105–6
Thai Red Curry with Beef and Kabocha Squash, 225
Steamed New Potatoes with Lemon-Caper Sauce, 205
Stir-Fried Black, White and Red Rice, 129–30
Stir-Fried Flank Steak with Bok Choy, 226–27
Stock, Quick Fish, 329
Strawberries
Citrus-Strawberry Salad, 402
quick dessert, 435
Quick Marinated Strawberries, 418
Strawberries with Whipped Ricotta, 438–39
Strawberry Soufflé Pancake, 337
Stuffed Mussels, 25
Summer Fruit Salad with Feta and Cilantro, 77
Summertime Basil Bass, 311
Sunset Salsa, 384
Super-Juicy Roasted Chicken with Garlic and Thyme, 255
Super-Rica Rajas, 158–59
Sweet Cinnamon Tomatoes, 208
Sweet Polenta-Orange Cake, 420
Sweet potatoes
Black Bean and Sweet Potato Stew, 148–49
Fijian Prawns with Sweet Potatoes in Coconut Curry, 318–19
Roasted Sweet Potatoes with Red Pepper–Chile-Lime Butter, 204
Spicy Sweet Potato Soup, 48
Sweet Potato Gratin with Chipotles, 205
Swiss chard

Roasted Chickens Stuffed with Orzo on a Bed of Rainbow Swiss Chard, 262–63

Swiss Chard with Peppers and Walnuts, 187

Whole-Wheat Spaghetti with Chard, 106–7

Swordfish, Baked, with Roasted Red Pepper Vinaigrette, 307

T

Tabbouleh, Spicy Citrus Couscous, 83

Tagines

Lamb Tagine with Dried Apricots, 245–46

Tagine of Meatballs and Peas, 250–51

Tamales, Fresh Corn, 151–52

Tandoori Chicken, 268–69

Tandoori Quail with Tropical Fruit Chaat, 290–91

Tangerine-Bourbon Chicken Breasts, 264

Tapenade, Black Olive, 3

Taro, 196–97

Tarts

Asparagus Tart, 365

Mary Risley's Fresh Fig and Plum Tart, 409–10

Tarte Tatin of Celery Root, Leek and Potato, 173

Tecomate and Poblano Chile Crostini, 13

Tequila

Grilled Tequila-Chipotle Shrimp, 321

Tequila Carrot Cake, 415–16

Tequila–Fresh Pineapple Cheese Pie, 425–26

Teriyaki Marinade, 271

Thai Chicken Soup with Coconut Milk and Galangal, 56

Thai Red Curry with Beef and Kabocha Squash, 225

Three-Cheese Pizza with Arugula, 176–77

Tofu

Tofu, Cucumber and Chive Soup, 33

Yellow Curry with Mixed Vegetables, Tofu and Thai Basil, 174

Tomatoes

All-American Spaghetti Sauce, 127

Black Bean and Sweet Potato Stew, 148–49

Braised Chicken Wings with Tomato, Porcini and Sage, 279

Cianfotto Lucana (Eggplant, Tomato, Pepper and Potato Stew), 149–50

Cornish Game Hen with Tomato-Olive Sauce, 292

Delfina's Spaghetti, 95–96

Duck Bolognese, 123–24

French-Style Cobb Salad, 79

Frisee and Corn Salad with Fried Tomatoes, 75–76

Frittatas with Prosciutto and Plum Tomatoes, 358

Ginger-Tomato Rasam, 51–52

Huevos a la Flamenca, 362

Italian-Style Tomato Sauce, 125

Killer Red Sauce, 391

Marinara Sauce, 168–69

Pan-Fried Breakfast Tomatoes, 349

Pappardelle with Arugula, Cherry Tomatoes and Breadcrumbs, 101

peeling, 95

Plaka Greek Salad, 72

Potato Gnocchi with Asparagus and Tomatoes, 181

Ranchero Sauce, 360–61

Rancho Sarsa, 382

Roasted Beet and Tomato Relish with Chermoula Flavors, 373

Salsa Fresca al Fresco, 385

Scorpion Tomato Relish, 378

Sicilian Tomato Pesto with Linguine, 104

Spaghetti with Marinated Fennel, Tomato and Olives, 96

Spicy Tomato Barbecue Sauce, 394

Sunset Salsa, 384

Sweet Cinnamon Tomatoes, 208

Three-Cheese Pizza with Arugula, 176–77

Tomato and Almond Pesto, 128

Tomato and Hot Pepper Relish, 6

Tomato and Pancetta Sauce, 126

Tomato, Lemon, Green Olive and Onion Salad, 71

Tomato-Lime Soup with Tapenade, 35–36

Tomato Sauce, 391

Turkey, Corn and Roasted Bell Pepper Enchiladas with Chipotle Sauce, 296–97

Zchug, 388

Tortillas. *See also* Enchiladas

Cazuela de Huevos Rancheros, 360–61

heating store-bought flour, 361

Morel Quesadillas with Mild Red Chile, 16–17

Trio Fruit Crumble, 436–37

Tropical Fruit Chaat, 291

Trout, Asian Pear and Horseradish Cream Crostini, Smoked, 15

Truffle oil, 121

Tuna

Basque-Style Fisherman's Stew, 331

Grilled Tuna Salad with Bok Choy and Papaya, 91

Penne with Three Herbs, Capers and Tuna, 89

Tunisian-Style Grilled Lamb Chops, 244

Turkey

Best Way Roast Turkey, 294–95

Boulevard's Staff Turkey Breast, 293

brining, 295

Curried Turkey Salad with Apple and Walnuts, 87

Green Beans and Turkey in Asian Black Bean Sauce, 298

Penne with Butternut Squash, Turkey, Currants and Spinach, 105–6

Spicy Asian-Style Cabbage and Turkey, 299

Turkey, Corn and Roasted Bell Pepper Enchiladas with Chipotle Sauce, 296–97

Turkey Soup with Wild Rice and Escarole, 58–59

Turnips, Orecchiette with Broccoli Rabe and, 103–4

Tzatziki, 17

U

Ultimate Lemon Meringue Pie, 406–7

Umami, 298–99

V

Vanilla-Scented Chicken and Mushrooms Simmered in Coconut Milk, 275–76

Vanilla Shrimp with Avocado-Tarragon Dip, 22–23

Veal Braised with Cognac, 230

Vegetables. *See also* specific vegetables

Asian, 196–97

grilling, 212–13

Kasha and Vegetable Casserole, 153

Malaysian Coconut Curry of Autumn Vegetables, 175–76

Marinated Vegetables in a Grill
Pan, 212
Mexican Minestrone with
Cilantro Pesto, 42–43
pinzimonio, 82
Polenta Baked with Vegetables,
170–71
Potée of Cabbage, Potatoes,
Turnips, Carrots, Onions and
Sausage, 252
Pot Roast with Caramelized
Onion Sauce and Roasted
Winter Vegetables, 220–21
Roasted Onions, Potatoes,
Carrots and Fennel, 214
Roasted Winter Roots with
Whole Garlic Heads, 150–51
Yellow Curry with Mixed
Vegetables, Tofu and Thai
Basil, 174
Vegetarian Corn Biryani, 156–57
Velvet Pound Cake, 421
Vietnamese "Shaking" Beef
Salad, 88–89
Vinegar, Basil, 85

W
Waffles, Kirk Webber's, 338
Walnuts
Christmas Nut Chews, 428
Curried Turkey Salad with
Apple and Walnuts, 87
Egyptian Haroset, 395
Michelle Anna Jordan's Soft
Polenta with Walnuts, 144–45
Oatmeal Cake with Walnut
Topping, 416–17
Oatmeal-Walnut–Chocolate
Chip Cookies, 427
Pan-Grilled Steaks with Toasted
Walnuts and Roquefort-
Shallot Butter, 216
Roasted Chicken with Garlicky
Skin and Walnuts, 256
Swiss Chard with Peppers and
Walnuts, 187

Walnut Wonder Bars, 431–32
Watermelon Sherbet, 439
Water spinach, 197
Wheat berries
cooking, 447
Wheat Berries with Ricotta,
Almonds and Honey, 334
White Bean and Pesto Dip, 4
White Bean and Roasted Garlic
Soup, 41–42
Whole-Wheat Spaghetti with
Chard, 106–7
Wild Mushroom Bread Pudding,
167
Wild Mushroom Omelet, 354
Wild Mushroom Soup, 47
Wild rice
cooking, 447
Turkey Soup with Wild Rice
and Escarole, 58–59
Wilted Cabbage Salad with
Bacon and Cashel Blue
Cheese, 90
Wine
cooking with, 372
matching food and, 170
pairing cheese and, 18
Red Wine Marinade, 226
Red Wine Vinaigrette, 72
Winter Wild Mushroom Risotto,
143–44

Y
Yellow Curry with Mixed
Vegetables, Tofu and Thai
Basil, 174
Yorkshire Pudding, 219–20

Z
Zarzuela's Patatas al Ajillo
(Potatoes with Garlic), 202
Zchug, 388
Zesting, 376
Zucchini
Greek Taverna-Style Zucchini
with Lemon, 209

Mexican Zucchini and Corn
Gratin, 211
Zucchini with Apple and Mint,
210
Zuni Cafe's Chocolate Pots de
Crème, 400

Chefs/Restaurants

A

Advincula, Noel, 54
Alamilla, Johnny, 265
Alberti, Jean, 270
Anderson, Jean, 78
Anzu, 167
Atlas Peak Vineyards, 320
Autumn Moon Cafe, 90, 168, 347

B

Bakeshop, 407
Bauer, Michael, 22, 212, 398
Bay Wolf, 366
Beardsley, John, 281
Bennett, Lynne, 298, 299
Betelnut, 115
Bette's Oceanview Diner, 337
Bijan, Donia, 75, 172, 193
Bistro Don Giovanni, 93, 123
Bistro Viola, 355
Bizou, 331
Black Cat, 427
Boulevard, 215, 235, 293
Braker, Flo, 341, 399, 409, 410, 412, 421, 423, 426, 429, 432, 436, 441, 451
Brennan, Georgeanne, 3, 9, 21, 25, 30, 39, 65, 73, 74, 77, 85, 89, 91, 112, 142, 146, 150, 176, 189, 190, 203, 205, 206, 209, 214, 231, 236, 243, 244, 252, 254, 256, 305, 315, 316, 318, 322, 325, 333, 339, 349, 354, 386, 393, 405, 437, 451
Brown, Barney, 115
Brown Derby Restaurant, 65
Buenviaje, Brenda, 97

C

Cadwallader, Sharon, 187, 335
Cafe Kati, 98, 186, 338
California Culinary Academy, 87, 318
Caputo, John, 375, 386
Carroll, John, 407
Case, Kimberley, 410
Chapeau, 8
Charanga, 26
Chavarria, Marie, 406
Chenel, Laura, 65
Chesarek, David, 427
Chez Panisse, 253, 294, 372
Chiang, Cecilia, 115
Child, Julia, 158
Chu, Philip, 60
Citron, 38
Clingman, Curt, 269
Columbus Ristorante, 292
Cosmopolitan Cafe, 374
Cost, Bruce, 119
Cox, Jennifer, 15
Cunningham, Marion, 88, 170, 233, 333, 340, 342, 344, 345, 353, 363, 379, 390, 392, 396, 399, 407, 416, 417, 422, 424, 428, 431, 434, 451

D

Danko, Gary, 145, 371, 376
Davis, Robin, 41, 78, 79, 85, 130, 148, 153, 161, 218, 220, 226, 261, 287, 312, 323, 334, 393, 394, 451
Delfina, 95
Denton, Jody, 330
des Jardins, Traci, 303, 371, 379
Dine, 262
Ditano, May, 292
Dona Tomas, 13
Drori, Julia, 381
Drysdale, Gordon, 68
Duggan, Tara, 98, 113, 182, 240, 313, 324, 327, 358, 451

E

Elisabeth Daniel, 257, 377
Elite Cafe, 284
Emma Restaurant, 210
Eos Restaurant & Wine Bar, 200
Evers, Ridgely, 2

F

Falcone, John, 320
Farallon, 399, 402
Fearing, Dean, 70
Field, Carol, 141
Firefly, 253, 266
Fletcher, Janet, 12, 19, 32, 45, 62, 96, 101, 102, 103, 107, 125, 126, 127, 128, 129, 139, 179, 228, 237, 255, 279, 307, 310, 333, 364, 438, 451
Fleur de Lys, 164
Foothill Cafe, 238
Forsha, Sean, 58, 87, 105, 296
42 Degrees, 215, 234
Franz, Mark, 402

G

Garibaldi's On College, 381
Gary Danko restaurant, 18, 145, 371, 376
Gasco, Lucas, 26
Gingrass, Anne, 140
Gordon's House of Fine Eats, 68
Grand Cafe, 47

H

Haig's Delicacies, 274
Hawthorne Lane, 140, 399, 401
Heffernan, Kerry, 90, 168, 347
Helm, Maria, 66, 414
Hensperger, Beth, 350
Herrera, Tilde, 132
Hiremath, Laxmi, 28, 50, 51, 84, 131, 133, 134, 135, 136, 156, 182, 248, 258, 268, 290, 403, 451

I

Infusion, 30
Insalata's, 199
Iron Horse Vineyards, 4

J

Jardiniere, 303, 371, 379
Jojo's, 269
Jordan, Michele Anna, 144

K

Kasper, Lynne Rosetto, 334
Keller, Hubert, 164
Keller, Loretta, 331
Kinch, David, 207
King, Niloufer Ichaporia, 160
Kokkari, 270
Krahling, Heidi, 199

L

L'Amie Donia, 75, 172, 193
Left Bank, 399, 419
Lemongrass, 33
Levine, Steven, 374
Levy, Brad, 253, 266
Link, Donald, 284
Loha-unchit, Kasma, 118
LuLu, 330
Lusardi, Mark, 210
Lyle, Lauren Elizabeth, 366

M

Malicki, Mark, 4
Mallorca, Jackie, 397
Mansion on Turtle Creek, 70
Martes, Daniel, 381
Masters, Shanna, 430, 439, 442
McClaskey, Julia, 262
McGlynn, Colleen, 2
McMahan, Jacqueline, 20, 34, 36, 42, 48, 57, 70, 78, 109, 131, 145, 151, 152, 154, 155, 159, 162, 191, 194, 195, 205, 208, 211, 260, 280, 282, 308, 321, 333, 343, 348, 350, 356, 359, 360, 361, 368, 371, 378, 382, 383, 384, 385, 386, 387, 389, 391, 404, 406, 415, 425, 433, 434, 452
Middione, Carlo, 371, 380
Millennium, 143
Mojo, 284
Moki's Sushi and Pacific Grill, 76
Montage, 15
Mott, Weezie, 138

N

Nan Yang, 60
Neilson, Lesli, 63
Nuevo Latino, 265

O

Oakes, Nancy, 215, 235, 293
Oakville Grocery, 80
O Chame, 116
Ong, Alexander, 14
Oritalia, 97

P

Pastis, 302
Patterson, Daniel, 257, 377
Pelchat, Marcia, 298
Perez, Angel, 80
Peyton, Nick, 18
Pham, Mai, 33, 56, 59, 86, 88,
    92, 100, 114, 136, 174, 197,
    198, 224, 225, 272, 276, 278,
    328, 452
Piatti, 11
Plue, Nicole, 401
PlumpJack Cafe, 66
Ponzu, 281
Postrio, 367

Q

Queluz Palace, 314

R

Reddington, Richard, 8
Richman, Alison, 325, 336
Rick & Ann's, 339, 410
Risley, Mary, 46, 219, 409
Rodgers, Judy, 110
Rosenthal, Mitchell and Steven,
    367
Rose Pistola, 27
Rossi, Chris, 38

S

Santa Fe Cooking School, 343
Sarvis, Shirley, 165, 217, 230,
    232, 264, 286, 300, 306, 309,
    311, 314, 319, 326, 452

Saul's Deli, 395
Savitsky, Dona, 13
Scala, Donna, 93, 123
Sent Sovi, 207
Shafer, Jerry, 238
Sinskey, Robert, 66
Sinskey Winery, 66, 414
Socca, 375, 386
Soriano, Denis, 47
Spieler, Marlena, 4, 5, 6, 7, 9, 16,
    18, 21, 24, 29, 35, 37, 44, 49,
    53, 56, 67, 68, 71, 74, 82, 83,
    94, 122, 163, 173, 175, 181,
    186, 189, 201, 204, 209, 216,
    226, 227, 245, 246, 250, 257,
    270, 273, 274, 275, 289, 330,
    333, 346, 352, 357, 362, 365,
    370, 373, 388, 395, 430, 438,
    440, 452
Spinoso, Pino, 149
Stoll, Craig, 95
Stoyanof's, 242
Striffeler, Philippe, 167
Super-Rica Taqueria, 158

T

Tante Marie's Cooking School,
    46, 219, 409
Tantillo's, 336
Tiramisu, 149
Tucker, Eric, 143

U

Universal Cafe, 179

V

Vardy, David, 116
Vera, David, 318
Vivande, 371, 380

W

Waters, Alice, 372
Webber, Kirk, 98, 186, 338
Weil, Carolyn, 407
Weir, Joanne, 6, 17, 19, 26, 72,
    82, 104, 111, 120, 222, 242,
    332, 420, 452

Whitelaw, Amy, 419
Wong, Arnold, 200
Woo, Gary, 76

X

Xanadu, 14
XYZ, 325

Z

Zaft, David, 19
Zare, Hoss, 188
Zare restaurant, 188
Zarzuela, 26, 202
Zeitouni, Mark, 355
Zepos, Daphne, 19
Zuni Cafe, 110, 400

Table of Equivalents

The exact equivalents in the following tables have been rounded for convenience.

US/UK

oz=ounce
lb=pound
in=inch
ft=foot
tbl=tablespoon
fl oz=fluid ounce
qt=quart

Metric

g=gram
kg=kilogram
mm=millimeter
cm=centimeter
ml=milliliter
l=liter

Weights

US/UK	Metric
1 oz	30 g
2 oz	60 g
3 oz	90 g
4 oz (¼ lb)	125 g
5 oz (⅓ lb)	155 g
6 oz	185 g
7 oz	220 g
8 oz (½ lb)	250 g
10 oz	315 g
12 oz (¾ lb)	375 g
14 oz	440 g
16 oz (1 lb)	500 g
1½ lb	750 g
2 lb	1 kg
3 lb	1.5 kg

Oven Temperatures

Fahrenheit	Celsius	Gas
250	120	½
275	140	1
300	150	2
325	160	3
350	180	4
375	190	5
400	200	6
425	220	7
450	230	8
475	240	9
500	260	10

Liquids

US	Metric	UK
2 tbl	30 ml	1 fl oz
¼ cup	60 ml	2 fl oz
⅓ cup	80 ml	3 fl oz
½ cup	125 ml	4 fl oz
⅔ cup	160 ml	5 fl oz
¾ cup	180 ml	6 fl oz
1 cup	250 ml	8 fl oz
1½ cups	375 ml	12 fl oz
2 cups	500 ml	16 fl oz
4 cups/1 qt	1 l	32 fl oz

Length Measures

⅛ in	3 mm
¼ in	6 mm
½ in	12 mm
1 in	2.5 cm
2 in	5 cm
3 in	7.5 cm
4 in	10 cm
5 in	13 cm
6 in	15 cm
7 in	18 cm
8 in	20 cm
9 in	23 cm
10 in	25 cm
11 in	28 cm
12 in/1 ft	30 cm